**PEARSON
BACCALAUREATE**

D1495835

Theory of Knowledge

DEVELOPED SPECIFICALLY FOR THE
IB DIPLOMA

SUE BASTIAN

VIVEK BAMMI • CRAIG HOWARD • JULIAN KITCHING
JOHN MACKENZIE • DENNIS OBERG
MANJULA SALOMON • DAVID WILKINSON

ALWAYS LEARNING

PEARSON

Pearson Education Limited is a company incorporated in England and Wales, having its registered office at Edinburgh Gate, Harlow, Essex, CM20 2JE. Registered company number: 872828

www.pearsonbaccalaureate.com

Text © Pearson Education Limited 2008

First published 2008

20 19 18 17 16 15 14 13 12

IMP 10 9 8 7 6 5

ISBN 978 0 435994 38 9

Edited by Liz Cartmell with thanks to Philippa Tomlinson
Designed by Tony Richardson
Typeset by Tech-Set Ltd
Original illustrations © Pearson Education Ltd 2008
Illustrated by Tech-Set Ltd
Cover design by Tony Richardson
Picture research by Susi Paz
Cover illustration © Pearson Education Ltd 2008
Indexed by Rosemary Dear
Printed in China (GCC/05)

Websites
There are links to relevant websites in this book. In order to ensure that the links are up-to-date, that the links work, and that the sites are not inadvertently linked to sites that could be considered offensive, we have made the links available on our website at www.pearsonhotlinks.co.uk. When you access the site, the express code is 4327P.

Acknowledgements

The publisher would like to thank Ric Sims for his professional guidance.

The authors and publisher would like to thank the following individuals and organizations for permission to reproduce photographs:

© akg-images p.92; © Alamy / Adam Eastland p.263 ('The Thinker'); © Alamy / Allstar Picture Library p.46 (David Beckham's head); © Alamy / Arcaid p.70 (Leicester University); © Alamy / Art Kowalsky p.270 ('The Birth of Venus'); © Alamy / Blaine Harrington III p.63 (Henry Moore sculpture); © Alamy / David Anthony p.241; © Alamy / David Levenson p.255; © Alamy / Dennis Cox p.266 (mandala); © Alamy / ImageState p.35; © Alamy /IML Image Group Ltd p.259 (sculpture); © Alamy / INTERFOTO Pressebildagentur pp.222(Nelson Mandela), 266 (Madonna and child); © Alamy / Israel images p.214; © Alamy / Jeff Morgan Hay on Wye p.304; © Alamy / Jupiter Images p.46 (woman reading); © Alamy / Keren Su / China Span p.252; © Alamy / Lazyfruit Pictures p.30; © Alamy / Lebrecht Music and Arts Photo Library p.249 (Immanuel Kant); © Alamy / Lordprice Collection p.268 (WW1 recruitment poster); © Alamy / Mary Evans Picture Library p.249 (John Stuart Mill); © Alamy / Mediacolor's p.28; © Alamy / Patrick Ward p.63 (Giacometti sculpture); © Alamy / Pictorial Press pp.113, 238; © Alamy / ReligiousStock p.261; © Alamy / Roy Garner p.211; © Alamy / Steven Poe p.263 (Fang sculpture); © Alamy / Stock Connection Blue p.53; © Alamy / Visual Arts Library (London) pp.194, 270 ('The Dwarf Sebastian de Morra'); © Dennis Oberg (outdoor sculpture); © Chantal and Eddy Verbeeck p.146; © Corbis / Alinari Archives pp.265, 269; © Corbis / Christie's Images p.263 (Emperor Jimmu); © Corbis / Eleanor Bentall p.222 (Frederik de Klerk); © Corbis / Kai Pfaffenbach / Reuters p.245; © Corbis / Reuters p.218; © Corbis / Shelley Gazin p.188; © Dina Graser p.164; © Dreamstime p.7; © Empics pp.67 (rod and model of the head), 83, 130; © FreeImage p.13; © Getty Images pp.196, 234, 235; © Getty Images / AFP p.206 (mourners); © Getty Images / Hulton Archive p.77; © Imi Hwangbo p.226; © iStockPhoto pp.9, 197; © iStockPhoto / Alexander Hafemann p.87; © iStockPhoto / Alexey Stiop p.268 (Ancient Egyptian art); © iStockPhoto / Anthony Baggett p.70 (All Souls' College); © iStockPhoto / Chris Schmidt p.232; © iStockPhoto / Gary Alvis p.259 (plate); © iStockPhoto / George Peters p.206 (happy society); © iStockPhoto / Hedda Gjerpen p.263 (Poseidon); © iStockPhoto / Ian Hamilton p.57 (rectangular road signs); © iStockPhoto / Lee Pettet p.57 (warning signs); © iStockPhoto / Mher Ajamian p.259 (binoculars); © iStockPhoto / Plesea Petre p.259 (flower arrangement); © iStockPhoto / Soren Pilman p.259 (rose); © IWM p.110 (Menin Road 1917); © Leslie Coate p.110 (Frank Bastable); © NASA p.46 (astronaut's suit); © PA pp.57 (Microsoft executives), 209; © S. Harris p.122, 126, 254; © Science Photo Library p.169; © Science Photo Library / J Gerard Sidaner p.253; © Science Photo Library / Philippe Plailly Eurelios p.184; © Science Photo Library / Science Source p.180; © The Royal Society p.151.

The authors and publisher would like to thank the following for permission to use © material:

p.x, 'On Educating Children' from *Essays* by Michel de Montaigne, translated with an introduction by J. M. Cohen (Penguin Classics, London, 1958). Copyright © J. M. Cohen 1958. Reproduced by kind permission of Penguin Books Ltd; p.2, extract from *Schools across Frontiers: the Story of the International Baccalaureate and the United World Colleges* by A D C Peterson, by permission of Open Court Publishing Company, a division of Carus Publishing Company © 1987, 2003; p.11 extract from a speech by H. G. Wells, to the Royal Institution of Great Britain, on November 20th, 1936, by permission of A P Watt Ltd on behalf of The Literary Executors of the Estate of H. G. Wells; p.12, extract from 'Who Says We Know: On the New Politics of Knowledge' by Larry Sanger, co-founder of Wikipedia. An Edge Original Essay; p.27, grateful acknowledgement to William James for his quote; p.27, extract from John Resnick, Creator and Host, *Legends of Success*, Syndicated Radio Program; p.28, extract from 'Harvard's baby brain research lab' by Roger Highfield, http://www.telegraph.co.uk/earth/main.jhtml?view=DETAILS&grid=&xml=/earth/2008/04/30/sm_babies03.xml, copyright © 2008, *The Daily Telegraph*; p.39, originally published in German under the title *Leben des Galilei*, copyright © 1940 by Arvind Englind Teaterforlag, a.b., renewed June 1967 by Stefan. S, Brecht; copyright © 1955 by Suhrkamp Verlag, Frankfurt am Main, translation copyright for the play and texts by Brecht © 1980 by Stefan S. Brecht, reprinted from *Life of Galileo* by Bertolt Brecht, translated from the German by John Willett and edited by John Willett and Ralph Manheim, published by Arcade Publishing, New York; p.40, extracts from *The Divine Mistress* by Samuel Edwards, grateful acknowledgement to Samuel Edwards for his quotes; p.42, extract from *Action in Perception* by Alva Noë, The MIT Press, 2005; p.45, extract from *Philosophical Inquiry* by Matthew Lipman, Ann Margaret Sharp and Frederick S. Oscanyan, IAPC, Montclair State University, http://www.montclair.edu/iapc; p.47, grateful acknowledgment to Brandon Rogers for permission to reproduce an extract from his exercise; p.49, extract from *Action in Perception* by Alva Noë, The MIT Press, 2005; p.50–51, extract from 'Sleights of Mind' by George Johnson, *The New York Times*, 8/21/2007 © 2007 The New York Times. All rights reserved. Used by permission and protected by the copyright laws of the United States. The printing, copying, redistribution or retransmission of the Material without express written permission is prohibited; p.52, from *Blink* by Malcolm Gladwell. Copyright © 2005 by Malcolm Gladwell. By permission of Little, Brown & Company/ from *Blink* by Malcolm Gladwell, Allen Lane, 2005, copyright © 2005 by Malcolm Gladwell. Reproduced by permission of Penguin Books Ltd.; p.59, extract from Jennifer Van Ezra, in the column 'Nexus', *Equinox*, 99 (1998), grateful acknowledgement to Jennifer Van Ezra for her quote; pp.59–60, extract from 'Mixed Feelings' by Sunny Bains, *Wired Magazine*, April 2007, copyright © 2007 by Sunny Bains; p.61, extract from blog by Dr. Jerome Groopman, http://www.jeromegroopman.com, copyright © 2007 by Jerome Groopman. Reprinted by permission of William Morris Agency, LLC on behalf of the Author; p.65, extract from *Philosophy In The Flesh: The Embodied Mind and its Challenge to Western Thought* by George Lakoff and Mark Johnson, copyright © 1999. Reprinted by permission of Basic Books, a member of Perseus Books Group; p.75, extract from 'The Guilt Free Soldier: New Science Raises the Spectre of a World Without Regret' by Erik Baard, *The Village Voice*, 22nd January 2003, copyright © 2003 by Erik Baard, a science writer in NYC; p.76, extract from *Upheavals of Thought: The Intelligence of Emotions* by Martha C. Nussbaum, copyright © 2001 by Martha C. Nussbaum; p.77, extract from 'Mokusatsu' by Heathcote Williams, copyright © 1988 by Heathcote Williams. Reproduced with permission of Curtis Brown Group Ltd, London on behalf of Heathcote Williams; p.78, extract from *The Atlas of the World's Languages in Danger of Disappearing* by Stephen A. Wurm, copyright © 2001, used by permission of UNESCO; p.79, extract from Resolution 12 of UNESCO's thirtieth general conference in 1999, copyright © 1999, used by permission of UNESCO; pp.80–81 , extract from 'The Roots of Language and Consciousness' by Roger Lewin, in id. (ed.), *In the Age of Mankind* (Washington D.C.: Smithsonian, 1988), copyright © 1988 by Roger Lewin; p.81, the excerpt first appeared in the article 'Proud Atheist' by Steve Paulson. This article originally appeared at http://www.salon.com; pp.82–3, extract from 'Aping Language: a skeptical analysis of the evidence for nonhuman primate language', by Dr. Clive Wynne, psychology professor at University of Florida, http://www.skeptic.com/eskeptic/07-10-31.html, copyright © 2007 by Clive Wynne; p.84, extract from *The Language Instinct* by Stephen Pinker, copyright © 1994 by Steven Pinker. Reprinted by permission of HarperCollins Publishers; p.85, extract from 'Language Barriers', *The Economist*, copyright © The Economist Newspaper Limited, London (19 August 2004); p.85, extract from Gay, Kathlyn. *Bigotry*. Berkeley Heights, NJ: Enslow Publishers, Inc., 1989, pp. 91–92; pp.86–7, extract from 'The secret language of Chinese women' by Edward Cody, *Washington Post*, 29th February 2004, copyright © 2004, The Washington Post. All rights reserved. Used by permission and protected by the Copyright Laws of the United States. The printing, copying, redistribution, or retransmission of the Material without express written permission is prohibited; p.112, extract from *Ypres 1914–1918: A Study in History Around Us* by Leslie Coate, grateful acknowledgement to Leslie Coate for his quote; p.113, extract from *Problems of Philosophy* by Bertrand Russell, copyright © 1959, by permission of Oxford University Press; p.115, Montaigne, M. de. (1958). *Essays*. Translated with an introduction by J. M. Cohen (Penguin Classics, London, 1959). Copyright © J. M. Cohen, 1958. Reproduced by permission from Penguin Books Ltd; p.118, extract from *The End of Education* by Neil Postman, copyright © 1995 by Neil Postman. Used by permission of Alfred A. Knopf, a division of Random House, Inc. / Reprinted with kind permission from the Markson Agency; p.120, extract from *Real Science. What it Is and What it Means* by John Ziman, copyright © 2000, Cambridge University Press; p.125, grateful acknowledgement to Konrad Lorenz for his quote on specialism; pp.127–8, extract from 'Two Kinds of Knowledge: Maps and Stories' by H.H. Bauer, *Journal of Scientific Exploration*, 9/2 (1995), 247–75, copyright © 1995 by H.H. Bauer; p.128, extract from 'Storytellers at the Crossroads: the challenge of narrative intelligence to identity, community and education' by Apostolos Doxiadis, IBAEM regional conference for educational leadership teams. American Community School of Athens, 14 Oct 2006, copyright © 2006 by Apostolos Doxiadis; p.130, extract from 'Never the Twain Shall Meet', *The Economist*, copyright © The Economist Newspaper Limited, London (31 January 2002); p.130, extract from *Ever since Darwin: Reflections in Natural History* by S.J.Gould, copyright © 1992, André Deutsch; p.131, from *Leonardo's Mountain of Clams and the Diet of Worms* by S J Gould, published by Jonathan Cape. Reprinted by permission of The Random House Group Ltd; p.131, from 'Of Two Minds and One Nature' by Shearer and Gould, *Science*, 286: 1093 (1999). Reprinted with permission from AAAS; p.133, extract from *A Mathematician Reads the Newspaper* by John Allen Paulos, copyright © 1996, Perseus Books Group; p.135, from 'Philosophical Problems of Mathematics in the Light of Evolutionary Epistemology' by Yehuda Rav, from *Eighteen Unconventional Essays on the Nature of Mathematics*. Edited by Reuben Hersh. Springer: New York, 2006, p.84. © 2006 Springer Science + Business Media, Inc. With kind permission of Springer Science and Business Media; p.140, grateful acknowledgement to Rodney Dangerfield for his quote; p.145, table from *Basic Concepts of Geometry* by W. Prenowitz and M. Jordan, copyright © 1965, Blaisdell-Ginn; p.146, from EVES. **ACP An Introduction to the History of Mathematics* Akron Edition, 6e. © 2006 Brooks/Cole, a part of Cengage Learning, Inc. Reproduced by permission http://www.cengage.com/permissions; p.148, extract from 'The Study of Mathematics' in *Mysticism and Logic, and Other Essays* by Bertrand Russell, reprinted with kind permission of The Bertrand Russell Peace Foundation Ltd; p.151, Professor Lord May speaking on the BBC programme *Chaos*, copyright © 1988 by Robert May; p.153, reprinted with kind permission of United Nations Environment Programme; p.153, extract from *Climate science: sceptical about bias* by Richard Black, copyright © 2007, BBC; p.155, from *Consilience* by Edward O. Wilson, copyright © 1998 by Edward O. Wilson. Used by permission of Alfred A. Knopf, a division of Random House, Inc; p.157, extract from 'In the Mind's Eye' by K.C. Cole, *Discover Magazine*, April 1985, copyright © by K.C.Cole; p.163, extract from 'Umbrellaology' by J. Somerville, *Philosophy of Science*, 1941, copyright © 1941, University of Chicago Press; p.164, extract from *The Life of the Cosmos* by Lee Smolin, copyright © 1997, Weidenfeld & Nicolson, a division of The Orion Publishing Group / by permission of Oxford University Press, Inc; p.168, extract from *The Structure of Scientific Revolutions* by T.S. Kuhn, copyright © T.S. Kuhn 1970, University of Chicago Press; p.171, extract from *Conjectures and Refutations: The Growth of Scientific Knowledge* by Karl Popper, copyright © 1965, published by kind permission of the estate of Karl Popper; p.175, extract from *What Is This Thing Called Science?* by Alan Chalmers, copyright © 1982, McGraw-Hill; p.175, extract from 'The End of Science' by Theodore Schick, *Skeptical Inquirer*, March/April 1997, copyright © 1997, used by permission of the Skeptical Inquirer Magazine (http://www.csicop.org); p.178, extract from an interview with Sheldon Glashow in *New York Times*, October 22nd 1989, grateful acknowledgement to Sheldon Glashow for his quote; p.178, extract from *The Ascent of Man: A Personal View* by Jacob Bronowski, published by BBC Books. Reprinted by permission of The Random House Group Ltd, copyright © 1973; p.183, extract from *Cambridge News*, 26/02/2005, http://www.cambridge-news.co.uk/ cn news huntingdon/displayarticle.asp?id=180014; copyright © 2005, Cambridge Newspapers Ltd; p.184, from *Newsweek*, 11th April © 1969 Newsweek, Inc. All rights reserved. Used by permission and protected by the Copyright Laws of the United States. The printing, copying, redistribution, or retransmission of the Material without express written permission is prohibited; p.185, extract from *Betrayers of the Truth: Fraud and Deceit in the Halls of Science* by William Broad and Nicholas Wade, reprinted by permission of Sll/Sterling Lord Literistic, Inc. Copyright © 1982 by William Broad; p.185, extract from *The Skeptic's Dictionary: A Collection of Strange Beliefs, Amusing Deceptions, and Dangerous Delusions* by R.T. Carroll, copyright © 2003 by Robert Todd Carroll, reprinted with permission of John Wiley & Sons, Inc; p.186–7, extract from Wikipedia article 'Trofim Lysenko', retrieved April 30th, 2008, from Answers.com Web site: http://www.answers.com/topic/trofim-lysenko; p.187, extract from *On Being a Scientist: Responsible Conduct in Research* by National Academy of Engineering, Institute of Medicine, National Research Council and National Academy of Sciences, reprinted with kind permission of the National Academies Press, © 1995, National Academy of Sciences; p.187, extract from an interview with Craig Venter, *New Scientist*, 2626 (2007), http://www.newscientist.com/channel/life/mg19626263.000-editorial-get-ready-for-synthetic.life.html, copyright © 2007, New Scientist Magazine; p.188, extract from *Genius: The Life and Science of Richard Feynman* by James Gleick, copyright © 1992 by James Gleick. Used by permission of Pantheon Books, a division of Random House, Inc; p.188, reprinted with permission from Richard Feynman, *The Physics Teacher*, Vol. 7, Issue 6, 313–20, 1968. © 2008, American Association of Physics Teachers; p.189, extract from 'On Science and Uncertainty' by Lewis Thomas, *Discover Magazine*, October 1980, copyright © 1980 by Lewis Thomas; p.192, extract from *History as a System and Other Essays towards a Philosophy of History* by Jose Ortega y Gasset. Copyright © 1941, 1961 by W. W. Norton & Company, Inc. Used by permission of W. W. Norton & Company, Inc; p.193, extract from 'Science and Human Behaviour' by B.F. Skinner in N. Block (ed.), *Readings in the Philosophy of Psychology*, Vol. 1, Harvard University Press, 1980, 40–1, copyright © 1980 by B.F. Skinner, reprinted with permission from B.F. Skinner Foundation; p.193, extract from Sir Alfred Julius Ayer, quoted on p.141 of *An Introduction to Philosophical Analysis* by John Hospers, copyright © 1997, Routledge; p.195, extract from pp.38–9 of *Suicide: A Study in Sociology* by E. Durkheim, copyright © 1970, Routledge and Kegan Paul; p.195, extract from *The Theory of Social and Economic Organization* by M.Weber, grateful acknowledgement to M. Weber for his quote; p.196–197, extract from 'Hitting it off, thanks to algorithms of love' by John Tierney, from The New York Times, January 29 © 2008 The New York Times. All rights reserved. Used by permission and protected by the Copyright Laws of the United States. The printing, copying, redistribution, or retransmission of the Material without express written permission is prohibited; p.199, extract from 'Numbers guy: are our brains wired for math?' by Jim Holt, *The New Yorker*, 3rd March 2008, copyright © 2008 by Jim Holt; pp.203–5, extract from Hayakawa. *Language in Thought and Action*, 5E. © 1989 Heinle/Arts & Sciences, a part of Cengage Learning, Inc. Reproduced by permission. www.cengage.com/permissions; p.209, extract from 'Searching for politics in an uncertain world: an interview with Zygmunt Bauman' by D. Leighton, *Renewal* 9/2 (1995): 247–75; p.218, extract from an interview with Wimar Witoelar, grateful acknowledgment to Wimar Witoelar for permission to reproduce his interview replies; p.223, 103 words from p. 213 from *Idea of History* by Collingwood, R.G. (1993). By permission of Oxford University Press; pp.223–4, extract from *A History of Europe: Ancient and Medieval*, Vol 1 (London: Eyre and Spottiswoode, 1935), grateful acknowledgement to H.A. L. Fisher for his quote; p.224, extract from *Civilizations: Culture, Ambition, and the Transformation of Nature* by Felipe Fernandez-Armesto, copyright © 2002, The Free Press. Reprinted with kind permission of David Higham Associates; pp.224–8, extract from an interview with Judith P. Zinsser, by Manjula Salomon, grateful acknowledgment to Dr Zinsser for permission to reproduce her interview replies; p.229, 232, extracts from *The Great Transformation* by Karen Armstrong, copyright © 2006 by Karen Armstrong. Used by permission of Alfred A. Knopf, a division of Random House, Inc; p.234, extract from 'Aborigines Accept Australia's Apology', Sky News (http://news.sky.com/skynews/article/0,,30200-1305185,00.html), 12 March 2008. With kind permission from Sky News Online; p.244, extract from 'The Morality Play' by Julian Baggini and Jeremy Stangroom, in *Do You Think What You Think You Think?*, copyright © 2006, Granta. Found in *The Philosophers' Magazine* at http://www.philosophersnet.com; p.246, extract from *The Blank Slate: The Modern Denial of Human Nature*, Steven Pinker, 2002, London, copyright © Steven Pinker, 2002. Reproduced by permission of Penguin Books Ltd/from *The Blank Slate* by Steven Pinker, copyright © 2002 by Steven Pinker. Used by permission of Viking Penguin, a division of Penguin Group (USA) Inc; p.253, extract from 'The Lie Detector' by Lewis Thomas, copyright © 1980 by Lewis Thomas, from *Late Night Thoughts On Listening To Mahler's Ninth* by Lewis Thomas. Used by permission of Viking Penguin, a division of Penguin Group (USA) Inc; p.254–5, excerpted with permission from Carol Gilligan, 'Woman's Place in Man's Life Cycle,' *Harvard Educational Review*, Volume 49:4 (November 1979) pp. 431–446. Copyright © by the President and Fellows of Harvard College. All rights reserved. For more information, please visit http://www.harvardeducationalreview.org; p.255, extract from 'No Magic, No Mystery', from *Ethics for the New Millenium* by Dalai Lama and Alexander Norman, copyright © 1999 by His Holiness The Dalai Lama. Used by permission of Riverhead Books, an imprint of Penguin Group (USA) Inc/ Copyright © 1997 by His Holiness the Dalai Lama, reprinted with permission of The Wylie Agency, Inc; p.257, extract from Alexander Solzhenitsyn's acceptance speech at the 1970 Nobel Prize Awards, © The Nobel Foundation 1970; p.257, extract from 'Reality' by Robert Muir, http://robmuirpoems.blogspot.com; p.260, extract from *The Birthday Party* by Harold Pinter, copyright © 1994, Grove Press, and with kind permission from Faber and Faber Ltd; p.260, extract from 'The Artistic Problem' in *Art* by Clive Bell, by kind permission of The Society of Authors as the Literary Representative of the Estate of Clive Bell; p.261, extract from *The Social Function of Art* by Radhakamal Mukherjee, copyright © 1948, Philosophical Library New York; p.262, extract from the translation of 'Ono no Komachi', reproduced with kind permission of Jan Lacure; p.262, extract from *Beowulf*, translated by Seamus Heaney. Copyright © 2000 by Seamus Heaney. Used by permission of W.W.Norton & Company, Inc. and of Faber and Faber Ltd; p.263, extract from 'When you are old' by W.B.Yeats, with the permission of AP Watt Ltd on behalf of Gráinne Yeats; p.263, extract from 'When I am old' by A. Maley in A. Maley and A. Duff (1989), *The Inward Ear: poetry and language in the classroom*, Cambridge: CUP. © Alan Maley 1989. Reproduced with permission; p.264, extract from *Newsweek*, 3 June © 1996 Newsweek, Inc. All rights reserved. Used by permission and protected by the Copyright Laws of the United States. The printing, copying, redistribution, or retransmission of the Material without express written permission is prohibited; p.264, extract from 'Intellectual Analysis and Aesthetic Appreciation' by Louis Arnaud Reid, *Journal of Philosophical Studies*, 1/02 (1996), 199–210, short text extract © Royal Institute of Philosophy. Reprinted with permission from Cambridge University Press; p.264, grateful acknowledgment to Benedict Clark for permission to reproduce his communication; p.266, extract from 'The Artistic Problem' in *Art* by Clive Bell, by kind permission of The Society of Authors as the Literary Representative of the Estate of Clive Bell; pp.269, extracts from *Mathematics and Art-perspective* by J. O'Connor and E. Robertson, copyright © 2003 by J. O'Connor and E. Robertson, http://www-history.mcs.st-andrews.ac.uk/history/HistTopics/Art.html; p.271, extracts from 'The impact of photography on painting' by Philippe Garner, copyright © 2000 by P. Garner, http://www.theimpactofphotography.blogspot.com/feeds/posts/default, accessed 27th December 2007; p.272, extract from 'Truth in Painting' by Giff Constable, copyright © 2000 by G. Constable, http://www.constable.net/currentart/essay5-20-2000.html; p.273, extract from Alexander Solzhenitsyn's acceptance speech at the 1970 Nobel Prize Awards, © The Nobel Foundation 1970; p.274, extract from 'Art, Truth and Reality' by Louis Arnaud Reid, *The British Journal of Aesthetics*, 4/4 (1964), 321–31, by permission of Oxford University Press; p.275, extract from 'The Arts, Knowledge and Education' by Louis Arnaud Reid, *The British Journal of Educational Studies*, 15/2 (1967), 119–32, by permission of Wiley-Blackwell Publishing; p.276, extract from 'Art: the Ultimate Luxury' by Shakti Maira, *Design Today*, December 2002-January 2003, reprinted with kind permission from Shakti Maira, author of *Towards Ananda: Rethinking Indian Art and Aesthetics*; p.276, extract from *Art Since 1960* by Michael Archer, new edition, © 1997 and 2002 Thames & Hudson Ltd., London. Reprinted by kind permission of Thames & Hudson; p.277, extract from Langer, Susanne K. *Philosophical Sketches*. pp.76. ©1962, The John Hopkins University Press. Reprinted with permission of The John Hopkins University Press; p.277, extract from 'The Cultural Importance of the Arts' by Susanne Langer, in M.F. Andrews (ed.), *Aesthetic Form and Education* (Syracuse: Syracuse University Press, 1958), 1–8, with kind permission from Syracuse University Press; pp.295, extracts from Preface to *Collected Essays* by Aldous Huxley. Copyright © 1959 by Aldous Huxley, renewed 1987 by Laura A. Huxley. Reprinted by permission of Georges Borchardt, Inc., for the estate of Aldous Huxley; p.302, extract from *The Age of the Essay* by Paul Graham, copyright © 2004 by Paul Graham, http://www.paulgraham.com/essay.html, accessed 3rd February 2008; p.304, extract from *The Importance of Non-fiction Writing by School Students* by Will Fitzhugh, grateful acknowledgement to Will Fitzhugh for his piece on the non-fiction writing; p.305, extract from *Climate of Fear: The Reith Lectures 2004* by Wole Soyinka, copyright © 2004, Profile Books.

The publisher would like to thank the International Baccalaureate Organization (IBO) for permission to reproduce its intellectual property.

This material has been developed independently by the publisher and the content is in no way connected with nor endorsed by the International Baccalaureate Organization.

Every effort has been made to contact copyright holders of material reproduced in this book. Any omissions will be rectified in subsequent printings if notice is given to the publishers.

Contents

Introduction

Over the years, you may have had teachers who loved their subjects and taught them with great enthusiasm whether literature, biology, art, maths, history or anything else in school. You might have wanted to share in their delight, to feel the same way about a formula or a cell or a colour or a poem instead of just writing something in your notebook to use in the next test. To be in their presence was an inspiration, to share in their joy was a vicarious thrill.

The co-authors of this book, eight teachers, love this subject which is given the formidable title of Theory of Knowledge (or TOK for short). The word 'love' is used intentionally, since intense pleasure and respect and wanting to bring its essence more and more into our own lives, and the lives of our students, make it exactly the right word. We, the authors, continue to learn more about its possibilities and we want to do right by what it demands of us as scholars and teachers. This is called passion and should be courted in your own life as you go forward into college and university and then out into the world to take up your own professional responsibilities. Work that touches both your heart and your mind is the right kind of work for you, and will help you fulfil your nature.

It is unlikely that as authors we can touch your life in the way that the right teacher in the right classroom on the right day can make a difference, even though it is our hope and our ideal in writing this book. Yet, we are speaking to you in these chapters out of our deep commitment to the value of thinking about what is true and what is false in life, about the differences among data, information, knowledge and wisdom, and the different ways of putting this understanding to work in the world.

As you open the pages of this book, it is important to say something about the title of the course. The term 'theory of knowledge' has one meaning in university philosophy departments, another in the International Baccalaureate (IB) programme. At the university level, theory of knowledge is called epistemology – itself an intimidating name – one of the central areas of philosophy. Some of the others (so it is widely agreed) are metaphysics, logic and ethics. Aesthetics and political philosophy are obviously connected to ethics since they are concerned with values and judgements. Then there are philosophies of this and philosophies of that if the department is a large and diverse one: philosophy of language, philosophy of maths, philosophy of science, philosophy of social science, philosophy of history and so on. There may even be a philosophy of business or a philosophy of crime. These topics could be treated historically, from the earliest years of Plato or Lao-tzu or they could be treated as problems such as the mind-body problem or the nature of causality or the existence of God.

TOK in the IB programme is a course that looks at the nature of knowledge across various fields or disciplines. It also explores the way we come to have that knowledge and how it is used in our personal, professional and political lives. But, to clarify further, let it be said what TOK is NOT.

TOK is NOT meant to prepare you to study philosophy nor to master other people's thoughts. You are to reflect on your own learning and what you include in your system of beliefs. It is NOT a course in current affairs, a general studies course, or a rambling session on the meaning of life even though topics can be taken from daily affairs and your experience outside the classroom.

It is NOT a course where a teacher needs to have a degree in philosophy or where teachers must be the experts and have the last word. We are all thinkers all of our lives if our minds are working well, so there may be a new kind of provocative exchange between teacher and pupil. The best teachers of TOK are those who themselves are reflective or curious about competing knowledge claims and who admit that most of the time we live in a world of degrees of certainty and uncertainty. Yet we must make decisions – some trivial, some of very great importance – about what to do with whatever knowledge we have.

It is NOT a course that will give you seven points, but it is foundational and basic for every TOK diploma student. You might not understand why this is so until several years later when you begin to 'make a living' and need to think and speak across subject areas and cultural differences in addressing global issues. Thus, it is NOT a course that will have an immediate bread-and-butter dimension to it, but it will give you a capacity of mind and a skill that will soon become apparent (and beneficial) in your higher education.

So, yes, TOK is a course in critical thinking, but it is NOT an activity where, behind closed doors, students criticize their teachers and what they are taught. It is NOT a course with an external exam but it does ask you to demonstrate your thoughts on paper with an essay, and then again to show your understanding about 'knowledge at work in the world' through a verbal presentation. So while TOK is NOT a course in philosophy as such, it is philosophical in so far as it is concerned with the justifications of knowledge claims and beliefs in all of their forms.

TOK asks that teachers and students get a feel for the power of questions, for how tricky they can be, what counts as a good question and a good answer as a way of sorting out the good stuff from the dross on the Internet. TOK should also help you realize that sometimes to ask a real question is to break a spell or to start a train of thought that leads to a long and winding road.

Thus, TOK asks us to tackle such particular questions as:

- What does it mean to know something in maths and science and history?
- Where does this knowledge come from and how secure is it?
- Are these the same kinds of knowledge? Why or why not?
- Why are logic and reasoning so important?
- When do my feelings count as knowledge?
- Is the scientific method the best or only way to gain an understanding of ourselves in the social sciences?
- Can we ever say that we have knowledge in the strict sense in the realms of art, ethics and religion?
- How does language help or hinder the pursuit of knowledge?

And so on… At its best, this kind of inquiry results in 'the examined life' as opposed to those who do not know what they think, or why – a terrible waste of a mind.

Teachers love TOK because when it works well we can see young people beginning to move from a school life of memorizing and test-taking to becoming aware of themselves as knowers. It is a wonderful experience for a teacher to see students grow in self-awareness and autonomy with a thoughtful view about how to test ideas through argument and to watch them learn to:

- believe strongly with good reasons
- debate pros and cons
- generalize with prudence
- deduce consequences
- identify assumptions
- make responsible ethical decisions
- meet criticism and mete it out to oneself and others with due respect for opposing opinions.

In doing so as your teachers we understand once again why we chose teaching as our life's work and how special it is to have young people in our charge. When we see your natural ability to think take a sharper edge, we all draw closer to the ideal of a liberal education if liberal means anything like its root meaning which pertains to freedom. Without sorting out all the ambiguities of the word *liberal*, two of its meanings 'freedom from' and 'freedom to' can be mentioned. The *freedom from* total reliance on knowledge by authority, second-hand ideas, all the results of other people's thinking, and *freedom to* think things through for yourself, to revise, to refine, to reject or to reaffirm all the things in your heart and your head and then to express those views with clarity and thoughtfulness. Few things feel better than to be able to stand up for yourself in front of others and sway them with your position when you know what you think and you know why.

The IB is 40 years old at the time of printing this book. And yet in this relatively short time, it has gained the respect of the best colleges and universities in the world for its academic rigour, its generality and its depth, three qualities not easy to bring together. The list of higher education schools now recognizing the IB is impressive, what some have called 'blue ribbon' status. This is a good thing.

But, as IB students and teachers, we have an additional responsibility. We must pay as much attention to the International part of our name as to the Baccalaureate, the academic. This is in spite of the fact that most schools and most students, it must be admitted, are concerned primarily with the 'B' of the IB, its academic side, in order to gain admission to colleges and universities.

It is not surprising that the IB has found the task of meeting its international ideals to be a complex one, even as its membership spreads to well over 120 countries. There is first of all the semantic difficulty of definition. What is an international education? What makes an organization international? What makes a school international? What makes a syllabus or a classroom or an exam international? Do we know it when we see it or do we know through intuition or analysis? This is a good TOK question in itself. How many answers to this question are acceptable?

Yet, the concept of an international or a global education is not new. (Are the terms *international* and *global* synonymous?) Read the passage below by Michel Montaigne, writing in 1572.

Mixing with the world has a marvelously clarifying effect on judgement. We are all confined and pent up within ourselves and our sight has contracted to the length of our noses. When someone asked Socrates of what country he was, he did not reply, of Athens, but of the world. This great world… is the mirror into which we must look if we are to behold ourselves from the proper standpoint.

From *On Educating Children* by Michel de Montaigne

International education did not catch on in the sixteenth century and the various definitions within the IB in its early years did not take us far, so we continue to face the challenge today. But the need is now more urgent, so let us fast-forward to our recently retired (2006) Director General of the IBO, George Walker, who has written a series of articles during his tenure summarized as: 'International Education is an Idea Whose Time has Come'.

He begins by telling us what an international education is NOT. (Yes, echoes of what TOK is NOT, but not so surprising a tactic when you consider how medicine and other fields of study use ruling out as a first line technique.) An international education is NOT:

- teaching groups of students of different nations
- studying the geography and customs of other countries
- feasts and festivals
- student foreign exchange programmes
- having strong modern language departments.

All of these are worthy but, on their own, they do not produce young people who have learned to see through the eyes, minds and hearts of others. Nor do such bits and pieces of education totally prepare you for a world where current geographic and political boundaries and economic assumptions are being replaced by new realities, and where values, often not our own (whatever they may be), are central to all decisions of global significance.

So the IB has now gone one step further to infuse its programmes with a greater international (and global) dimension by drawing up a Learner Profile. If this profile were put into place, and reached critical mass, imagine what a world that would be.

Exercise

IB learners should strive to be:

- inquirers
- thinkers
- principled
- caring
- balanced
- knowledgeable
- communicators
- open-minded
- risk-takers
- reflective.

Are all of these features familiar or even clear to you? Do you recognize them when you see them? Can you recognize them in yourself? How many have you exhibited since breakfast this morning? What are their opposites?

- ignorant
- selfish
- extremist
- closed-minded
- apathetic
- others…

Below is one TOK view of the characteristics of the Learner Profile combined with those of the generalized Ideal Knower that appears at the end of each chapter in this book.

It may be that the first thing that occurs to you is that this Learner Profile is about students, but it was pretty clear that the framers meant teachers too! We are also meant to exhibit such qualities. So you can apply this taxonomy to your teachers as well if you dare.

Applying the Learner Profile to TOK Knowers

In the decades of growth of the International Baccalaureate a prototype-learner has evolved. Here are some of the qualities that the IB Ideal Learner seeks.

Here we have applied these *qualities of mind and heart* that are the distinguishing characteristics of the IB Learner Profile to the Ideal Knower in Theory of Knowledge.

- **Inquirers** – inquiry is the flame that lights the intellectual journey of the knower. In gaining knowledge skills, the TOK knower seeks to be an independent thinker. The TOK knower is a life-long learner.
- **Knowledgeable** – the TOK knower acquires a broad base of knowledge across disciplines and issues as a life-long learner. They develop a depth of concept and approach.
- **Thinkers** – the TOK learner seeks to be active, reasoned, creative and ethical in their decision making.
- **Communicators** – the TOK learner takes a collaborative approach to the business of knowing and learning. The construction and expression of ideas is intrinsic to communal learning. A TOK communicator operates in more than one language and in several modes of communication including technology, and cultivates a language appropriate to each Area of Knowledge.
- **Principled** – a TOK knower seeks to understand, through an ethical framework, a respect for individuals and groups. Their life is a crucible of ethical responsibilities and conduct.
- **Open-minded** – the TOK knower appreciates the perspectives and values of groups other than their own. They develop the habits of mind that come from employing multiple perspectives and use these to seed their experiences. The knower retains an identity with their own traditions while engaging with others' values.
- **Caring** – the TOK knower seeks the habits of heart that nurture the sense of service and altruism towards others and towards the environment.
- **Risk-takers** – TOK knowers are intellectual risk-takers. They engage in unfamiliar intellectual and pedagogic fields with the readiness to learn new ideas, new frameworks and new approaches with courage. TOK knowers are flame carriers.
- **Balanced** – TOK knowers understand and seek the holistic equilibrium of body–mind–spirit in their daily lives. Their inner stability rests on this tripos.
- **Reflective** – a TOK knower's life is a life examined. They are aware of the power of self-evaluation in deploying strengths and monitoring limitations.

But even more astounding – to the degree that all of us have these qualities, the IB claims that we are ipso facto *international-minded*. That bears some thinking about. It doesn't just say if you have a multicultural faculty or classroom or if you teach this and that in your programme, or if everyone knows two or three languages, you have achieved international mindedness. By logical extension, it says that schools in Wichita, Kansas, USA; Copenhagen, Denmark; Santiago, Chile or Abu Dhabi with largely local populations can be *internationally minded* as much as the United World College, Singapore with 80 different nationalities. What would be your opinion about this definition of internationalism if asked in a college or university interview?

Impossible? Not at all. Idealistic? Certainly. But we need our ideals in this young organization whose future is brighter than its history is long. (Forty may seem old to you but think about it on a history time line and you can see that the IB is still very new and still very innovative.) We have to keep saying over and over what we are about – to remind ourselves of our ideals. In a way, an educational programme is a movement suffused with ideals and values. You have joined this movement consciously or not. And any movement needs many voices. The IB needs your voices for a better world. Have you any notion of the philosophy or mission of the IB or have you signed up only for your own purposes? Does the notion of an educational movement seem strange to you?

The IB mission statement

The International Baccalaureate aims to develop inquiring, knowledgeable and caring young people who help to create a better and more peaceful world through intercultural understanding and respect.

To this end the organization works with schools, governments and international organizations to develop challenging programmes of international education and rigorous assessment.

These programmes encourage students across the world to become active, compassionate and lifelong learners who understand that other people, with their differences, can also be right.

But in order to become part of a working international community – and to be glad of it – an IB education, and by implication the TOK course, must include activities and ideas as a matter of course that encourage awareness of, and commitment to, the solutions to global problems of a cast and character possibly widely different from what we can now imagine on our own. In part this means that voices of diversity are no longer a value for their novelty; they are necessary for our salvation – everyone's salvation. Please think of this when you make your selections for your presentation topics.

In each of our cultures, in each of the several worlds we occupy, we are offered paradigms of skill, integrity, courage, leadership and creativity. We have no trouble recognizing some of the following as exemplars of Ideal Knowers, each in their field.

David Beckham	Sachin Tendulkar	Yao Ming	Tiger Woods
Nelson Mandela	John F. Kennedy	Vandana Shiva	Mother Theresa
Shah Rukh Khan	J. K. Rowling	Oprah Winfrey	Bono of U2
Galileo	Marie Curie	Watson & Crick	Albert Einstein

1 Choose one from each group that you recognize and identify what makes them an exemplar.

Mother Theresa   compassion

_____   _____

_____   _____

_____   _____

_____   _____

2 Could you identify your own TOK learner profile?

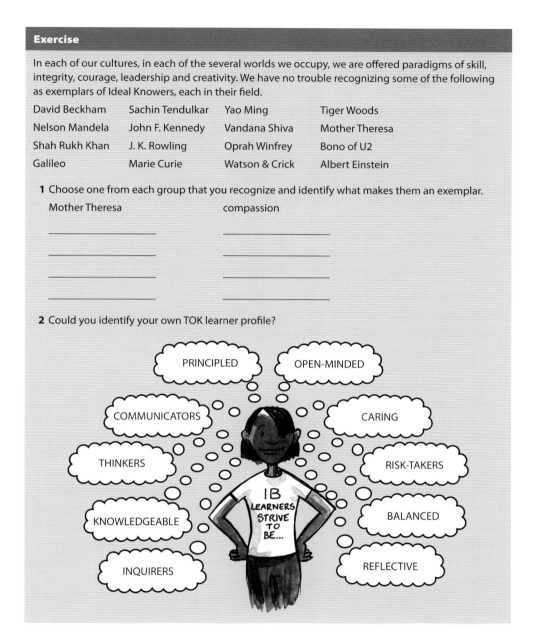

Think about the world's trajectory, not just Iraq or Korea or Darfur at the time of this writing, not just the dominance or decline of the US or the power or passivity of the UN; think about the *vroom* of technology – each day a newer, swifter something appears. It doesn't matter if we like it or not. A lot of people do and a lot of people are using it, for better or for worse, to talk across borders where traditional geopolitical national identities begin to seem quaint. We better learn how to understand this; we better learn how to feel at home here. It is the special mission of the IB to prepare young people to live within a pluralistic community of many voices, all possibly chattering at once in every kind of boundary-crossing conversation. You, our student, look to us to get you ready – we are your teachers. You are entitled to be prepared by us to comprehend the great world beyond your street, your neighbourhood, your culture, your nation, as a result of the expanded perspectives we arouse and shape in you. Some of this we have tried to do with our chapters in this book.

The world we pass on to you is not likely to become better – nor your place in it – without the recognition that the job falls squarely in our laps. It may well be that our IB schools and teachers and students will be the ones to promote perspective taking and international-mindedness – not the politicians, not the media moguls, not the generals nor the corporate tycoons, and not the keepers of the religious flames.

Why should we be internationally minded?
- 'They' have something we want – resources/power/security.
- 'They' have something we admire – style/confidence.
- 'They' are worth studying, as an exercise – things go their way/they are the 'chosen'.
- We are part of a human family and we have much in common.
- 'They' may have perspectives we need to understand.
- Conflicts might be avoided with a broader understanding of 'them'.

Why should we not be internationally minded?
- Our local culture/nation has enough to offer.
- Our values and loyalties will be eroded by exposure to others.
- Cultures could homogenize and our individuality will be lost.
- Our culture will pay the cost for internationalism.
- Our culture has the least to gain from internationalism.
- The other side wants to take our resources and gives in return their values imposed on us.

In a real sense, then, you have the whole world in your hands. We are asked to think today and tomorrow and on and on about how our teaching can be relevant to issues of global significance that you face now, and others that we can see only dimly, if at all. You know the list – war, environment, poverty, terror, energy, global warming and so on. It's a long list. It touches us all. It's in our front gardens. But it is you who can dispel indifference and ignorance; it is you who can broaden horizons. It is you who can find unity in diversity and hear its message and sound its echo. We teach. We make a difference. You learn. You can make that difference happen.

Please note that PT refers officially to the Prescribed Titles from which students choose one on which to write for their TOK grade. In everyday terms you sometimes will hear 'essay topics' or 'essay questions' used. The word 'topic' is also used informally by some teachers to refer to presentations.

An introduction to Theory of Knowledge

What is Theory of Knowledge and why does it matter?

Imagine a group of idealistic men and women from several countries sitting around a table back in the sixties asking, What should our young people know and be able to do by the time they leave school? That's like asking, Why do we go to school?

Now imagine you had a blank slate and could design your own course of school studies the way you can after you leave and move on to college and university. Would you include Theory of Knowledge (TOK)? Before you could give an intelligent answer, you would have to know what it is, and what value it holds for you and for others.

It should be no surprise that the IB was born against the backdrop of the tumultuous sixties. And even though educational debates might lack the drama of the other movements of that era, there were radical notions at play in those early IB meetings. After all, these visionary pioneers were turning their backs on their own country's school systems in favour of a programme of international awareness, even compassion, linked to the highest academic rigour and recognized by the best institutions of higher learning around the world.

But first the reformers needed a curriculum and a testing system independent of any particular culture. The initial choices were easy. A mother tongue and a second language were obvious for an international diploma and they quickly agreed on the need for science and maths requirements; then at least one of several humanities or social science courses; and, finally, the arts were the finishing touch of the hexagon that later became their logo. And to make the IB a distinctive programme, and not just a collection of courses, as was the case with the British 'A' and 'O' levels and the American Advanced Placements courses, the Extended Essay and CAS were added. Yet, to bring it all together, it was also crucial that there should be one academic course, a keystone course that unified the IB diploma. But what should it be?

International agreements are not easy to reach. This reality emerged with the French insisting that every student should take philosophy and the British strongly vetoing the idea. The quarrel was protracted but both sides at last seized upon the idea that every student should follow a course, not in philosophy as such by mastering the great books, but in philosophical thinking based on the students' education to date. Thus, What is science? What is art? What is good evidence? Is there such a thing as an ethical fact? When do your feelings count as knowledge? are typical TOK questions. So TOK became the great compromise and the basic design of the IB diploma was complete. Today, TOK is hailed as the unique feature of the IB programme. It is widely emulated by national schools for the quality of thought that it generates about the purpose, methodology and proofs of each discipline or field of study.

With TOK it was hoped that each IB diploma holder would not only gain a thoughtful awareness of the knowledge they had so far acquired in school, plus the way knowledge 'works in the world', but also the grounds for their personal belief systems. And that they would come to realize that this knowledge, which seems so certain and final in their textbooks, and is imparted with almost gospel credibility in the classroom, is the answer to questions someone once asked in curiosity, wonder or doubt.

Alec Peterson, Godfather of TOK, one of the founding fathers of the IB, its first Director General and himself a TOK teacher, stated that the aim of the course was to counteract two weaknesses which were seen in most upper secondary schools:

1 **The failure to make explicit in the minds of students the different forms which academic learning and knowledge take.** What matters is not the absorption and regurgitation of facts but the development of powers of the mind or ways of thinking which can be applied to new situations and new facts as they arise.

2 **The tendency for students to study their different subjects in watertight compartments**. In doing so, they fail to be able to relate science and art to one another, or to make connections between literature and history. The ability to see how different specialized approaches to a single problem can occur is very important.

In short, the definition of an educated person within the IB was someone who knew how to apply knowledge to novel situations for which there were no ready-made answers.

In Peterson's words

> *Within the IB, the nature of the TOK course is to encourage reflection upon what the student has learned both inside and outside the classroom. For even a broad and intensive curriculum can be studied as though the subjects were in watertight compartments and unrelated to ordinary experience. No matter how good the curriculum is in its parts, we have not done fully right by our students if we deny them the chance to make an integrated sense of their high school life and the virtues and limitations of their learning, and to bring it to critical light. TOK makes a start in this direction.*

> From *Schools Across Frontiers: the Story of the International Baccalaureate and the United World Colleges* by A.D.C. Peterson, by permission of Open Court Publishing Company, a division of Carus Publishing Company © 1987, 2003

TOK A course that examines the origins, methods and validity of the various Areas of Knowledge and Ways of Knowing and how they relate to one another.

TOK is a thoughtful reflection on what students claim to know and believe and what others profess as knowledge.

The IB hexagon

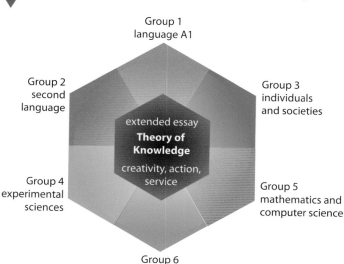

Group 1
language A1

Group 2
second
language

Group 3
individuals
and societies

extended essay
Theory of Knowledge
creativity, action, service

Group 4
experimental
sciences

Group 5
mathematics and
computer science

Group 6
the arts

Critical thinking does not mean finding fault. The spirit of inquiry is meant to bring about more appreciative ways of looking at the subject areas around the IB hexagon.

The teaching may be different from that found in other subjects, since the memorization model of learning is replaced by the question and discussion model.

There may not be one right answer to a question but there are standards for judgement in the expression and defence of beliefs and knowledge claims. And some reasons may be better than others.

Assessment is based on an externally marked essay written on one of ten Prescribed Topics (PTs), plus an internally assessed presentation to the class on 'knowledge at work in the world'.

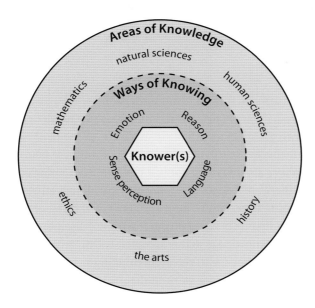

The traditional TOK diagram

The traditional TOK diagram

Exercise

Based on what you have read so far, role play with others a 30-second 'sound bite' in which you respond to someone in a university admissions office or a summer job interview asking you, 'What is TOK, anyway?'

All the parts of this course radiate out from the central question, What is knowledge? While nowhere in the syllabus do we consider this question on its own, we shall do so in the next chapter. We talk about Ways of Knowing where knowledge is linked to Reason, Emotion, Sense perception and Language and Areas of Knowledge where knowledge is already organized into maths, natural sciences, human sciences, history, ethics and the arts. Students tend to talk about these Areas of Knowledge as subjects or courses in secondary school but elsewhere, especially in universities, they are described as disciplines or fields of study each with its own:

- definition
- way of thinking
- set of problems
- object of study
- vocabulary
- methods
- proofs
- experts.

It is crucial to your success in TOK that you understand what a discipline means, since the course is organized, in large part, around the Areas of Knowledge, in other words, disciplines. In order to get a feel for what a discipline is in the real world, it is good to know that real people make their living as scholars within these fields of study and in that sense the disciplines are dynamic, not just collections of knowledge. In fact, as in any social group, there are leaders and followers and cliques all performing their scholarly work according to certain written and unwritten rules, acquiring knowledge, explaining it and defending it (because disputes within a discipline are endless). While there is always a body of knowledge that is accepted within any discipline, there are also people working at the cutting edge of research, thinking new thoughts and debating the issues of the day and publishing their work in the magazines or periodicals associated with each field of study.

So it is not surprising that some people get prizes, money and fame and some do not. Some work in the trenches of everyday activity, while others make the discoveries and breakthroughs. Some are in and some are out, some are lucky, some are not. Some get to ask the questions and give the answers and others have to fall in line. Yet, at the same time, all scholars and practitioners use questions, doubts, theories, facts, imagination, intuition, reason, passion, patience, evidence and intellectual honesty as they try to make sense of the world and tell us about it.

Exercise

Match each discipline with the following simple identifiers. (Note the simplicity of the list. In the real world, there are many hyphenated or overlapping disciplines such as astro-physics, bio-chemistry, art history, cognitive psychology, political anthropology, ethics of science etc.)

_____	Logic	a)	numerical relationships
_____	Economics	b)	judgements of right and wrong
_____	History	c)	valid reasoning
_____	Ethics	d)	past events
_____	Aesthetics	e)	lawful events in the natural world
_____	Maths	f)	behaviour of people and animals
_____	Science	g)	events in the social world
_____	Psychology	h)	power and policy
_____	Politics	i)	judgements of beauty
_____	Human sciences	j)	distribution of material goods and services

A good presentation topic is to consider what the cutting edge issue of the day is for each discipline and who are the leaders in any particular field, and why.

What's in a name?

Have you ever wondered why the course is called Theory of Knowledge? Other names that have been suggested for the course include:

- Forms of Knowledge
- Maps of Knowledge
- Realms of Knowledge
- Problems of Knowledge
- Knowledge Issues
- Ways of Understanding.

You should note that the name 'Theory of Knowledge' is not meant to imply that there is only one theory about knowledge. *Theory* comes from the Greek word for *theatre* as a way of seeing something, so 'Looking at Knowledge' might be an equivalent for 'Theory of Knowledge'. What other names might you suggest? Pathways to Knowledge? What does each variation emphasize?

But more importantly than what TOK is are the habits of mind that are formed in the student from the experience of honest critical thought. After all, it is the student who is at the centre of the TOK diagram as the knower. And it is the mission of the IB that all of its diploma students will acquire the intellectual honesty and powers of judgement which are characteristic of the thinking student and that these characteristics will be emblematic of the IB education. (See the Learner Profile on page ix to match your idea of what it means to be educated with what the IB has proposed.)

What do you think of one teacher's description of her TOK students on their graduation day?

> *Students come to us at the beginning of the year who have studied something of great human significance in art, literature, the sciences, maths and history – all the hexagon subjects. Experience is then deepened with the exposure to new, challenging and relevant ideas from other disciplines, other groups or a voice not earlier heard. They internalize a feeling for more than one way of seeing the world. They find their voices in discussion with others. They know the limitations of any single voice. They are immersed in a community of intercultural and interdisciplinary thought. They have begun to master the skills of integrating these diverse perspectives because they know what counts as a good question and the beginning of a good answer. And they know that a question can be asked with admiration and awe as well as from challenge and confrontation. They are comfortable with ambiguity and prepared to live in a world of uncertainty. They sense when action or restraint in judgement is called for; they are comfortable in disagreement and poised in conflict.*
> *This is a splendid portrait of a young person with empathy, with openness to growth, glad for the stimulation of new ideas, and with an appreciation of differences as a treasure house. All of this has become part of their instinctive responses to novel situations. They are ready to take the next step. They are ready to graduate.*

Compare the personal view given above with the more textbook version of a critical thinker versus a non-critical thinker shown below. Both have value. Which do you prefer?

Critical thinker	Non-critical thinker
They are honest with themselves and recognize what they do not know.	They pretend they know more than they do, ignore their limitations, and assume their views are error-free.
They regard problems and controversial issues as exciting challenges.	They regard problems and controversial issues as nuisances or threats to their ego.
They strive for understanding, keep curiosity alive, remain patient with complexity and invest time to overcome confusion.	They are impatient with complexity and would rather remain confused than make the effort to understand.
They set aside personal preferences and base judgements on evidence.	They base judgements on first impressions and gut reactions. They are unconcerned about evidence and cling to their own ideas in the face of a challenge.

Knowledge profile
Who are you?

Man is made by his beliefs. As he believes, so he is.

Bhagavad Gita 500 BCE

You are very likely to ask yourself more than once in your life, Who am I? What do I believe? What do I want to do? What do I need to know in order to do it? Self knowledge, as such, is not taught in school even though we come to know ourselves better through the way we react to the experience of learning both in and out of the classroom. Before delving into the Ways of Knowing which we'll explore in Chapter 3, it is good to recall the words of Socrates, 'Know thyself'.

Exercise

One wise man said, 'If you want to know someone, you have to know their memories.' Does this mean that you are your memories? Another person said, 'If you want to know someone, don't ask about what they love, find out what they hate.' Does this mean you are what you hate? Consider:

- You are what you know.
- You are what you believe.
- You are what you do.
- You are what you hope for.
- You are what you feel.
- You are how you think.

How true is any of this? Is the list complete? What would you add? What are the differences? What difference does it make in your life to believe or not believe something? How might it make you a different person?

Don't tell me what you believe in. I'll observe how you behave and I will make my own determination.

Alex Trebek

Note how your actions are affected by your belief that:
- No one is watching you.
- It is going to rain.

- Your chair is broken.
- You are invisible.
- Your father is mad at you.
- Your opinions are worth nothing.
- You are weightless.
- You are good-looking.
- You can dance.
- You can't dance.
- Nobody likes you.
- Everybody likes you.
- You are smart.
- You are not smart.
- The world will end tomorrow.
- God is watching you every minute.

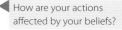

How are your actions affected by your beliefs?

Another distinction among people is the way they go about finding out what they need to know. In the US the state motto for Missouri is the 'show-me' state meaning that people there are reluctant to believe anything that they don't see with their own eyes. In short, seeing is believing.

Consider the story below which is about a husband and wife as an example of two different kinds of 'knowers'. In philosophical terms, one is the *empirical* and the other is the *rational*; in simpler terms, one relies on *observation* and *experience* while the other relies on *logic* and *reasoning*.

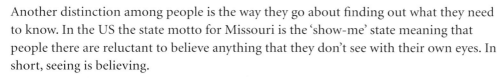

Once upon a time there was a woman who thought she heard a burglar downstairs. She woke up her husband…

Woman: *Honey, I think someone is in the house. Please go and look.*

Man: *There's no one in the house. If someone were in the house the alarm would have gone off. Go back to sleep.*

Woman: *Maybe someone cut the wires.*

Man: *Don't be silly. The dog would have barked.*

Woman: *Maybe they chloroformed the dog. Please go look for me.*

So down he went, and looked around, then came back up…

Man: *There, I've looked. No one is in the house.*

Woman: *Well, did you look everywhere?*

Man: *Yes.*

Woman: *Did you look in the kitchen?*

Man: *Yes.*

Woman: *Well, maybe when you were in the kitchen, he was in the living room.*
And so on…

The message of the story is that one kind of person, by and large, figures things out in his head and reaches a conclusion, a very satisfactory one for him. If there were a burglar, the dog would have barked; the dog did not bark, therefore there is no burglar. This is a very neat *syllogism* or piece of logic. In contrast, the wife cannot accept the first premise because she depends upon the *seeing is believing* kind of evidence. For every reason the husband gives, the wife will find a doubt. For every possibility the wife gives, the husband will find it inconceivable. While no one is purely only one kind of knower, or uses only one kind of approach, these two tendencies, *going and looking* versus *sitting and thinking* characterize some of our own ways of forming our beliefs, becoming certain of our opinions or even changing our minds upon occasion.

Two approaches to belief

The following do not all mean the same but each column belongs to a family of meaning.

Rational	Empirical
Logic	Experience
Reasoning	Observation
Sitting and thinking	Going and looking

Changing your mind

Exercise

A Name one thing that you used to believe and now do not.
B Name one thing that you believe now that you think you will believe forever.
For A, ask yourself:
- What made you believe it in the first place?
- Was the belief rational or empirical or both or neither?
- How did you come to change your belief?
- How strong was the belief?
- How important was the belief?
- What might occur to make you believe it again?
- What difference would it make in your life if this belief turned out to be true?

For B, ask yourself:
- What makes you believe it in the first place?
- Is the belief rational or empirical or both or neither?
- Could anything make you change your mind?
- Would it be rational or empirical or both or neither?
- How strong or important is the belief?
- How many other people believe the same thing?
- What difference would it make in your life if this belief turned out not to be true?

Some of the beliefs you might have mentioned could have powerful emotional components to them. For instance, a) it feels good to know something and b) miserable not to know something when you want to or when you have to: (c) to feel awful to lose a belief or (d) to think you will never know something important no matter what you do.

Exercise

Consider how you might complete the following sentences.
- It felt really good when I finally found out that…
- How I wish I had known…
- If I could only still believe that…
- I don't think I will ever really know about…

We also have attitudes of awe and/or pity for those who know a great deal or very little. So, it is not just self-knowledge that is valuable but the way others know us, or think they know us, or believe us or trust us. Because we live in a world with others, there is an other-relatedness to what we know and believe and how we talk about it. Do people see you as gullible or sceptical? As rational or empirical? How far are you from the total ignoramus or the ideal knower if such people exist?

We certainly act as if we know a great many things (even when we find out we don't) and many of us intuit a difference between genuine knowledge with its compelling grounds for belief and that of mere opinion. At this point we suppose that knowledge is the better thing. However, this seems to invite exploration. And at this point, and with this difference in mind, we have the foundations for our TOK course.

Today's world: trust

Why do we usually assume that people who tell us something are telling the truth? Do you usually believe strangers on the streets? Do you always trust everyone fully? If not, how do you decide who to trust and who not to trust? Could your trust be eroded? Can it be re-established? On what grounds do we decide to double-check someone's statements or advice? Do we trust some people more than others? How do we decide? Are there some sorts of knowledge that we must trust others to give us? Could we possibly gain all the knowledge and beliefs that we have if we did not trust others?

To be a successful knower implies that we must develop a nose for unreliable information. To be a good gatherer of knowledge is in large part to be able to judge the conditions of trust.

Do you usually believe strangers on the street? ▶

Ideal knower

The Buddha (circa 563–483 BCE)

Buddha was not a prophet, saint or god; he was a wise teacher and even taught his followers to doubt him.

In Buddhism, there are two kinds of faith: preliminary faith (the trust with which we begin) and verified faith (the confirmation of preliminary faith). Here are some of the words of Buddha:

Do not believe in anything simply because you have heard it.

Do not believe in traditions because they have been handed down for many generations.

Do not believe in anything because it is spoken and rumoured by many.

Do not believe in anything simply because it is found in your religious books.

Do not believe in anything merely on the authority of your teachers and elders.

But after observation and analysis, when you find that anything agrees with reason, and is conducive to the good… then accept it and live up to it.

O monks, just like examining god in order to know its quality, you should put my words to the test. A wise person does not accept them merely out of respect.

Shakyamuni Buddha

Student presentation

1 Does it matter if what we believe is true?

Give each person three short articles of varying credibility. They might be:

a an absurd news article to provoke disbelief such as Elvis on the Moon

b an article mixing fact and fiction, perhaps treating one cultural group negatively

c a more dependable article, but which is still interpretive (for example, a passage from a history textbook).

Discuss these questions after reading the articles:
- Do you believe the article? Why or why not?
- What is its source? What is its evidence?
- Does it matter if what you believe is true?
- What if you believed or rejected the article? What would it justify?

2 Expand on the exercise on page 4 by interviewing your teachers, then presenting the following to the class:
- What was their major field of study in college or university?
- What were some supporting disciplines?
- How are the disciplines described?
- How was the choice arrived at?
- What is the history of the disciplines?
- Who are the major figures?
- What are the current problems of knowledge or knowledge issues in the various disciplines?

Note: This list can be revised in several ways to suit the situation.

Essay questions

1 We cannot understand what a person means by what he says without knowing a good deal about his beliefs.

2 What beneficial role might doubt play in forming beliefs? Discuss.

What is knowledge?
The quest for knowledge

It is said from time to time that ignorance is bliss, but this is not so. The pattern of our lives as students and teachers involves us in years of schooling and sometimes years of continued struggle to master a discipline and gain a reputation in the public realm. Or, at the personal level, to find out what is worth knowing and what is worth forgetting. Francis Bacon, an Elizabethan philosopher, believed that *knowledge is power* and, whether you believe that or not, the quest for knowledge is endless and daily. One could almost say that it is part of the human condition.

All men by nature desire to know.   Aristotle

What is knowledge? sounds simple enough. We all know roughly what it is to know and to be correct; to be wrong, to doubt and to be only partially right. If you've thought about knowledge at all, you may hold some view close to what can be called the 'Trivial Pursuit' model. That is, knowledge is seen as facts which are more or less simple, discrete, non-controversial and displayed through recall. This model is generated and confirmed by much of your school experience and, certainly, exploited by television game shows. People with a lot of this kind of knowledge are often called clever and those with less of it are often called something not so complimentary.

In the world outside the classroom, knowledge-seeking never stops. Governments appoint commissions, armies rely on intelligence, scientists conduct research, doctors constantly retrain, teachers carry on with professional development, wrestlers study their opponents, journalists check their sources, musicians look for better ways to compose, philosophers clarify concepts, gamblers study the odds and so on. We speak about *life-long learning* or *learning how to learn* as qualities more valuable than acquiring a mountain of facts that may not be relevant when the time comes to use them.

A young woman's vision of her autonomy

I remember the day I went away to university. My uncle told me that because of the luck of the draw, I had very little of the structures of my life under my control. Not my place of birth, my gender, my height, my looks, my genes and so forth, and that everyone in the world wanted my mind and my money. Keep them both to yourself, he said. I didn't accept his cynicism but on the first day of class when the professor quoted Einstein to me, my uncle seemed just a little bit wiser:

If most of us are ashamed of shabby clothes and shoddy furniture, let us be more ashamed of shabby ideas and shoddy beliefs.

Albert Einstein

And I knew then that the ideas and beliefs that would become the furnishings of my mind were in my control, just the way I was furnishing my new apartment. I decided to go for quality and get rid of the clutter. I would believe what is worth believing and no more.

In one sense there is an implicit command in TOK to find out things for yourself. After all, the knower is at the centre of the diagram (see page 3). In addition, people are increasingly inclined to find out what they need to know from all kinds of places, often online, and not necessarily with deference to experts who pronounce from on high. The near universal student use of the Wikipedia open source encyclopedia on the Internet is one of the most obvious examples, especially when compared to that of the leather bound Encyclopedia Britannica, once the pride of every middle class home in the English speaking world. And the long hours spent in libraries consulting stacks of books, the standard practice of earlier generations, is now almost as quaint as carbon paper. While expert opinions are still sought today, especially with the aid of the Google search engine, increasingly it is the individuals themselves who weigh the various authorities and come to their own conclusions. Just ask doctors about their Web-savvy patients who come into their offices with handfuls of printouts from the Internet.

In the Middle Ages, we were told what we knew by the Church; after the printing press and the Reformation, by state censors and the licensers of publishers; with the rise of liberalism in the 19th and 20th centuries, by publishers themselves, and later by broadcast media—in any case, by a small, elite group of professionals.

But we are now confronting a new politics of knowledge, with the rise of the Internet and particularly of the collaborative Web—the Blogosphere, Wikipedia, Digg, YouTube, and in short every website and type of aggregation that invites all comers to offer their knowledge and their opinions, and to rate content, products, places, and people. It is particularly the *aggregation* of public opinion that instituted this new politics of knowledge.

From 'Who Says We Know: On the New Politics of Knowledge' by Larry Sanger, co-founder of Wikipedia. An *Edge* Original Essay.

So here is the challenge for the TOK student: in this new world, the skill of speed of access is not what is needed as much as the skills of discernment and discrimination. What best supports an argument or helps solve a problem? How can I ask the right question? Where do I go for the answer? How can I tell the difference between the reliable and the slipshod? The subjective and the objective? The biased and the fair? Those skills must be valued and practised; they are not inborn. So at the very least we should ask, What are the sources and dependability of our knowledge?

The world of Wikipedia: can it make the grade?

There are some things that seemingly everybody knows: that the earth goes around the sun, that humans have two eyes, that aeroplanes can fly and a lot of other facts too tedious to mention since, after all, everybody knows these things. Then there is *background* or *common knowledge* which seemingly a majority of people accept, yet a significant number of people do not: statements about global warming, evolution, who destroyed the World Trade Center, the Holocaust and so forth. To be able to establish society's **common knowledge** and to establish what is true and false for the majority is an awesome power when you realize that this kind of knowledge shapes whole generations of people in their education, influences research and legislation and brands some people and groups as mad if they don't believe as the majority does. To give an example, Linus Pauling was a two-time Nobel Prize winner but his fame could not protect him from public ridicule when he began to make extravagant claims about the power of vitamin C as a near cure-all.

How this common knowledge is mastered and shaped into disciplines is one thing but more importantly, how it can be posted onto the Web by nearly anyone, and then spread throughout the entire world, is one of the real technological and knowledge revolutions of our time.

Common knowledge
Knowledge accepted by a majority of people but rejected by a significant minority.

Exercise

Take a moment to think about how technology affects the construction and spread of knowledge.

Probably some of your teachers began their careers with manual typewriters and used their own book collections or the public library as their major sources of knowledge. They probably also hand-cranked purple ink mimeograph handouts for their students that smelled slightly of dizzy-making fumes. The move to electric typewriters and the photocopying machine prior to the computers and the Internet today surely has had an impact on what and how much we can know in ways still to be understood. Perhaps a teacher would like to speak about this change or you might want to explore it for your TOK presentation.

Wikipedia is a challenge to traditional teaching and learning, to the authority of the professor, the textbook, the library, the publishing house, the documentary video, indeed, every form of mediated knowledge vetted by some expert, real or imagined. Until recently, these were the voices who said, This is good to read. This is knowledge. This you should consult. This you may footnote. Just imagine the difference between the textbook you are reading now and its very same contents posted on a wiki site. In five or ten years, the paper version will be much as it is now in contrast to the online document which will have been either improved or tampered with depending on your point of view. Both have value.

A page from Wikipedia – the free online encyclopedia

As Larry Sanger says: 'A giant, open global conversation has just begun, one that will live on for the rest of human history; its potential for good is tremendous'. Add to this, one of the champions of the free and open exchange of ideas, John Stuart Mill, who argued in *On Liberty*, that an unfettered vigorous exchange of opinion is the very best means known to man as a way to improve our grasp of truth. Where better to find the vigour of argument than in the infosphere of the Internet?

Yet, in opposition, voices of concern say that there is too much back and forth, too much noise and dissent about everything on the Web. With Wikipedia and the proliferation of the blog culture, there is a lot less of what 'we all know' as time goes on. And in so far as a common culture of ideas depends on a large body of common knowledge, giving a voice to everyone, fair and equal as that may be, presents a threat to the unity and coherence of that common knowledge along with any standards of reliability.

Of course, we want our encyclopedias, and all our sources of knowledge, to be as reliable as possible. Ideally we would like to read an encyclopedia, believe what it says and arrive at knowledge, not error. According to one leading account of knowledge called 'reliabilism', knowledge is true belief that has been arrived at by a 'reliable process' (for example, getting a good look at something in good light) or through a reliable indicator of truth (for example, the proper use of a calculator) but not necessarily a reliable person. Note the contemporary similarity here to Plato's classical definition where Knowledge = Justified True Belief.

But reliability is a comparative quality. Does something have to be *perfectly* reliable in order to be reliable? To say that an encyclopedia is reliable is to say that it contains an unusually high proportion of truth versus error, compared to other publications. But it can still contain some error and perhaps a high enough proportion of error such that you should never use just one reference work if you want to be sure and safe about your information. Are second opinions always to be sought if there is no perfect encyclopedia?

Exercise

- A question to think about in terms of perfect reliability is one from science (see page 158). It is concerned with the use of Newtonian mechanics in engineering, which rests on a mathematical description of reality (Newton's Laws) that does not perfectly describe gravitation. Yet, in almost all cases it is reliable enough. How do scientists determine that it is reliable enough?
- Do you think it is possible that there will be a perfect encyclopedia some day? Would you know it if you saw it?
- If there were a perfect encyclopedia, could you get knowledge just by reading, understanding and believing it?
- If you think that encyclopedias should state the truth, do you mean the truth itself, or what the best informed people, or experts, take to be the truth? Or even what the general public takes to be the truth?
- Do you ever consider getting a second opinion on your second-hand knowledge in the way people sometimes do with medical care?
- Do you think encyclopedias should be free (like some on the Internet) or should there be a subscription or purchase fee?

By the time this book is published Wikipedia, one of the most frequently visited websites at the time of writing, may have changed drastically or even no longer exist. In fact, one of the founders has left to start another online source of information. However, the birth of such a rapidly successful phenomenon in your time is a valuable example of how knowledge comes to be organized and presented to a mass audience. But for now, most of the debate swirling around the growth and use of Wikipedia is not its reliability, which according to several studies in recent years shows its error ratio to be just a hair below that of the Encyclopedia Britannica, but that it initially had no special role for experts in its content production system. In fact, Wikipedia's defenders go so far as to say that expertise is not necessary, a commitment to a position that some call 'dabblerism'. This goes against the view that special knowledge or credentials should give experts special authority in contrast to the wisdom of the masses. The professors in academia have been furious.

Of course questions arise. If Wikipedia ignores the need for expert guidance, how then does it propose to establish its own reliability? Either it does so from external reports (in which case it chooses authorities to establish its credentials) or its reliability may come from Wikipedia's internal contributors who form the benchmark for truth. But then, is this too self-serving, perhaps even a form of *relativism*, which means that truth and its reliability are 'socially constructed' by crowds, anonymous or not, whose credentials are irrelevant to their entries? As we shall see in the following pages, there are difficulties whenever truth is relative, namely, *true for you but not for me*. Moreover, one has to ask, if the writer of any piece has no degree or credential, does the supposed truth have credibility just because the writer is sure of it?

In summary, Wikipedia, in its infancy, is deeply egalitarian and is proud of its creed of *epistemic egalitarianism* which states that we are all fundamentally equal in our authority or right to articulate what should pass for knowledge. The only grounds on which a claim can compete against other claims are to be found in the content of the claim itself, never in who makes it. In fact, Wikipedia gives quite clear instructions for anyone who wishes to post original entries or to edit those of others.

Since nearly 85 per cent of students cited Wikipedia in their footnotes in recent TOK essays, it is important, if not imperative, that those involved in the assessment process have an intelligent and defensible position about Wikipedia sources and statements.

Although only anecdotal, the following type of experiment has been carried out any number of times by those wishing to test the accuracy of Wikipedia. Someone places a number of false entries on the website hoping to slip them in unnoticed, either for the sheer challenge of fooling the editorial team or possibly to undermine the site's reputation. Yet the 'troll' (Internet slang) is often surprised to find that the Wikipedia editors have not only found the offending entry within hours, but have deleted it and sent a message back requesting an end to the posting of inaccurate material.

Exercise

- Compare the Wikipedia encyclopedia movement of today with that of the philosophers of the Enlightenment in France in terms of their motives and successes in collecting all that mankind should know.
- Discuss the issue that Wikipedia is not egalitarian in any admirable way if the equality of its sources results in a sloppy information architecture that gives everyone equal access to creating and receiving mediocre information.
- Compare the egalitarianism philosophy of the Wikipedia policy and practices with that of the Reformation's devastating criticism of the exclusive right of the Catholic Church to deliver the meaning of scripture and to mediate God's word to the masses.

The origins and nature of knowledge

Knowledge does not exist in a social vacuum. In every discipline or Area of Knowledge there are scholars who have more authority than others. And certainly those outside the discipline have even less expertise or fewer credentials. The previous pages brought to your attention the schism between the more traditional reliance on knowledge by authority and the freedom provided by Wikipedia for anyone to contribute to what is known about the world. Indeed, there is a movement coming out of Germany and France that studies how socio-cultural factors influence the development of beliefs and opinions. This movement is called 'the sociology of knowledge' and is concerned with the dependence of knowledge upon social position. That is, who gets to say what is knowledge is a function of your standing in society. As a knower yourself, you should be thinking about whether who proposes an idea has any bearing on whether it is true or false. (See the appeal to authority fallacy in Chapter 7: Reason, page 106, and the Semmelweis case study in Chapter 10: Natural science, page 160.)

The origins of knowledge are many, but the proofs of knowledge are few, and maybe only two.

Sue Bastian

Origins, Proofs and Areas of Knowledge

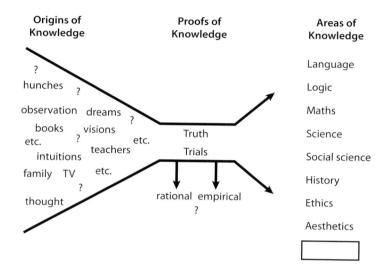

On the left of the diagram, you can see many different *Origins of Knowledge*, and the possibilities are far more numerous than the diagram shows. You could not count the origins, although it is a good exercise to consider where your own ideas come from, at least those that you need to prove to yourself or to others. Now look on the right at the *Areas of Knowledge*. Here you can see there is that last entry, an empty box: this can stand for knowledge that perhaps falls outside the standard forms or is a combination of disciplines. While looking at this diagram, think about the reality that all knowledge is the answer to a question someone once asked. Knowledge begins in doubt and wonder and is a triumph of passing hurdles known as truth tests or achieving proofs of various kinds.

In other words, someone once asked a question, had a doubt, a belief, a hunch, an intuition or a hypothesis (on the left) and if it was eventually accepted as knowledge (on the right) by you or others, it had to have had some justification (the centre piece). The demand of others, *How do you know?* and your own demands for proof, justification, compelling evidence or similar notions is an understandable one. That is how things go. After all, why should anyone believe what I say just because I said it? Who am I? Perhaps if I am a prince in a world of paupers, no one will argue with me, but that does not make me right and it does not make my subjects believe me. So we must turn to that narrow middle section, the proofs and the truth tests. These are the hurdles that I, and others, must overcome in order to convert, say, a doctoral dissertation thesis, or my personal conviction, into something deemed knowledge. I have to meet standards outside myself. Your certainty may drive you to find the answer and establish your knowledge claim, but your feeling of certainty in itself cannot make it true for others.

Once upon a time Galileo had a bright idea that grew into a belief that was formed into a hypothesis that was tested and confirmed by the telescope. That is, he was trying to move from the left to the right of the diagram, from his *acquaintance* with the skies to a *description* of the skies that others could know about. He was trying to prove his ideas to the doubting masses, many of whom refused to even look through the lens of the new instrument. In fact, the most important changes in knowledge have always been met with resistance. Would you have looked in the telescope or passed it by, dismissing it as a crazy idea?

Knowledge by acquaintance and knowledge by description

The example of Galileo above talks about acquaintance and description, an idea that is often linked to the British philosopher, Bertrand Russell. At a basic level, it looks like this:

1   Knowledge by Description   similar to   Knowing That   >   Public
2   Knowledge by Acquaintance   similar to   Knowing How   >   Private

Let's look at each of these in more detail below.

Knowledge by description

The first, **knowledge by description**, is public knowledge, knowledge of facts, including the knowledge of the disciplines, since it describes the world using statements or, as philosophers say, *propositions*. If you cannot describe or say anything about a state of affairs that can be understood, then that state of affairs cannot be known to anyone else, unless we begin to inhabit a new kind of world of mind-reading. (Whether mind-reading is possible is an interesting notion for a TOK presentation.) Thus, language or some form of public expression is crucial to getting your idea into the public realm.

As an example, think of a mining accident where a single observer (you) experiences the reality of the situation and then communicates the findings to those waiting above ground. 'There are 12 men located at level B.' Whether I believe you (or not) has several assumptions built in: that you can see things for what they are, that the conditions of seeing are adequate, that you can describe them accurately, that you are a truth-teller and that I can understand you.

Overall, the statement (or proposition) 'there are 12 men located at level B' is thought to be *objective*, meaning that another person equally endowed with vision and understanding of the language, etc. would report the same or a closely similar version of reality. However, the details about the miners' well-being might be more problematic; that is, are they dead or alive; what are their immediate needs; what should be done next? These judgements go far beyond the initial report of finding the trapped workers. Where things begin to become *subjective* is where your opinions, feelings or point of view might colour the report. For instance, 'The miners have been located at level B' is a different kind of factual statement to 'The miners are suffering horribly' which is more interpretive. Knowledge by description takes as its goal the more objective propositions, but most of us realize that our statements about reality are usually a combination of fact and interpretation.

 Knowledge by description This is explicit knowledge expressed as facts about the world.

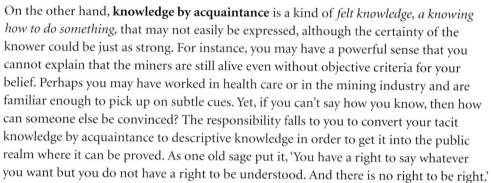

Knowledge by acquaintance

Knowledge by acquaintance This is tacit knowing, from familiarity or a feeling that is difficult to express.

On the other hand, **knowledge by acquaintance** is a kind of *felt knowledge, a knowing how to do something,* that may not easily be expressed, although the certainty of the knower could be just as strong. For instance, you may have a powerful sense that you cannot explain that the miners are still alive even without objective criteria for your belief. Perhaps you may have worked in health care or in the mining industry and are familiar enough to pick up on subtle cues. Yet, if you can't say how you know, then how can someone else be convinced? The responsibility falls to you to convert your tacit knowledge by acquaintance to descriptive knowledge in order to get it into the public realm where it can be proved. As one old sage put it, 'You have a right to say whatever you want but you do not have a right to be understood. And there is no right to be right.'

Knowledge by acquaintance, or know-how, is best shown, not explained. Just watch a master gardener pottering around his plants or consider a bicycle racer taking a curve, a painter mixing tones and hues to get just the right shade of blue, or a footballer placing a kick or a person understanding his pet. They know just what they are doing but may not be able to explain it. Also, think how this distinction between acquaintance and description, the *knowing how* versus the *knowing that*, works itself out in your daily life. You won't get any prizes in school if you can't answer the questions in class or on the test. Your silence may be taken for ignorance or fear or shyness but not knowledge. Yet *knowing how* to do something, for example, getting along with your teacher or your classmates, may be just as valuable in overall terms of success in school.

It is not surprising that *knowledge by description* is more often taken for real knowledge and given pride of place in the academic world. If *knowledge by acquaintance*, important as it may be at the 'life as lived' level, cannot be described, proven and codified into book learning, it is sometimes seen as a poor relation by comparison,

Knowing how versus knowing that

The two statements below typify the debate about what constitutes knowledge. The first excludes anything that might be considered private knowledge (similar to the public knowledge by description), while the second (similar to knowledge by acquaintance) takes the intuitive into consideration.

> *If you can't say it, you don't know it.*
> Hans Reichenbach (German philosopher of science, 1891–1953)

> *I know more than I can say.*
> Michael Polanyi (Hungarian philosopher of science, 1891–1976)

Look at the two columns set out below. The terms in each column have been grouped together because they seem to have a resemblance. Do you agree with the grouping? You may be able to address this question more clearly as you answer each of the true or false questions that follow.

Knowledge by acquaintance	**Knowledge by description**
knowing how	knowing that
tacit	articulated
subjective	objective
private	public
can be shown	must have reasons/evidence/proofs
can originate in experience	can originate in experience
may give certainty	may give certainty
baking bread	recipe for baking bread
savoir	*connaitre*
wissen	*kennen*
saber	*conocer*

Place T (true) or F (false) or D (debatable) in the space next to the question.

_____ **1** Knowledge by description is more than a mental state.

_____ **2** Language is the usual medium of expression in knowledge by description.

_____ **3** Experience can be a source for knowledge in either knowledge by acquaintance or knowledge by description.

_____ **4** Not all experience can be put into words.

_____ **5** There can be no knowledge by description without evidence.

_____ **6** Evidence is a sufficient condition for knowledge by description.

_____ **7** Evidence is a necessary condition for knowledge by description.

_____ **8** Knowing how to do something is always capable of being said.

_____ **9** Language is a sufficient condition for knowledge by description.

_____ **10** Language is a necessary condition for knowledge by description.

_____ **11** Knowledge by acquaintance may be inarticulate.

_____ **12** If something is true, then this means that you know it.

_____ **13** The certainty reached in descriptive knowledge is greater than that reached in any other way.

_____ **14** You can know something but not believe it.

_____ **15** You can believe something without knowing it.

_____ **16** Experience is not identical to knowing.

_____ **17** A man who guesses the horses right for every race, but cannot say how he does it, has no real knowledge by description.

_____ **18** Every experience in life results in knowledge.

_____ **19** A therapist can know more about your behaviour than you do.

_____ **20** A male doctor can know more about giving birth to children than a woman who has ten children.

_____ **21** The doctor who has suffered a ruptured appendix knows more about the condition than a doctor who has not suffered the pain.

_____ **22** 'More people can get into this bus' is a statement of knowledge by description.

_____ **23** Experience is a sufficient condition for knowledge.

_____ **24** Feelings are a sufficient condition for knowledge.

_____ **25** It is possible to know something that isn't true.

Think about the following question where both kinds of knowledge, *acquaintance* and *description*, are at play: 'Can a male obstetrician know more about childbirth than a woman who has had eight children?' Now imagine this scenario. The woman is in labour. The doctor says that it will be several hours yet until the birth. The woman shouts that the baby is coming now. The doctor says that it is impossible because sufficient dilation has not occurred.

In this scenario, of course, it all depends on what you mean by 'knowledge', and that is just the point. These kinds of situations happen frequently in life where knowledge by acquaintance (having had eight children) gives a kind of *knowing how* from the woman's point of view versus the doctor's *knowing that* with the scientific reliability of his or her knowledge. Who gets to say? Would it make a difference if the doctor were female, with or without children? How can the two perspectives combine for the best possible outcome? What do you make of the phrase, 'the art and science of medicine'?

The basis of knowledge – rationalism and empiricism

Some people have a disposition towards logic while others lean towards sense experience in finding out what they want to know. Think back to the story on page 7 about the husband who reluctantly goes downstairs in the middle of the night to search the house in response to his wife's pleading. Rational Husband thought he could figure out things in his head to reach a conclusion, while Empirical Wife wanted to see for herself, or at least have her husband go and look for her. In this example, we were talking about psychological tendencies to confirm our beliefs and answer the questions we ask ourselves about reality. Is there a stranger in the house or not? We can extend this notion from the psychological to the philosophical and introduce the *rational* and the *empirical* as the basis for, or proofs of, knowledge.

In this section we will confine ourselves to the first two paradigms: the *rational* (the power of reason) and the *empirical* (the power of perception). These two contrasting views were explored at least as far back as the Indian Vedas, dating to 1500 BCE, the earliest philosophical texts in existence. When you consider that there is still discussion and debate today (see the section on The Baby Lab on page 28) it is not surprising that we will not settle this difference for ourselves in several short paragraphs. However, throughout this book the concepts of the empirical and the rational will be deepened and clarified as we examine the nature of evidence in each of the Areas of Knowledge.

Rationalism

One of the figures in the history of thought closely associated with the rationalist school of philosophy is René Descartes. Imagine the year 1741 and a young French soldier huddled by a wood-burning stove at his post in the Netherlands. Before his military duty was over, he would give the world one of the most famous (if not always well understood) phrases in philosophy, *cogito ergo sum,* I think therefore I am, and he did it through the power of reason right there in that little room. What was the point? Well, Descartes wanted to see if anything he had been taught could survive the challenge of doubt. Before long, the casualties were his teachers, his books, the deception of his senses, the possibility of dreaming and even an evil genie fooling him. In short, almost everything. Then with utter clarity, he realized that no matter what else he had consigned to the knowledge rubbish bin, he was a person doubting. That he could not deny; *I doubt, therefore I am.* Because his reason told him that he existed with such clearness, Descartes began to rely on the rigour of reason, and reason only, as a method to establish anything that could be known with certainty. In a way, as in mathematics, the *cogito* was his axiom, his starting point and his principle of verification. This epiphany (or was it a logical intuition?) gave him the confidence to build a system of knowledge using reasoning as its primary source and its form of validation.

Only reason can give the certainty that Descartes sought. Much of the strength of the rational position will be seen in further chapters, especially Chapter 7: Reason and Chapter 9: Mathematical knowledge.

Empiricism

Although the line between the two schools of thought, the rational and the empirical, can be vague, and the terms can be used in either looser or stricter ways, the following story might make the point that the empirical way to prove knowledge seems much closer to common sense. Long ago, a young monk was listening to older senior monks who were discussing how many teeth were in a horse's mouth. Because this was the Middle Ages when 'logic-chopping' was the way to reach conclusions (in other words, arguing over seemingly minor points) the older monks began to reason about the nature and essence of a horse, spinning out complicated deductions to reach their conclusion. Just then the young monk said: 'I have an idea, let's get a horse and look in its mouth and actually count them'. The elders were not pleased that their methods were called into question by the so-called new boy on the block.

But more than proving knowledge claims, a full-blown empirical position states, in brief, that all of our knowledge is built up on sense impressions as if a person were a blank slate to be written upon by experience. This concept of *tabula rasa* was given to us by

Rationalism
Rationalism as a philosophy states that reason has precedence over all other ways of acquiring knowledge, or more strongly, that it is the unique path to knowledge. It is traditionally contrasted with empiricism.

Empiricism The view that the senses are primary with respect to knowledge.

the Englishman, John Locke, (1632–1704) and is a powerful notion about how we know what we know and how we prove what we want to establish. By extension, this position says that the empirical process begins right from birth and that all that we know up until today is taken in by our senses as raw material to be worked up into ideas by the mind (see Chapter 4: Sense perception). In contrast, the theory of rationalism is closely connected with *innate ideas* meaning that we are born with some kind of 'implicit knowledge' that allows us to know the world independent of our sense experience.

The difference between these two positions, the rational and the empirical, is one of the most fundamental in any theory of knowledge. It will be interesting to see how they both work themselves into knowledge claims from the various Areas of Knowledge.

Knowledge claims

Knowledge claim This simply means that you are saying something that you believe to be true. This phrase will be used extensively throughout this book. It is a good thing to begin to see the differences and similarities of knowledge claims that come out of the Ways of Knowing and the various Areas of Knowledge.

By now, after several years of full-time education, you know many things. And if the previous pages have been of help, you should be able to see immediately what kinds of good reasons you might have for what you say that you claim to know and choose to believe. These may include:

- logic
- perception
- intuition
- self-awareness
- memory
- authority
- consensus
- revelation and faith.

Whatever the justification, it is important to be able to see the similarities and the differences between the knowledge claims that you and others profess.

In the following exercise, try to see if the propositions can be proven true or false or both or neither. While the statements are simple ones, they stand as representatives of their kind. You might also want to make your own list of 'I know' statements and test your understanding of *empirical* and *rational* propositions and the concepts of *knowledge by acquaintance* and *knowledge by description*.

Exercise

Look at each of the propositions below and decide whether it can be proven true or false or both or neither. Imagine that someone is asserting each one as knowledge, not merely believed or held as an opinion.

1 I know   it is raining.
2 I know   it is raining or it isn't raining.
3 I know   2 + 2 = 4.
4 I know   two apples and two apples make four apples.
5 I know   my brother is my sibling.
6 I know   how to speak French.
7 I know   I will pass the test.
8 I know   girls are better at TOK than boys.
9 I know   murder is wrong.
10 I know   my tooth hurts.
11 I know   she doesn't like me.
12 I know   God exists.

Now that you've tried the exercise, let's look at each of the propositions in turn.

1 Despite the similarity in subject matter between 1 and 2, 1 is empirical and needs sense experience to prove it true or false. While contentious people might get into the semantics about drizzling or pouring or sprinkling or other forms of precipitation, either it is or it is not raining once the linguistic difficulties have been ironed out.

2 Unlike 1 which required going and looking to prove it one way or the other, this proposition is true under all conditions. Thus, it is called a rational or a logical truth. There is no need to do anything more to prove it, once you have understood the language, since your mind tells you that it has to be true. As a double check to clarify its status, try thinking of what could prove it false.

3 Similar to 2, this is a rational proposition true at all times within the mathematical framework of base 10. It is coherent with all other statements of its kind, ($7-4 = 3, 248 \times 5 = 1240$ etc.) all of whose truths depend on one another. Pen and paper or the mathematical mind is all that is needed to establish its truth. What possible thought or observation could show it to be false?

4 There may be a surface similarity between 3 and 4 but a moment's thought should persuade you that this is an empirical statement about the physical world, not a rational statement about mathematics. The frequent use of this statement in student essays as a mathematical truth does not make it so; the subject here is about apples, not numbers (the numerals are adjectives). While the statement may be an illustration or a demonstration beloved of junior school teachers and TOK students, it is not a proof. Just consider: do two drops of water plus two drops of water make four drops of water?

5 Again, this is a rational proposition true by definition. You may try to avoid the clarity of its truth by talking about relatives living or dead, or adopted brothers or in-laws through marriage, but either someone is your brother or not, and if not, the *sibling* predicate is irrelevant. But if he is your brother, then he is your sibling. Again, try to think of a counter-instance that would invalidate the statement.

6 It should be obvious that this is a 'knowing how' statement, not 'knowing that', and as such belongs to knowledge by acquaintance. Just like baking bread or dowsing for water, either you can do it or you cannot, and the proof is in the performance. Thus, it is a variant on the empirical statements of proving to someone else (or yourself) that observation will carry the day, not reasoning.

7 This statement is either true or false but, as such, it is not verifiable. Its value to this exercise is to promote discussion about whether any statement about the future can be claimed to be true or false in advance of its occurrence (not at all a trivial matter). Consider 'I know they will win the World Cup', 'I know they will never catch me' or 'It will not rain on my wedding day'.

8 This proposition could be classified as empirical since, in principle, it could be established as true or false by looking at all the evidence. You may not agree with others about what 'better' means or what would count as evidence, or even if all the evidence is available. But there is a strand of the human sciences that makes this

kind of comparative statement with great frequency so it seems to belong to the class of what can be known by sense experience.

9　Here it is understandable that some will think, 'Aha! This is an opinion, not a proposition that can be labelled true or false by empirical means.' If this judgement is so, which seems likely, then ask yourself, could you reason your way to an understanding of knowledge about any wrongdoing? Or would you classify this statement as a belief rather than, as the speaker did, assert it as knowledge?

10　The interesting point about this statement is that it may be one of those truths that is only true for you and nobody else. How can you prove it? Why would you have to prove it? This assertion is one of the most interesting on the list. What if your dentist said that your tooth could not hurt, that he had given you lots and lots of painkiller? Is there privileged knowledge we have about our own bodies? Think once again about the woman giving birth on page 20. Could you imagine pain that wasn't there? What would be the difference between imagined pain and real pain? Or phantom pain? Some hospitals now use charts of smiley and frowning faces to help patients indicate their degree of pain on a scale of 1 to10. How could these charts help, if at all?

11　Anyone stating this proposition as knowledge, not opinion or belief, is likely to be countered with, How do you know? And indeed, that is the question, how would you know? Would this be an instance of knowledge by acquaintance or perhaps you have only met the person and are not acquainted at all. Social scientists study liking and non-liking behaviour and we know from our own experience what both look like, so we are not totally in the dark here. Yet, how would you prove this to someone who did not believe you, who thought you could be mistaken?

12　It is no surprise that any statement about the existence of non-physical entities can cause consternation when stated as knowledge rather than opinion or belief. What is the justification if the object said to be known cannot be seen or is not of this world? This concern is relevant not only to many statements central to religious creeds, but to the entire spiritual realm. We must tread carefully here and recognize that what we wish to assert is of the utmost importance, but possibly of great debate. Whether propositions about religious beliefs can be justified true beliefs is at the heart of the matter. First, we must consider the possibility of an innate idea about spiritual matters as a source, if not a proof, since the idea cannot be proven empirically. For those interested to know more about this fascinating area of knowledge claims and beliefs, you might research the various proofs for the existence of God.

Exercise

What do you make of these propositions? Are they more rational or empirical?

- Every event has a cause.
- All people are created equal.
- Whatever has shape has size.
- Every cube has twelve edges.
- I see with my eyes.
- There is life on Mars.

Truth

Truth is a tricky word. What is truth? On the everyday level we seem to have no problem dealing with the concept. (It is ten o'clock. No, that's not true. Yes, it is.) However, some confusion may lie in the overuse of the word as an intensive, so consider the following:

- A true friend
- True to his wife
- A true likeness
- The true meaning of democracy
- The door hangs true
- True to life
- True diamonds
- The whole truth
- Nothing but the truth
- Truth tables in maths
- I love you truly
- The truth hurts

Try to translate the 'truth' terms above into something synonymous with loyal, straight, accurate, real and so on. Yet no matter how the word 'truth' is used in daily conversation, when we come to apply it to knowledge claims there are some definite parameters. One thing we can say right away is that truth is a judgement we make about a proposition. *The cat is on the mat. It is raining. Every event has a cause.* Someone says P is true, someone else says that it is not. That's not all there is to it but it's a good beginning.

As a minimum, you should be able to bring an understanding of three basic truth tests to the treatment of an essay topic such as: *Discuss the characteristics and the merits of the three different truth tests: the correspondence, coherence and the pragmatic and how they might intertwine in some way.*

Each truth test with its elaborate theories deserves pages and pages that we cannot go into here but for our purposes you need to have some introductory understanding. So as you read these preliminary explanations, you should see where each connects with the rational and the empirical basis of knowledge. The coherence truth test links to rationalism, while the correspondence truth test links to empiricism. You can decide for yourself about the pragmatic truth test.

The correspondence truth test

The theory behind this truth test is similar to the empirical basis of knowledge and, indeed, they are connected in many ways other than capturing our commonsense idea of the truth. Here we have something like a matching game. A statement is uttered about a state of affairs (a fact) and the words either match or fit or agree with or correspond to the facts (the state of affairs). You can probably think of many more examples than the one shown in the drawing on the next page, 'The cat is on the mat.'

Either the cat is or is not on the mat and the words either match that state of affairs or they do not. If you wanted to argue this point you might look at the problems associated with the definition of facts and the definition of matching but for our purposes the basic idea is laid down.

The correspondence truth test ▶

The coherence truth test

The power of this truth test is not as easily seen as the previous one but if you think for one minute how any single statement or proposition fits in with other statements you take as true, then you can see the power of this theory of truth. In the drawing below, it is obvious that any mathematical operation fits within a system but just as well, the seemingly simple truths about a shark found in Lake Windermere can be rejected because of the previously held knowledge that sharks are found only in salt water. So the listener is entitled to discount the statement, or at least question its truth, based on the logic of the situation. As we shall see in Chapter 10: Science, the great theories, the paradigms of science, hang together through their coherence. In short, statements under the coherence test pass muster by their rational agreement with one another, even though each individual proposition or law within the system is tested by how it relates to the state of affairs of the real world. So we can see that the correspondence and the coherence truth tests work together in giving us knowledge of the world that we can count on and find useful.

The coherence truth test ▶

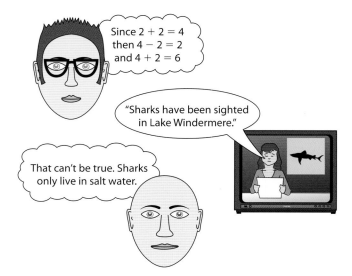

If you wanted to argue against the coherence truth test, you might say that all the statements taken together within a coherent system could hang together but still be wrong fact by fact. One example is that of the classical world view that the earth was the centre of everything as opposed to the current view, the helio-centric paradigm, that the sun is at the centre of what is now rightly called the solar system.

The pragmatic truth test

This truth test offers up some complexity since its primary value is what happens as a result of believing something to be true, not its actual truth as per the previous two theories. Thus the question is: does the idea work for you? For example, take the statement that the car will not start because the computer switch is not engaging. This is condition A. After some work on the transmission, the car starts. Does the success of this repair guarantee the truth of A, the diagnostic statement, or did the mechanic coincidentally alter something else (condition B) unknowingly? In any case, the car started, so A is considered true.

The supporters of this view claim that usefulness is the primary truth value, while critics say that if you do not really know what actually caused the car to start, how does pragmatic truth of A help you the next time? Where this theory becomes quite interesting is with beliefs that are held to be true because they are useful when we can never know the final truth. One example is believing that God exists or any number of other profoundly important issues where the actual truth may never be known in the strong sense of 'knowing'.

A brief story from the life of William James, one of the founders of the pragmatic theory of truth, taken from his book *The Will To Believe*, might clarify the above explanation. James was reared in a family plagued with emotional instability and developed painful symptoms himself which led him to thoughts of suicide as a release from his suffering. Yet during his crisis of 1869–70, the idea of personal freedom took hold of him and he avowed that his first act of free will would be to believe in free will, to believe that he could change his life. This idea would work for him thus proving, for him, its truth. Critics attack this view of the pragmatic truth test by saying that too much subjectivity or wishful thinking works itself into this theory.

Perhaps the quotation below might clarify the pragmatic theory of truth that the idea that works is the true one.

> *Grant an idea to be true, what concrete difference will its being true make in anyone's actual life? How will the truth be realized? What experiences will be different from those which would be the case if the belief were false? What, in short, is the truth's cash value in experiential terms?*
>
> William James

Exercise

Which truth tests would you apply to test the truth of the following:
1 = coherence (logical truths)
2 = correspondence (observational truths)

_____ **a**   Metals expand when heated.

_____ **b**   It is raining.

_____ **c**   It is raining or it is not raining.

_____ **d**   A triangle has three sides. (The sum of the interior angles of a triangle = 180 degrees.)

_____ **e**   All white cats are white.

_____ **f**   All white cats are deaf.

_____ **g**   The population of Tokyo is larger than that of Hong Kong.

_____ **h**   All wives have husbands.

_____ **i**   Mars has no moons.

_____ **j**   Mars is a planet.

_____ **k**   The best team will win the World Series.

_____ **l**   If Bert is a younger son, then he is a brother.

_____ **m**   If Bert is a younger son, then he is a sibling.

_____ **n**   It is now raining in Rio.

_____ **o**   The hydrogen atom has one electron.

_____ **p**   You are either here or somewhere else.

_____ **q**   There is an invisible elephant in this room.

Do babies come into the world mentally equipped with certain systems for ordering and understanding it?

Today's world: the Baby Lab

At the world's leading baby brain research lab at Harvard University, Elizabeth Spelke's team is conducting experiments that reveal not only that humans are born with a range of innate skills, but that our prejudices are formed within the first few months of life.

The lift doors open and Belinda Burnett carries her baby, Freya, into a bright and welcoming lobby, carpeted in maroon with walls of custard yellow and midnight blue. Playthings are scattered about – a magnet board, basketball hoop and bins of toys. Behind the glass wall of an office, stuffed animals gaze out, prizes for taking part in what are euphemistically called 'games'…

Welcome to Spelkeland, or, to give it its proper name, the Laboratory for Developmental Studies at Harvard University's Department of Psychology, run by the cognitive psychologist Prof Elizabeth Spelke, which is dedicated to understanding what shapes the most powerful known learning machine – the infant mind. Great philosophers have mused for millennia about human consciousness and how it makes sense of its surroundings. Like any good scientist, Spelke has turned philosophical hot air into firm experimental data that suggests that we are born with a significant amount of 'core knowledge' hardwired into our brains.

Spelke is arguably the most influential figure in the relatively new field of baby brain research, and has been named by _Time_ magazine as one of America's best in a list of 'brilliant researchers who are the envy of the world'. One prominent British experimental psychologist, Prof Bruce Hood of the University of Bristol, says she has 'revolutionised infancy mind research'. The psychologist and writer Steven Pinker, Spelke's colleague at Harvard, is another who acknowledges her profound impact, and says her ingenuity has shown that 'babies are smarter than we thought'…

We are natural-born mathematicians – for example, six-month-olds can distinguish the quantities eight from 16, and 16 from 32. Babies will infer that a rolling ball will keep moving. They also know that when that ball rolls behind a screen it should pop out the other side. And although they can only babble, babies tell us that the germ of our instincts about age, gender and race are laid down in the cradle…

When Spelke's research began, the dominant thinking was that of the influential Swiss developmental psychologist Jean Piaget who, after keeping meticulous diaries of the behaviour of his own three children in the 1930s, believed that babies were not empty vessels to be filled but little boffins primed to devour and exploit any and every experience. Even so, doctors of that time thought that babies had such a diminished consciousness they had no sense of pain, so did not need anaesthetic if undergoing surgery…

…an intellectual war that still rages over whether we emerge from the womb as general-purpose learning machines that soak up details of our environments, or, as Spelke believes, are born 'precocious', so we can immediately do things that are key to survival (just as newly-hatched chicks and fish can immediately do things such as navigate, or find and recognise food).

© _The Daily Telegraph_ 2008

Student presentation

1 The work of Dr Spelke at Harvard's Baby Lab addresses long-standing philosophical questions about the origins of human knowledge regarding space, objects, motion, unity, persistence, identity and number. How does Dr Spelke prove her theories about innate ideas through empirical scientific methods?

2 Compile a list of a dozen songs from the last 50 years and play the CD in class. Engage everyone in identifying the knowledge issues in each song. Songs you might use are:
   - Bob Dylan's 'Blowing in the wind'
   - 'How Can I Sing Like A Girl?', 'Which Describes How You're Feeling' and 'Narrow Your Eyes' by They Might be Giants
   - 'No One' by Alicia Keys.

Essay questions

1 The test of truth is whether or not reality confirms what one thinks. Do you agree? Justify your response and show what someone who disagrees with you might say.

2 Compare and contrast knowing a friend to knowing how to swim, knowing a scientific theory and knowing a historical period. What conclusions about the nature of knowledge can you reach?

Ways of Knowing
The TOK four… and more

The TOK syllabus lists the Ways of Knowing as:

- Language
- Reason
- Emotion
- Sense perception.

Without getting into whether babies are born with these Ways of Knowing (innate) or acquire them from experience (blank slate), we want to look at how they work together so seamlessly that usually we are not even aware of them. But, in addition, to fill out the picture, three other important concepts will be touched upon in this introduction: memory, testimony and imagination. Each can provide fruitful topics for TOK presentations for those who wish to look further into these related fields of study. Perhaps you will come to the conclusion that they are Ways of Knowing each in their own right.

How the Ways of Knowing work together (Emotion, Sense perception, Reason, Language)

As this heading indicates, it is not easy to separate out the four TOK Ways of Knowing for any human activity.

The Ways of Knowing in action

Emotion, Perception, Reason and Language all work together to make Will dedicated to his football training

Consider the sport of football or any similar activity which a player (let's call him Will) cares about immensely. Because of his *emotional* drive, Will gets up early to practise, suffers defeat with stoicism, celebrates in victory and cares enough to watch video after video of professional players as well as those of his team. He notes the opponents' tactics and his own moves and compares them to when they win and when they lose. His *perceptions* are heightened when surprise strategies catch his eye and the other team moves down field together in pursuit of the ball. He *reasons* out the best counter-offence and talks it over (*language*) with his mates and the coach, all of whom analyse and concoct new ideas. Plans are made such as: if you do this, then that will happen, so we will do this and see if it happens. Schemes are drawn, positions are named, simulations take place, observations are made and conclusions are reached. Good luck and high fives are exchanged and they're ready to take the field once more in high spirits.

A snapshot of history

Now consider a brief account of the four Ways of Knowing involved in creating a history book that might span years, perhaps centuries, and involves numerous different people leading up to the book you eventually hold in your hands. It is fairly easy to identify where perception is at play, but not as obvious that emotion is taking place in this sequence. Yet, if no one cared enough to look and to record the event it would be the same as if it never happened. As you go through the list below, try to tease out the four Ways of Knowing: language, sense perception, reason and emotion.

- An event happened.
- An eyewitness saw it.
- A scribe wrote it down.
- A citizen read it and told a friend.
- The friend was fascinated and read more.
- Her friend heard about it and asked questions.
- The friend read more and searched further.
- A historian pieced the story together.
- An academic read it and passed it on to a publisher.
- The publisher read it, liked it and printed it.
- A critic compared it to other books and selected it for the prize list.
- The librarian read the list and bought the book for the school library.
- The History teacher selected the book for the classroom and taught it.
- You read it and liked it or didn't like it.

To finish the brief, if you liked the subject area or the book, you might go further and write your Extended Essay on the same or a similar topic. If you are indifferent, you will probably forget you read it after the exam is over. But throughout the ages the play of reason, perception, language and emotion, intertwined in the stages above, produced that history book and your knowledge as surely as anything else you can name. And it all started with someone caring enough to look, to notice, to record and to preserve it for others.

In addition to sports and the writing of history, dozens of occupations (from office work to figure skating, to string quartets, to medical research) weave these Ways of Knowing together in various proportions. It is good to examine them on their own to further our understanding of the unique contribution that each makes to what we know (and we will do this in later chapters) but first let's look at memory, testimony and imagination.

Memory, testimony, imagination
Memory

'It's a poor sort of memory that only works backwards', the Queen remarked in *Through the Looking Glass* and hardly anyone knows what this means exactly. But then memory is more a mystery than a clearly understood concept or function even though all that we know or are justified in believing at any given moment resides in that part of the mind or brain we call our memory. Yet memory is seldom talked about in TOK, since we spend most of our time concerned with how we come to know or believe in something, not how any particular proposition comes to sit in our memory and to be called up when needed. Perhaps we can all agree with David Reisman's view that 'people tend to remember best the things they have felt most deeply', but not much else.

Questions arise about this memory apparatus. How did any memory come to be part of our mental inventory? How forceful or faint is the memory? How is it recalled and upon what stimulation? How much of the storehouse and the recall of our ideas are within our control? How reliable are these images or ideas? Does any particular memory correspond to a state of affairs in the world? If so, how can we check on this correspondence since the memory is something filed away from the past? Or does our confidence in any idea or proposition in memory take its strength from fitting in with other things in our mind, more akin to a coherence theory of ideas fitting together? (Think back to the correspondence and coherence truth tests from Chapter 2.)

Memory is one of those mental features we can't choose to accept or avoid, even as we know that we and others are often mistaken, that memory is a 'fond deceiver' and that self-interest and wishful thinking may play a huge role. On the other hand, we often try in vain to recall what does not come to us – the answer to a test question, a French verb or where we left our keys. Most of us know the agony of failed memory at just the wrong time even though Gerald Brenan says, 'a bad memory is the mother of invention'. Can you think what he means by these words? Compare his statement with the reality of photographic memories.

Pre-literate and oral cultures have excellent memories and societies sometimes called primitive often have staggering capacities for remembering. Certain Polynesian communities can recite family trees which go back dozens of generations. In a similar vein, in the late Middle Ages, the Inquisition found it was not enough to burn books because so many people had learned most of the Scripture by heart. Even today in India it is said that if all written and printed copies of the *Rigveda* (about as long as the *Illiad* and *Odyssey* combined) were lost, the text could be restored at once by scholars from memory.

It has been argued that the memories of literate peoples have been impaired by print because they know that they don't need to burden themselves with what they can find in a book or on the Internet. School children are seldom asked to memorize poetry or lists of countries of the world the way they once did. Yet students in India not so long ago could memorize a textbook and reproduce it word for word in an examination room.

Oddly enough, one great advantage of memory loss, if it can be thought of in that way, is that we don't need to carry around masses of obsolete information in our heads; the mind is left free to process new data and move on to still more data. In a complex changing world where students must process, not store, data, this is an indispensable asset. Then again, studies suggest that much of memory lies too deep for access (think of Freudian psychoanalysis) or that we remember a great deal of what we no longer care about, say, the telephone number of an old boyfriend or girlfriend. Some things we are told we will never forget, for example, how to ride a bike. Think how Marcel Proust, the French author, created an entire literary masterpiece of twentieth century fiction, *A la recherché du temps perdu,* by delving into the past, stimulated by the single memory of a madeline biscuit. Yet we also hear of short- and long-term memories deteriorating with old age or Alzheimer's disease. What is your first memory and why are some so vivid they will never be forgotten?

The field of memory study is fascinating in its own right. So to cite this mind/brain function as a possible Way of Knowing, however briefly, is mostly a signal to be aware of the centrality of memory in our expressions of what we know. Surely all of us have personal experiences of remembering and not remembering which can be brought forward as examples for critical reflection. Thus, a further exploration of memory attached to knowledge issues can be an interesting topic for TOK Presentations.

Testimony (or Knowledge by Authority)

In reality, most of what we know comes from other people. We entrust ourselves to others from our earliest years: our parents, followed by our teachers and friends, added to which are computers, television and books etc. What or who else are the authorities we count on for what we come to believe? The proportion of knowledge gained by a well-educated person learned through testimony or authority may outweigh all others combined. What should we think about this reality?

Although the term *testimony* should be understood in this book as somewhat synonymous with *knowledge by authority,* in other contexts they have different meanings. Testimony is sometimes meant as a legal term, a religious profession or an expression about transcendent or paranormal experiences. Knowledge by authority often has a power implication that is not directly tied to the concept of knowledge passed on from others. Take a moment to sort out the different meanings here and to find examples of each distinction.

Most of our school life, whether as students or teachers, is spent accepting or passing on the wisdom of the ages (or the knowledge of the day) from people we take as experts or who, at least, seem to know more than we do. We simply do not have time to gain all of what we need to know directly for ourselves. And nearly all of us as students are susceptible to a teacher's influence by tone, selection and emphasis. This dependency continues as adults when we select our reading material, our television political broadcasts, our educational programmes and websites for our information. These offerings are called 'mediated' knowledge, since others have vetted them and they are not experienced directly (or immediately) by ourselves. 'How do you know that?' someone might ask. '*They* said so', you reply. How many *theys* are there in your world?

Take a common piece of knowledge and explore the extent to which it is based on what others have told you.
- Everything consists of atoms.
- The burial place of King Tutankhamen is in the Valley of the Kings in Egypt.
- J.R.R. Tolkein wrote *The Lord of the Rings*.
- The earth is round.
- Indonesia has more Muslims than any other country in the world.
- Eating too much fat is unhealthy.
- In the middle of Australia is a large monolith called Uluru (once known as Ayer's Rock).
- Bees do a little dance to give directions to the best flowers.
- Tokyo is the capital of Japan.

With thanks to Tim Sprod

Consider how many of your answers are versions of 'Somebody told me and I believed them', compared to 'I saw it for myself' or 'I worked it out' or 'I just feel it is true'. Do any of the explicit TOK Ways of Knowing come into play here? Imagine you are trying to convey the truth of the propositions above to someone who doesn't yet know them, or who doesn't believe you. What do you say when they ask, 'And how do you know that?'

Or turn things around and take the position that you are being told these things and you ask, 'How do you know?' For example, if someone claims to have seen a picture of an atom taken by an electron microscope you can ask how he knows that the picture shows what it purports to show. If he claims to have seen King Tutankhamen's tomb, you can ask how he knows that it wasn't the tomb of someone else. The aim of the exercise is not to show how silly all these questions might be that no one really doubts, or to generate an unhealthy scepticism, but to point out how even the four Ways of Knowing themselves often rest on testimony.

Naturally to stand on the shoulders of authorities is a great convenience; indeed, it is a blessing, since how much could we learn or prove all on our own? But a dependence on others can also be an epistemological disadvantage. Think of all the people who were once wrong because someone told them that the world was flat. Think of all the people today who purport to tell us about our diets, our nutrition and our health in the ever-changing world of do-this-do-that self-help publishing.

Much as it does not become us, we are gullible or impatient sometimes, or afraid to think, or find it too much work. The worst may be too lazy and the best too busy. 'Just give me the answer', we hear people say. So if this is the case, then it follows that we all become knowers by being born, nurtured and raised within a community of knowers, people who tell us things, which is, perhaps, what Knower(s) means to convey at the centre of the TOK diagram.

Another way of looking at the pervasiveness of testimony over time is to consider a great engineering feat of the past (Notre Dame Cathedral in France, the Borobodor temple in Java or the Taj Mahal in India) and look at the role of testimony in that achievement. Think how it was possible for such complex structures to be built, how they came to be so perfect given how much can go wrong with communication and cooperation. Yet, there they are. What did the builders need to know and how did they come to know it?

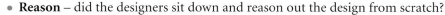

- **Reason** – did the designers sit down and reason out the design from scratch?
- **Emotion** – did they feel the splendour of the design?
- **Sense perception** – did they see the blueprint in nature and copy it? Probably some element of each of these entered into it.
- **Language** – the main elements of the design were all passed on through the language of testimony. The designers drew on the achievements of many others, possibly right back to the first lean-to makers aeons earlier. Each little improvement arising from reason, perception, emotion or language was adopted into the architect's repertoire and passed on to the builder through testimony. No wonder accuracy and honesty are celebrated virtues.

Let's go back to our question first posed in Chapter 2 – what are the sources and dependability of our knowledge? In other words, where do you go when you want to know something? What do you do? Encyclopedias (especially Wikipedia) and Google (think how this word has so quickly become a verb!) are nearly always first on the list, the most obvious knowledge by authority that we can name. Then take a look at the TOK Ways of Knowing: Sense perception, Reason, Language and Emotion. It's true that we see, think, speak and feel all the time when searching for an answer, in trying to find out what's what, in trying to prove or disprove something, but at the same time we are fortunate not to have to check every assertion we encounter provided that we are critical thinkers.

As critical thinkers:

- We know that the person whose word we take should really be an authority (the chemist may not be an expert in politics).
- We recognize what to do when two authorities differ (i.e. medical doctors).
- We recognize when two statements can have no defining criteria. (The only God is Allah versus the only God is Jehovah.)
- We remember that knowledge by testimony and from authority is always a secondary, not a primary, source of knowledge (secondary does not mean second-rate).
- We accept all secondary knowledge at our own risk.
- We have the confidence and techniques to sort out the fallacies from the factual.

The wider meanings of testimony may be explored as possible TOK presentation topics, since they all relate one way or another to issues of evidence. In many countries, testimony is a form of evidence that is obtained from a witness making a solemn statement or a declaration of fact. The role of opinions and inferences is relevant here. There are many kinds of evidence admitted as testimony: documentary evidence, physical evidence, digital evidence, exculpatory evidence, scientific evidence, demonstrative evidence and even hearsay (in UK law). Each has its own criteria for validity.

Many kinds of evidence can be admitted as testimony

In religion, testimony may involve an inward belief or outward profession of personal religious experience. Christians use the term to show how they became believers or 'how God has appeared or demonstrated his presence' either to a congregation of believers or to non-Christians so they might 'come to know' the religious encounter. Many such testimonies are available on the Internet from a variety of religious sects.

In other religions, Muslim and Mormon believers testify as a profession of faith. Such testimonials are often confirmed by a personal experience or a revelation that is taken as evidence of God's manifestation or existence. In Mormonism, testifying is also referred to as 'bearing one's testimony', an interesting set of words.

Finally, there is an autobiographical genre called 'testimonial literature' – usually first person accounts of oppression or living in war and violence. These stories often present evidence of human rights abuses as offered to international human rights tribunals. There is a strong association here with Latin America, especially Chile and Argentina, thus the Spanish term 'testimonio', although the writings of Frederick Douglass in the US are considered one of the earliest English language works in this style. How these literary works constitute evidence is worthy of greater study and possible TOK presentation material.

Imagination

One of the most famous remarks about imagination comes from Albert Einstein:

> *Imagination is more important than knowledge. Knowledge is limited. Imagination encircles the world.*

Similar to poetry, such quotations compress meaning into a few words. Perhaps trying to interpret what Einstein might have meant would be a good way to begin to think about this faculty of mind that brings new knowledge to us. To continue with two quotations linking imagination to memory, compare Samuel Johnson's words:

> *Imagination selects ideas from the treasures of remembrance and produces novelty only by varied combinations.*

with those of Samuel Butler:

> *Imagination depends mainly on memory but there is a small percentage of creation of something out of nothing with it. We can invent a trifle more than can be got at by mere combination of remembered things.*

Note how both ideas dip into memory for new ideas but Butler says there is a bit of something created 'out of nothing', and that is the seeming miracle of imagination, something out of nothing. No wonder the fullest introduction to Ways of Knowing requires at least a few words about imagination even though it is not formally part of the TOK syllabus. This omission was brought to our attention by students who chose the 2006 essay topic *Compare the roles played by Reason and Imagination in at least two Areas of Knowledge*. Interestingly, they criticised the TOK programme authors for excluding imagination as a Way of Knowing.

Exercise

What would be the arguments for imagination being a Way of Knowing equal to Language, Emotion, Sense perception and Reason?

Consider the quote from William Blake, 'What is now proved was once only imagined', a concept that could describe the progression pictured by the diagram on page 16.

In this diagram, a private thought or hunch passes from private to public knowledge and becomes part of the disciplines (or knowledge by description) only by meeting the truth tests within the relevant Areas of Knowledge. But does the formation of a knowledge claim always start as an act of imagination? Some would say probably not. The scientist, for example, may form a hypothesis based upon a careful review of existing literature and research. Or in medical practice, the senior doctor leading the rounds in a hospital or lecturing the medical students often begins with 'Imagine a patient…' Then the team proceeds to form a serious list of what might be the medical problem followed by a critique examining why or why not each of the problems might be the real cause. As the diagram shows, 'The origins of knowledge are many…'

For yet another take on imagination, consider the Wikipedia definition: 'Imagination is the innate ability and process to invent partial or complete personal realms within the mind from elements derived from sense perception of the shared world'. Think about these words: from the shared world. Wouldn't this be difficult to establish if imagination is, finally, some quality of mind that exercises freedom to evoke new worlds? Or some quality of mind that expresses highly individualistic thoughts even though the existing world will always serve as a baseline of comparison or validation?

And while imagination seems free from objective restraints, and is certainly necessary for social relations (empathy), a person whose imagination runs wild beyond the laws of reason or what is possible in the practical world can quickly be regarded as insane. The same limitation comes to be clear very soon in the world of science, to take one Area of Knowledge. A hugely imaginative hypothesis, if proven, might change the law, theory or even the paradigms within science, yet if it is too far from the established facts or too ahead of its time, it may have no audience and no chance for years of being tested within the discipline. (See the Semmelweis case study in Chapter 10: Natural science and the Galileo exercise at the end of this chapter). It is now quite easy to revere Galileo and to marvel at Semmelweis's discovery of childbed fever but in their times they were reviled as lunatics. Galileo was jailed and it is possible that Semmelweis committed suicide. These are just two examples in the history of intellectual thought where knowledge is finally triumphant but not without a struggle and a human price to be paid. (Carry out research into Linus Pauling, the double Nobel Prize winner who was labelled a heretic.)

 You can find out more about Linus Pauling by visiting www.heinemann.co.uk/hotlinks and entering the express code 4327P.

Finally, while the power of imagination cannot be denied in the formation of new knowledge, it is not always easy to tell the difference between imagined or internally created worlds and perceived reality, the sensed external world. Empirically-inclined people take the sensed external world as the real one but some people (and cultures) see this so-called real world as an illusion while the world given to the mind's eye has equal or greater validity. Think about exploring the concept of *maya* within the Buddhist tradition, the concept of *dreamtime* of the Australian Aborigines and the Parable of the Cave by Plato.

In conclusion, let us see what an IB student has to say about imagination in response to the essay topic: *Compare the roles played by Reason and Imagination in at least two Areas of Knowledge.* (You should note the excellent introduction to this essay.)

In exploring the roles played by reason, a logical thought process or realistic way of implementing ideas and theories into practice within the context of society, as well as imagination, defined as the moment of inspiration, or what forces humans to think beyond the boundaries of the theoretical frameworks of the societies in which they live, in various areas of knowledge, two important assumptions are made. The first is the idea that reason and imagination do in fact play different roles in different areas of knowledge. The second is that imagination and reason are fundamentally different from each other. While reason and imagination may seem very different, I would argue that they share underlying similarities. Throughout this essay, I will explain that although they play different roles, the relationship between the two is comparable in several areas of knowledge, particularly in the areas of mathematics, art and ethics.

…However, there is much more to mathematics than the practice of reasoning. In fact, imagination also plays a role in this field. In order to visualize problems at any level and to make new connections between natural occurrences and numbers, thereby creating new theories and concepts, it is essential for the mathematician to think beyond the limitations and constraints of what is known. John Nash, winner of the 1994 Nobel Prize in Economics, and one of the best pure mathematicians of the twentieth century, is a good example of a mathematician who was considered to be exceptional precisely because his ideas were original. It was Nash's extraordinary imagination which allowed him to think outside the box and thus discover or create the Theory of Games.

…Advances in numerous fields were made possible as a result of Nash's discovery, as its widespread application produced revolutionary results, impacting politics, economics and evolutionary biology. These far-reaching implications of Nash's theory demonstrate the extent to which reason and imagination are not only complementary in mathematics but allow it to be applied to other aspects of human life.

…Unlike mathematics, art is an area of knowledge that is generally assumed to use imagination alone. The role played by imagination is indeed significant, as it is the basis of an artist's visualization of abstract ideas and emotions, then conveyed through an artistic medium. A fine example of an artist whose imagination guided him to produce some of the greatest symphonies ever composed was Ludwig von Beethoven. As a musical genius and composer of extremely complex pieces, Beethoven had begun to lose his hearing before the age of thirty but continued to create masterpieces long after he had lost his ability to hear his works-in-progress. Beethoven thus had no choice but to rely on his imagination to compose pieces that still transmitted the intensity of his emotions so effectively and were so widely appreciated.

…Ethics is another area of knowledge where the role of both reason and imagination together are indispensable. While imagination ensures that thoughts get beyond time and culture, or context, allowing thinkers to introduce new concepts, reason is essential to effectively apply these ideas in a way that appeals to the common people of the era…Professor Mohammed Yunus is an example of an activist who has succeeded in making a difference by fusing imagination and reason, in terms of social ethics. Founder of the Grameen Movement and 'the world's banker to the poor', Yunus, winner of the 2006 Nobel Peace Prize, joins his ideas of capitalism with social responsibility through the concept of micro-financing. He strongly believes that poverty should not exist at all. Acting on the idea that even the poorest deserve the chance to maintain their dignity, his life's work has been to prove that the poor are credit-worthy. In this way, Yunus has impacted the global ethical framework, through his imaginative yet applicable ideas.

In conclusion, the roles of imagination and reason are significant in the areas of mathematics, art and ethics, though are certainly not limited to these areas of knowledge. The common relation between the two can be described as imagination fuelling reason, while reason, in turn, supports the imagination. While reason is a way of knowing and imagination may not technically be perceived as such, what makes them so complementary is that each is a creative function of the mind. Inspired ideas are not necessarily unreasonable, for as Plato, the ancient Greek philosopher stated in his dialogue, The Republic, 'necessity is the mother of invention'. In order to implement new ideas of the imagination, one must consider ways unheard of in the context of society, thus forcing reason to be creative.

Ways of Knowing applied to Galileo's trial in 1633

Each of the four Ways of Knowing, Sense perception, Reason, Language and Emotion, is involved in the conflict between Galileo and the ecclesiastical authorities.

Bertolt Brecht, wrote *The Life of Galileo* (1943), a play that in part shows the resistance of the Catholic Church in 1633 to Galileo's discoveries about the heavens. Question 1 below is based on the play itself and is an exercise in how the four Ways of Knowing are often intertwined in any conflict. Question 2 is an exercise designed to help you see how the Ways of Knowing are present in our personal lives. Question 3 asks you to think of yourself within the context of your Knower Profile.

▲ A stamp commemorating the life of Bertolt Brecht

1 Look at the extract below and then show, using the extract to illustrate your answer, how the positions held by the two sides are derived from a combination of each of the four Ways of Knowing.

> **Sagredo:** *Looking through the telescope, half to himself*. The crescent's edge is quite irregular, jagged and rough. In the dark area, close to the luminous edge, there are bright spots. They come up one after the other. The light starts from the spots and flows outwards over bigger and bigger surfaces, where it merges into the larger luminous part.
> **Galileo:** What's your explanation of these bright spots?
> **Sagredo:** It's not possible.
> **Galileo:** It is. They're mountains.
>
> * * * * *
>
> **Mathematician:** One might be tempted to answer that, if your tube shows something which cannot be there, it cannot be an entirely reliable tube, wouldn't you say?
>
> * * * * *
>
> **Galileo:** … Our proposition, Andrea?
> **Andrea:** As for floating, we assume that it depends not on a body's form but on whether it is lighter or heavier than water.
> **Galileo:** What does Aristotle say?
> **The Little Monk:** 'Discus latus platique…'
> **Galileo:** For God's sake translate it.
> **The Little Monk:** 'A broad flat piece of ice will float on water whereas an iron needle will sink.'
> **Galileo:** Why does the ice not sink, in Aristotle's view?
> **The Little Monk:** Because it is broad and flat and therefore cannot divide the water.
> **Galileo:** Right. *He takes a piece of ice and places it in the bucket.* Now I am pressing the ice hard against the bottom of the bucket. I release the pressure of my hands. What happens?
> **The Little Monk:** It shoots up to the top again.
> **Galileo:** Correct. Apparently it can divide the water all right as it rises.
>
> * * * * *
>
> **The Inquisitor:** Practically speaking one wouldn't have to push it very far with him. He is a man of the flesh. He would give in immediately.
> **The Pope:** He enjoys himself in more ways than any man I have ever met. His thinking springs from sensuality. Give him an old wine or a new idea, and he cannot say no.
>
> Bertolt Brecht, *The Life of Galieo*, translated by John Willett and Ralph Manheim,
Methuen Drama, an imprint of A&C Black Publishers.

2 Think of a personal experience which involved a similar inability to make another person understand a position or opinion that you hold. Describe the arguments used in the conflict and try to analyse them in terms of the four Ways of Knowing.

3 Imagine that Galileo's testimony in the seventeenth century about the heavens and the empirical evidence he offers for what he sees with his telescope is the latest technology of the day. Then read the quote below. Would you have looked in the telescope as invited or would you have walked on by? Who in the text of the play above do you most identify with? Are there analogous situations today?

> *My Dear Kepler*
>
> *What would you say of the learned here, who, replete with the pertinacity of the asp, have steadfastly refused to cast a glance through the telescope? What shall we make of this? Shall we laugh, or shall we cry?*
>
> Letter from Galileo Galilei to Johannes Kepler
With thanks to Brian Kahn

Today's world: memory research

As an introduction to the Ways of Knowing this chapter cited memory, imagination and testimony as worthy of your attention in addition to the TOK selection of language, reason, sense perception and emotion. We also talked about the difficulty of separating these Ways of Knowing from one another, since in daily life they so often work together to help us make sense of the world. Now we offer you an institution that is itself a crossover among Ways of Knowing and Areas of Knowledge: the Centre for Interdisciplinary Memory Research (CMR) located at the Kulturwissenschaftliches Institut in Essen, Germany.

C. P. Snow once lamented that there was such a huge gulf between the sciences and the humanities that the two could not even talk to one another, even though the world sorely needed the thinking from both sides to be brought together. Here, at this fairly new international and interdisciplinary centre, scholars from the sciences and the humanities come from all over the world to share their ideas and test their hypotheses.

With cutting edge neuroimaging technology and the advent of neuro-biological work on the brain, traditional explanations of memory storage are being left behind. What we have as a result is a wealth of clinical data to help us understand this fascinating function of our species that is still largely a mystery. There are multiple projects happening at the centre that you might research for your TOK presentations.

But research is not just necessary from the standpoint of scientific inquiry. In view of the demographic shift in ageing modern societies, memory research is also a necessity in the humanities. In the decades to come, memory-related health problems like dementia and Alzheimer's disease will increase markedly (afflictions that could easily enter your own life with ageing parents or grandparents, or even yourself someday). Apart from the personal dimension, this medical challenge also has enormous sociological and economic dimensions.

The centre is also looking into how memory is formed in general and how it varies in individuals, about which little is known. Another research agenda is the transmission of memories from one generation to the next, and the long-term effects of the collective experience of violence and post-traumatic syndrome. Research is also taking place into the role of memory in reaffirming our individual identities in this time of rapid global change. Perhaps with reference to the past and to the anchor that our store of memories gives us, we can learn more about ourselves as we move through adolescence into maturity, middle and old age.

Finally, it is interesting to note how the memoir as a literary genre has increased in popularity during this same 20-year period of the growth of the CMR. You might want to return to the question posed in Chapter 2: how true is it that you are your memories?

Ideal knower
Gabrielle Émilie, Marquise du Châtelet-Laumont (1706–49)

I feel the full weight of the prejudice which so universally excludes us from the sciences; it is one of the contradictions in life that has always amazed me, seeing that the law allows us to determine the fate of great nations, but that there is no place where we are trained to think... Let the reader ponder why, at no time in the course of so many centuries, a good tragedy, a good poem, a respected tale, a fine painting, a good book on physics has ever been produced by women. Why these creatures whose understanding appears in every way similar to that of men, seem to be stopped by some irresistible force, this side of a barrier. Let the people give a reason, but until they do, women will have reason to protest against their education... If I were king, I would redress an abuse which cuts back, as it were, one half of human kind. I would have women participate in all human rights, especially those of the mind. It would seem as if they were born only to deceive, this being the only intellectual exercise allowed them. The new education would greatly benefit the human race. Women would be worth more and men would gain something new to emulate... I am convinced that either many women are unaware of their talents by reason of the fault in their education or for want of intellectual courage. My own experience confirms this. Chance made me acquainted with men of letters who extended the hand of friendship to me... I then began to believe that I was a being with a mind...

Judge me for my own merits, or lack of them, but do not look upon me as a mere appendage to this great general or that great scholar, this star that shines at the court of France or that famed author. I am in my own right a whole person, responsible to myself alone for all that I am, all that I say, all that I do. It may be that there are metaphysicians and philosophers whose learning is greater than mine, although I have not met them. Yet, they are but frail humans, too, and have their faults; so, when I add the sum total of my graces, I confess I am inferior to no one.

From *The Divine Mistress*, Samuel Edwards, 1970. Signed by Mme du Châtelet to Frederick the Great of Prussia

Gabrielle Émilie was:
- the translator of *Oedipus Rex*
- the author of *The Elements of the Philosophy of Newton* (this remains the authoritative French translation of Newton's work)
- the author of *Institutions de Physiques* (the works of Liebniz)
- the interpreter of the work of René Descartes
- a mathematician and scientist
- a wife and mother
- the lover of Voltaire.

Student presentation

1 Ranging from scientifically trained physicians to what might generically be called 'alternative' medical practitioners, and depending upon the culture or the individual situation, consider how the patient's beliefs and demands might conflict with the doctor's convictions, and how a patient might use the various Ways of Knowing to reach a decision about treatment.

2 Think about, then present to your class, how the various Ways of Knowing, including testimony, memory and imagination, might contribute to what can be called a good explanation in any of the Areas of Knowledge or in a situation of personal involvement.

Essay questions

Two recent Prescribed Titles (PTs) include:

1 Is it possible to justify a hierarchy of different Ways of Knowing and, if so, on what basis?
© International Baccalaureate Organization 1999

2 It is an oversimplification to claim that some Ways of Knowing give us facts, while others provide interpretations?
© International Baccalaureate Organization 2006

Sense perception

What is perception?

A popular and understandable theory about perception goes something like this: you open your eyes and - presto! - you enjoy a richly detailed picture-like experience of the world, one that represents people and things in sharp focus, uniform detail and high resolution from the centre out to the periphery. Let us call this the snapshot model of sense experience.

From *Action in Perception* by Alva Noë, The MIT Press, 2005

Throughout this chapter, we use 'perception' to mean the same as 'sense perception' in the interests of brevity.

Five senses or more?

Traditionally we think about our perception as being bound up with the sensations of the apparatus of our sight, hearing, taste, smell and touch, with sight being privileged among the five. After all, well over half of our sensory input to the brain concerns this one sense. Yet a fuller picture of this description shows us that the **sensorium** of most people should be listed this way:

1 visual sense – sight

2 auditory sense – hearing

3 gustatory sense – taste

4 olfactory sense – smell

5 cutaneous sense – touch

6 kinesthetic sense – movement

7 vestibular sense – balance

8 organic sense – hunger, thirst etc.

And those with even a passing acquaintance with physics will know that the range of wavelengths of light to which our eyes are sensitive comprise only a small fraction of the electromagnetic spectrum as a whole. What we cannot sense, we cannot perceive, so there are clear human biological limitations to this Way of Knowing. Would you have any idea of space if you could not see? Would you have any sense of objects if you could not feel? Would you have any idea of causation?

Sensorium Part of the brain or the mind concerned with the reception and interpretation of sensory stimuli.

Exercise

Try to imagine a world where in just a small part of the animal kingdom the following is true:

- ants – can detect small movements through 5cm of earth
- bees – have chemoreceptors on jaws, legs and antennae; 5000 lenses in each eye; bellies which detect the magnetic field
- buzzards – can see small rodents from a height of 15,000 feet
- chameleons – can see in two different directions at once
- crabs – have eyes on the end of stalks; hairs on claws to detect water currents
- dolphins – can hear frequencies up to at least 100,000 Hz; use echolocation for movement
- elephants – have a hearing range between 1 and 20,000 Hz
- grasshoppers – have hairs all over the body to detect air movement

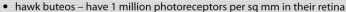

- hawk buteos – have 1 million photoreceptors per sq mm in their retina
- jellyfish – have 24 eyes
- star-nosed moles – have six times more touch receptors in their nose than in the human hand
- penguins – have flat cornea for underwater vision; can see into the ultraviolet range
- pigeons – have lateral eyes to see 340 degrees
- rabbits – have 17,000 taste buds in their tongue
- seahorses – each eye moves independently
- scorpions – can have as many as 12 eyes
- snakes – use their tongue to bring smells into the mouth; have no ears; sound waves travel through bones in their heads

As Professor Noë of the University of California Berkeley tells us, people who study perception, whether in the arts, in psychology or in philosophy, usually take their start from the snapshot model. But then the puzzle we all face is how do we enjoy such a visual experience when our actual direct contact with the world in the form of information on the retina is so limited? The limitations are familiar. There are actually two retinal images, not one; the images are distorted, tiny and upside-down; the resolving power of the eye is weak; the retina is nearly colour-blind and its powers of discrimination are few.

Exercise

As you read this, your eyes are rapidly flickering from left to right in small hops, bringing each word sequentially into focus. When you stare at a person's face your eyes similarly dart here and there. Try to detect this frequent flexing of your muscles as you scan a page, a face or a scene.

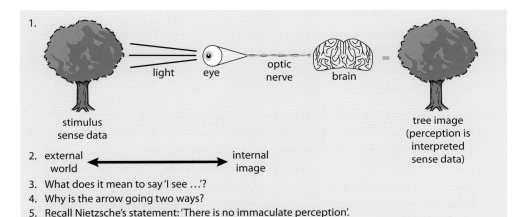

1.

| light | eye | optic nerve | brain | = |

stimulus sense data

tree image (perception is interpreted sense data)

2. external world ←→ internal image
3. What does it mean to say 'I see …'?
4. Why is the arrow going two ways?
5. Recall Nietzsche's statement: 'There is no immaculate perception'.
6. Recall 'seeing is believing'. Should we also say 'believing is seeing'?

There is more to seeing than meets the eye!

Have you ever watched a jittery video made with a hand-held camera that made you almost ill? With our eyes constantly darting back and forth and our body hardly ever holding still, that is exactly what our brain is faced with. Yet despite all these alternating snapshots and grey-outs, we usually perceive our environment as perfectly stable. This is the problem faced by visual theory. How do we see so much on the basis of so little? There are knowledge issues and implications for daily life attached to this question, which we will explore in later pages.

Related questions include:
- Why do we have differing perceptions?
- Why do we see what cannot be?

- Why do we not see what is in front of us?
- How do context and culture affect our perceptions?
- How do we ever think or see 'outside the box'?
- And perhaps, subsuming them all, is the TOK essay question in recent years: '*We have eyes to see with, ears to hear with - why then do we err?*'

What really happened?

It's a safe bet that nearly every country in the world that promotes professional or amateur sports, or sends a team to the Olympics, uses the video camera and instant replay technology. The first seems to capture what really happened: the pitch that went wild, the foot over the line or how the matador speared the bull. Long after any event people can study 'what really happened'.

An interesting combination of digital video and computer technology now allows a new use of the instant replay where an individual can sometimes evaluate a performance in the middle of the game. For example, after each time at bat, David Ortiz, the star hitter of the 2007 World Series winning Boston Red Sox, flips open his laptop in the dugout to study his hits and strikes, and the pitches thrown to him, before the next time up.

Sports like so much else are an interesting combination of concealment and revelation, yet with an instant replay it can be seen in sumo wrestling if any part of the body except the soles of the feet touched the ground; at Wimbledon the camera can show points won or lost with games sometimes reversed; at the Kentucky Derby, the horse that won by a nose in the photo finish can be given the blanket of roses because that's what 'really happened'.

Think about this for a moment. At Wimbledon, the ball did or did not go out. The umpire makes the call. Hundreds of other people are watching and the court is rocked with cheers and jeers for the good or bad call. Which is it? The single opinion will not do. It is time for the instant replay. Magically, we see the play again. We see it in stop-time, from above, from below, from every point of the compass. What an admirable determination to get at the truth. And, yes, the ball is in. The umpire raises his hand. But for some, even the instant replay falls short and the issue remains shrouded in ambiguity. They are not satisfied. They saw what they saw. And they know what 'really happened'.

The single look is what the artist Willem de Kooning called 'the slipping glimpse'. The first look may be seeing what we want to see. But the second look is hard-edged, gimlet-eyed.

What causes this uproar? No matter what the differences among us, no matter the imperfections of our faculties, no matter the obstruction of the sightline, almost everyone has a point of view and almost everyone in the world thinks that some things 'really happened'. And we all want to know or think we know.

Next consider this fashionable art scene.

One evening a young woman went to an opening night at a contemporary art gallery showing the works of Duane Hanson, the realist sculptor.

It was crowded and she couldn't find her boyfriend in the mob, so she asked the waiter the way to the buffet table where she was meant to meet him. A second later she realized she had talked to a piece of sculpture. This gaff embarrassed her so much that she turned giggling to the security guard and confessed her mistake. But he was a statue, too. She couldn't believe her eyes. She couldn't stand it. She ran out of the door and headed straight for home where she knew what was real and what wasn't. The gallery was too spooky. She hardly knew 'what really happened'.

On seeing things as they really are

There are fascinating debates represented in the exercise you have just completed that you might use as a presentation. However, for our purposes in the examples on the previous pages, something happened or it didn't, something was real or it wasn't. In all cases, we want to know. We want to be right. We want to win. We want to be safe. We want to feel good. We want 'seeing is believing' to be true. We don't want to be fooled. All of which adds up to our need to find out what is really there and what things really mean. We need to have meaning in the world.

Perception as the search for meaning

One of the axioms of perception that this chapter assumes is that the human mind involuntarily creates meaning from stimuli. This is an activity that goes on in spite of your will or desire. For example, as an English speaker, you cannot help but find meaning in the words of a headline from the *The Times* newspaper. In contrast, as an English speaker, it is unlikely you can find meaning in the front page of the Japanese newspaper *The Mainichi Shimbun*. It is all squiggles on a page. One of the easiest inferences we can draw here is that perception is not objective and unlearned, but that it is context and culturally dependent and directed towards making sense of the world.

Could you read *The Mainichi Shimbun*?

Not so familiar now!

Exercise

You can easily watch your mind in action, searching for meaning, with the following simple activity. Cut out a dozen or so pictures from magazines of contemporary interest removing all written text. Then cut out an equal number of words or phrases from advertisements. Place them in two separate piles. Keeping the two collections separate, get a small group of people together and ask them to turn over a picture at the same time as randomly turning over a word or phrase, mating one with the other.

Although the combinations are left to chance, most pairs will express a meaning so uncanny as to suppose that someone had planned it. (This is not unlike reading your horoscope or a Chinese fortune cookie. Most messages seem to have a good fit.)

As an alternative to the exercise outlined above, you could play a game where a familiar face, for example that of Britney Spears or David Beckham, is pasted on top of an astronaut's suit. What should be utterly familiar (the face) is now not so easy to identify, since the meaning has been scrambled (see the picture opposite). Most of us know about this phenomenon from not being able to identify our dentist in the supermarket or our teacher on the street. Movie directors use this ploy all the time. The mind goes whirring… where, where, where have I seen that person before… since the lack of meaning, the lack of closure, causes a disturbance in mental equilibrium.

> *The solution of mystery remains one of the most irresistible of all human temptations.*   Anon

The myth of the mental instant replay

Sometimes people think of visual perception as operating like a television camera, recording the full details of a scene on a tape that is labelled and filed in the brain. If someone asks you what you did last Friday night, you go to your mental file, retrieve the tape dated last Friday and the process of memory unfolds as a replay in your mind. The UK and other legal systems lend support to this concept in the courtroom when a person's fate is determined by the 'replay' capability of an eyewitness. However, several studies, numerous films and your own class experiments will show that eyewitness testimony in both real and simulated conditions is very often inaccurate. Such accounts are shockingly vulnerable to manipulation by emotion, social stresses and position, or the way a question is asked and other factors. As shown in *The Principles of Visual Perception*, one man in a five-person police line-up was placed under a small sign saying *Wanted Dead or Alive* and he was selected as the criminal many more times than the others. The sign itself had not registered with those identifying the supposed culprit. All in the line-up were innocent.

Exercise

- Why is eyewitness evidence admitted in many courts of the world, but not hearsay evidence?
- Why is it that a signature on a contract often carries more weight than a handshake and the spoken word?
- What might be some of the other factors referenced above that would skew perception?
- Can you imagine that your own fate, or victory, or happiness could depend on the variables of perception?

Perception and multiple perspectives

The exercise below was designed by Brandon Rogers, a TOK teacher at Atlanta International School. Perhaps you might like to make a set of cards, using the list below, and have a go at this activity in your class.

Exercise

You will be given a card. On it, you will find a witness or a person connected to the following event involving a car accident. Consider the various perspectives and the various meanings that each perspective brings to the interpretation of the event. What kinds of questions would you ask of those involved? What would you expect to be asked?

The list of people involved includes:
- driver of car A
- driver of car B
- witness with her child in the playground
- witness about to cross the street
- witness sitting in burger joint
- witness in the car behind car A
- police officer arriving on the scene after the accident

- solicitor hired by the driver of car A
- solicitor hired by the driver of car B
- journalist assigned to report the incident for the local newspaper
- therapist of the driver of car A
- priest of the driver of car B
- the manufacturer of car A
- the manufacturer of car B
- the mother of the driver of car A
- the paramedic called to the scene after the crash
- director of transportation for the city
- the judge for this case.

Approach the event shown in the artwork from the perspective of the person given to you on your card. Then, in a small group, briefly address and compare the following questions.

1 What Ways of Knowing seem most important to you? How do those apply specifically to this situation?

2 What details/aspects about this event do you notice or pay attention to? Why?

3 What biases do you bring to your understanding/knowledge of this event?

4 What problems of knowledge result from this perspective? In other words, what don't you know, what can't you know, what prevents you from knowing, what might be flawed about what you know or think you know?

5 Find someone else in your group whose 'knower' has knowledge that is valuable to you. Why is this person important to your perspective?

6 Find someone else in your group whose 'knower' has knowledge that might conflict with yours. Why/how does it conflict?

7 What questions come to mind? What do you want to know?

8 What Ways of Knowing do you emphasize?

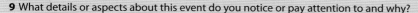

9 What details or aspects about this event do you notice or pay attention to and why?

10 What biases do you bring to your understanding/knowledge of this event?

11 What problems of knowing or knowledge issues result from your perspective? In other words, what don't you know? What can't you know? What prevents you from knowing?

12 What might be flawed about what you know or think you know?

13 Find someone else in your group who has knowledge that is valuable to you. Why is this person important to your perspective?

14 Find someone else who has knowledge that might conflict with yours? Why or how does it conflict?

15 What are the knowledge issues introduced by this exercise, i.e. what ramifications, problems, and/or questions follow from this?

16 What does this exercise suggest/imply about the knowledge we have, the knowledge we use and/or the knowledge we manipulate?

17 What contemporary, 'real-world' examples can you think of that illustrate these issues?

18 What examples from your life outside the classroom can you think of that illustrate these issues?

There's more to seeing than meets the eye

Along the same lines of seeing/not seeing what is there, recent work in the psychology of sense perception brings attention to **change blindness** and **inattentional blindness**.

According to Philosophy professor, Alva Noë:

> … consider the following familiar sort of gag. I say to you as you tuck into your lunch: 'Hey isn't that Mick Jagger over there?' You turn around to look. When you do, I snatch one of your French fries. When you turn back you're none the wiser. You don't remember the exact number or layout of fries on your plate and you weren't paying attention when the fry was snatched. Your attention was directed elsewhere.

> It turns out that this sort of failure to notice change is a pervasive feature of our visual lives. Usually when changes occur before us, we notice them because our attention is grabbed by the flickers of movement associated with the change. But if we are prevented from noticing the flicker of movement when the change occurs, we may fail to notice the change. What is striking – and this will become important later on – is the fact that we will frequently fail to notice changes even when the changes are fully open to view. Even when we are looking right at the change when it occurs, something we can test with eye trackers, we may fail to see the change.

The fact of *change blindness* is widely thought to have several important consequences. Firstly, perception is, in an important sense, *attention dependent*. You only see that to which you attend. If something occurs outside the scope of attention, even if it's perfectly visible, you won't see it. In one study perceivers are asked to watch a video tape of a basketball game and to count the number of times one team takes possession of the ball. During the film clip, which lasts a few minutes, a person in a gorilla suit strolls onto the centre of the court, turns and faces the audience and does a little jig. The gorilla then slowly walks off the court. The remarkable fact is that perceivers often do not notice the gorilla. This is an example of *inattentional blindness*.

 Change blindness and inattentional blindness Changes which occur in the visual field which go unnoticed by the perceiver.

 You can see the video by going to www.heinemann.co.uk/hotlinks and entering the express code 4327P. You will see the relevant link.

Secondly, as we have already said, perception is selective and 'gist-dependent'. Changes that affect the meaning of any scene are more likely to be noticed; other changes are ignored. Thirdly, it seems that the brain does not build up detailed internal models of the scene… contrary to the assumption that we have in our brain a complete, coherent representation of the scene.

Dr David Dennett, one of the most respected practitioners in the field, asks in *Perception in Action*:

> Why do normal people express such surprise when their attention is drawn to their limitations? Surprise is a wonderful dependent variable and should be used more often in experiments; it is easy to measure and shows that the subject expected something else. People are shocked, incredulous, dismayed; they often laugh and shriek when I demonstrate to them for the first time how mistaken their beliefs about their perceptions really are.

Surprise may require explanation, but at the same time we know that perception is not passive since we have to peer, squint, move our heads, lean forward, adjust lighting, put on glasses etc., knowing that if none of these adjustments are performed, the scene will not come through to us. We constantly have to work to see what is there. And, finally, it is worth noting that artists, magicians, stage designers and cinematographers, people who live by the maxim that the hand is quicker than the eye, would not be surprised by *change blindness* and other such factors. Why should they be? Our perceptual access to the world may be robust, but it is also fallible. How could anyone really think otherwise?

Tricks of the mind

It was Sunday night on the Las Vegas Strip, where earlier this summer the Association for the Scientific Study of Consciousness was holding its annual meeting at the Imperial Palace Hotel… After two days of presentations by scientists and philosophers speculating on how the mind construes, and misconstrues, reality, we were hearing from the pros: James (The Amazing) Randi, Johnny Thompson (The Great Tomsoni), Mac King and Teller — magicians who had intuitively mastered some of the lessons being learned in the laboratory about the limits of cognition and attention…

Apollo, with the pull of his eyes and the arc of his hand, swung around my attention like a gooseneck lamp… When he appeared to be reaching for my left pocket he was swiping something from the right. At the end of the act the audience applauded as he handed me my pen, some crumpled receipts and dollar bills, and my digital audio recorder, which had been running all the while. I hadn't noticed that my watch was gone until he unstrapped it from his own wrist…

A recurring theme in experimental psychology is the narrowness of perception: how very little of the sensory clamour makes its way into awareness… Secretive as they are about specifics, the magicians were as eager as the scientists when it came to discussing the cognitive illusions that masquerade as magic: disguising one action as another, implying data that isn't there, taking advantage of how the brain fills in gaps — making assumptions, as The Amazing Randi put it, and mistaking them for facts.

Sounding more like a professor than a comedian and magician, Teller described how a good conjuror exploits the human compulsion to find patterns, and to impose them when they aren't really there.

'In real life if you see something done again and again, you study it and you gradually pick up a pattern,' he said as he walked onstage holding a brass bucket in his left hand. 'If you do that with a magician, it's sometimes a big mistake.'

Pulling one coin after another from the air, he dropped them, thunk, thunk, thunk, into the bucket. Just as the audience was beginning to catch on — somehow he was concealing the coins between his fingers — he flashed his empty palm and, thunk, dropped another coin, and then grabbed another from a gentlemen's white hair. For the climax of the act, Teller deftly removed a spectator's glasses, tipped them over the bucket and, thunk, thunk, two more coins fell.

As he ran through the trick a second time, annotating each step, we saw how we had been led to mismatch cause and effect, to form one false hypothesis after another. Sometimes the coins were coming from his right hand, and sometimes from his left, hidden beneath the fingers holding the bucket.

He left us with his definition of magic: 'The theatrical linking of a cause with an effect that has no basis in physical reality, but that – in our hearts – ought to.'

*****

… 'It's "The Truman Show", ' said Robert Van Gulick, a philosopher at Syracuse University… who had come to the conference to talk about *qualia*, the raw, subjective sense we have of colours, sounds, tastes, touches and smells… a question preoccupying philosophers is where these personal experiences fit within a purely physical theory of the mind.

Like physicists, philosophers play with such conundrums by engaging in thought experiments. In a recent paper, Michael P. Lynch, a philosopher at the University of Connecticut, entertained the idea of a 'phenomenal pickpocket', an imaginary creature, like Apollo the thief, who distracts your attention while he removes your *qualia*, turning you into what's known in the trade as a philosophical zombie. You could catch a ball, hum a tune, stop at a red light – act exactly like a person but without any sense of what it is like to be alive. If zombies are logically possible, some philosophers insist, then conscious beings must be endowed with an ineffable essence that cannot be reduced to biological circuitry…

One evening out on the Strip, I spotted Daniel Dennett, the Tufts University philosopher, hurrying along the sidewalk across from the Mirage, which has its own tropical rain forest and volcano… For years Dr Dennett has argued that *qualia*, in the airy way they have been defined in philosophy, are illusory. In his book *Consciousness Explained*, he posed a thought experiment involving a wine-tasting machine. Pour a sample into the funnel and an array of electronic sensors would analyse the chemical content, refer to a database and finally type out its conclusion: 'a flamboyant and velvety Pinot, though lacking in stamina'.

If the hardware and software could be made sophisticated enough, there would be no functional difference, Dr Dennett suggested, between a human and the machine. So where inside the circuitry are the ineffable *qualia*? [You might like to look at the 2007 TOK essay topic: 'Can machines know?']

Retreating to a bar at the Imperial Palace, we talked about a different mystery he had been pondering: the role words play inside the brain. Learn a bit of wine speak – 'ripe black plums with an accent of earthy leather' — and you are suddenly equipped with anchors to pin down your fleeting gustatory taste impressions. Words, he suggested, 'are like sheepdogs herding ideas.'

Additional thoughts about perception and meaning

However, regardless of magic, point of view, expectations, gender, age, etc., the concept of the mind as an objective recorder is based on a false premise about the *purpose of perception*. The study of visual perception clearly reveals that perceptual processes are not structured to record data but to organize meaning. Sense data are not perceived as isolated fragments; the mind organizes them in meaningful and relevant ways into a web of beliefs about what is real and what isn't. In memory storage, itself a dynamic and young field of investigation, sense experience is assimilated into a field of meaning from its interwoven relationships with other experiences

In comparison to the instant-replay notion, this operation might at first seem to be a weakness. But for the most part it functions as an advantage. If you had to record and maintain all data as separate fragments, you would soon become paralysed from dealing with a chaos of inputs with nothing connected to anything else. Seeing-as-meaning prevents you from expending time and energy on separate stimulations as if they were unique and unrelated to anything else. Thus, in one sense, perception is a streamlined survival process.

The miracle of the mind is that it copes so well with a jumble of inputs and is able to organize sense data so that most of the time your world is reasonably coherent, predictable and stable. By regarding perception as a program for processing data (and not for recording it) you can understand why there is often great disparity among the meanings we assign to experience. Yet, there is similarity as well, since the need for shared perceptions is fundamental to the human condition. The necessity to bond depends on perceiving things somewhat the same way, as in, 'I'm glad you see what I mean'. Think how wonderful it is for two people to laugh at the same thing or detest the same thing. These shared perceptions bring us closer.

Although research is not conclusive, the drive for meaning exists from the first days or weeks of life. Scientific studies show that infants prefer patterned cards to plain ones and respond more to the configuration of the human face than to scrambled features. Obviously, because a baby's survival is involved more with the human face than with any other stimulus, it is understandable that the face has more meaning. But interestingly, people never lose their need to perceive the human face. Think about the weirdness of masks and the challenge one teacher felt when her students all showed up wearing dark glasses. The school rules had failed to ban this oddity, taking for granted that teachers and students would disclose themselves to one another by showing their faces. Ask yourself if you could learn from an instructor who wore a bag over his head or if he could teach you while you wore a bag over your head? What is the power of the human face?

Reading faces

Some people appear to be able to read faces better than others. Malcolm Gladwell, in his book *Blink*, talks about a policeman, John Yarbrough, who was with the Los Angeles Sheriff's Department. Time and again he could tell if a perpetrator would attack or shoot when armed. Yarborough recounted one incident:

> *He had the gun in his right hand. He was on the curb side. I was on the other side, facing him. It was just a matter of who was going to shoot first. I remember it clear as day. But for some reason I didn't shoot him… If you looked at it logically, I should have shot him. But logic had nothing to do with it. Something just didn't feel right.* [This is a classic example of knowledge by acquaintance/ knowing how in contrast to knowledge by description/knowing that!]

From *Blink* by Malcom Gladwell, Allen Lane, 2005 © Malcom Gladwell 2005. Reproduced by permission of Penguin Books Ltd.

Elsewhere in the same book, Gladwell talks about the 'theory of thin slices', where a little knowledge can go a long way. He speaks about the high success rate of predicting divorce among couples within fifteen minutes of observing their conversations with one another and perceiving certain features and facial expressions.

At an even more intuitive level of perception, there are studies coming out of the Harvard Graduate School of Education indicating that the good teacher can be spotted within a period of two to three minutes of observation. Such an evaluation is not, as previously thought, dependent upon multiple classroom visits by a supervisor over a long period of time. Is there anything in your perceptual experience of teachers to suggest the soundness of this form of reading faces and behaviour? Consider this hypothesis in terms of the rising popularity of speed interviewing and speed dating.

All of us read faces all day long. When someone says, 'I love you', the face should show it. When someone smiles, you see subtle clues signalling the message of the smile: the flirt, the grin, the nod, the smirk. The face communicates in such an extraordinarily efficient way that some people think there are ways to interpret facial expressions that transcend cultural differences. Do you think it is possible in Papua New Guinea, New York or Japan that expressions can be interpreted in such a way that ensures your safety and well-being? And how is it that some people are so adept at finding the meaning in a smile?

But what if we don't find meaning?

Other questions arise. If the mind is so preoccupied with the search for meaning, how does it respond if it does not find it? Why do you think so many people find abstract art disturbing? Remarks such as 'my five-year-old could do this' or 'hang it upside down and you couldn't tell the difference', camouflage the reality that the viewer just doesn't get the point. And that irritation, and even anger, takes over and dominates when meaning disappears.

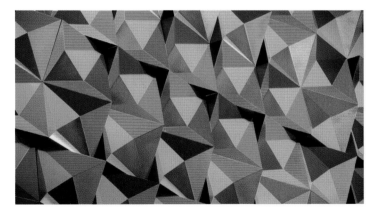

Can you find meaning in abstract art?

Or, on a more simple level, think how you react when someone tells you a riddle or a joke then walks away. Or consider the 'magic eye' puzzles that were fashionable a few years ago. How long before you looked up the answer? This will tell you something about your own ability to tolerate lack of meaning.

Much of joke-telling and other tension-related activities that end in laughter depend on our willingness to tolerate frustration and suspense up to a point. Laughter almost always expresses tension relief. Certain people, artists and other creative types, can usually handle more meaninglessness, that is, more perceptual uncertainty in their lives because they respond to stimuli by generating new meanings. Think only of the stereotype of the crazy artist or the mad scientist – people who are not satisfied with the conventional interpretation of images. No wonder they meet public opposition.

It is not overly dramatic to remind ourselves of the cost to health and sanity from a radical loss of meaning when nothing makes sense in a normal way. Paranoia, delusions of grandeur, catatonia or schizophrenia are afflictions where the world becomes so distorted that pathologies take over, perhaps representing a retreat from a senseless world. 'Crazy-making' is a clinical concept that could be explored in your presentations.

Organizing principles

However, the average person feels comfortable with familiar meanings and is secure in thinking that he knows what is going on. The world, by and large, does not disturb his mind and he organizes his perceptual stimulations according to some fundamental principles, one of which is called *the law of simplicity*. As an example, look at the figures below from Carolyn Bloomer's *Principles of Visual Perception*:

Circles?

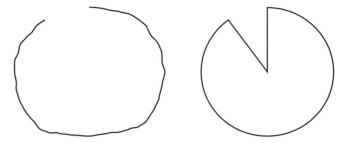

Are they circles? Not really. The first is not complete. It is also irregular and a little lumpy, a bit squarish; in fact, a funny kind of figure, but most of us keep referring to it as a circle and do not invent a new name for it. The second is a circle with a piece cut out. But whatever you say about them, you keep coming back to their circular qualities, an instance of the *law of simplicity*. A circle is the simplest category of meaning that your mind can come up with to fit the stimulus. Of course, if the features become too borderline, you would need to rename the item, something we are faced with constantly in classifying the world. As an analogy, think about how similar this situation is to the quandary of considering what could be a new planet, Eris, which is 27 per cent more massive than Pluto, yet has been called the dwarf planet. How far does Eris stretch our definition of a planet? What shall we now call Pluto?

The law of simplicity is so basic that it has been codified in science as the *law of parsimony,* which states that the best scientific explanation is the simplest one that fits the data. A classic example is the theory proposed by Copernicus to take the Sun as the centre of the universe, and not the Earth, as was the case with Ptolemy's model. Copernicus's conception was simpler. It worked better.

Scientific discovery nearly always involves leaping beyond our perceptual limitations. Einstein – like Columbus – was 'out of his senses'. After all, sensible people clearly see that the Sun rises and that the Earth is flat. They have to be taught that this is not so. As Sir Arthur Eddington observed, any true law of nature is likely to seem irrational to rational man. In the end all good science and the true key to knowing the universe will lie in knowing ourselves.

The Gestalt Principle

This law of simplicity was applied to the human mind by psychologists who gave us the term *gestalt*, a German word meaning 'form'. Not only did the Gestaltists find that the mind perceives the simplest possible form but also that it tends to see the 'best' or most 'correct' possible form. This means that we tend to see things not as they really are but as our minds think they should be. By extension, we make mental corrections all the time, not only in irregular circles but in proofreading and any number of other instances. Carolyn Bloomer offers the simple but telling example where 'chack' (a non-word) was placed in two different contexts. In a sentence about poultry raising it was misread as 'chick'; in a sentence about banking, not surprisingly, it was misread as 'check' (the US spelling was used). Your own problems with proofing your essays should give even more weight to this notion. It is interesting that, to date, most spell checkers cannot deal with the meaning of a sentence.

Nor has the computer, at the time of this writing, had much success in filling in fragments (which our own minds do so swiftly). For example, imagine you see a deer in the woods – it is behind a screen of trees so that what you are actually seeing is only bits and pieces of what you, nevertheless, can identify as an intact living animal. Even though recognizing the deer as a deer is effortless for us, it is not a trivial accomplishment for the brain. Teaching robots to recognize objects in real life from fragments – what we do in a flash – has proved to be a most difficult task for artificial intelligence designers.

Context

Context is enormously influential in how we see the world. We don't see any single thing as it is, we see it in a setting where it does or does not belong. Novelty in context can be exciting but it can also be disturbing. Take a look at some of René Magritte's work for good examples of this, for example, 'The Portrait'.

The context of any problem determines how you will see clues and often influences our thinking well below our level of awareness. Solutions are reached and discoveries are made by giving attention to the slightest clue, but such clues do not announce themselves. 'We need to know what to look for in foreign countries,' said Immanuel Kant (where a foreign country can mean anything unfamiliar). And 'Chance favours the prepared mind,' said Louis Pasteur. But how can we prepare ourselves if discovery or problem solving depends on the open or imaginative mind that isn't hindered by the context of the clue?

The history of scientific discovery is full of chance observations. Alexander Fleming was not the first to notice mould in his bacterial growth, but he was the first to recognize the significance of the ring around the mould's growth where the bacteria had died. Because of his fresh eye we have the benefit of penicillin today. Likewise, a fact out of context is a nuisance to most people, but Wilheim Roentgen, a German physicist, discovered X-rays by paying attention to a fogged photographic plate when working with his vacuum tubes. A week later, he took an X-ray photograph of his wife's hand which clearly revealed her wedding ring and her bones. The photograph electrified the general public and aroused great scientific interest. Roentgen used the 'X' to indicate that it was an unknown type of radiation. The name stuck.

One remarkable example of the power of the context is the informal experiment reported by the US newspaper *The Washington Post* called 'Pearls Before Breakfast'. The famous violinist, Joshua Bell, agreed to perform classical solos on the platform of the underground metro system at L'Enfant Plaze station. The hypothetical question to be answered was: what would happen if one of the world's greatest violinists performed incognito before a rush hour audience of over a thousand people? The answer was not surprising. Next to no one paused to listen or, seemingly, even to notice.

Perceiving the whole

Another feature of perception, according to the Gestalt theory, is that we perceive whole configurations, not parts. We do this so rapidly that the process is below conscious awareness. For instance, as you read you are perceiving words and phrases, not individual letters. This finding is exploited by the speed-reading schools of the world where people are taught to grasp entire chunks of words at a time. You only struggle with the letters when the words as a whole elude you.

> **What is**
>
> **wrong with this**
>
> **this line?**

Finally, the mind appears to fill in sense data in such a way that we can create a whole from fragments, as shown in the high contrast figure below. The image is reduced to black and white which eliminates the outside contours and the degrees of shading that we ordinarily expect to find. The fact that you can organize an image so easily from fragments emphasizes how we readily fill in the blanks.

To recap in brief, the mind organizes meaning according to these processes:
- attraction of a stimulus – you pay attention
- differentiation of stimulus –a figure versus a background relationship
- focus on stimulus – the details of the thing
- naming the stimulus – closure.

What's in a name?

How much better people feel when they name something. Some people will not eat a food, no matter how appealing it may be, if they cannot name it. In medicine, we want names for our illnesses as well as names for our treatments. In schools, we name the constellations, the continents, the countries and the cities. Little children name the parts of their bodies: the nose, eyes, head and hands – often in nursery rhymes. Adults name stamps, birds, rocks, antiques and cars. What do you know when you know the name of something ?

Depending on the name given to those in this photo, what would be the chances of someone investing in their company? Imagine they were called The Young Inventors, The Geeks from the Blue or Microsoft Executives. What would be your interpretation of the photo without a caption? Bill Gates is in the lower left corner.

The Microsoft Corporation executives, 1978. Would you have invested?

Signs and graphics

Advertising and city services, to mention just two areas, follow the four processes listed on page 56 quite closely, using logos and signage that attract our attention and give nearly instant closure. The need for advertisers to get our attention means we are bombarded with neon signs, flashing banners on websites and sultry young women perched on car bonnets – anything to distract us from our business and be drawn towards them. The insignia for the Red Cross is about as perfect a symbol as has been created. It is immediately identifiable and conveys the meaning of the organization at a glance. Consider how swiftly the graphics below send their message.

Bloomer seems to suggest that, in contrast, great art is the kind that provides a sort of renewable closure – not too simple and not too obscure, both of which can turn a viewer away. The masterpieces seem to allow for multiple viewings, each time offering something new. Not only has the artist expressed multiple meanings, but the work allows you to project different meanings onto the painting, symphony, novel, etc. at different stages in your life. Although it is easy to speak of great art, as if we all agreed on these examples, these comments are not meant to exclude films, television shows and even cartoons. In short, anything that provides a range of renewable closure experiences.

What movies or songs bear repeating not only for their familiar pleasure, but for the newness with each experience? Ask your parents, grandparents and teachers what artistic expressions have been so rich that they could return to them again and again.

Optical illusions and paradoxical perceptions

Optical illusions fascinate us, challenging our default notion that what we see is really real. They demonstrate that all of our perception is an illusion. Because all incoming sensory information is an interpreted representation of the world, our eyes lie to us and our brain knows it. It is the playful child in us that makes illusions so entertaining, but knowledge issues abound if we cannot believe our eyes.

Macbeth asked, 'Is this a dagger I see before me?' Was he seeing things? And if it was a dagger, what could it mean or portend? Other illusions present not one, but multiple images, some of them contradictory. Ambiguous illusions offer a switch between alternatives, for example, is it an old lady or a young girl? Is it a duck or a rabbit? Another popular example is the Rubin vase, which is either an urn or two faces. Some people see the alternatives rapidly and the switches are under their control. Others who fix on one image are more under the control of the graphics and cannot see the duck for the rabbit. Ambiguous figures demonstrate our ability to shift between figure and ground, the basis for the two different interpretations of the figures. They exemplify the fact that sometimes the same perceptual input can lead to very different representations.

Paradox illusions offer impossible objects. Most students are familiar with the castle staircase of the Dutch mathematician/artist M.C. Escher. It appears to be going up forever – seemingly it cannot get you anywhere or, conversely perhaps, it can take you anywhere. It certainly raises significant questions about the relationship between perception and rationality.

Consider the devil's pitchfork and the impossible triangle below. At first glance, there they are, a pitchfork and a triangle. But wait a minute… something isn't right. The two-dimensional images represent an object that cannot possibly exist. Slow down and run your finger around the lines. You will be baffled. And as with many puzzles you will be simultaneously frustrated, tormented and attracted by an illusion that is dependent on a cognitive misunderstanding that adjacent edges must join.

All of these illusions (and more) disturb the mind and interfere with the necessity to interpret the world as swiftly as possible so that we can take some kind of action. After all, you cannot stop to compute if what you see before you may be a lion or a bear or a snake. You need to name the image and, quite possibly, run for your life.

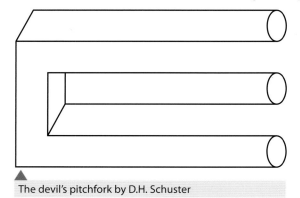

The devil's pitchfork by D.H. Schuster

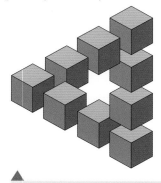

The impossible triangle of Oscar Reutersvärd

Perception and research: two projects

Getting in touch

Participants in a recent psychological study will probably never look at mannequins – or their own bodies – in quite the same way again. Before the study, they knew their arms belonged to them and synthetic ones didn't, simply because seeing is believing. Now they're not so sure.

Researchers at Carnegie Mellon University in Pittsburgh asked subjects to keep their eyes on a rubber arm that was sitting on a table in front of them. With the subject's left arm hidden from view by a screen, the researchers simultaneously stroked both the rubber hand and the subject's hand with a paintbrush. Even though they knew their own hand was being stroked behind the screen, nearly all the subjects experienced the same bizarre sensation: they felt the fake hand was actually their own.

According to Matthew Botvinick, the PhD psychology student who co-authored the study with adviser Jonathan Cohen, awareness of self seems to depend on intricate conversations between the brain and a range of sensory inputs that it constantly receives. If those conversations become garbled by contradictory messages, the brain is even willing to stretch the bounds of where the body ends and the outside world begins in order to draw a coherent picture.

'It's like ventriloquism,' says Botvinick, who was so spooked by the illusion when he tested it on himself that he let out a yelp and threw the fake hand across the room. 'In the experiment, when something touches the fake hand, you feel it, so the rubber hand appears to be an object with which you sense. And when there is an object of that kind, it's usually part of you. That seems to be one basis of self-identification.'

To confirm that the subjects were experiencing a true shift in their perception of themselves, researchers asked them to run their right index finger along the underside of the table until it was directly underneath their left one. Those who had experienced the rubber hand illusion invariably missed their real finger altogether and pointed more closely to the fake hand.

'When you look at your hand, it doesn't feel as if your brain might be going through all kinds of complicated computations to arrive at the conclusion that this thing is yours,' says Botvinick. 'You just know it's your hand.'

Jennifer Van Ezra in 'Nexus', *Equinox* no. 99 (July 1998)

A sense of direction

For six weird weeks in the fall of 2004, Udo Wächter had an unerring sense of direction. Every morning after he got out of the shower, Wächter… put on a wide beige belt lined with 13 vibrating pads – the same weight-and-gear modules that make a cell phone judder. On the outside of the belt were a power supply and a sensor that detected Earth's magnetic field. Whichever buzzer was pointing north would go off. Constantly.

'It was slightly strange at first,' Wächter says, 'though on the bike, it was great.' He started to become more aware of the peregrinations [adjustments] he had to make while trying to reach a destination. 'I finally understood just how much roads actually wind,' he says. He learned to deal with the stares he got in the library, his belt humming like a distant chainsaw. Deep into the experiment, Wächter says, 'I suddenly realized that my perception had shifted. I had some kind of internal map of the city in my head. I could always find my way home. Eventually, I felt I couldn't get lost, even in a completely new place.'

Continued

The effects of the 'feelSpace belt' – as its inventor, Osnabrück cognitive scientist Peter König, dubbed the device – became even more profound over time. König says while he wore it he was 'intuitively aware of the direction of my home or my office. I'd be waiting in line in the cafeteria and spontaneously think: I live over there.' On a visit to Hamburg, about 100 miles away, he noticed that he was conscious of the direction of his hometown. Wächter felt the vibration in his dreams, moving around his waist, just like when he was awake.

Direction isn't something humans can detect innately. Some birds can, of course, and for them it's no less important than taste or smell are for us. In fact, lots of animals have cool, 'extra' senses. Sunfish see polarized light. Loggerhead turtles feel Earth's magnetic field. Bonnethead sharks detect subtle changes (less than a nanovolt) in small electrical fields. And other critters have heightened versions of familiar senses – bats hear frequencies outside our auditory range, and some insects see ultraviolet light.

We humans get just the five. But why? Can our senses be modified? Expanded? Given the right prosthetics, could we feel electromagnetic fields or hear ultrasound? The answers to these questions, according to researchers at a handful of labs around the world, appear to be yes.

It turns out that the tricky bit isn't the sensing. The world is full of gadgets that detect things humans cannot. The hard part is processing the input. Neuroscientists don't know enough about how the brain interprets data. The science of plugging things directly into the brain – artificial retinas or cochlear implants – remains primitive.

So here's the solution: Figure out how to change the sensory data you want – the electromagnetic fields, the ultrasound, the infrared – into something that the human brain is already wired to accept, like touch or sight. The brain, it turns out, is dramatically more flexible than anyone previously thought, as if we had unused sensory ports just waiting for the right plug-ins. Now it's time to build them.

How do we sense the world around us? It seems like a simple question. Eyes collect photons of certain wavelengths, transduce them into electrical signals, and send them to the brain. Ears do the same thing with vibrations in the air – sound waves. Touch receptors pick up pressure, heat, cold, pain. Smell: chemicals contacting receptors inside the nose. Taste: buds of cells on the tongue.

There's a reasonably well-accepted sixth sense (or fifth and a half, at least) called proprioception. A network of nerves, in conjunction with the inner ear, tells the brain where the body and all its parts are and how they're oriented. This is how you know when you're upside down, or how you can tell the car you're riding in is turning, even with your eyes closed.

When computers sense the world, they do it in largely the same way we do. They have some kind of peripheral sensor, built to pick up radiation, let's say, or sound, or chemicals. The sensor is connected to a transducer that can change analogue data about the world into electrons, bits, a digital form that computers can understand – like recording live music onto a CD. The transducer then pipes the converted data into the computer.

But before all that happens, programmers and engineers make decisions about what data is important and what isn't. They know the bandwidth and the data rate the transducer and computer are capable of, and they constrain the sensor to provide only the most relevant information. The computer can 'see' only what it's been told to look for.

The brain, by contrast, has to integrate all kinds of information from all five and a half senses all the time, and then generate a complete picture of the world. So it's constantly making decisions about what to pay attention to, what to generalize or approximate, and what to ignore. In other words, it's flexible.

In February, for example, a team of German researchers confirmed that the auditory cortex of macaques can process visual information. Similarly, our visual cortex can accommodate all sorts of altered data. More than 50 years ago, Austrian researcher Ivo Kohler gave people goggles that severely distorted their vision: the lenses turned the world upside down. After several weeks, subjects adjusted – their vision was still tweaked, but their brains were processing the images so they'd appear normal. In fact, when people took the glasses off at the end of the trial, everything seemed to move and distort in the opposite way.

Later, in the 60s and 70s, Harvard neuro-biologists David Hubel and Torsten Wiesel figured out that visual input at a certain critical age helps animals develop a functioning visual cortex (the pair shared a 1981 Nobel Prize for their work). But it wasn't until the late 90s that researchers realized the adult brain was just as changeable, that it could redeploy neurons by forming new synapses, remapping itself. That property is called neuroplasticity.

This is really good news for people building sensory prosthetics, because it means that the brain can change how it interprets information from a particular sense, or take information from one sense and interpret it with another. In other words, you can use whatever sensor you want, as long as you convert the data it collects into a form the human brain can absorb...

From 'Mixed Feelings' by Sunny Bains, published in *Wired* Magazine, April 2007

Today's world: perception and medicine

The text below is taken from Dr Jerome Groopman's blog, Jerome Groopman.com, 13 April 2007. Dr Groopman is the Dina and Raphael Recanati Chair of Medicine at Harvard Medical School and the author of *How Doctors Think*.

There is an art to medicine that involves creative thinking, self-doubt, sensitive perception, and engaged dialogue with a patient and their family, drawing out key information and weighing its importance. It is hard to say how this can be 'measured,' but it *can* be better taught and modelled. I know that there are many times when I fall into cognitive traps and still have a long way to go to improve 'performance' after some 35 years in medicine.

The question remains, who is a good doctor, and, moreover, who is the right doctor for any individual? The best answer that I have found for myself and my family is a doctor who thinks with us, explains clearly what is in her mind, how she arrived at her working diagnosis, and why the offered treatment makes sense for us as individuals. She may refer to guidelines and 'best practices,' but clearly takes into account the spectrum of human biology and customizes our care to fit both our clinical needs as well as our emotional, social, and psychological dimensions based on astute perception.

I feel strongly that it is time to integrate cognitive psychology (the study of perception) into the curriculum. Physicians are making decisions all the time under conditions of uncertainty with limited data. The human mind is wired to take shortcuts, and our biases and emotions can strongly colour our reasoning. Scant attention is paid to this critical cognitive dimension, which underlies misdiagnosis. Over the past years, many medical educators have proposed algorithms and illness scripts to medical students and residents. These are based on prototypes, typical patients with diseases that have typical symptoms and findings on physical examination or laboratory testing. As the letters in the New England Journal of Medicine articulate, such illness scripts and algorithms are very seductive, because, working under time pressure, and with incomplete data, it is much easier to follow than to lead, much easier to just grab on to the algorithm or illness script rather than take the time to think expansively. This is not to say that such algorithms are worthless. But they have to be put into context, consulted and evaluated, but not automatically adopted. As several of the medical educators write in the New England Journal of Medicine, illness scripts can paradoxically foster misdiagnosis by causing anchoring errors and premature closure.

I am heartened by the increased debate around these issues. Every misdiagnosis I made was painful – most painful, of course, for the patient, but, also for me. As physicians, we are constantly trying to do our best. We know that we are imperfect, and will always fall short. So, we need to work in an environment that allows us to think better, and we need to be educated in self-awareness, both about our cognitive processes and how our emotional state can affect our judgement.

Ideal knower

Helen Keller, American author and activist and the first deaf/blind person to graduate from college (1880–1968)

Can any of us imagine how the world might seem to Helen Keller, deaf and blind since the age of two? How could any of us hope to be as strong and as optimistic as her? Where would we find the courage to manage the world and find delight in its beauty? She is an inspiration to so many, yet like us she still has normal human failings. She loses her temper when she doesn't get her own way and ignorance irritates her – she even complains about doing her homework!

Doubtless it will seem strange to many that the hand unaided by sight can feel action, sentiment, beauty in the cold marble and yet it is true that I derive genuine pleasure from touching great works of art. As my fingertips trace line and curve, they discover the thought and emotion which the artist has portrayed. I can feel in the faces of gods and heroes hate, courage and love, just as I can detect them in living faces I am permitted to touch.

… A medallion of Homer hangs on the wall of my study, conveniently low so that I can easily reach it and touch the beautiful sad face with loving reverence. How well I know each line in that majestic brow – tracks of life and bitter evidences of struggle and sorrow; those sightless eyes seeking even in the cold plaster, for the light and blue skies… but seeking in vain; that beautiful mouth, firm and true and tender. It is the face of a poet… Ah, how well I understand his deprivation… In imagination I can hear Homer singing as with unsteady hesitating steps he gropes his way from camp to camp – singing of life, of love, of war… it was a wonderful glorious song and it won the admiration of all ages. I sometimes wonder if the hand is not more sensitive to the beauties of sculpture than the eye.

… Another pleasure that comes more rarely than the others is going to the theatre. I enjoy having a play described to me while it is being acted on stage far more than reading it, because then it seems as if I were living in the midst of stirring events. … I think only those who have escaped the death-in-life existence… can realize how isolated, how shrouded in darkness, how cramped by its own impotence is a soul without thought or faith or hope. Words are powerless to describe the desolation of that prison-house, or the joy of the soul that is delivered out of its captivity. When we compare the needs and helplessness of the blind before Dr Howe began his work, with their present usefulness and independence, we realize that great things have been done in our midst. What if physical conditions have built up high walls about us? Thanks to our friend and helper, our world lies upward; the length and breadth and sweep of the heavens are ours!

From *The Story of My Life* by Helen Keller

Student presentation

1 Compare the three different ways that you perceive the world as:
- a member of a species
- a member of many groups
- a unique individual.

2 How can you learn something about perception-as-meaning from the way you organize the contents of your hard drive or your desktop?

Essay questions

1 Compare and discuss the following two quotes in the light of your understanding of human perception:

It seems that the human mind has first to construct forms independently before we can find them in things. Knowledge cannot spring from experience alone, but only from the comparisons of the invention of the intellect with observed fact.

Albert Einstein

The subtlest and most pervasive of influences are those which create and maintain stereotypes. We are told about the world before we see it. We imagine most things before we experience them.

Walter Lippman

2 What can be meant by the Panchatantra saying, 'Knowledge is the true organ of sight, not the eyes'? Is it necessary to have clear ideas to see?

Emotion
An introduction to emotion

Why do we want to touch some sculptures and stand away from others? Why do some songs evoke such vivid memories in our minds? Why are we attracted to some human faces but not to others?

'Reclining Mother and Child' by Henry Moore

A sculpture by Giacometti

Sing, Goddess, the wrath of Achilles.

Homer, *The Iliad*

Of all the Ways of Knowing described in the TOK subject guide, the emotions are perhaps the most misunderstood. We all have emotions, and while we may not be able to describe the physiological processes by which they occur, we certainly know how they feel to us. We have all felt happy, jealous and tense, and while we may have trouble explaining to others how those emotions feel to us, we may think ourselves quite good at identifying them when we see them in others. On the basis of the outward manifestations of emotional behaviours, psychologists and neuroscientists have developed some categories of emotions:

We are probably pretty good at identifying emotions in others

- primary or universal emotions: happiness, sadness, fear, anger, surprise and disgust
- secondary or social emotions: embarrassment, jealousy, guilt and pride
- background emotions: well-being or malaise, calm or tension, fatigue or energy, anticipation or dread.

Primary or universal emotions are the basic emotional mechanisms common to all people in all cultures. We are wired at birth with primary emotions. Secondary or social emotions are socially conditioned by the conventions of a given culture at a point in time. Background emotions are frequently not conscious but often form the psychological context for the rest of our behaviours.

I think she's mad at me

One of the reasons emotions have been misunderstood by TOK students (and almost everyone else) is because they are frequently considered to be opposed to other ways of knowing, and therefore an impediment to knowledge. How many times has someone said to you something like:

'Stop crying, you're being irrational!'
or
'You have no reason to be angry!'
or
'There is no reason to be afraid!'?

The assumption behind these admonitions is that we are capable of controlling emotions and because we are free to do so, we are responsible for the consequences if we do not. (Consequences such as irrational thinking, distorted perceptions and exaggerated language.)

When we control these emotions, what are we really controlling? Are we controlling the feeling or the behaviour that comes from the feeling? The inward experience of fear, or the outward expression of it? Can we be filled with rage, yet behave calmly and rationally? Can we be scared to death, yet behave with nonchalance? Surely to some extent we can, especially with practice and over time, as we become well integrated into the culture in which we find ourselves. We have all freely invoked emotions in order to control others and get what we want. We have seen 'temper tantrums' during which children kick and scream and throw things around. On a more sophisticated level, we have also tried to manipulate those whose favour we seek by 'emoting' in specific ways that influence their behaviours. We have feigned sadness, or pretended to be happy, or surprised. In those cases it might be said that we are modelling the behaviours that accompany those emotions that we have observed in others in order to get the desired result – generally the approval or sympathy of someone who we can influence in no other way. However, there is something irrational (and even futile and unkind) about telling someone who is genuinely angry or sad or afraid to stop having that emotion because it is inappropriate. Some emotions are not voluntary.

Exercise

Think back over the past week and make a list of the times and circumstances when you felt some kind of primary or secondary or background emotion. Now, think back over today and try to remember any time when you did not feel any emotions at all. Do you think there might be a connection between emotion and memory?

Reason and emotion

Cool-headed people have prefrontal damage.

Antonio Damasio

Reason has frequently been seen as the defining characteristic of human beings, the one faculty we do not share with animals. Reason has further been conceived as existing in a separate part of the brain from emotions, independent of what we do with our bodies, and holding a higher position in determining the truth of what we claim to know. Nature itself has been viewed as essentially rational, with its laws existing independently of man but discoverable through the use of human reason. The effective application of reason requires dispassionate thought – inquiry uncontaminated by the emotional biases and excesses of human desire. However, recent developments in cognitive science have called these assumptions into question and have changed our understanding of reason. The cognitive scientists George Lakoff and Mark Johnson have summarized these changes in *Philosophy in the Flesh: The Embodied Mind and its Challenge to Western Thought*.

How cognitive science has changed our understanding of reason

- **Reason is not disembodied...** but arises from the... same neural and cognitive mechanisms that allow us to perceive and move around.
- **Reason is evolutionary**, in that abstract reason... makes use of, rather than transcends, our animal nature... it places us on a continuum with them.
- **Reason is not "universal"**... that is, it is not part of the structure of the universe... it is a capacity shared universally by all human beings.
- **Reason is not completely conscious, but mostly unconscious**.
- **Reason is not purely literal but largely metaphorical and imaginative.**
- **Reason is not dispassionate, but emotionally engaged.**

From *Philosophy in the Flesh: The Embodied Mind and its Challenge to Western Thought* by George Lakoff and Mark Johnson, reprinted by permission of Basic Books, a member of Perseus Books Group, 1999

In the past, scientists who wanted to investigate how the human brain worked were limited to examining the brains of cadavers, and to making rough correlations between what neurological damage they found and the behaviours of the person whose brain they examined. While this process was cumbersome and approximate, it did result in some advances in how we view the relationship between the brain and the body. The invention of MRI (magnetic resonance imaging) and PET (positron emission tomography) scans that can illuminate the electrical processes of a living brain as it reasons, perceives, communicates, feels and remembers has brought new understanding of the relationships between the brain and the mind and the body. It has helped to articulate the implications of our 'embodied' minds in ways that traditional philosophical and psychological thinking cannot.

Because our brains exist only in particular physical bodies, located in particular places and at particular times, they are not biologically different from other organs of our bodies that have evolved over time to their present state. Just as perception, emotion and language have evolved through time, so has reason – and all have evolved in conjunction with one another. We reason with categories that come from the experience of having a body that is constituted the way our bodies are constituted. Our eyes are located in the 'front' of our head (hence the concept 'front'), which is situated on a body a specific distance from the ground (hence the concept 'up'). We walk upright on two legs and, compared to the dog that walks beside us, our senses of smell and hearing are retarded. When we walk in the front door of a theatre, we find ourselves in the back of it and the North Pole always sits on 'top' of the maps we make to conceptualize our earthly space.

Our minds and our ways of knowing the world are dependent on the ways in which our bodies have evolved through time.

Furthermore, we are not directly conscious of most of what our brains do when we see and hear, or when we remember or think or speak. Nor are we conscious of the neuro-physiological processes of bodily movement, even though we can attend to certain movements, as when we dance or perform on a balance beam in gymnastics. We can practise certain movements and train our muscles to remember what we do but, as we perform, we are not directly conscious of our brain activities. Nevertheless, we depend upon those unconscious processes to shape how we conceptualize all aspects of our experience. Our bodies frame our experiences and act as the vehicle through which we live and through which we come to know our world. Those unconscious processes shape how we comprehend what we experience, and constitute our 'unreflective common sense' (Lakoff and Johnson, 1999).

We are not always conscious of the role the emotions play in our lives either, except when our emotions 'run away with us' and cause us to make bad choices. Most of us have been taught that good decisions are the product of dispassionate and objective thought. We have all made bad choices in the heat of an athletic contest or in an argument with a friend or family member when our passions are running high, so it is easy to see how emotions might be considered an impediment to rational deliberation. On the other hand, what if our emotions were not operating at all – could we still make good and appropriate decisions?

The strange case of Phineas Gage

The study of the anatomy and functioning of the human brain presents special problems, unlike the study of other parts of the body.

The distinguished neuroscientist and philosopher Antonio Damasio recounts the strange case of Phineas Gage who, in 1848 at the age of 25, was injured in a freak accident while working on a railroad construction crew.

In order to lay a flat and level rail bed, it was necessary for Gage and his crew to blast through the rocky terrain outside a small Vermont town. Gage, an extremely capable worker and leader of his men, took special pride in the delicate task. This consisted of drilling a hole in the rock and filling it half full of blasting powder, inserting a fuse and covering the remainder of the hole with sand. Once loaded with sand, Gage used a three foot seven inch round iron bar, tapered at one end, to tamp the sand tightly against the powder so that the blast went into the rock instead of back out of the hole. After loading the charge and setting the fuse, Gage was momentarily distracted and, before his assistant could fill the hole with sand, he began tamping directly on the blasting powder. This ignited and blew the iron rod into his left cheek, upward through the left orbital cavity and out of the top of his head. Because of the shape of the iron bar and its tapered end, the bar blew cleanly through Gage's head, doing apparently minimal but unknown damage.

Gage was able to walk and talk and function normally immediately after the accident, and within two months was medically healed, save for some lingering infections. Unfortunately, his behaviour was changed radically by the injury, which damaged no other aspects of his mental functioning. Prior to the accident, Gage was physically athletic, very decisive, rational, efficient and popular with both his men and the company for whom he worked. He was considered a righteous member of his community and had a bright future ahead of him. However, after his accident, even though he retained all of his former physical and intellectual skills, he became so uncouth, profane, irritable and aggressive that his former employer would not hire him back. The problem was not his ability to do the job, but his anti-social behaviour. Gage subsequently roamed about the country taking odd jobs but was never able to hold a position for long because of his complete lack of discipline. Eventually, he joined the Barnum Museum in New York City and allowed himself to be displayed in the circus freak show. He died of a series of epileptic seizures in San Francisco in 1861.

Some years after Gage's death, his body was exhumed and his skull, along with the iron bar, were placed on display in the Warren Medical Museum of the Harvard Medical School, where it remains to this day. Through modern medical imaging techniques and some remarkable forensic investigations, the parts of Gage's brain that were destroyed have been approximately identified as the ventromedial region of the prefrontal cortex, damage to which would have:

> … *compromised his ability to plan for the future, to conduct himself according to the social rules he previously had learned, and to decide on the course of action that ultimately would be most advantageous to his survival.*
> From *Descartes' Error: Emotion, Reason, and the Human Brain* by Antonio R. Damasio, Vintage. Reprinted by permission of the Random House Group Ltd.

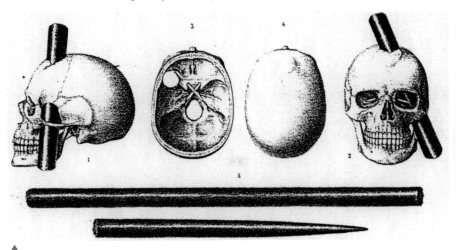

The bar that penetrated Phineas Gage's skull

Phineas Gage's skull and a model of his head

Another investigation of prefrontal brain damage

The insights gained from an examination of the brain of Phineas Gage led Damasio to investigate a number of living subjects who suffered similar prefrontal brain damage.

One such patient, named Elliot, suffered from a benign brain tumour located just above the eye sockets, which put pressure on the frontal lobes. The tumour and the surrounding damaged tissue were surgically removed. After the surgery, Elliot began exhibiting uncharacteristic behaviours that made it impossible for him to return to work and, since he was receiving disability payments, the referring physicians wanted to know if he was suffering from a real disease, or if he was merely malingering.

His behaviour was much like that of Phineas Gage in so far as he went from being a successful businessman with a happy family to someone whose life was utterly dysfunctional. While all of his other mental and intellectual capacities were intact, he could no longer follow a schedule, dress himself or make basic decisions. At his office, he would spend hours deciding by which criteria to file documents, never reaching a conclusion. From time to time, he would start reading what he should have been filing and become so engrossed in the documents that he would forget his task. His business judgement, formerly so acute, had vanished, and he found himself unable to choose between those business partners who were honest and those who were not. He lost his business, his wife and his family and because he was no longer able to learn from his mistakes, he was unable to live independently.

Yet Elliot was intelligent and aware of what was going on around him. He could keep track of current events and could recall the relevant facts and details of his business and family life. His intelligence was well above average and his memory excellent. He could recall the details of his recent misfortunes and, when recounting them, could do so dispassionately, almost as if they had happened to someone else. He acknowledged his recent actions but was in no way embarrassed by them.

On the other hand, he could not make decisions about things in his own life and was unable to formulate any plans for his future. When his brain was examined by computerized tomography and magnetic resonance imaging, the damage revealed was to the prefrontal cortices only, the rest of his brain remained undisturbed, much like that of Phineas Gage. Both men could reason normally, neither could make a decision. It was as if each choice in a field of possible choices was valued exactly the same, and while Elliot could reason about the consequences of all of them, his reasoning had no end and culminated in no decision.

As Damasio interviewed Elliot, he realized that he had never seen him display any emotions and could describe the horrible events that had befallen him as if he were a pure spectator. He had complete rational understanding of what had happened and could return to those events with equanimity and recount them in detail – but he could not relate to them emotionally. Damasio commented: 'We might summarize Elliot's predicament as to know but not to feel.'

Acting on our feelings

Imagine a situation in which you act before you 'decide' to act (in which you feel but do not know). You are walking alone down a dark, narrow street in a city late at night, when you see a large and imposing figure coming towards you, moving in a distinctly threatening manner. Before you can reason through your options of possible actions, of which there are few, you find yourself already across the street, your mouth dry, your skin prickly and hot and your heart racing. You increase your pace and hug the wall, trying to make as little noise as possible and to become invisible. You are completely in the moment and focused on the figure coming towards you. Your body has already responded to the possible threat before your mind is aware of what your body is doing. You have never been in this situation before, so you don't 'know' how to act.

Fortunately for you, the approach of the aggressive-looking man provokes sympathetic nervous system activation, which affects the internal environment of your body by acting on smooth muscles and hormonal levels. You are already well into your response to the threat before you become aware that you are afraid. You experience the emotion of fear as a feeling of being aware that your body is changing. You are equally capable at that moment of running or fighting for your life. As the man draws near, you feel like you will explode. But the man passes you by on the other side of the street without incident and you walk to the well-lit train station at the end of the street, where you sit on a bench under a light until you can catch your breath and stop shaking.

Maybe you laugh at yourself for overreacting but you know in your heart you will never walk down that street again. Not in the dark, not in the light, not alone, not with someone, not ever. Your body and your brain are hard-wired for survival and, just as your brain keeps your body regulated in a state of homeostasis or functional balance (within which your body operates most efficiently) without your knowledge or consent, it also responds to certain stimuli in the world with a primary emotion – in this case fear – that occurs prior to any thought but which then shapes all subsequent thought about the circumstances of this and all similar instances like it.

Once you stop shaking, you may begin to devise rules for yourself about what you will do in similar cases in the future, such as familiarize yourself with the geography of strange cities before you explore them alone at night, or rethink the advisability of walking in certain neighbourhoods alone at any time. When you next encounter a similar circumstance, your knowledge of what to do will be conditioned by the secondary emotion, which was formed when you made the systematic connections between the aggressive man, the dark and unfamiliar street and primary fear.

Emotions and judgement

> *Thinking is a form of feeling… feeling is a form of thinking.*
>
> Susan Sontag

In the example above, the choices available to you were quite narrow and there was no opportunity to deliberate anyway. Much of life proceeds in this fashion, with your body responding before you have a chance to think about the possible choices available. When you become hungry, the choice that you *will* eat is made before any deliberation about *what* you will eat. We all move out of the way of oncoming traffic without much deliberation. In fact, most of us would be hard pressed to recall many of the details of our trip to college, school or work this morning, even though the trip was full of decisions and deliberations as we made our way. Most of us tend to be on 'auto pilot' during such times, with our minds wandering aimlessly until something focuses our attention. However, there are other kinds of decisions over which we agonize, deliberate, counsel and procrastinate in an attempt to get it right. As to these kinds of decisions, Antonio Damasio suggests there are at least two possibilities, which he calls:

- the **high reason** view of decision making on the one hand and
- the **somatic marker** hypothesis on the other.

High reason The high reason view of decision making is one that values 'objectivity' and a dispassionate view of the relevant courses of action. Logic is its powerful tool.

Somatic marker *Soma* means 'body' in Greek. A somatic marker is a bodily feeling (either positive or negative) that is experienced prior to making a decision and that influences that decision.

The 'high reason' view of decision making

The 'high reason' view is probably familiar to you, or soon will be, as you select a college or university and a major area of study. It is the point of view that someone other than you might take with respect to your future – someone who does not share your emotional history and cannot know how you really feel and who proceeds to give you advice. The high reason view, as its name suggests, values pure reason and logical deduction above all else and it assumes that in order to get the best results, emotions and passions must be set aside (since they cannot be objectively verified) and a pure 'cost/benefit analysis' must be calculated. Of course this assumes the analyst can be cool headed and objective, or at least that the analyst values a kind of disembodied rational analysis.

Exercise

Before you begin this exercise, you might want to consider these preliminary questions:

What are the criteria you will use to select your college or university? What will be your major field of study and how will it influence your choice of institution? Is cost a factor and how will you pay for it?

1 List each of the colleges or universities and the areas of study you are considering.
2 Where are they located? Are they urban, suburban or rural? In warm climates or cold? Near to home or far away?
3 What are the academic experiences you hope to have and how do you know you can get them at your institution? What are the social experiences and how can you get them?
4 What is the quality of the faculty and curriculum?
5 List the benefits you hope to gain upon graduation from each institution.
6 List the cost of each benefit.
7 How do you know the benefits outweigh the costs?
8 When you have made these deliberations, rank order your choices from most preferred to least preferred.

Leicester University, Faculty of Engineering, 1959–63

All Soul's College, Oxford University

While the list on the previous page is not exhaustive by any means, it is probably long enough to demonstrate that if the power of pure reason is all you have to work with, you are going to be at the project for at least as long as it will take you to graduate. The preliminary questions alone would be enough to stall most of us. For example, assuming you can isolate the academic and social experiences you hope to have in higher education, how can you value them one against the other? By what calculus will you determine the cost of the benefit of a university's curriculum, and weigh it against an as yet unknown future value? You may not realize the benefit of an excellent faculty member until years after you graduate.

The pure weight of the details of gains and losses will swamp your ability to attend to them and remember them, constantly postponing your decision until it is too late. Remember Elliot's inability to decide which criteria to use to file his documents? All criteria were valued equally and he could not move from indecision – even though he could give rational and sensible reasons for each criterion he considered. Is it possible that the one criterion you value the most is not on the list because it is not susceptible to rational analysis? The high reason method of decision making does not allow you to consider questions that do not have rational answers. Fortunately, we are almost never reduced to reason alone when we deliberate about important decisions.

The 'somatic marker' hypothesis

Let's say, for example, that one of the universities you are considering is in a city much like the one in which you were frightened by the aggressive-seeming man. When you visit this university, it is a grey and dark December afternoon and you are on your own walking around, looking at the gothic architecture. The university has many appealing qualities: it is small; it has an excellent undergraduate curriculum with famous professors in your field of study who actually teach undergraduates; it is urban and yet close to beautiful countryside; but for some reason you have a bad feeling about the place and you cannot quite articulate why. It's physical, it centres in your gut and you know that no matter how many attractive features the place might have, you will never have the completely positive image of it you hoped for. You are already unfavourably disposed and, while you have not crossed it off your list, you have a nagging bias against it. All other things being equal, you may well choose another university.

We all experience these kinds of 'gut' feelings, although we are not always aware of them at the time, and they help us make decisions. Damasio calls them 'somatic markers'. They are somatic because they are about the body and markers because they mark an image. In this case, the image is of a dark and narrow urban street and the body feeling is the primary emotion of fear. You have formed a systematic connection between categories of objects and situations on the one hand (darkness, narrow city streets, aggressive-seeming men) and primary emotions (in this case fear) on the other. Notice that this negative gut feeling comes quickly, fleetingly, but unmistakably, *before* you apply any kind of cost/benefit analysis. Your attention has been focused on the possible negative consequences of attending this university in this city and has sounded an alarm that, by itself, might not be enough to make you reject it, but has certainly biased your possible choices. If the somatic marker is strong enough, it may lead you to immediately reject the contemplated choice, thereby not only protecting you from possible danger but also eliminating a possible alternative. Without a somatic marker, you are as likely to deliberate among possible choices indefinitely, as you are to ever come to a decision.

> *In short, somatic markers are a special instance of feelings generated from secondary emotions. Those emotions and feelings have been connected, by learning, to predicted future outcomes of certain scenarios. When a negative somatic marker is juxtaposed to a particular future outcome the combination functions as an alarm bell. When a positive somatic marker is juxtaposed instead, it becomes a beacon of incentive.*

> From *Descartes' Error: Emotion, Reason, and the Human Brain* by Antonio R. Damasio, Vintage. Reprinted by permission of the Random House Group Ltd.

If our attention is focused in such a manner by emotions, and if our emotions occur prior to our thoughts, rather than in competition with them, emotions might actually be said to be preconditions for our thoughts, essential valuing mechanisms programmed by evolution to seek pleasure and avoid pain, in the most fundamental of terms. Emotions frame our conscious awareness such that we rationalize our choices after we make them. Certainly, we can override our emotions, and choose to postpone gratification in order to obtain a more beneficial result, which is what we do when we exercise will-power, but the emotional frame of reference for the eventual choice is made before we devise our rational strategies for achieving our aims. Without an emotional impulse, we would wander endlessly through the barren landscape of rationality without ever coming to a decision.

The role of education and culture in the formation of both adaptive and maladaptive somatic markers cannot be over emphasized: it is primarily through education and socialization that the number of stimuli grows and becomes rationally coherent.

Emotional images

Homeostasis The coordinated and mostly automated physiological reactions required to maintain healthy balance in a living organism.

In the example given above, the original impulse was one of fear, a primary emotion, caused by a specific image, a dark and threatening shape in a narrow and confining space. We are unlikely to forget the categories of dark, aggressive shapes in conjunction with confined spaces that produced the original primary emotion of fear. When they present themselves again in some similar conjunction, the normal emotional state of **homeostasis**, in which the brain efficiently manages the body's emotional levels between pain and pleasure, is disturbed. This may only be briefly but we feel a negative 'gut' feeling towards the new situation.

The reaction can be reinforced by such unrelated experiences as going up a dark staircase in a strange building or watching a scene from an old horror movie set on a dark street of a nineteenth century European city. We may not feel the primary emotion of fear with the intensity we did originally but such a stimulus can certainly change our mood or our predisposition to choose among alternative courses of action – with or without our being consciously aware of it.

In fact, any mental image can have the same effect. As we walk along through a pleasant neighbourhood, our minds wandering through memories, our body's emotional equilibrium can be upset by a random mental image, a daydream. Have you ever awakened in the early morning from a dream you can't quite remember but from which you have a lasting mood that carries through the day? Such emotional states are constantly being evoked as we experience the variety of mental images of our conscious lives. We are literally swimming in emotional images and we are as aware of most of them as a fish is aware of the water in which it swims.

Intuition

As we swim in our emotional images, we are constantly confronted with making choices. Which images are worth our attention? How do we know what we *ought* to notice, out of all of the images that present themselves to our conscious minds? When we turn our attention to a particular image, for example, the sound of the motorcycle idling in the car park, or the whisper of our friend's instructions about chemistry homework, what do we miss? How do we decide what to notice and therefore what to value? Since our decisions happen in fractions of seconds, it's all we can do to keep track of even the most important - as our minds wander to the sounds of the idling motorcycle, we are transported to another scene of rolling hills and fence posts whipping by as we accelerate through the lanes. When did you say that homework is due?

The images of normal consciousness are rich and infinitely engaging. While our somatic markers help us sort out the ones that will lead to positive outcomes from those that will lead to negative ones, they may also operate subliminally (i.e. outside of the scope of our normal intentions and beneath the view of our ordinary consciousness). When they do, we call them **intuitions**, by which we mean the immediate apprehension of a solution to a problem or an insight into a situation without the intervention of any reasoning process.

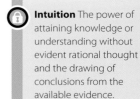

Intuition The power of attaining knowledge or understanding without evident rational thought and the drawing of conclusions from the available evidence.

How often this happens is difficult to say but we have all experienced the intuitive flash, which is so intense and immediate that we cannot deny its unusual character. Sometimes those intuitions lead to good results, though sometimes they do not. More common than the intense flash, perhaps, is the gut feeling that things are not quite right, which results in our not pursuing a course of action, or at least in our taking the time to engage rational processes to validate the impulse, or on the other hand, that things have a good feel to them and that the time for positive action is now. In either case, all intuitions take place in the context of our lived experiences, and our personal histories, and within the constraints and possibilities of both our culture and our own biology. In this respect, they are perhaps not qualitatively different from other emotional markers that allow us to make decisions.

In an interesting experiment conducted by Antonio Damasio at the University of Iowa, and reported by Malcolm Gladwell in his fascinating book *Blink: The Power of Thinking Without Thinking*, subjects are asked to play a card game in which they are presented with four decks of cards: two red decks and two blue. They are asked to turn over cards one at a time from any of the decks and, as they do so, they are either paid a sum of money or penalized a sum of money. The decks have been rigged in such a way that the red decks, while paying high rewards, also have high penalties and the only way to win is to take blue cards at a lower payout and penalty rate.

Once players have turned over about 50 cards, they start to develop a 'hunch' about what is going on, and while they haven't figured out the precise reinforcement schedule, they know something is not right with the red decks. When players have turned over about 80 cards, they recognize the patterns of payout and penalty and can articulate why the blue decks are preferable. This is a normal process of trial and error, followed by reasoning and formulating an explanation and, if that was all there was to the experiment, it would be of little interest. However, the Iowa psychologists also hooked each player up to a machine that measured the activity of stress response in the sweat glands of the hands. As the gamblers played the game, they started to develop stress responses after turning only ten cards from the red decks – 40 cards before they could report their hunch that something was wrong with the red decks. At about the same time their hands began to sweat, they also changed their strategies, without being conscious of having done so, and started picking more cards from the blue decks and fewer from the red. The emotional response came first, then the changed behaviour and finally the conscious rationalization.

This experiment clearly shows that the process by which we become aware of our environment is one in which our bodies respond to the world first, with some sort of emotion that results in a feeling that tags the situation as potentially aversive or beneficial. If our culture and brains are healthy, we learn to respond in ways that preserve our existence (and our genetics) on into the future. Intuitions are stronger instances of the same process, and have long been linked with creativity and with artistic and scientific breakthroughs, in which artists and scientists make interesting and unpredictable choices that result in inventions that redefine who we are and how we understand our world. Of course, a mathematician who invents some part of a mathematical world does not do so outside of the context of the existing mathematical world of which he is a well initiated and trained member. Great novels happen within the context of an existing range of expectations. Similarly, a musician's intuitions about how to play a certain piece of music have been informed by years of experience playing the way everyone else plays before it ever occurs to him to improvise, and the audience must have a certain level of sophistication to realize what has just happened.

So while intuitions may appear to be random events, much like the rest of our conscious and unconscious experience, they are not recognized as intuitions unless the person having them is prepared and attentive. How many times did the grey-eyed goddess Athena whisper into Odysseus's ear before he heard her message? While the flash of intuition may seem a random and fortuitous event, it occurs in a well rehearsed context of expectation shaped by the other Ways of Knowing: reason, language, and perception.

Exercise

The International Baccalaureate Learner Profile wants us to be both *principled* and *open-minded*. Since these two virtues may conflict, consider the following questions:

- When we say we have faith in a god, or in a person or in an institution, is our certainty intuitive or rational or some combination of both? Can we always be both open-minded and faithful?
- When we argue, along with Plato, that what we mean by knowledge is justified true belief, do our beliefs have both rational and emotional justifications? Are we open-minded about certain beliefs to which we are emotionally committed?

In summary

We have seen that emotions can interfere with our reasoning processes, bias our perceptions and colour our language. Emotions can reinforce a prejudice for social and intellectual conformity and can sharply limit what we can perceive and how we communicate our perceptions to others. But without emotions, everything in our perceptual field has the same value and consequently goes unnoticed. Without emotions, we cannot 'pay attention' to any one thing because we cannot choose to focus our consciousness in a way that brings meaning to an otherwise cacophonous world. Our consciousness is forever restless, constantly and quickly flitting from one mental image to another, evaluating and choosing and endowing experience with meaning. That we remember certain events and not others, that we see some objects and not others, that we speak with one accent or inflection and not another is because our brains are emotionally connected to the world through our bodies.

◀ We see some things and not others

Today's world: deeper questions, deeper dilemmas

As we learn more about neuroscience and about how our brain's chemistry works, more human (and anti-human) possibilities present themselves. Science seems to be giving us a new kind of 'self-control.' Consider the following dilemma.

The Guilt-free Soldier: New Science Raises the Spectre of a World Without Regret

At the University of California at Irvine, experiments in rats indicate that the brain's hormonal reactions to fear can be inhibited, softening the formation of memories and the emotions they evoke. At New York University, researchers are mastering the means of short-circuiting the very wiring of primal fear.

The web of your worst nightmares, your hauntings and panics and shame, radiates from a dense knot of neurons called the amygdala. With each new frightening or humiliating experience, or even the reliving of an old one, this fear centre triggers a release of hormones that sear horrifying impressions into your brain. That which is unbearable becomes unforgettable too. Unless, it seems, you act quickly enough to block traumatic memories from taking a stranglehold.

Some observers say that in the name of human decency there are some things people should have to live with. They object to the idea of medicating away one's conscience.

(But) the scientists behind this advance into the shadows of memory and fear don't dream of creating morally anaesthetized grunts (infantry soldiers). They're trying to fend off post-traumatic stress disorder, or PTSD, so that women who've been raped can leave their houses without feeling like targets. So that survivors of terrorist attacks can function, raise families and move forward. And yes, so that those young soldiers aren't left shattered for decades by what they've seen and done in service.

Adapted from an article by Erik Baard in *The Village Voice*, 22 January 2003.
Erik Baard is a science writer in New York.

Ideal knower

Martha C. Nussbaum (1947–)

Martha C. Nussbaum is the Ernst Freund Distinguished Service Professor of Law and Ethics at the University of Chicago. She is also one of the most prominent philosophers in the US today.

Dr Nussbaum draws on her wide-ranging expertise in philosophy, psychology, law, divinity, anthropology, music, literature, Asian and gender studies and the classics when she says that emotions such as love and grief, far from irrational distractions, are 'intelligent responses to the perception of value'.

> Emotions shape the landscape of our mental and social lives… like 'geological upheavals'. They mark our lives as uneven, uncertain, and prone to reversal… their urgency and heat, their tendency to take over the personality and to move it to action… a person's sense of passivity before them; their apparent adversarial relation to 'rationality' in the sense of cool calculation… their close connection to one another as hope alternates uneasily with fear…
>
> In light of these features, it might seem strange to suggest that emotions are forms of judgement. And yet… all these features… are best explained by a modified version of the ancient Greek Stoic view according to which emotions are forms of evaluative judgement that ascribe to certain things and persons outside a person's own control. Emotions are thus, in effect, acknowledgments of neediness and lack of self-sufficiency.
>
> [Yet]… if emotions are suffused with intelligence and discernment, and… contain within themselves an awareness of value and importance, they cannot… be sidelined in ethical judgement as has so often been the case in the history of philosophy.
>
> From *Upheavals of Thought: The Intelligence of Emotions* by Martha C. Nussbaum

Student presentation

1 In recent times a Danish newspaper published some unflattering cartoons of the Prophet Mohammed. You have all read of the consequences and probably considered some of the arguments offered by both sides as you tried to make some sense of the episode. For this presentation, you will need a group of five students to role play the following scenario:

You are the editorial board of a large urban newspaper near your school. You are meeting to decide whether to publish the Danish cartoons in your newspaper. As you meet, you will need to develop the rationale for making your decision, taking into account the likely consequences of publication and the equally serious consequences of a decision not to publish. You must come to a consensus and you must explore the relevant knowledge issues in the process.

2 Identify a recent discovery in neuroscience and discuss its social and ethical implications. What sorts of knowledge issues does it raise?

Essay questions

The following Prescribed Titles from previous years invite a consideration of emotion as a Way of Knowing. Some of them even hint that emotion might be a precondition for knowing anything at all.

1 Should a knower's personal point of view be considered an asset in the pursuit of knowledge, or an obstacle to be overcome?

© International Baccalaureate Organization 2002

2 Sometimes we hear reasoned arguments that oppose a view to which we are emotionally committed; sometimes we hear a passionate plea for a view we have good reason to reject. Bearing this in mind, discuss the importance of reason and emotion in distinguishing between belief and knowledge.

© International Baccalaureate Organization 2005

Language

An introduction to language

Language is a dramatic gift bequeathed to humans. It can be wonderfully inclusive, enveloping its speakers in a glow of belonging and common perceptions. Yet, unfortunately, language can also be a source of exclusion, misunderstanding and conflict, as dramatized in the following extract from the poem 'Mokusatsu' by Heathcote Williams:

Asked what he would undertake first,
Were he called upon to rule a nation,
Confucius replied: 'To correct language…
If language is not correct,
Then what is said is not what is meant,
Then what ought to be done remains undone;
If this remains undone, morals and art will deteriorate;
If morals and art deteriorate, justice will go astray;
If justice goes astray,
The people will stand about in helpless confusion.
Hence there must be no arbitrariness in what is said.
This matters above everything.'

Asked to surrender in World War Two,
The Japanese employed the word 'mokusatsu'
In replying to the Potsdam ultimatum.
The word given out by the Domei news agency
Was interpreted in Washington as 'treat with contempt'
Rather than 'withholding comment' – pending a decision
Its correct meaning.
The Americans concluded that their ultimatum had been rejected;
The boys in the back room could play with their new toy
A hundred and forty thousand people lay around in helpless confusion.

Today 'peace' is mis-translated, and means a seething stalemate
Instead of calm;
'Strength' is mis-translated, and means paranoid force
Instead of right-minded confidence.
Reproduced with permission of Curtis Brown Group Ltd, London on behalf of Heathcote Williams.
Copyright ©Heathcote Williams 1988

◀ The atomic bomb drops on Hiroshima

Heathcote Williams's poem is a reminder of the statement in the TOK subject guide that 'the acquisition (learning) of a first language occurs so easily for most people, and communication with others is so natural, that the influence of language in shaping thought is not obvious'.

In this chapter, we will become aware that language functions as much more than a medium of communication in human societies, and moulds the interaction of humans in multiple ways. We will examine the many aspects of language and its impact upon the construction of knowledge and our identities as knowers including:

- the emergence of dominant global tongues and the disappearance of several indigenous languages
- theories on the origins of human language
- the debate on animals' ability for language
- the question of whether human language is innate or learned
- the links between language and culture, in particular gender and social values
- the significance of visual and symbolic language
- the appearance of new forms of communication, such as 'net language', in our times.

The following questions underlie the knowledge issues that will be examined in this chapter:

- How does language shape human thought?
- Does language assist or limit our search for knowledge and truth?
- What different functions does language perform? Which of these are most relevant in creating and communicating knowledge?
- If people speak more than one language, is what they know different in each language? Does each language provide a different framework for reality?
- Is it possible to think without language?

The case of the disappearing languages

The *Ethnologue: Languages of the World* (edited by Raymond G. Gordon) lists 6912 living languages in the world. Of these, it is estimated that about half are under threat of disappearing in the near future. A study funded by the United Nations Educational, Scientific and Cultural Organisation (UNESCO) points out that 'the past 300 years or so have seen a dramatic increase in the death or disappearance of languages', with serious consequences for humanity:

> The loss of any language means a contraction, reduction and impoverishment of the sum total of the reservoir of human thought and knowledge as expressible through language.

Used by permission of UNESCO

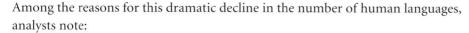

Among the reasons for this dramatic decline in the number of human languages, analysts note:

- speakers shifting to dominant languages, such as English, French, Spanish, Mandarin and Hindi
- speakers' own preference of shifting to other languages that they consider more 'prestigious' and 'modern' than their own languages
- socio-political factors, including language policy, language indoctrination through education, repression and pressure to use the official and national languages over local languages
- economic pressures and migratory trends
- epidemics and natural disasters.

Exercise

Working in a group, locate the language maps of Africa, Asia and the Americas on the website http:// www.ethnologue.com.

On these maps, each dot represents the primary location of a living language that is listed in the *Ethnologue.* After a careful examination of the maps, discuss the following questions:

1 What, in your opinion, would explain the areas and countries on each map with the greatest concentration of living languages?

2 Identify those areas and countries which you think are at greatest risk of the 'death or disappearance of languages'.

3 Link your answer for question 2 to the reasons listed above for the decline in human languages: which of these factors would best explain the endangering of languages in different regions of the world and why?

At its thirtieth general conference in 1999, UNESCO reaffirmed the importance of linguistic and cultural diversity in the globalizing world. The following are selected recommendations from Resolution 12 from the conference:

> *Recommends that Member States:*
>
> *(a) create the conditions for a social, intellectual and media environment of an international character which is conducive to linguistic pluralism;*
>
> *(b) promote, through multilingual education, democratic access to knowledge for all citizens, whatever their mother tongue, and build linguistic pluralism; strategies to achieve these goals could include:*
>
> - *the early acquisition (in kindergartens and nursery schools) of a second language in addition to the mother tongue, offering alternatives;*
> - *further education in this second language at primary-school level based on its use as a medium of instruction, thus using two languages for the acquisition of knowledge throughout the school course to university level;*
> - *intensive and trans-disciplinary learning of at least a third modern language in secondary school, so that when pupils leave school they have a working knowledge of three languages – which should represent the normal range of practical linguistic skills in the twenty-first century...*
>
> Used by permission of UNESCO

- In a paragraph, explain whether you agree with the call for the preservation of linguistic and cultural diversity, and some of its policy recommendations in the resolution. Would you, for example, support the goal of a 'working knowledge of three languages' for all school-leaving students?
- Why has the IB adopted the three official languages of English, French and Spanish? Could a strong case be made for the inclusion of other official IB languages, such as Mandarin, Arabic and Hindi? Set up a panel discussion in class to look at the reasons and arguments in favour of, or against, the inclusion of additional languages.

Counter-argument and debate

While you have read arguments in favour of the retention of the diversity of languages, others may claim that the move towards greater uniformity of national or even global languages may offer several advantages. The possible benefits could include:

- a global language for trade and commerce, including all nations in an equal exchange of goods and services
- a boost to national unity for countries recovering from colonial rule or internal divisions
- an avenue for social mobility and advancement for formerly disadvantaged groups.

The class should be divided into two groups, one arguing for the advantages of language uniformity or 'homogenization', and the other supporting the case for linguistic diversity. After hearing the case for both sides, conduct a poll in the class to understand where you and your peers stand on this debatable issue.

The origins of human language

How did the splendid capacity and creativity of human language emerge in the first place? Is language a uniquely human trait? Is language an innate ability or is it learned from society? As with many other knowledge issues, these questions continue to arouse controversy and debate, informing our notions of identity as a species and as individuals shaped by our natural and cultural environments.

Roger Lewin claims that:

> … human speech is the most powerful channel of communication in the world of nature, far outstripping anything produced elsewhere in the animal kingdom… more than anything else, language makes Homo sapiens something extremely special in the world.

From *In the Age of Mankind* by Roger Lewin, Smithsonian, 1988

The world of language enables humans to communicate wide-ranging experience:

> … from the mundane orbit of practical affairs, through the personal universe of deep emotions, to the intellectual and spiritual sphere of abstraction, mythology, and religion…

Roger Lewin, see source above

Lewin also points to two explanations for the evolution of human speech and language. The first claims that the development of technology that accompanied the hunting and gathering stage played a vital role in the creation of more efficient communication:

> … subsistence technology – which, from an archaeological point of view, principally means the development of stone tools – [became] more and more complex… all of which was accompanied by a virtual tripling of the size of the human brain – from some 400 cubic centimeters in the earliest australopithecines to more than 1200 cubic centimeters in modern Homo sapiens; [thus] technology is envisaged as the driving force of the evolution of the human brain. And language is assumed to be an essential part of the evolutionary innovation that made mankind successful…

From In the Age of Mankind by Roger Lewin, Smithsonian, 1988

More recently, however, a different explanation places greater emphasis on the social aspects of human evolution. Ralph Holloway, an anthropologist at Columbia University, points out that 'brains evolve in both material and social contexts… I regard the development of language as more closely bound up with social affect and control than with hunting behaviour involving signalling and object naming'. Lewin sums up that 'having moved away from a self-evident explanation – namely, better communication in the world of practical affairs – the origin of human language now occupies a much less tangible terrain, that of social complexity'.

Steven Pinker, a cognitive psychologist at Harvard University, agrees that language is:

> … certainly one of the distinctive traits of Homo sapiens. But I don't think language could have evolved if it was the only distinctive trait. It goes hand in hand with our ability to develop tools and technologies, and also with the fact that we cooperate with non-relatives. I think this triad – language, social cooperation and technological know-how – is what makes humans unusual. And they probably evolved in tandem, each of them multiplying the value of the other two.

Extract first appeared in the aticle 'Proud Athiest' by Steve Paulson.
This article originally appeared at www.salon.com

Do animals share human capacities for language?

The 'uniqueness' of human language appears obvious: it is manifested in the communication of the vast and limitless repertoire of knowledge that structures our existence as a species. However, many researchers have argued that animals are not devoid of the capacity for language, and their studies offer rich insights into the building blocks of language.

Read the exercise on the next page. As you read the extract below, keep the questions in mind:

In August 1969 the pre-eminent journal *Science* published a paper which, in its own way, marked as giant a leap for mankind as the first moon landing a month earlier. Allen and Beatrice Gardner of the University of Nevada reported that, for the first time in human history, they had conversed with a member of another species. Washoe, a female chimpanzee who had been reared in a trailer in the Gardner's backyard, had a vocabulary of over 100 words that she used to effectively communicate with her caregivers.

Until Washoe, every 'speaking beast' had been shown to be just a circus trick. Parrots might be trained to repeat certain phrases, but they had no understanding of what they were saying. Dogs could respond to commands, but they had no grasp of grammar. But Washoe… didn't just respond to rote commands, she could correctly respond to novel combinations of words. And she created her own little sentences like *gimme sweet, come open* and *listen dog*. Taken out on a lake, Washoe saw a swan for the first time and signed water bird for this unfamiliar creature.

The Gardners succeeded where so many before them had failed because they had the brilliant insight to teach Washoe to use her hands to communicate instead of her vocal chords. The Gardners trained Washoe in the sign language used by the deaf in North America: ASL (American Sign Language). Washoe inspired legions of imitators… [and] one ape language project maintained its scientific respectability.

Duane Rumbaugh's system, in which the chimpanzees communicated by pressing buttons on a keyboard, had always been subjected to tighter experimental control than the ASL-based attempts at ape language. In 1980 Duane Rumbaugh and Sue Savage-Rumbaugh started working with a new species of ape: bonobos – also known as pygmy chimpanzees. According to Savage-Rumbaugh, the moment the special keyboard was set up in front of Kanzi (an adopted infant bonobo) to start his language training, he began using the signs on the keys to communicate. On the very first day he pressed 12 of the keys over 120 times. He asked for *banana, juice, raisin, peanuts, chase, bite, tickle, orange, outdoors, swing, cherry, ball* and *sweet potato*. There was even evidence that Kanzi could combine signs meaningfully. He indicated *raisin peanut* and *sweet potato tickle* and seemed grateful when given each of these things. Kanzi went on to master rapidly the 256 signs, which was the most that could be fitted conveniently onto a portable keyboard.

Starting in the mid-1980s the Rumbaughs started claiming that Kanzi had mastered the rudiments of grammar. In a major study carried out when Kanzi was eight-years-old, his comprehension of over 600 different sentences was tested. An experimenter went behind a one-way mirror (so that she could not convey any non-verbal cues, such as eye movements, to Kanzi) and asked him to carry out a command. For example, Kanzi was asked to do such things as 'Go put some soap on Liz', 'Put on the monster mask and scare Linda'… as far as possible the experimenters tried to formulate commands that were unlikely to have previously arisen in Kanzi's daily life. In a majority of cases Kanzi did as he was asked to do. Kanzi, concluded the Rumbaughs, 'clearly processed semantic and syntactic features of each novel utterance'. In other words, here was a non-human ape who understood meaning and grammar.

When I first heard of Kanzi's achievements I was very excited indeed. I really felt that our understanding of the nature of the world and our place in it as human beings had been altered by what this bonobo had done. But when I studied the complete report of what Kanzi had been asked to do and started going carefully through the 660 commands he had been given and how he had responded to each one, my excitement changed to disappointment.

For a start, Kanzi did not show the increase in sentence length that is typical of children learning language. And it turns out that to complete many of the requests that were put to him Kanzi did not need to understand grammar… To test grammar what are needed are pairs of reversible commands like: 'Dog bites man' and 'Man bites dog'. Just knowing those three words – man, bites and dog – is not enough to comprehend the difference between these two statements. For that difference to be understood grammar is crucial.

Of the 660 commands that Kanzi was given, a mere 21 formed pairs of 'man bites dog', 'dog bites man' variety that constitute a critical test of grammatical comprehension. Savage-Rumbaugh and her colleagues reported that Kanzi responded accurately to 12 of these 21 pairs – a modest 57 per cent correct. On closer inspection, however, it became clear to me that their method of coding Kanzi's responses was unreasonably generous. To take one example: they commanded Kanzi to 'Pour the juice in the egg'. Kanzi proceeded to pick up the bowl with the egg in it, sniff it and shake it. They repeated the command three times – each time changing the wording slightly – before Kanzi did what they asked him to do. They nonetheless scored his response as correct. When they asked Kanzi to 'Pour some water on the raisins', he held a jug of water over a lettuce. This was coded as correct… When Kanzi was given the two commands, 'Make the (toy) doggie bite the (toy) snake' and 'Make the snake bite the doggie', in both cases the snake ended up in the dog's mouth but both responses were coded as correct. Re-scored to exclude these false positives, Kanzi achieved less than 30 per cent correct.

The point here is not to deny Kanzi's achievements – what other non-human can convey so much to his caregivers, or understand so much of what they say to him? – but to quantify them correctly. The point is not to see whether Kanzi does something involving toy dogs and snakes when asked to 'Make the doggie bite the snake', but to see if he understands grammar. And, on any assessment not tinted with rose-colored glasses, Kanzi just doesn't get it… Somewhere in the history of our kind there must have been the first beings who could rearrange tokens to create new meanings, to distinguish *Me Banana* from *Banana Me*. But the evidence from many years of training apes to press buttons or sign in ASL, is that this must have happened sometime after we split off from chimps, bonobos and gorillas. Since then, we have been talking to ourselves.

Extracts from 'Aping Language: a skeptical analysis of the evidence for non-human primate language' by Dr Clive Wynne, Professor of Psychology at University of Florida
www.skeptic.com/eskeptic/07-10-31.html

Exercise

- Of the evidence presented for 'non-human language' in the article, which do you find most convincing or persuasive and why?
- What, in your opinion, is the dividing line between human and non-human language?

A young chimp remembers the location of numbers on a screen and correctly recalls the sequence

You can find this information on Tetsuro Matsuzawa by visiting www.heinemann.co.uk/hotlinks and entering the express code 4327P.

Exercise

- The author comes to the conclusion that 'no beasts, no matter how fortunately circumstanced, can make known their thoughts through language'. Do you agree?
- Research further on the case being made for language capacities in other species such as dolphins, whales and bees. To what extent might these studies modify our understanding of the uniqueness of human language?
- Refer to the work of Tetsuro Matsuzawa, director of the Primate Research Institute of Kyoto University in Japan, and the related article 'Chimps beat humans in memory test'.

Is human language innate or learned?

An enduring knowledge issue arises from the question, 'Do humans learn more from 'nature' (their innate or inborn biological and genetic inheritance) or from 'nurture' (education from society and culture)?' A similar debate underlies differing theories about our acquisition of language: is the capacity for language 'hard-wired' into our brains, or does culture determine the formation and shape of language use? The following excerpts present the case for both sides of the argument. After reading them carefully, you as the knower can decide whether you lean more toward the nature or nurture side of the fence.

Extract A

In any natural history of the human species, language would stand out as the preeminent trait... Language is not a cultural artifact that we learn the way we learn to tell time or how the federal government works. Instead it is a distinct piece of the biological makeup of our brains. Language is a complex, specialized skill, which develops in the child spontaneously, without conscious effort or formal instruction, is deployed without awareness of its underlying logic... I prefer the admittedly quaint term 'instinct'. It conveys the idea that people know how to talk in more or less the sense that spiders know how to spin webs.

[Linguist Noam] Chomsky called attention to two fundamental facts about language. First, virtually every sentence that a person utters or understands is a brand new combination of words, appearing for the first time in the history of the universe. Therefore a language cannot be a repertoire of responses; the brain must contain a recipe or program that can build an unlimited set of sentences out of a finite list of words... The second fundamental fact is that children develop complex grammars rapidly and without formal instruction and grow up to give consistent interpretations to novel sentence constructions that they have never before encountered. Therefore, he argued, children must innately be equipped with a plan common to the grammars of all languages, a Universal Grammar, that tells them how to distil the syntactic patterns out of the speech of their parents.

Chomsky attacks what is still one of the foundations of twentieth-century intellectual life – the 'Standard Social Science Model', according to which the human psyche is moulded by the surrounding culture... I think it is fruitful to consider language as an evolutionary adaptation, like the eye, its major parts designed to carry out important functions.

Exercise

What arguments are presented by Pinker and Chomsky to support their claim that human language is an 'instinct' or an innate ability? Do you find their evidence convincing?

Extract B

Take heart, those of you who struggled with maths at school. It seems that words for exact numbers do not exist in all languages. And if someone has no word for a number, he may have no notion of what that number means.

The Piraha, a group of hunter-gatherers who live along the banks of the Maici river in Brazil, use a system of counting called 'one-two-many'. In this, the word for 'one' translates to 'roughly one' (similar to 'one' or 'two' in English), the word for 'two' means 'a slightly larger amount than one' (similar to 'a few' in English), and the word for 'many' means a 'much larger amount'. In a paper just published in *Science*, Peter Gordon of Columbia University uses his study of the Piraha and their counting system to try to answer a tricky linguistic question.

The question was posed by Benjamin Lee Whorf in the 1930s. Whorf studied Hopi, an Amerindian language very different from the Eurasian languages that had hitherto been the subject of academic linguistics. His work led him to suggest that language not only influences thought but, more strongly, that it determines thought.

Dr Gordon… spent a month with the Piraha and elicited the help of seven of them to see how far their grasp of numbers extended. Using objects with which the participants were familiar (sticks, nuts and… small batteries), he asked his subjects to perform a variety of tasks designed to measure their ability to count. Most of these tests involved the participant matching the number and layout of a group of objects that Dr Gordon had arranged on a table.

In the tests that involved matching the number and layout of objects they could see, participants were pretty good when faced with two or three items, but found it harder to cope as the number of items rose. Once it was beyond eight, they were getting it right only three-quarters of the time…Things were worse when the participants had to remember the number of objects in a layout and replicate it 'blind', rather than matching a layout they could see. In this case, the success rate dropped to zero when the number of items became, in terms of their language, 'many'.

The Piraha are a people who have steadfastly resisted assimilation into mainstream Brazilian culture. Their commerce takes the form of barter, with no need to exchange money. Exact numbers do not exist in their language simply because there is no need for them. And in this case, what you do not need, you do not have. At least in the field of maths, it seems, Whorf was right.

From 'Language Barriers' ©*The Economist* Newspaper Limited, London (19 August 2004)

Extract C

One of the most powerful forces in keeping prejudice alive is language – words and how they are used. Words shape thought; they can be used as propaganda and to spread opinions or beliefs. Words can intimidate or frighten, or be direct threats of violence. More than anything else, words reinforce stereotypes and perpetuate racism and bigotry.

Colour symbolism, for example, is very much a part of US culture. The word *white,* or whiteness as a concept, usually symbolizes a positive quality, while *black* or blackness connotes a negative. Just take a quick look through a thesaurus or dictionary and you will find such terms as *blacklist, blackmail, black deeds, black sheep, black mark,* and so on – all linked to unfavourable images. Many more such terms subtly but unmistakably put across the idea that 'black is bad'. On the other hand, whiteness is more often associated with positives such as 'purity' and 'cleanliness'.

Since white Protestant Anglo-Saxons are the dominant group in the US, many forms of expression have their roots in WASP myths or prejudicial ideas about groups of people. Take a look at history books that describe various groups. Writers have used 'loaded' words to distort or to justify conquests of Native Americans. For example, if whites won battles, they have been called victories; if Native Americans won battles, they have been called 'massacres' by 'savages' rather than, say, 'a battle to defend homelands'.

From 'The Language of Bigotry and Racism' in *Bigotry* by Kathlyn Gay, Enslow Publishers, 1989

Paradigm
A philosophical and theoretical framework of a scientific school, or other discipline; theories, laws and generalizations are formulated and experiments are performed in support of them.

Exercise

- Do extracts B and C support the claim that language is shaped and determined by culture? Would these excerpts validate the Sapir-Whorf hypothesis, which states that 'language determines our experience of reality'?
- In class, discuss the 'nature' versus 'nurture' debate which presents two contrasting **paradigms**. From the perspective of the study of human language, which paradigm would you support to a greater extent and why? Is it possible to offer a 'synthesis' or combination of the two paradigms? (Use the responses as the basis for a class debate).
- Another class discussion… extract C points out that language often becomes the basis for constructing stereotypes and discrimination. Could you suggest ways in which language could become more 'neutral', or are there other avenues for reducing and removing the effects of propaganda and negative images of other groups?

Language and gender: 'Nu Shu', China's secret female language

In the previous section, we looked at the relationships between language and culture, and how these could structure elements of discrimination and prejudice. In human history, one of the longest-lasting forms of inequality relates to gender. The following passage relates to language and gender discrimination in traditional society in a Chinese province.

Nowadays, it would be called empowering women. But back then, centuries ago, it was just a way for the sworn sisters of this rugged and tradition-laden Chinese countryside to share their hopes, their joys and their many sorrows.

Only men learned to read and write Chinese, and bound feet and social strictures confined women to their husband's homes. So somehow -- scholars are unsure how, or exactly when -- the women of this fertile valley in the southwestern corner of Hunan province developed their own way to communicate. It was a delicate, graceful script handed down from grandmother to granddaughter, from elderly aunt to adolescent niece, from girlfriend to girlfriend -- and never, ever shared with the men and boys.

So was born nushu, or women's script, a single-sex writing system that Chinese scholars believe is the only one of its kind.

"The girls used to get together and sing and talk, and that's when we learned from one another," said Yang Huanyi, 98, a wrinkled farmer's widow whom scholars consider the most accomplished reader and writer among a fast-dwindling number of nushu practitioners. "It made our lives better, because we could express ourselves that way." ...

Much remains unknown about nushu. Its origins, reaching perhaps as far back as the third century, have been the subject of scholarly exchanges among a handful of researchers in China and elsewhere. They know it was used in Hunan's Jiangyong County, in south central China...

What seems clear is that nushu was fostered by the region's ancient custom of "sworn sisters," whereby village girls would pledge one another fealty and friendship forever. The tight sorority, which included growing up together in cobbled village lanes and gathering with adult women to weave and embroider, inevitably was shattered when the time for marriage came. Tradition dictated that a bride go away to her groom's home -- and that is where nushu came in.

Three days after the wedding, the adolescent bride would receive a "Third Day Book," a clothbound volume in which her sworn sisters and her mother would record their sorrow at losing a friend and daughter and express best wishes for happiness in the married life ahead. The first half-dozen pages contained these laments and hopes, written in nushu that the groom couldn't read. The rest were left blank for the bride to record her own feelings and experiences -- in nushu -- for what would become a treasured diary. ...

Most important to the women who learned it, sometimes memorizing letters written on the palms of their hands because of a lack of paper, nushu liberated them from illiteracy.

The way nushu came to light some 20 years ago also has been clouded in competing theories.

Lin Lee Lee at the University of Minnesota has written that a Jiangyong County woman visiting relatives in Beijing in 1982 astounded them by singing and then writing a language and script they could not understand. The relatives passed along their amazement to scholars, she said in a conference presentation, and research into the strange female writing system began.

But Zhou Shuoyi, 78, a self-described countryside intellectual who lives in nearby Yongzhou city, said he knows better, and he explained why.

One of his ancestors, a grandmother six generations back, wrote a poem titled "Educate the Girls." The poem, handed down from generation to generation, was translated into nushu by local village women, he said, and his aunt brought the nushu version to his father's house sometime in the 1920s as a subject of curiosity.

Zhou's father, a schoolteacher, was impressed by the strange writing he couldn't understand and urged the young Zhou to investigate. Later, working for the Jiangyong County cultural department in the 1950s, Zhou said he discovered a number of elderly peasant women still mastered nushu. ...

"At that time, many grandmothers could sing it, write it and read it," he said in an interview. "In society at that time, there was injustice between men and women, and women needed this language as a way to express themselves."

Zhou reported his findings to authorities in Beijing, but by then the Cultural Revolution had convulsed China. ...in 1979, when calm had returned, Zhou said, he went back to work at a local museum and resumed his interest in nushu, eventually learning to read and write. ...

"Now a lot of people are studying it, and a lot of people come here to ask about it," he said.

From 'The secret language of Chinese women' by Edward Cody, *Washington Post*, Sunday, February 29, 2004

Exercise

Hold group discussions on the following:
- In what ways can language be an 'empowering' experience for its users?
- What is the role of language in creating and reinforcing social distinctions, such as gender?
- Can you think of other examples of disadvantaged groups in society using language as a means of expression and survival?
- Aldous Huxley observed in 1947 that 'words form the thread on which we string our experiences'. What experiences did the women of Hunan 'thread' through the creation of 'nu shu'? Do you think it enabled them to live happier lives?
- Do women still need a different language today?

As a class:
- Construct a poem which expresses the sentiments of the women who used 'nu shu'.
- Split up into two groups – male and female. Both the 'women's group' and the 'men's group' should gather together and decide on a topic of conversation which is of particular interest to them. A recorder in each group should note the stories or terms that seem to predominate in the conversation. After 15 to 20 minutes, each group should report to the class and compare the 'language' used by them. Did you observe substantial differences and what might that imply for gender differences (or similarities) in our times?
- Write a reflective journal of 250 to 300 words on how gender has shaped your experiences as a knower, particularly in the use of language.

'Nu Shu' written in Nu Shu (right to left)

Proverbs and aphorisms Brief pithy sayings that express a truth or widely held belief, for example, 'absence makes the heart grow fonder'.

Language and culture: proverbs and aphorisms

Rice terraces in Bali

Languages are shaped by their physical and social environments, giving them their richness and diversity. **Proverbs** and **aphorisms** preserve the wisdom of cultures, while at the same time revealing their concerns and important values. The culture of the Indonesian island of Bali is known for its incredible artistic talents, which extend beyond dance, painting and sculpture to the use of language itself. After reading the Balinese proverbs and expressions that follow, we will examine the messages that they convey.

1 'Get grasshoppers, bring fire.'
Some Balinese collect grasshoppers and bring them home to cook over a fire and eat them. The proverb refers to one who would bring the fire along while collecting the grasshoppers; figuratively, this refers to a person who spends money as quickly as he earns it.

2 'A cotek fish is joined to a layur fish.'
A *cotek* is a very common short fish, while the *layur* is a much longer fish. The meaning here refers to gossip – as it spreads, the story gets longer and exaggerated out of all proportion.

3 'Like the life of rice. When empty it stands up. When full it looks down.'
This refers to a 'know-it-all' type. He has an empty head (like a young rice stalk) but he stands up and talks a great deal. A wise person, on the other hand, looks down at his feet; his head is full (like mature rice) but it bends over. He may know a lot but he says little.

4 'Like eating krupuk; a lot of noise.'
Krupuk is a large, crispy cracker which makes a lot of noise when eaten, but it is rather spongy and is mostly air. The expression is used to refer to a 'loud mouth' – a person who makes a lot of noise but says nothing at all.

5 'Sere has a bad burned fish smell but it has lots of uses.'
Sere is a fermented fish paste that smells bad but lends a delicious flavour to dishes when used properly. The expression refers to a person who may be undesirable looking in a village but who is very useful and important to the life of the community.

6 'That person is like a dry kepundung.'
A *kepundung* is a fruit with an unattractive appearance but a delicious taste. This refers to a person who may be externally unattractive but who is in reality very good and interesting.

7 'Like a crow naming himself.'
When a crow makes its characteristic cawing sound, it seems to be calling itself by its own name. This refers to a person who tells a lot of interesting stories but mostly about himself. Most of his stories are probably lies but the audience cannot tell whether they are true or false.

8 'If you rinse out your mouth and spit upwards, the spit will fall on you.'
This is said of a person who talks about his own problems to others. People criticize him for not keeping his misfortunes to himself.

9 'Like an earthquake, it starts itself.'
This refers to a person who acquires knowledge or skill by him or herself, inspired toward learning by internal or intrinsic motivation (the ideal knower!)

10 'Like carrying a dog on your hip.'
Babies in Bali are usually carried on the hip before they can walk. Carrying a dog that way is very bad since an animal should not be carried that high, violating the Balinese idea of elevation being linked to status. This proverb refers to a person who spoils someone endlessly.

Some sayings in Balinese are very similar to expressions used in other cultures:
- 'If you have an itch, scratch it' (take advantage of an opportunity).
- 'Talking about spilled tuak' (tuak refers to palm beer and this saying corresponds to 'there's no point in crying over spilt milk').
- 'A puppy barks but it never bites' (similar to 'his bark is worse than his bite').
- 'Like a hill seen from afar; nice looking' (corresponding to 'the grass is always greener on the other side of the fence').

From Fred B. Eiseman, Jr., *Bali Sekala and Niskala*, Vol. II Periplus

Exercise

Discuss the following as a class:
- Classify the proverbs and expressions that you read into two categories: desirable human behaviour and undesirable human behaviour. What does this classification tell you about the values of Balinese culture?
- Which of the proverbs and sayings made the greatest impression on you and why?
- The Balinese use the metaphor of rice to contrast a wise and an 'empty' person (see proverb number 3). Is this an appropriate metaphor? Could you suggest other metaphors to explain the same idea?

The language of symbols

Human language is enriched by its multi-sensory nature, drawing upon all the senses to create a combination of expression and meaning. Visual images have the capacity to deeply influence our thinking, since they seem to enter the subconscious layer of our minds and to create powerful responses to the world around us. Not surprisingly, all cultures have used symbols to communicate some of their most cherished ideals, beliefs, fears and hopes.

You are going to examine traditional symbols from several Asian and Western cultures, some of which continue to be highly significant. Then you can look at the use of symbols in our times to communicate messages and ideas that seem to resonate with contemporary concerns and lifestyles.

Have a look at the following symbols drawn from Asian religions and philosophies, which have had a profound influence upon ideas, beliefs and aesthetics.

The Yin Yang

The Yin Yang represents the Daoist symbol of the continual interaction of cosmic and universal forces and was later adopted by other Chinese philosophies such as Confucianism. Yin (moon) stands for the passive, cold, female elements while Yang (sun) is seen as the masculine force, characterized by heat and movement. These aspects can be extended to any other pairs of opposites, such as day and night or enlightenment and ignorance. However, these forces are seen as dynamic and complementary, leading to harmony. The symbol arose from the Daoists' close observation of nature, a world of continual flux and change which seems to find a balance and equilibrium.

The Yin Yang

The Lotus Flower

This is an important symbol in the Hindu, Buddhist and Egyptian religions. In Hinduism and Buddhism, the lotus symbolizes the human quest for enlightenment and spiritual freedom; the lotus has its roots in muddy waters (the material world and human imperfection), yet manifests as a perfect blossom. In the Egyptian tradition, the lotus symbolized the sun, because it bloomed at daytime and closed at night, and the sun was an object of veneration and worship.

The Lotus Flower

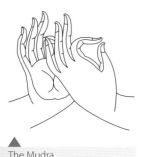

The Mudra

The Mudra

The Mudra uses a variety of hand gestures to represent different spiritual truths in Hinduism and Buddhism. For example, mudras in the Buddhist tradition symbolize the Buddha calling the earth to witness his conquest of Mara (temptation) and the achievement of enlightenment; setting the wheel of Dharma (Buddhist teaching) in motion; and the emphasis on meditation as spiritual practice.

Now examine the following symbols used in Western cultures or in international contexts.

The Absolute

The Absolute

The Absolute is represented by the straight line and is one of the five basic elements in Western symbolism. The straight vertical line stands for unity, oneness, the self, the number 1, authority, power and the absolute. When placed between other signs, it has a dividing meaning. In logic, for example, it sets up the proposition 'either A or B but not both'.

The Five Pointed Star

The Five Pointed Star

This star has no crossing lines and is a commonly used symbol with multiple connotations. It is used in the flags of 35 countries, first appearing in the national flag of the US in 1777. For nearly all armed forces in the world, the golden five pointed star is the symbol of military rank and power and is closely related to symbols for Venus as the morning star and the goddess of war. It is also a symbol of many ideologies and belief systems: with the hammer and sickle it represents communism; with palm leaves, scientology; with the crescent moon, Islam.

The Swastika

The Swastika

The Swastika has become notoriously associated with Hitler and Nazi Germany but is actually a very old symbol, used by early civilizations in Mesopotamia and the Indus Valley. One theory is that the swastika represents the sun, the highest god and the supreme power and life force. In India, where the swastika is associated with both Hinduism and Buddhism, it is derived from the Sanskrit words 'su' (good) and 'asti' (to be), with the suffix 'ka'. Commonly found in Turkey and Greece, the swastika had many different names in Europe, including 'Hakenkreuz' in Germanic areas and 'fylfot' in England; here the meaning of the symbol revolves around notions of power, energy and migration. It was used to indicate electric power plants in the nineteenth and twentieth centuries, and even by a brewery, but these were discontinued after Hitler used it as a national symbol from the 1920s to 1945.

 You could consult two websites which you will find by visiting www. heinemann.co.uk/ hotlinks and inserting the express code 4327P.

Exercise	
• Extend the study of symbols by carrying out your own research.	
• Working in pairs, your class could generate an extensive list from the index on these sites and fill the classroom with a colourful collage of human creativity in the use of pictorial signs	

Exercise

- Contrast the Yin Yang symbol with the Absolute. In which aspects or areas of knowledge do you think these symbols would be most useful? Do they represent complementary forms of critical thinking or do you prefer one as the appropriate symbol for critical thought? Write down your reasons.
- Why do religions and political ideologies use symbols? Could these be considered as forms of 'propaganda'?
- The Swastika is an example of a symbol that may have very different connotations in different cultures. Why is this the case? Are there other examples of symbols that may be 'read' in different ways?
- What, in your opinion, are appropriate symbols for 'knowledge', 'critical thinking', and 'Theory of Knowledge'. (You could discuss this in groups and share your illustrations with the class.)
- Research and present in class the important visual symbols that you see around you today. These could relate to commercial advertisements, political parties or ideologies, environmental messages, public campaigns or prevalent belief systems. Has the 'symbolic landscape' changed in the world in the last 50 years and does this reflect changing beliefs and concerns? Do you think these changes are for the better?
- Visual images and symbols are often seen as vital elements in constructing 'propaganda'. Do you accept this premise? What is the distinction between knowledge and propaganda?

Exercise

Look at the list of commonly used text and business terms in today's world (see below):
- In your opinion, does the appearance of 'net language' point to a greater empowerment of its users or does it indicate a corruption and debasement of language?
- Is change in language inevitable or should we retain elements of language structure and usage from the past?
- What other changes can you see emerging in our use of language in the near future?

Today's world: net language – empowerment or corruption?
Nothing seems to better symbolize the globalized world today than the converging communication networks powered by emails, chat rooms and instant messaging, bringing an ever greater swathe of humanity within their seductive web. The impact on language is already evident in the adoption of several short hand terms that reflect the quickening pace of communication.
Some examples of commonly used text and business terms include:

2moro – tomorrow	WYWH – wish you were here
2nite – tonight	AFAIC – as far as I'm concerned
BRB – be right back	CLM – career limiting move
B4N – bye for now	DD – due diligence
BFF – best friends forever	DRIB – don't read if busy
DBEYR – don't believe everything you read	EOM – end of message
FUD – fear, uncertainty and disinformation	ESO – equipment smarter than operator
IMHO – in my humble opinion	GMTA – great minds think alike
JK – just kidding	HIOOC – help, I'm out of coffee
LOL – laughing out loud (or lots of love)	IANAL – I'm not a lawyer
LYLAS – love you like a sister	LOPSOD – long on promises, short on delivery
NP – no problem	MYOB – mind your own business
OT – off topic	NRN – no reply necessary
POV – point of view	OTP – on the phone
RBTL – read between the lines	QQ – quick question
SITD – still in the dark	RFD – request for discussion
TMI – too much information	STD – seal the deal
TTYL – talk to you later	TIA – thanks in advance
TYVM – thank you very much	WIIFM – what's in it for me?
VBG – very big grin	WOMBAT – waste of money, brains and time

Ideal knower

Jalal ud-din Rumi

Jalal ud-din Rumi (1207-1273 CE) was born in Afghanistan. He wrote in the Persian language and moved with his family early in life to Anatolia (modern Turkey).

The name 'Rumi' comes from 'Rum', meaning 'Roman', since Anatolia was part of the old Roman Empire. A mystic of the Islamic Sufi order and a poet, Rumi is regarded as the greatest literary figure in the Islamic world and today he is one of the best-selling poets in America and other Western countries.

Jalal ud-din Rumi

The popularity of Rumi can be ascribed to the language of love and tolerance that subtly emerges in his poetry. This is a language that the world thirsts for today, to overcome the barriers and conflicts emerging from globalization and to reassert our common humanity. Rather than a 'clash of civilizations', Rumi's poetry stands as a clarion call for the 'dialogue of civilizations' and unity. This thirteenth-century poet speaks to our times and, in the process, covers many themes addressed in the TOK course as well.

The following is a sample of Rumi's verse taken from *Unseen Rain, Quatrains of Rumi*
Translated by John Moyne & Coleman Books, Shambhala, 2001

On wisdom and love, the two springs of knowledge:

Inside wisdom, a bright-flowing, analytic power.
Inside love, a friend.
One a psychic source, the other plain water.
Walk out into the indications
of where you must go.

On the journey of the knower:

Keep walking, though there's no place to get to.
Don't try to see through the distances.
That's not for human beings.
Move within,
But don't move the way fear makes you move.

On religious unity:

Two hands, two feet, two eyes, good,
as it should be, but no separation
of the Friend and your loving.
Any dividing there makes other untrue
distinctions like 'Jew', and 'Christian' and
'Muslim'.
Sometimes visible, sometimes not,
sometimes devout Christians, sometimes
staunchly Jewish.
Until our inner love fits into everyone,
all we can do is take daily these different
shapes.

On perception:

Don't forget the nut, being so proud of the shell,
The body has its inward ways,
the five senses. They crack open,
and the Friend is revealed.
Crack open the Friend, you become
the All-One.
I am so small I can barely be seen.
How can this great love be inside me?
Look at your eyes. They are small,
but they see enormous things.

On the global citizen:

If you want to live, leave your banks,
as a small stream enters the Oxus,
miles wide,
or as cattle moving around a
millstone
suddenly circle to the top of the sphere.

On love, renewal and union:

Listen if you can stand to.
Union with the Friend means not being who you've been,
being instead silence: A place: A view
where language is inside seeing.
When your love reaches the core,
earth-heavals and bright eruptions spew in the air.
The universe becomes one spiritual thing, that simple,
love mixing with spirit.
Life is ending? God gives another.
Admit the finite. Praise the infinite.
Love is a spring. Submerge.
Every separate drop, a new life.

Student presentation

1   Advertising as authority: propaganda or useful information?
    Here you can consider historical examples (Nazism or Soviet Russia are favourites) as well as contemporary examples of political and commercial advertising. The title lends itself to multiple perspectives on the positive and negative aspects of advertising.

2   Lost in translation: the problems of translating texts, poems or songs from one language to the other.
    This topic is a good avenue for your voice since you can contrast passages in your first and second (and third) languages. Hearing three versions of a song from the 'Lion King' in English, French and Dutch is an entertaining exploration in the subtle nuances and variations in meaning (and emotion) that different languages embody!

Essay questions

Two recent Prescribed Titles (PTs) include:

1   'All of the other Ways of Knowing are controlled by language.' What does this statement mean and do you think it is a fair representation of the relationship between perception, emotion, reason and language?

© International Baccalaureate Organization 2004

2   Would you classify mathematics, logic and music as languages? Justify your answer, considering the extent to which they resemble or differ from natural language and the role they play in the acquisition of knowledge.

© International Baccalaureate Organization 1997

7

Reason
Reason as a knowledge force…
a balance of extremes

Science is built up of facts, as a house is with stones. But a collection of facts is no more a science than a heap of stones is a house.

Henri Poincaré (1854–1912)

You live in a world consisting of extreme thinking and actions. Cultures and societies have produced a significant number of reasoning gems for society to wonder at. Consider, for example, the social science work of Gustave Le Bon (1841–1931). In his 1896 study of crowd behaviour (*The Crowd: A Study of the Popular Mind*) he asserted the following:

> … *a large number of women whose brains are closer in size to those of gorillas than to the most developed male brains. This inferiority is so obvious that no one can contest it for a moment; only its degree is worth discussion… Women… represent the most inferior forms of human evolution and… are closer to children and savages than to an adult, civilized man. They excel in fickleness, inconsistency, absence of thought and logic, and incapacity to reason. Without a doubt there exist some distinguished women, very superior to the average man but they are as exceptional as the birth of any monstrosity, as, for example, of a gorilla with two heads; consequently, we may neglect them entirely.*

Gustave Le Bon

In this day and age, how such an idea could be accepted in the academic community is clearly beyond any reasonable imagination. The irony of this passage is that the reason given for women being 'the most inferior forms of human evolution' is 'absence of thought and logic, and incapacity to reason'! As a TOK student you are left to review a multitude of judgements and knowledge claims that are questionable. Having the ability to measure and balance the justification for ideas in a well thought out manner becomes a necessary skill.

Reasoning, logic and critical thinking form a knowledge force, and the interplay of sound reasoning with the other Ways of Knowing is significant. Reason can fill in the gaps that other Ways of Knowing sometimes leave. It allows the scientist to understand how things work within sub-atomic particles beyond the normal range of human sight perception. Reason allows political figures to assess values and to balance them with emotional commitment in the hope of coming to a compromise that will leave conflicting sides at peace. Critical thinking and reason allows you to register the artist's intent and hence to appreciate the hidden beauty of a painted canvas and the message that it communicates.

The multifaceted nature of reason

If the world were a logical place, men would ride side saddle.

Rita Mae Brown (1944–)

The formal and informal use (and misuse) of reason in your day-to-day existence is ever present. You may not recognize it but it's there. A typical day in the world of the Jansen family can help you to identify the ways people connect to what is reasonable.

Exercise

Mr Jansen walks into the supermarket for his Tuesday afternoon shopping visit. He has a keen eye for a bargain and immediately sees a sign placed in the fresh fruit section. Without hesitation he puts five apples in his shopping trolley while happily mumbling to himself, 'That's a reasonable deal!'

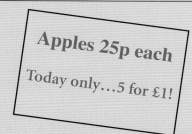

Apples 25p each
Today only...5 for £1!

Later that same afternoon, Mr and Mrs Jansen's third grade son, Liam, is getting Monday's mathematics quiz back. He notices that question four, 'What is 25 × 5?' is marked as incorrect. He had given the answer 100.

At about the same time, Mrs Jansen, the Theory of Knowledge teacher, is grading papers at Parkville High School. Two girls enjoying a short break between classes are standing outside the entrance to the room and begin a conversation, which Mrs Jansen overhears:

Abigail: *Hey, anyone who likes you will send you flowers.*

Brianna: *Well, George did send me those lovely roses for Valentine's Day.*

Abigail: *OK, he sent you flowers, so you know that he really likes you!*

Mrs Jansen sighs and knows that next week's lesson covering 'Logic and Everyday Thinking' is clearly coming at an appropriate time.

---

1   Are you surprised that Mr Jansen should find the '5 for £1' price to be reasonable? Does the fact that Mr Jansen will benefit from a cheaper price for the five apples imply that the deal is reasonable? Is it reasonable for the supermarket to set the price of apples in such a way? Explain.

2   Liam's answer is clearly incorrect but how does this relate to the apple price of 5 for £1?

3   Is it obvious that Abigail and Brianna's argument relating flower giving and liking is logically flawed? Explain.

Reason comes into question for each of the family members in a different context. Liam experiences the rather formal process of reason in the strict mathematical sense. His answer is incorrect and any thoughts otherwise will be quickly corrected by Liam's teacher or classmates. Liam's father, however, has a similar problem, but with a result that ends in a twist. The business logic of 'cheaper by the dozen' makes Mr Jansen a happy customer. And the supermarket manager will no doubt be a happy businessman in that he can increase his bottom line profit margin by selling more apples. In this business context, one apple costing 25p does not imply that 5 apples cost £1.25, but the *business* interpretation of 'to add' is nonetheless seen as being quite reasonable.

Finally, Mrs Jansen works with students who communicate on an informal basis and do so without regard to the formal side of reason and logic. Abigail and Brianna have casually discussed a personal situation and ended up coming to a conclusion which is not valid. You will be given a chance to show this in one of the exercises that follow.

The Jansen family experience allows you to view reason (i.e. being logical) from two different perspectives. One sees reason as being formal, as in the strict mathematical sense. A second view sees reason as being less formal but nonetheless typical of the way people structure thinking and communicate ideas to each other. The various Areas of Knowledge depend upon the structure and correctness that sound reason provides, and in this way reason does act as the glue that holds knowledge claims together. Here you don't want to forget about those situations where the truth of a proposition is determined by its *coherence* with a set of other propositions.

The manner in which reason is presented varies from a formal approach that you find in mathematics and science to one that is less formal in outward appearance but is nonetheless complex. Such arguments often deal with elaborate moral and political judgements and present a serious challenge to you. These arguments can be clouded by appeals to emotions and by a range of attempts to manipulate your thinking. By looking at various examples we can see that the application of correct reasoning is not a simple matter. It is indeed easy for the knower to be taken in by an argument that is not reasonable.

The formal side of logic and reason

We are approaching a new age of synthesis. Knowledge cannot be merely a degree or a skill... it demands a broader vision, capabilities in critical thinking and logical deduction without which we cannot have constructive progress.

Li Ka-shing (1928–)

Formal reasoning can be established in two ways:
- deductive methods
- inductive methods.

Deductive reasoning is a rule-governed method which allows a specific conclusion to be drawn from a set of general statements. A classic example of a deductive argument follows:

> *All TOK students must write an essay.*
> *Marlene is a TOK student.*
> *Therefore, Marlene must write an essay.*

Inductive reasoning allows a general conclusion to come from a collection of specific cases. A typical example of inductive reasoning might go as follows:

The 1st positive odd integer is 1, and $1 = 2(1) - 1$

The 2nd positive odd integer is 3, and $3 = 2(2) - 1$

The 3rd positive odd integer is 5, and $5 = 2(3) - 1$

The 4th positive odd integer is 7, and $7 = 2(4) - 1$

Hence, the nth positive odd integer can be written as $2n - 1$.

These two methods of reasoning are used throughout the knowledge forming process. The scientist and historians, for example, will use deductive and inductive reasoning to establish knowledge claims and this is explained later in some detail with respect to the work of a scientist.

Determine whether each of the following represents a form of deductive or inductive reasoning.

Example	Deductive or inductive reasoning?
1 The scientists in Prague formulated the experiment on cold fusion. They got positive results on the first three trials. Scientists in Tokyo, Moscow and Helsinki also claimed similar positive results on individual trials. The editor of *The Journal of Modern Chemistry* concluded that the results claimed by the Prague group were worthy of publication.	
2 Juan said that his computer was not able to open the physics experiment database file. He decided that it was because of a faulty hard drive or because of the settings on his security firewall. He checked the hard drive and it was functioning properly. So he concluded that his problem was because of firewall settings.	
3 Ms Kim said that anyone who did not do the assignment would get an F grade for the term. Marie did not do the assignment. I am not surprised that she got an F.	
4 The first five terms in the sequence are 5, 7, 9, 11 and 13. The next term following 13 is 15.	
5 Each of the first six test slides that Dr Brandon looked at had tested positive. It appears as though the entire population of mice has been infected with the virus.	
6 I was trying to check my solutions of $x = 3$ and $y = 5$, so I plugged it into the first three equations in the system. All three equations yielded true results. I felt that I could go ahead and write $x = 3$ and $y = 5$ down as a final solution for the entire system of six equations.	
7 That new student couldn't answer any of the questions that Mr Gardner asked in class. I was talking to him yesterday and he said that his family has been moving house all week. I also know that he was at school late yesterday for the first basketball game. I don't think he read that assignment from *Hamlet*.	
8 I started to do my homework last night around 7 p.m. The phone rang just as I started. It was Jenny. She was upset because she had had an argument with Henry. Then at 7.20 p.m. the phone rang again. This time it was Ingrid. She had forgotten her physics assignment and wanted to know if I had it. At 7.30 p.m. the phone rang again. This time it was Mr Waddell. He wanted to know if I would be on the sixth form committee. At that point in time, I just gave up on homework. I knew that I wouldn't get any done with the way that phone was ringing.	

Both inductive and deductive reasoning can be analysed through formal means. It is interesting to note that the TOK courses established in the early days of the IB assumed that students studied the formal analysis of reasoning and logic. The study of formal logic could occupy weeks of class time. This is no longer the case but it is appropriate to take a brief look at how the formal study of logic and reason is done.

Deductive arguments and symbolic logic analysis

Formal logic and arguments can be fortified in a structural manner by the use of symbolic interpretation. Any argument consists of **statements.**

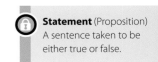

Statement (Proposition)
A sentence taken to be either true or false.

Statement examples:
- Paris is a city in Italy.   (false)
- $1 + 3 = 4$ (true)
- Shut the door, please.   (not a statement)
- What time is it?   (not a statement)

Consider two simple statements represented by letters p and q:

p: the hat is too big q: the sock is too small

These statements can be combined into compound statements using some basic symbols.

Compound examples:

The hat is not too big.	$\neg\, p$
The hat is too big and the sock is too small.	$p \wedge q$
The hat is too big or the sock is too small.	$p \vee q$
If the hat is too big, then the sock is too small.	$p \Rightarrow q$

Simple and compound statements (or propositions) can be combined to form **arguments**. A deductive argument consists of a set of premises followed by a conclusion. Consider the following simple deductive argument:

If Mr Mustard is elected President, then our taxes will decrease.
Mr Mustard is elected President.
Therefore, our taxes will decrease.

Argument A combination of statements such that a given set of premises leads to a conclusion. Logical arguments can be inductive or deductive.

To perform a symbolic analysis of this argument, parts of the argument can be labelled as follows:

Major premise: If Mr Mustard is elected President, then our taxes will decrease.
Minor premise: Mr Mustard is elected President.
Conclusion: Our taxes will decrease.

Next, statements can be labelled using letters:

p: Mr Mustard is elected President.

q: Our taxes will decrease.

Using these labels along with the symbol '$\Rightarrow$' to represent *if…, then…* our argument now takes on its symbolic form:

Major premise: $p \Rightarrow q$
Minor premise: p
Conclusion: $\therefore\ q$

This argument has three parts which are made up of two statements. If we want to consider all the true–false possibilities of p and q, then we quickly see that four different cases can occur:

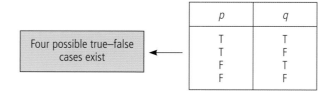

p	q
T	T
T	F
F	T
F	F

Four possible true–false cases exist

Symbolic logic allows us to apply rules to the structure of these simple statements that have been built into compound statements and arguments. We now consider the symbolic structure of our argument as follows:

The conjunction of the *premises* gives rise to the *conclusion*.

or: $[(p \Rightarrow q)$ and $p]$ implies q

or in symbols: $[(p \Rightarrow q) \wedge p] \Rightarrow q$

The next step is to consider the truth value of this argument for all four possible cases at hand. But before we can construct the truth table for the entire argument, we must first be aware of two fundamental truth tables as shown below:

1 The conditional (if p then q)

p	q	$p \Rightarrow q$
T	T	T
T	F	F
F	T	T
F	F	T

2 The conjunction (p and q)

p	q	$p \wedge q$
T	T	T
T	F	F
F	T	F
F	F	F

The truth table representing the argument follows:

p	q	$p \Rightarrow q$	$(p \Rightarrow q) \wedge p$	$[(p \Rightarrow q) \wedge p] \Rightarrow q$
T	T	T	T	T
T	F	F	F	T
F	T	T	F	T
F	F	T	F	T

Notice that the last column of truth values consists of all true values.

The interpretation is now that the entire argument which is represented by the heading of the last column is true for all individual truth value cases of p and q. The conclusion is that the argument is *valid* (i.e. logically correct). Had one of the entries of the last column of the truth table analysis been false, then the argument would be classified as *invalid*. This type of analysis may already be familiar to students in Standard Level Mathematical Studies.

The *truth* of the argument itself is another matter to consider. It must be carefully noted that the truth of an argument is not the same as validity. Consider the following **valid** argument:

> *The moon is made of Wensleydale cheese.*
>
> *Ms Oregano's pet Dachshund is part of the moon.*
> _____
> *Therefore, Ms Oregano's Dachshund is made of Wensleydale cheese.*

This argument is valid even though each of the individual premises is false and the conclusion is false.

It is also possible that an argument could yield a conclusion that is true where the argument itself is **invalid**. The following argument consists of true premises and a true conclusion, but the argument itself is invalid:

> *Denmark is south of Norway.*
>
> *Germany is south of Norway.*
> _____
> *Therefore, Germany is south of Denmark.*

Valid argument
An argument that is logically correct, i.e. the argument's conclusion is true whenever all the premises are true.
Invalid argument
An argument that is not valid (also called a fallacy).

Identify the statements used in each argument below. Test the validity of each argument using truth tables.

1 If he likes me then he sends me roses.
   He sent me roses.
   Therefore, he likes me.

2 If it rains, then she will wear her hat.
   She is not wearing her hat.
   Therefore, it is not raining.

You can find the solutions in the Appendix on page 307.

Consider the argument shown below. Is the argument valid? Is the argument necessarily true? If not, then why not?

Whatever allows for peace is good for international relations.

Weapons of mass destruction allow for peace.

Therefore weapons of mass destruction are good for international relations.

Classic arguments – valid and invalid

Simple arguments can be set up and analysed using truth tables. Some classic results follow (Miller, Heeren and Hornsby in *Mathematical Ideas*, sixth edition).

Four classic valid arguments

Modus ponens	Modus tollens	Disjunctive syllogism	Reasoning by transitivity
$p \Rightarrow q$	$p \Rightarrow q$	$p \vee q$	$p \Rightarrow q$
p	$\neg q$	$\neg p$	$q \Rightarrow r$
$\therefore q$	$\therefore \neg p$	$\therefore q$	$\therefore p \Rightarrow r$

Two invalid arguments (formal fallacies)

Fallacy of the converse	Fallacy of the inverse
$p \Rightarrow q$	$p \Rightarrow q$
q	$\neg p$
$\therefore p$	$\therefore \neg q$

Combinations of these arguments emerge to form even more substantial arguments. Some scholars have gone to great lengths to explore these combinations. Charles Dodgson, also known as Lewis Carroll, produced *The Game of Logic* designed to help students explore and learn logic in a fun way. Consider the following set of premises:

1 *All IB students like to study.*
2 *If you don't get a place at university, then you do not earn high marks.*
3 *If you like to study, then you earn high marks.*

What is an appropriate conclusion for this set of premises? The analysis of this set could be accomplished by translating each statement into a conditional (if… then…) and by reordering statements. The following result occurs:

statement 1: *If you are an IB student, then you like to study.*
statement 2: *If you like to study, then you earn high marks.*

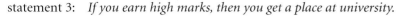

statement 3:   *If you earn high marks, then you get a place at university.*

This is true since $(p \Rightarrow q) \equiv (\neg q \Rightarrow \neg p)$ (see the Appendix on page 307)

Reasoning by transitivity now allows for a logical connection.

IB student $\Rightarrow$ like to study $\Rightarrow$ earn high marks $\Rightarrow$ get a university place

Thus, an appropriate conclusion for this particular set of premises would be:

If you are an IB student, then you get a place at university.

Exercise

Translate each of the following premise statements into conditional form.

1 All TOK teachers are promise breakers.

2 Promise breakers are untrustworthy.

3 One can always trust a person who wears clean socks

4 Anyone who is not a sceptic wears clean socks

Use symbols and reasoning connections to show that an appropriate conclusion would be:

If you are a TOK teacher, then you are a sceptic.

You can find the solutions in the Appendix on page 308.

The study of symbolic logic is worthy of an entire university course. You have been given a small taste of how symbolic means can determine whether an argument is indeed valid.

Do the symbolic arguments really matter?

In formal logic, a contradiction is the signal of defeat but in the evolution of real knowledge it marks the first step in progress toward a victory.

Alfred North Whitehead (1861–1947)

People who manage day-to-day affairs and actually think symbolically are, perhaps, few and far between. This should not, however, keep any TOK student from appreciating the processes that are at work. Indeed, the number of times that you use a simple argument is significant. Consider the following classic symbolic argument.

The disjunctive syllogism $p \lor q$
$$\frac{\neg p}{\therefore q}$$

The argument can easily be illustrated with words:

He will stay at home to study or he will work on his CAS project at school.
He did not stay at home to study.
So, he worked on his CAS project at school.

Now, how often do we use this type of argument? Consider the following event.

It's the end of the school day and Marcel realizes that he no longer has his jacket.

If you're Marcel, what are you to do? Marcel is thinking…

'Let's see. I either left it in the cafeteria or it's over in the art block. I'll go downstairs and look in the cafeteria.'

Two minutes later:

> Friend: *Have you found your jacket yet?*
>
> Marcel: *No, I haven't but I did check in the cafeteria and it wasn't there. It must be in the art block. I'll go and look.*

It's a typical scenario… it's more or less 'Marcel goes through a process of elimination'. Is this same type of reasoning used by knowers in a more formal way?

Dr Nosaer and the green grass question

Now consider the following method used by Dr Nosaer over in the biology laboratory. Dr Nosaer, being the perceptive individual that he is, has noticed that the grass growing in front of the school is green. His inquisitive nature has once again taken over and now he wonders why the grass is green. He decides to take a scientific approach to the question at hand, 'Why is the grass green?'

Dr Nosaer thinks it through and carefully forms a hypothesis, 'The grass is green because of the element of iron which is present in the soil.' He now devises an experiment to test this hypothesis. Grass is grown in two different pots. The conditions are carefully controlled. The soil in the first pot is tested to be iron-free. The soil in the second pot is iron enriched. The pots are placed in identical growing conditions. After a period of weeks, it is obvious that grass – *green* grass – is growing in both pots.

What is Dr Nosaer left to do? He has little choice but to conclude that his hypothesis is false. The grass is green but not because of the iron content in the soil. So now it might be time to regroup on the hypothesis front. Dr Nosaer quickly rethinks his position and creates a second hypothesis. This time he states, 'The grass is green because of the nitrogen levels in the air surrounding the growing grass.'

Once again Dr Nosaer goes back to the laboratory and devises a carefully controlled experiment to determine whether nitrogen levels do indeed influence the 'green factor' of the grass. Once again he finds that the grass grown under the two controlled conditions has the same green colour. Dr Nosaer has once again eliminated one of the possible causes for the green grass.

Dr Nosaer's list of possible causes of green grass is looking like this:

~~Iron Content in Soil~~
~~Nitrogen Levels in the Air~~
Outdoor Ground Temperature
…

Is this manner of reasoning any different than that of Marcel trying to find his missing jacket? Suppose that Marcel goes to the art block and finds his missing jacket. Is his carefully thought out method a clear-cut case of the disjunctive syllogism? The two arguments are as follows:

Marcel	**Dr Nosaer**
The jacket is in the cafeteria or the art block.	The grass is green because of the iron content in the soil or because of something else.
It is not in the cafeteria.	It is not because of the iron content.
∴ The jacket is in the art block.	∴ The grass is green because of something else.

Both Marcel and Dr Nosaer are getting to the truth of the matter by eliminating that which is not a possibility.

Now suppose that Dr Nosaer finds that 'ground temperature regulation' results in one pot of green grass (regular outdoor temperature 5°C) and no green grass (temperature of soil kept at 50°C).

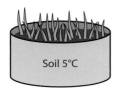

Dr Nosaer is pleased to note that his experimental result justifies his hypothesis. But has he *proved* that the grass is green because of the ground temperature regulation?

It should be clear that Dr Nosaer has not proved a thing. Indeed he is informed the following week by his scientific colleague, Dr La Cigol, that his experimental conclusions are flawed. Dr La Cigol explains to Dr Nosaer that his claim to have justification is not correct: the brown grass in the heated soil has resulted from a lack of moisture in the soil due to water evaporation caused by the high temperature. The control of the experiment was compromised and hence Dr Nosaer's analysis came to an incorrect conclusion.

Dr Nosaer's claim to know why grass is green is falsified. His problems included one of rather poor experimental control with a careless conclusion resulting from faulty reasoning. He wanted to conclude *low soil temperature ⇒ green grass*. Dr La Cigol stepped up to note an invalid argument and labelled it as 'post hoc ergo propter hoc'. In simple terms the post hoc fallacy is expressed as:

> *X* has occurred, followed by *Y*.
> *X* is the cause of *Y*.

Inductive reasoning

It would be difficult for you to function in any normal day-to-day context without making generalizations. Making general conclusions based upon a pool of evidence from personal experience is done by everyone. People leap from experiences to generalizations in order to make sense of the world. But this leap should be made with care. How many individual cases are sufficient to form a generalization? Consider the following hypothetical situation.

Exercise

You have been placed in a room sitting next to a machine which is labelled *The Super Predictor*. Two mysterious boxes A and B are placed before you. Box A is transparent and box B is opaque. You are told that box A contains £10,000 and you can clearly see the money in A. You are also told that B contains either nothing or one million pounds! You are not able to see into box B at all. You are asked to make one of the following choices:

The Super Predictor

Choice 2 =
£10,000 only

- Choice 1 = box B only
- Choice 2 = both box A and box B

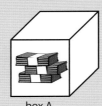
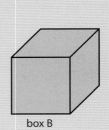

box A   box B

You smile and think, 'What a silly question!' However, before you choose, you are told, and you are to assume correctly, that *The Super Predictor* machine is a device that analyses the situation of those who are offered such a choice. The machine predicts that people who take Choice 1 (box B only) will win £1 million, and that those who take Choice 2 (both boxes) will only win £10,000 only.

You enquire as to the record of *The Super Predictor* so far. You are informed, correctly, that 1000 other patrons have been given, and have made a choice, and all have been subject to *The Super Predictor*, just as you have. Further, you learn that all visitors who selected Choice 2 (700 in fact) received only £10,000 (the contents of box A) while box B ended up being empty. And indeed, all those 300 visitors who selected Choice 1, box B only, received £1 million. What a machine! It's almost as though *The Super Predictor* has control over what goes into box B. Given this information you are asked to deliberate and decide. Which is the more reasonable choice? Why?

A person's experience is clearly no substitute for knowledge. Personal experiences are limited and any conclusions made about the world will be founded upon a tiny proportion of all possible cases. Conclusions made about social behaviour, gender, race or religious groups that are based upon a set of personal experiences are likely to end up being wrong. Furthermore, any conclusions made in the inductive sense are true only to a more or less probable degree. At the end of the inductive process a person can conclude no more than that it is reasonable to believe a conclusion, in light of the evidence that has been reviewed.

Invariably you are left to question whether you have a sufficient number of cases that are fairly representative of the idea, group or claim under consideration. Chapter 9: Mathematical knowledge will show that even in the most well defined and seemingly predictable situations, generalizations can go wrong. You may have already decided that it is wrong to generalize about people. Fallacious or hasty generalizations that can lead to erroneous inferences or unpleasant circumstances often begin as:

> Men can…, Women cannot…
> Blacks are…, Whites are not…
> Muslims will not…, Jewish will…

Informal reasoning and the fallacies that follow

The critical examination of ideas and knowledge claims requires energy and dedication. Informal reasoning lends itself to the day-to-day conversations and interactions you experience. It is easy to simply sit back and let someone else do the thinking. After all, things may go more smoothly when you simply accept claims and assertions made by the media, your friends, family or your teachers. Informal fallacies that occur are not about the logical structure of an argument presented but instead are concerned with the support embedded within an argument. This support may be inappropriate or irrelevant, may appeal to the emotions, or make dodgy connections between cause and effect. Informal fallacies often go unnoticed but can have a serious influence on the way you think and behave. Important decisions you have to make concerning education, economics, politics, health and welfare may be manipulated by people with a particular agenda or motive not shared by you.

The categories and lists of logical fallacies are many. Use of contemporary arguments concerning politics, economics, environmental or health issues will in all likelihood connect well to the fallacies and will serve as the basis for a relevant TOK presentation. Six commonly used fallacies include:

- red herring
- argumentum in terrorem (appeal to fear)
- post hoc ergo propter hoc (refer back to page 103)
- argumentum ad vericundiam (appeal to authority)
- slippery slope
- argumentum ad misericordiam (appeal to pity).

A brief explanation of each of these fallacies is given below.

Red herring

This fallacy results when an argument is given in response to a particular argument, but this response is not relevant to the issue at hand. By raising an irrelevant point, a diversion is created away from the original issue.

Example: The current data clearly shows that global warming is a serious issue and requires that nations work together to take appropriate measures with respect to the use of fossil fuels. But the leaders of those nations do not want to forget that the oil industry may stand to take serious losses in profits.

Argumentum in terrorem (appeal to fear)

A person will employ this fallacy in an attempt to earn support for a particular idea by creating a fear factor. This fallacy is commonly used in politics and marketing and is meant to create support for a particular idea or product by creating fear of a political or business enemy.

Example: Last night while surfing on the Internet, Carlos received a pop-up message which indicated that his computer 'has in all likelihood' been exposed to a computer virus. The message indicated that he should download the anti-virus software called *FreeVirus v 2.0* immediately. The message indicated that failing to do so 'could very well result' in the loss of his music, photo and video data files.

Post hoc ergo propter hoc

This expression translates from Latin as 'after this, therefore because of this'. In short, this refers to two particular events that happen in sequence. Event X happens first, followed by event Y. Since Y follows X, the fallacy claims that X is the cause of Y.

Example: The hurricane hit the southern region of the country two days prior to the national elections. When the election results showed that the Social Democrats had lost power, it became clear that the poor weather and resulting catastrophic conditions were to blame.

Argumentum ad vericundiam (appeal to authority)

This fallacy makes use of the authority or background of a person (often well-known) to support an action or assertion. Because a well-known person has certain positive qualities, the claim that this person makes is meant to be true. This fallacy is also commonly used in politics and advertising.

Example: Tyler gave his TOK presentation concerning the use of counter-terrorism measures taken by the government. It was clear that some of the measures had infringed upon certain civil liberties that were guaranteed by the government. Tyler's support argument for the use of such measures included the joint statement made by Missy JJ (hip hop artist) and Chase Beckhurst (football star). They stated, 'People can sleep better knowing that all possible measures are taken to prevent acts of terrorism.'

Slippery slope

If an argument makes reference to a particular event or action and suggests that this action will initiate a chain of further actions or events which will ultimately culminate in an undesirable event or action, then a fallacy results.

Example: The Prime Minister spoke today about immigration. He stated that the government was not prepared to allow for European-based immigrants who were coming from non-EU countries. The reason for doing so was that this would open the gates for immigrants from the Middle East and Northern Africa. This, of course, would mean that within a short time that immigrants from all parts of Africa and Asia would come streaming into the country.

Argumentum ad misericordiam (appeal to pity)

This form of persuasion attempts to use emotion (specifically sympathy) as opposed to factual evidence. This fallacy is commonly used by people trying to create pity for an individual or group. It represents an interesting point of debate in any discussion of the roles played by emotion and reason as counter-balancing Ways of Knowing. Judicial mercy may well consider that an appeal to pity is appropriate.

Example: Naseem should be president of the Student Council. Her campaign manager argued that she's the cleverest student in the class and a top athlete. He stated furthermore that she could really get things organised and get the whole student body to work for the common good. He finally added that she needs to be considered most of all because she's still pretty shaken up by the car accident, which wasn't her fault.

Investigate four other logical fallacies from the list shown below. Give a brief description of each using your own words along with a specific example of how each might be used.

- ad hominem
- golden mean fallacy
- begging the question
- ad baculum
- appeal to popularity
- ad ignorantiam
- composition
- black and white thinking
- gambler's fallacy
- guilt by association
- golden mean fallacy

- relativist fallacy
- two wrongs make a right
- dicto simpliciter
- non sequitur
- ad numerum
- cum hoc ergo propter hoc
- get on the bandwagon
- appeal to tradition
- weak analogy
- poisoning the well

Life's moments and unreasonable thinking

Judgements and decisions surround us in everyday situations. The exercise below presents a few hypothetical situations. Read each carefully. You may agree or disagree with any apparent decision or action taken by the individuals in each. It is not the point of this exercise, however, to simply agree or disagree and argue. Your assignment is to:

- identify each particular issue at hand
- state the apparent reason that the person concerned is using for making his or her judgement
- determine the knowledge issue (maybe 'factors related to the judgement' is appropriate in some instances) associated with the judgement or action.

To help you get started, here is a worked through example:

Hypothetical situation: Annalies (a second year IB student) threw the can from her soft drink on the ground just outside the cafeteria. I asked her why she did that. She said that she knew about the college rule of 'no littering' but that she did it because it was just one of Mr Clark's (the college principal) many rules she had broken that day. She said that she hated Mr Clark and had therefore decided not to follow any of his silly rules.

Issue: Should Annalies drop litter on the school grounds? She has decided to do this in spite of the known rule.

Reason: Even though she is aware of the rule she has decided to ignore it simply because it *is* one of the rules – she's breaking the rule for spite. This is very similar to someone who decides to *follow* every rule because 'rules should always be followed'.

Issue: 'Breaking all rules for spite' is making use of erroneous reasoning. In Annalies's case, call it a problem with 'what seems to be *reasonable.*' One of the primary reasons for having rules must be to make people think. Annalies is clearly not taking time to think about the reason for the 'no littering' rule. Littering to satisfy her ill feelings for the college principal may not weigh up against well thought out support for the rule. From a 'logical rigour' standpoint we could label her conclusion to litter as a non sequitur.

We can all probably think of good reasons why we should not drop litter. Is Annalies simply guilty of not considering all relevant factors? Maybe littering constitutes a health hazard to the community or excessive litter is expensive for the school to clean up. Maybe having older students dropping litter sets a bad example for younger students. Once an abundance of support (factual) surrounds a particular issue, the judgement you may make concerning that issue usually becomes more directed.

Exercise

Consider each of the hypothetical cases below carefully. Remember you need to:
- identify each particular issue at hand
- state the apparent reason that the person concerned is using for making his or her judgement
- determine the knowledge issue (maybe 'factors related to the judgement' is appropriate in some instances) associated with the judgement or action.

1 According to the poll taken by the mathematics class, 65 per cent of the student body decided to adopt a healthier life style (e.g. quit smoking, exercise regularly, etc.) after listening to Paula Radcliffe speak on health and fitness. Prior to the speech, only 15 per cent had shown a desire to live a healthier life.

2 Andrew gave £50 to those kids who were begging down at the tube station. He said later that he thought the little one was so cute and that she looked really sad.

3 The girls on the varsity team were not at all surprised when Hiroko did not show up for the conference championship game. Even though she was the second leading scorer on the team, they all knew how much she valued her music. The opportunity for her to play solo with the city symphonic orchestra was just too good to pass up.

4 Henri just loves Amy but could not believe that she got a tattoo on her neck last week. When she asked Henri what he thought about it, he told her that he thought it was beautiful. He just didn't have the heart to hurt her feelings.

5 Most students in our school felt that the new administration's discipline policy was too tough. Yoo Ri was the only student who voted in favour of the policy. He told me later that the discipline at our school was much more lax than that back home in South Korea.

6 Tony (Student Council President) told me that he was going to end his friendship with Nanda (Class Representative). They've been arguing quite a bit about the way things have been handled by the student council. Tony told me that no matter how he perceives the feelings of his fellow students, Nanda sees it differently.

From Teacher Support Material – Theory of Knowledge: Lessons from Around the World,
© International Baccalaureate Organization

Exercise

The following story is based upon a true event. The names and places have been changed. Discuss the story and identify the various knowledge issues it raises. Identify the fallacies used by different characters in the scenario.

Travis Smith is a 17-year-old sixth former at Arnold High School. He is a gifted student and has played key roles in the school's musical productions. He is captain of the school's athletics team and has earned first place awards in various speech and debating competitions. Travis is an all-round student, friend to all of his classmates and is a dependable employee at the local supermarket where he has worked part-time for the past year and a half. He is also gay.

The school community did not know that Travis was gay until the spring of his first year in sixth form. Travis decided not to attend the Easter ball. This decision seemed peculiar to many, as it was known that several of the most popular girls were hoping that Travis would ask them to be his date. Soon after the ball, vicious rumours started flying. 'Is it true that Travis Smith is gay?' could be heard in closed conversations around school. Just before the end of that school year, Travis made it clear to his friends – he was gay.

His decision to open up about something so personal was not an easy one. It could have been the steady flow of gossip that managed to somehow penetrate Travis's ears. Perhaps the pressure grew and eventually he gave in. Travis had talked things over with his parents. They totally understood and left him feeling supported and loved. For whatever reason, his decision was made and it was a costly one. Embarrassing and hurtful situations popped up one by one.

Word that Travis was gay reached the manager of the supermarket and Travis was fired within two days. The manager of the market cited complaints from customers about his work. The complaints were valid but they had come during Travis's first week on the job, which was now over a year and a half ago. No complaints had been made since that first week. To make things worse, the athletics season was just about to start and the members of the team had met secretly and voted to remove Travis as captain. Representatives from the team went to the coach and the school's head teacher and said that Travis should not be allowed to participate on the team for the coming season. One of the athletes claimed that 'gays always cause trouble'. The coach agreed and informed Travis that, under the circumstances, everyone on the team would feel more comfortable if he did not participate in the coming season.

Not all reactions were negative. Mr Niles, the speech and debate team sponsor, was supportive of Travis. He even went so far as to confront the members of the athletics team and called them 'complete idiots'. Ms Farmer, the theatre projects teacher, was also supportive. Some of Travis's friends told him that they wanted to remain friends. But after the class representative made it clear that he did not approve of Travis's sexuality, it seemed as though several of Travis's friends and classmates became distant. Hurtful messages were left on Travis's locker. Despite the fact that Travis did have the support of his parents and a few friends, he was left wondering whether he had made the right decision.

Travis's most difficult day came when he was called to the head teacher's office. The head told Travis that he was concerned about the situation. He explained to Travis that it was not the school's role to take any official stand in the matter. The head was, however, concerned that the whole affair was having a negative influence on attitudes and activities around school. He stated that the entire episode would snowball into a violent outcome and that students and teachers would be at risk…

The reason-emotion connection to an Area of Knowledge

Knowledge is not solely dependent upon reason. Reason works as a bond between other Ways of Knowing and helps to form knowledge claims. It also exists in its own right as an organised method of thinking. Self-evident rules or axioms allow for the formation of formal logic and as Bertrand Russell has noted, 'What is important is not the fact that we think in accordance with these laws but the fact that things behave in accordance with them; in other words, the fact that when we think in accordance with them we think truly…'

The knower must critically think through any knowledge formation process. This would include the gathering of appropriate support or evidence for a claim. And during this process, sensitivity to the context of evidence must be shown. This may rely on an ability to understand and interpret emotion as a Way of Knowing. Sound reasoning gives the knower a necessary means to allow for the selection of evidence based upon an emotional interpretation that clearly defies the knowledge ideal of evidence being made up of 'hard, objective fact'. Consider the example of a historian's collection of evidence used to establish events surrounding the Battle of Ypres in the First World War (in 1917).

1 The **eye witness account** of a British soldier who took part in the battle during October 1917.

Frank Bastable at age 86, 7th Battalion, Royal West Kent Regiment

Frank Bastable was able to share some of his recollections. He served with the 7th Battalion, Royal West Kent Regiment. In October of 1917 he took part in the Third Battle of Ypres:

There were these streams, or there had been, near where I was at Poelkapelle, but the shells had broken their banks. That's what made it so bad… there was mud everywhere. Me and the Sergeant pulled one bloke out. He was up to his neck in this shell-hole. We managed to get him out after a struggle, small north country chap he was, but he didn't seem to be able to walk. I don't know why. So, we just laid him down… we had to get on. I still wonder now whether or not he was alright afterwards.

From *Ypres 1914–1918: A Study in History Around Us* by Leslie Coate

2 **A photograph** of Menin Road just outside Ypres, September 1917.

The notorious Menin Road, looking directly eastwards to the front line, 27 September 1917. 'Hellfire Corner' seen signed here 1.5 km from Ypres was a particularly dangerous place because German guns were always trained on it and, despite the canvas screens used to hide movement, were almost always sure of hitting something because it was such a busy spot. The Germans came this close to Ypres in 1918.

3 'Dulce et decorum est', **a poem** by Wilfred Owen written near Ypres in 1917.

> Bent double, like old beggars under sacks,
> Knock-kneed, coughing like hags, we cursed through sludge,
> Till on the haunting flares we turned our backs
> And towards our distant rest began to trudge.
> Men marched asleep. Many had lost their boots
> But limped on, blood-shod. All went lame; all blind;
> Drunk with fatigue; deaf even to the hoots
> Of gas shells dropping softly behind.
>
> Gas! GAS! Quick, boys! – An ecstasy of fumbling,
> Fitting the clumsy helmets just in time;
> But someone still was yelling out and stumbling,
> And floundering like a man in fire or lime…
> Dim, through the misty panes and thick green light,
> As under a green sea, I saw him drowning.
>
> In all my dreams, before my helpless sight,
> He plunges at me, guttering, choking, drowning.
>
> If in some smothering dreams you too could pace
> Behind the wagon that we flung him in,
> And watch the white eyes writhing in his face,
> His hanging face, like a devil's sick of sin;
> If you could hear, at every jolt, the blood
> Come gargling from the froth-corrupted lungs,
> Obscene as cancer, bitter as the cud
> Of vile, incurable sores on innocent tongues, –
> My friend, you would not tell with such high zest
> To children ardent for some desperate glory,
> The old Lie: Dulce et decorum est
> Pro patria mori.

The historian's quest for the *truth* will require a serious review and analysis of all of the evidence at hand. Should the poetry of Wilfred Owen be included in that review? This poem is clearly an emotional account. Evidence of this kind can only be included when the historian assesses it and places it appropriately within the context of all evidence. An understanding of the balance between hard facts, reasoning and emotion allows this to be done. Which of the three pieces of evidence brings you closest to the truth of what the battle was like?

> *Common sense is the collection of prejudices collected by age eighteen.*
>
> Albert Einstein

In much the same way that the historian must be able to understand the context of historical evidence, an individual making a moral judgement will have to understand the context of human behaviour. You will surely be confronted with dilemmas. Reasoning skills will allow you to identify an individual's attempt to justify behaviour with a fallacy like an emotional appeal to pity. Your intellect may recognize such justification as an informal fallacy. But your ability to act in a reasonable manner necessitates that you focus on the real issue(s) at hand *and* weigh the true strength of such an appeal. Is it possible that a personal appeal may consist of a true hardship and should not simply be written off as an inappropriate justification? What exactly does it mean to say, 'use common sense'?

Suppose for example that you are the admissions officer for a university with one place open for admission. The records and personal statements of two students are on your desk.

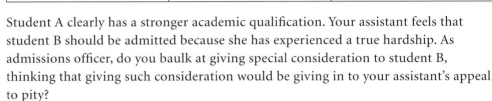

	Student A	Student B
School grade point average of 10:	9.75	9.15
IB Diploma score of 45:	38	34
Study area choice:	Humanities	Humanities
Personal background:	Affluent parents provided extra support and private tuition.	Parents abandoned child who grew up being HIV positive.

Student A clearly has a stronger academic qualification. Your assistant feels that student B should be admitted because she has experienced a true hardship. As admissions officer, do you baulk at giving special consideration to student B, thinking that giving such consideration would be giving in to your assistant's appeal to pity?

Fuzzy logic A form of reasoning used for problem solving (usually mathematical based) where decision making based upon imprecise data is required. Truth is allowed to assume a continuum of values.

Today's world: fuzzy logic

Aristotelian logic consists of arguments constructed of statements or propositions that are clearly classified as being either true or false. In today's world, the need to find solutions to technological, social and medical issues has created different approaches to the use of reason and 'being logical' that vary significantly from the bivalent propositional approach of Aristotle. One of the non-classical logics is **fuzzy logic**. This type of logic is devised to allow for an infinite set of truths. By assigning set values to any of the infinitely many numbers between 0 and 1, fuzzy logic allows for a range of logical interpretations to take place over any number of linguistically imprecise terms like 'almost' or 'many' or 'slightly'.

A simple concept like 'cold' is not one that can easily be defined in terms of a numeric scale or mathematical formula. Such a vague concept cannot simply be defined as any temperature of below −3°C or 0°C or even +3°C. To complicate matters, pre-existing conditions can add to the confusion. However, fuzzy logic can allow for a particular context of 'cold' to be taken into consideration. The idea of 'where a person is coming from' does make a difference. Consider the following situation. It's the middle of March and two men decide to travel to Brussels, Belgium. The first man is on a flight from Miami, Florida to Brussels. He is boarding a plane from an environment of 25°C (Miami). The second man leaves St Petersburg, Russia where the temperature is −10°C. Now assume that both men arrive in Brussels where the temperature is 5°C. Will the man from Miami find Brussels to be cold? What about the man from St Petersburg? The concept of 'a cold day' no doubt becomes relative to the weather recently experienced.

Technology makes use of fuzzy logic in the design of small machines like ordinary clothes washers and dryers or car braking systems or computer photo imaging software that will react to a range of variables and pre-existing conditions. Fuzzy logic also allows for scientists to work with imprecise data. Consider, for example, the need for a team of doctors to understand how epidemics spread. The world's battle with AIDS is being fought on an emotional front and remains a serious concern. The World Health Organization's collection of data in 1997 initially indicated that the number of AIDS cases was approximately 1.5 million. It soon became clear that because of delays or poor recognition of clinical cases that as many as 8.4 million was a more accurate figure. The problem of creating a mathematical model representing the spread of AIDS was obviously complicated by the imprecise data that was available. Thinking and problem solving using fuzzy logic was put to use by a team of scientists, doctors and engineers who were intent upon knowing how serious this health issue could be. Understanding the spread of AIDS came down to dealing not only with imprecise data measurements but with vague words like 'fever', 'infection', 'immune' and 'sexually very active'. The knowledge claims to be made were vital to the health and well-being of millions of people. This is no ordinary problem and finding a solution requires more than a casual respect for the Ways of Knowing at play.

Use of fuzzy logic is controversial. Mathematicians and engineers who reject its use claim that fuzzy logic is simply a glorified use of probability theory. Others claim that attempts to connect quantitative measure to qualitative judgements are not precise. But formal reasoning of the highest order allows for a method of critical thinking and problem solving that is able to adapt to the conditions surrounding a knowledge context. This includes the careful consideration of how the Ways of Knowing interact. The blend of reason, emotion, perception and language helps you to realize that true understanding does not come about through a black and white separation of means. The Ways of Knowing exist as a flexible and dynamic mechanism, and it is only by keeping this in mind that justification of beliefs can be brought to any substantial form.

Ideal knower

Bertrand Russell (1872–1970)

Bertrand Russell was a true intellectual and spent his life as a prolific writer, pacifist, philosopher, mathematician, historian and advocate of social reform. Russell served time in jail for his anti-war activities during the First World War. For his written work he was awarded a Nobel Prize in Literature, 'in recognition of his varied and significant writings in which he champions humanitarian ideals and freedom of thought' (The Nobel Foundation, 1950).

The following text is taken from *Problems of Philosophy* by Bertrand Russell (by permission of Oxford University Press).

◀ Bertrand Russell

Some… principles must be granted before any argument or proof becomes possible. When some of them have been granted, others can be proved, though these others, so long as they are simple, are just as obvious as the principles taken for granted. For no very good reason, three of these principles have been singled out by tradition under the name of 'Laws of Thought'. They are as follows:

1 The law of identity: *'Whatever is, is.'*

2 The law of contradiction: *'Nothing can both be and not be.'*

3 The law of excluded middle: *'Everything must either be or not be.'*

These three laws are samples of self-evident logical principles, but are not really more fundamental or more self-evident than various other similar principles: for instance, the one which states that what follows from a true premise is true. The name 'laws of thought' is also misleading, for what is important is not the fact that we think in accordance with these laws, but the fact that things behave in accordance with them; in other words, the fact that when we think in accordance with them we think truly…

… But in fact 'knowledge' is not a precise conception: it merges into 'probable opinion'… A very precise definition, therefore, should not be sought… all our knowledge of truths is infected with some degree of doubt, and a theory which ignored this fact would be plainly wrong.

Student presentation

1 Two students perform a skit concerning the upcoming presidential election in the Republic of Tokland. Five voters are interviewed and each has made a choice from one of the three possible candidates. Reasons are given for the selections made and, of course, more than one of the logical fallacies is at play. A serious critique is given from each voter's argument. Examples of voter reasoning from recent US presidential elections are reviewed.

2 Two students role play as ambassadors representing two feuding countries. Tensions have risen and a special session of the UN has been called in order to hear the arguments posed by each side. Both countries possess nuclear weapons and threaten the use of these weapons of mass destruction. The UN has asked that both countries use 'common sense' in dealing with this problem. Both countries interpret the use of common sense. Arguments are analysed and logical fallacies are noted.

Essay questions

Two recent Prescribed Titles (PTs) include:

1 If facts by themselves never prove or disprove anything, what else is involved in the proof of a statement?

© International Baccalaureate Organization 2003

2 One definition of knowledge is true belief based on strong evidence. What makes evidence 'strong' enough and how can this limit be established?

© International Baccalaureate Organization 2004

Areas of Knowledge: an overview

Knowledge today and yesterday

When we consider through what mists and how gropingly we are led to our knowledge of most things within our grasp, we shall assuredly conclude that it is familiarity rather than knowledge that takes away their strangeness, and if these things were presented to us newly, we should think them as incredible as any others, or even more so...

Montaigne

We have looked at some features and complexities of knowledge, and the distinctions that might be drawn between different kinds of knowledge, such as 'knowing that' and 'knowing how'. We have also examined a number of Ways of Knowing – human faculties that play crucial roles in making it possible for us to know anything at all. As a knower, you know many things with the help of these Ways of Knowing – perhaps more things than someone of your age might have known in the past. Would you agree with this? If so, what kinds of knowledge do you think you possess more of? Is it possible that you could have less?

The simplest schoolboy is now familiar with truths for which Archimedes would have sacrificed his life.

Ernest Renan

Exercise

Imagine the following situation: it has become possible in a science fiction world to send messages backward in time. Yet due to the current limits of this cutting-edge technology, only brief messages corresponding to roughly a single side of A4 paper can be transmitted. Your job is to prepare such a message to be sent back, say, 1000 years. Assume that any recipients will understand modern English.

What *knowledge* would you transmit in your message and how and why?

In the exercise above, you almost certainly identified items of knowledge which you thought would have special value to our ancestors. If so, is it fair to say that knowledge especially valuable for them is likely to have value for us? There are other considerations, of course; for example, knowing what people knew at that time, and whether your intervention will change the course of history. But such is often the nature of thought experiments, and we will return to this activity in a moment.

You should note that there might be a good presentation topic here: does (or should) knowledge develop according to what humans value (or fear, or exploit, etc.)?

What are the disciplines?

 Discipline An established branch of knowledge with its own subject area and methods of engaging it.

Valuable knowledge often resides in well-established subjects, or **disciplines**, such as economics, music, physics or mathematics. These are labels with which we are all comfortable, and you will be familiar with many of them from your IB studies. The IB diploma puts many of them into the six groups around the hexagon.

The IB hexagon

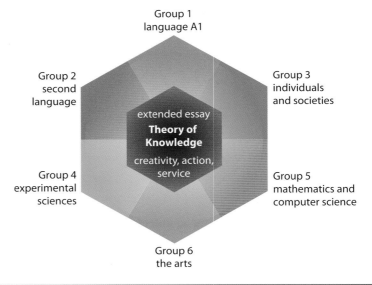

Group 1
language A1

Group 2
second
language

Group 3
individuals
and societies

extended essay
**Theory of
Knowledge**
creativity, action,
service

Group 4
experimental
sciences

Group 5
mathematics and
computer science

Group 6
the arts

Exercise

1 Make a list of the disciplines that are offered in your school's IB programme. What others are available? Do the six IB groups make sense to you? If so, on what basis?

2 Now look at the contents of your time-machine message (see page 115) and classify what you have chosen into these disciplines and groups. You could use the hexagon diagram above as a guide, although there may be other categories that you wish to use (such as ethics or technology).
  * What sort of distribution do you find?
  * What does your classification say about the value you place on different *kinds* of knowledge? Does it indicate the value of the *discipline* in itself?

3 The activity could be extended: think about people in the future (say 50 years from now) and their knowledge. What would they want to send back to us in the present? What would we hope to receive from them? Does this indicate anything about the projected value of disciplines in the future?

How do disciplines divide up knowledge?

A few years ago, TOK students were invited to respond to the essay title:

God may have separated the heavens from the earth. He did not separate astronomy from marine biology.

Jonathan Levy

To what extent are the classifications separating Areas of Knowledge justified?

© International Baccalaureate Organisation 2002

What is your first reaction to this? Do academic disciplines arise out of natural categories? This idea has been supported by a number of prominent thinkers through the ages, from the Greek philosopher Aristotle to the Swedish taxonomist Linnaeus, who also believed in the fixity of living species. But judgements about the importance of various disciplines show historical and geographical variation, and it is worth looking at some of the alternatives for a sense of perspective. For example:

* Two and a half millennia ago, the Chinese thinker and philosopher Confucius promoted training in archery in order to develop skills of discipline and precision, and also a course in 'good manners'.

- The ancient Greeks combined arithmetic, astronomy, music and geometry into a discipline called 'harmonics', but had no interest in foreign languages and would have considered it ridiculous to study them. Plato added a form of 'gym' to meet the ideal of a healthy mind in a healthy body.
- In medieval Europe, university faculties were often divided into religion, jurisprudence, medicine and the arts.
- Ultimately ill-founded subjects can die, such as alchemy, with its single unattainable goal of transmutating base metals into gold, but in the process it gave birth to modern chemistry.
- Adam Smith of Scotland considered himself a moral philosopher, more than a century before the term 'economics' became well-established.
- Modern biology emerged from 'natural philosophy', or the philosophy of nature.
- The origin of psychology as a discipline can be traced back only just over 100 years.

In modern times, **rhetoric**, logic and Latin as subjects have become rather neglected, at least in school curricula. An interesting presentation might be to give the arguments for and against the inclusion of such subjects in the modern curriculum. But insights from some subjects have influenced others to the extent that new titles have become common, such as economic history and evolutionary psychology.

Within the IB diploma, a course like Information Technology in a Global Society (ITGS) could only exist in the modern context. It was inconceivable not too many years ago. You can now write your Extended Essay in Peace and Conflict Studies – this would not have been possible until recently. Indeed, the TOK programme itself is a distinctive feature of the IB diploma alone (see Chapter 1: An introduction to Theory of Knowledge).

 Rhetoric The art of communication (through speaking or writing) with a particular emphasis on trying to persuade an audience or move them to action.

Disciplines and values

In some parts of the world, the perceived value of various disciplines such as economics and the arts is strongly influenced by traditional ideas about vocation. Have you ever heard a parent complain along these lines?

> *What on Earth do you think you're going to do with a subject like art?*
> *Forget about history, it's just about dates of battles and monarchs; but*
> *economics will help make you rich.*

Such comments might be heard in parts of the world where education can only be seen as more of a privilege than as a right. Under these circumstances, decisions about what disciplines to study can become particularly important when they are seen in terms of their direct career outcomes. Thus the value of a subject can vary between cultures, and is sometimes measured in very pragmatic terms.

Exercise

- What is it like in your school or college? TOK students were once asked if they measured the value of anything by its usefulness. What would be your reply? How would the best liberal arts universities in the world evaluate your worth based on the subject choices you have made?
- You might like to reflect on what a future IB diploma could look like – perhaps in 20 or even 50 years from now. You might also reconsider the question asked in Chapter 1: in designing your own course of studies, would you include a TOK course? Why?

You are probably aware of the expression 'the three Rs' as part of basic education – reading, writing and arithmetic (the Rs are only phonetic, as you can see!). In his book *The End of Education – Redefining the Value of School*, the American writer Neil Postman has suggested that a curriculum of the future should consist largely of 'the three As':

- Archaeology – knowledge of the history of our species and cultures.
- Anthropology – knowledge of the present variety of human cultures.
- Astronomy – knowledge of the universe and our place in proportion to it.

Exercise

Where would these subjects fit into the IB diploma? And what do you make of Postman's suggestion? What would a typical school day be like?

Disciplines and Areas of Knowledge

The Theory of Knowledge syllabus groups the disciplines into Areas of Knowledge. Six such areas are identified: the arts, ethics, history, the human sciences, mathematics and the natural sciences: they could be represented by the diagram which you saw in Chapter 1: An introduction to Theory of Knowledge.

The traditional TOK diagram ▶

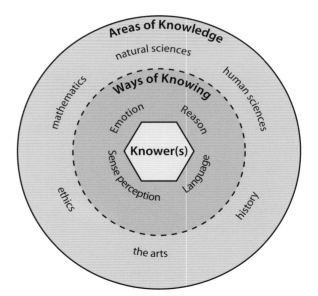

As with the Ways of Knowing, the list is not intended to be exhaustive, and it can be argued that there are other Areas. Interestingly, the Areas of Knowledge do not quite match the six subject areas around the hexagon. For instance, in TOK, history is given its own Area of Knowledge status, while the hexagon puts history in with the human sciences (Group 3). Also, consider that a student can earn the IB diploma without taking a history course. What do you think of that? A debate or discussion about how this state of affairs came about might also make a good presentation topic. Look again at the Areas of Knowledge – do you think there are important disciplines that don't fit anywhere? If so, why not? What about technology, for example?

Disciplines as cultures – a metaphor

In 1959, the British novelist and physicist C.P. Snow delivered a lecture called 'The Two Cultures' in which he lamented a yawning gulf, as he saw it, between those who were familiar with the sciences and those conversant in the humanities subjects. Perhaps you recognize this dichotomy today. Is there a preference for, or prejudice against, one or the other in your school or college, or among groups of students? Are mathematics and sciences considered 'hard' subjects; literature and the humanities as interesting but 'soft'? Snow considered the apparent antagonism between these 'two cultures' as a major hindrance to the application of knowledge to pressing global problems, such as poverty and inequality – instances of what in TOK we sometimes call 'knowledge at work in the world'.

The idea of disciplines as cultures is a metaphor, and it might help us to examine the relationships between all disciplines; not just the sciences and humanities. As an IB student, you are frequently encouraged to think in an 'internationally-minded' fashion, and this involves thinking about cultures and cultural matters. You might believe, for example, that some degree of cultural misunderstanding is inevitable in the world, but that efforts towards intercultural understanding are, nevertheless, worthwhile. You may well condemn xenophobic attitudes. Using the metaphor, you might conclude that confusion between practitioners of different disciplines is impossible to avoid completely, but efforts towards mutual understanding should be encouraged in order to promote a broader perspective on knowledge. The metaphor also allows us to revisit the issue of whether disciplines are natural or social constructs.

An anthropologist, interested in a culture, would be keen to examine aspects of a discipline such as beliefs and ideas, customs and practices, implicit values, common language and a hierarchy of status. There may even be a rough parallel here with 'knowing that' and 'knowing how' – discussed in Chapter 2: What is knowledge? What could be the corresponding aspects of academic disciplines?

The nature of disciplines

In the exercise on sending material to the past on page 115, you classified knowledge statements into disciplines by considering that the disciplines consist of established subject matter. This could correspond to the 'knowing that' of ideas and beliefs. Although there could be regions of overlap, it seems pretty clear that, for example, biology is about living things and history is about the past. Disciplines are surely about 'knowing that' certain things are the case. But disciplines have different methods and traditions as well, rather like the 'knowing how' of customs, practices and so on.

Knowing	Cultures	Disciplines
knowing that	beliefs and ideas	subject matter/content
knowing how	customs and practices	methodology

On first inspection, the methods seem to relate directly to the subject matter under consideration (experiments for finding out about the natural world; evaluating documents and witnesses for finding out about the past, etc.). So does it make any real difference whether we classify disciplines according to subject matter or methods? What is the relationship between them – aren't they just two sides of the same coin?

Disciplines as social institutions

As you read on into the chapters about the various Areas of Knowledge, much will need to be said about the methods employed. But as these methods must be shared and understood within each discipline, this demonstrates how scholarly activity should be seen in terms of agreed practices. Academic disciplines are constructions; they are not pure subject matter or disembodied methods. Rather, they are built and driven forward by human beings, with their attitudes, assumptions, standards and prejudices. Taking this broad conceptual view, a method provides practitioners with an agenda, a way forward, rules (both written and unwritten) for acceptable behaviour and much more. In short, it is the way they do things. There seems to be more to methods than immediately meets the eye.

Disciplines offer not only methods of approach but communities of scholars bonded by social practices. In the 1940s, the American sociologist Robert Merton elaborated some norms of behaviour to which scientists are expected to aspire. Here is a simplified summary:

Merton's Norms

Norm	Description – contributions to scientific work should:
Communalism	become part of public knowledge by full disclosure
Universalism	be judged independently of personal traits of the contributor
Disinterestedness	be made neutrally, impersonally and without regard for personal gain
Originality	offer something new to the existing body of knowledge
Scepticism	be subjected to systematic doubt by the scientific community.

Norms are expectations that are not always realized. In 2004 and 2005, the prominent Korean biomedical scientist Woo-Suk Hwang announced two breakthroughs in research into stem cells (cells that have the ability to differentiate into an unlimited variety of cell types and therefore can be used to repair tissues and organs). Firstly, he claimed to have cloned human stem cells, and secondly, to have developed such cells using the genetic material from specific donors, thus opening the door to the production of stem cells tailored to particular patients. For these apparent scientific and medical advances, Hwang was feted as a hero. Soon, however, awkward questions were asked about Hwang's methods and conclusions. Initially it became known that he had lied about the sources of the eggs used to create the stem cells, and eventually it was shown that his claims about specific lines of stem cells were not truthful – essentially that they had been faked.

This story demonstrates the importance of some of Merton's norms. Hwang breached the norm of *communalism* in failing to tell the truth about his work, concealing certain practices. The enormous personal prestige afforded to him through his work perhaps tempted him into fraudulence, and undermined a *disinterested* stance, as he had much to gain as an individual from his alleged breakthroughs. The story underlines how vital it is that members of the scientific community maintain their *sceptical* stance, no matter who is making the claims, and that *originality* must be tempered with *honesty*.

Returning to the idea of disciplines as cultures, figures such as Hwang, through showing disrespect for the professional rules, lay themselves open to being ostracized by the very community to which they belong.

Exercise

1 To what extent do you think that these norms apply to other Areas of Knowledge? What about the arts, for example? Could we define disciplines in terms of how scholars are expected to behave?

2 Try running an Internet search on some or all of the following items. One of them might provide the trigger for a presentation topic:
- Lysenko and vernalization
- Irving and the Holocaust
- Fleischmann and Pons and cold fusion
- Blondlot and N-rays
- Mitogenic radiation
- Geller and Randi

Consider the following prescribed essay title:

Discuss and evaluate the ways in which the beliefs of researchers might count as evidence for or against their results.

© International Baccalaureate Organisation 2003

In 1962, the American philosopher and historian of science, Thomas Kuhn, proposed a model for the way science proceeds. He suggested that, most of the time, scientists work within a set of shared beliefs and assumptions that help to set the agenda for research and the acceptable methods for interpreting results. This kind of activity he named **normal science**, and the accepted beliefs and assumptions formed what he called a **paradigm**. As time goes on, however, findings accumulate that are not consistent with the current paradigm, and eventually it is overthrown and replaced by a new paradigm that better resolves the inconsistencies. He called this process a 'paradigm shift' and scientific activity during this period **revolutionary science**. Examples of such paradigm shifts would be major, but rare, changes such as the acceptance of the sun-centred model of the solar system, of atomic theory in chemistry, and continental drift in the earth sciences. Kuhn's ideas emphasize again that scholarly activities take place in a shared social context.

Normal science
Scientific activity that takes place within the constraints of a paradigm.
Paradigm A comprehensive set of beliefs and assumptions which is not questioned during day-to-day enquiry in a science discipline, and that provides context and meaning to discoveries.
Revolutionary science
Scientific activity taking place during the shift from an old disintegrating paradigm towards a new one.

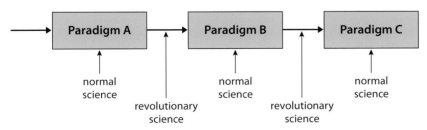

How science proceeds – according to Thomas Kuhn

Kuhn was talking specifically about the natural sciences, and explicitly denied the existence of paradigms in the human sciences, claiming that there was much more fundamental and everyday disagreement in these disciplines. What is your experience with this? In Group 3 of the diploma, if you are studying economics, psychology or social and cultural anthropology, have you encountered more contradictory ideas or diverse methods than in your Group 4 subject(s)? Whatever seems to be the case, perhaps it is worth revisiting the thought that the paradigm model could be applied more widely to the academic disciplines. An idea such as this could be explored in response to the following prescribed essay title:

> *'Human beings are not aware of their assumptions or basic beliefs, much as fish are unaware of the water in which they live.' Discuss.*
>
> ©International Baccalaureate Organization 1997

Paradigms, including their embedded assumptions and beliefs, can act as reliable guides to the process of discovery and channel our creativity, but they may also mislead us when new developments compromise their usefulness.

Disciplines as tools

Read the following enigmatic offering from Donald Rumsfeld, former American Defense Secretary, re-framed by some admirers as a poem:

> **The Unknown**
> As we know,
> There are known knowns.
> There are things we know we know.
> We also know
> There are known unknowns.
> That is to say
> We know there are some things
> We do not know.
> But there are also unknown unknowns,
> The ones we don't know
> We don't know.
>
> Donald Rumsfeld, Department of Defence news briefing, 12 February 2002

Although this was probably not exactly what Rumsfeld had in mind (he was more concerned with weapons of mass destruction and insurgency at the time), we could suggest that disciplines help us turn *unknown unknowns* into *known unknowns*, and thus increase the likelihood of their eventually becoming *known knowns*. They help us ask the right questions, guide us toward trusted methods, frame what are considered satisfying answers and provide a context for like-minded scholars.

IF NEWTON WAS A BOTANIST...

Ah, ha — the stem of an apple is not permanently fixed to the tree.

Consider the following recent prescribed essay title:

'Tell me how you're conducting your search and I'll tell you what you're looking for.' To what extent do the methods used in different Areas of Knowledge determine the object or the scope of the research that is possible?

To what extent do *different methods* result in *different outcomes*? It is sometimes the case that different disciplines approach a given topic from different angles – determined by different sets of concepts. This can lead to the application of different methods and the formulation of different questions. For example, taking the topic of human aggression, a neurologist might look for physical or chemical causes and might advocate a pharmaceutical or even surgical procedure; whereas a psychiatrist might concentrate on social causes and look to psychotherapy as an appropriate response. Contrastingly, a novelist might want to explore the truth about the topic through fiction.

Sometimes, disciplines seem to form a hierarchy of explanations in relation to one another. In the natural sciences, when explaining enzyme action in an IB biology course, you would make reference to the overall shape of the molecule caused by the sequence of amino acids that constitute it (diagram A). On the other hand, in IB chemistry you would be more concerned about the exact nature of the forces between them (diagram B). A physicist might try to explain all of this at a more fundamental level still, making reference to various sub-atomic particles (diagram C). But, although such a 'physics' explanation of enzyme action might be true, it would not be helpful to us in our quest to understand the topic as it refers to the 'wrong' concepts for the task. So it is treated here like a black box that we don't wish to open, filled with knowledge which is not appropriate to our goal. Disciplines assist us in knowing what kind of answers to give to questions, and what concepts to apply.

A: Biology

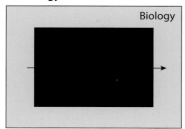

B: Biology ←→ Chemistry

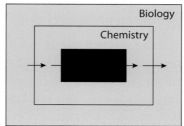

C: Biology ←→ Chemistry ←→ Physics

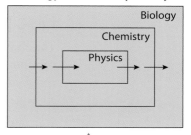

How disciplinary background affects findings

In the human sciences, namely twentieth century psychology, much effort was put into explaining behaviour solely in terms of stimulus and response. The workings of the mind itself were considered to be beyond current scientific explanation, and so they constituted another black box.

Disciplines and Ways of Knowing

Let's take a moment to return to basics. What does the word 'discipline' mean? When you stop to think about it, there is more than one meaning. Whereas we have been using it to describe academic subjects, this meaning is derived from an older notion of *disciples* initiated into *accepted practices*. In achieving this, the disciple must exercise 'discipline'. You have almost certainly heard about 'school discipline', and would probably agree that it can have positive or negative features and effects. We can now go on to explore this idea in relation to academic disciplines.

Consider the following two quotations from Albert Einstein:

> *The whole of science is nothing more than a refinement of everyday thinking.*
>
> ★★★★
>
> *Common sense is the collection of prejudices acquired by age eighteen.*

As our direct means to gaining knowledge, the Ways of Knowing might seem to be intimately bound up with common sense or everyday thinking. Are these two interchangeable? If they are, then we could ask:
- Do disciplines build on *truths* gained through the Ways of Knowing?
- Or do they act to correct *misunderstandings* and *falsehoods that arise from the Ways of Knowing?*

Exercise

Consider the following table and try to complete it:

Common sense	Disciplinary knowledge
Objects will stop moving unless continuously pushed.	Newton's laws of motion (physics)
Prices are fixed features of commodities.	
	heliocentrism (astronomy)
An insulated house keeps out the cold.	
Maggots arise spontaneously from rotting meat.	
	plate tectonics (geology)

Disciplines as guides to the truth

The above exercise suggests that, sometimes, there is a clear disjunction between common sense knowledge acquired through the Ways of Knowing, and knowledge accepted in the disciplines as true. Why should this be the case? Might the disciplines allow us to see beyond our own Ways of Knowing?

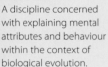

Evolutionary psychology

A discipline concerned with explaining mental attributes and behaviour within the context of biological evolution.

You will probably be familiar with the idea of evolution, which claims that our physical characteristics are the product of natural selection – in other words that our bodies are adapted for survival. In recent years we have seen the rise of the discipline of **evolutionary psychology**, which is based on the premise that our *mental capacities* also must also be products of evolution. According to this idea, the Ways of Knowing evolved in ways that helped us to survive, and may be better at this job than actually revealing the truth. For example, you might have mistaken a rock formation or a tree bending in the wind for an animal or another person. This is quite a common experience. Although in this case the *perception* is not true, it cannot have harmed prehistoric humans who were familiar with hungry predators, and on the rare occasion when it *was* true, it may have saved a life. The speed with which we feel emotions (such as fear) and the powerful command they exert on our lives might also be explained in terms of survival value. Even our reasoning abilities might be moulded by our social arrangements. Maybe here lies the explanation for some of the features and limitations of the human Ways of Knowing.

It could be argued, then, that modern disciplines to some extent serve as correctives for the shortcomings of the Ways of Knowing, and guide us on the road to truth – in other words, our Ways of Knowing need to be subjected literally to discipline. The American evolutionary psychologist Steven Pinker has explored this idea in his book *The Blank Slate: the Modern Denial of Human Nature*:

- Our everyday perceptions lead us to think that objects need to be continuously pushed (given impetus) in order to stay in motion; this is contradicted by Newton's first law of motion.
- We divide the world up into living and non-living, with the former possessing some special essence or 'life force'; this is contradicted by modern biochemistry.
- We separate humans from the rest of nature by referring to souls; this is contradicted by modern psychology.

- As toolmakers, we tend to look for the purpose of objects; this leads us astray when there is no such purpose.

So disciplines may generate findings that are counter-intuitive but perhaps closer to the truth.

> **Exercise**
>
> - It has been claimed by some that historians are fraudulent in so far as they make up causes for events retrospectively that satisfy our need for plausible stories but are no more truthful than many other possibilities.
> - Economists have been accused of applying theoretical statistical models that ignore 'inconvenient' but important aspects of the real world (see, for example, *The Black Swan* by N.N. Taleb).
>
> **1** Do you think that such claims undermine the idea that disciplines are reliable guides to the truth?
>
> **2** Re-read the quotation by the sixteenth century French writer Michel de Montaigne at the start of this chapter (page 115). Do you see any connection between it and this chapter? What do you think about the fact that it was written more than 400 years ago? Is there anything to be learned from this?

Disciplines and knowledge as a whole

In the previous section, we explored how disciplines might assist us by compensating for the limitations of our Ways of Knowing. But there are more ambitious goals – some scholars have looked forward to a time when it might be possible to unify all scholarly knowledge on some basis. You may have heard of the hopes of physicists to uncover a unified theory for gravity, electromagnetism and the two forces associated with the nucleus (such a unification is sometimes referred to as a 'big TOE' – a Theory of Everything!). An even more ambitious goal exists under a name that might be new to you – **consilience** – that all of the sciences, humanities and arts can be brought together in coherence as 'nature is organized by simple universal laws of physics to which all other laws and principles can eventually be reduced'. You can read more about this in *Consilience – the Unity of Knowledge* by E.O. Wilson, the renowned entomologist.

Consilience The goal of creating a common matrix of explanation across a wide variety of disciplines.

Rather than acting individually as the 'guardians of truth' (correcting our natural shortcomings), in this scenario the disciplines would merge into one massive interlocking, self-reinforcing matrix.

> **Exercise**
>
> - Do you think consilience will ever be possible? Why or why not?
> - Earlier descriptions of TOK spoke about the value and even the goal of unifying students' knowledge – what would this mean? What would it feel like to have such coherence in your knowledge?
> - Can you reconcile the idea of black boxes with consilience?

Now consider an alternative vision, as set out by the famous Austrian scholar of animal behaviour, Konrad Lorenz:

> *Every man gets a narrower and narrower field of knowledge in which he must be an expert in order to compete with other people. The specialist knows more and more about less and less and finally knows everything about nothing.*

A few hundred years ago, it was possible for an outstanding educated individual (sometimes referred to as a 'Renaissance Man') to keep abreast of developments across all the various disciplines, but the relentless expansion of knowledge has made this impossible in our age (can you connect this to the discussion of Wikipedia in Chapter 2: What is knowledge?). Rather than promoting connections and helping to dissolve the boundaries of the disciplines, perhaps this growth of knowledge is leading to an ever-increasing fragmentation into new and bewildering categories and sub-disciplines. What would this mean and how should we respond?

Diversity or unity: which is better?

There is often a strong impetus for approaches to learning and research that involve a number of disciplines. But what exactly is the nature of these **inter-disciplinary** approaches? There could be several. In the IB diploma, there are now a number of trans-disciplinary courses available, such as Environmental Systems and Societies, and Text and Performance, in which the subject matter and methodologies of two disciplines are to some extent dissolved in the interests of a new synthesis. Maybe there is a fruitful distinction between **trans-disciplinary** approaches that try to unify different disciplines, and **multi-disciplinary** ones that try to achieve understanding through a combination of the insights from separate subjects.

Exercise

Discussion about the question below might take place during your Group 4 Project – particularly during the planning phase.

- Are you being asked to work within your individual science subjects and then bring your conclusions to the multi-disciplinary table?
- Or to approach the topic simply as a science student among many, contributing to a common goal?
- Which do you think would be more effective?
- Is it more important to respect the diversity of disciplines or to attempt to merge them?

Multi-disciplinary approaches encourage a respect for disciplines as constructions that have stood the test of time; trans-disciplinary ones seek to transcend them. **Cross-disciplinary** studies extend the reach of one discipline by applying its concepts in another field, which may hence be enriched by new insights. For example, bio-politics would be concerned with introducing biological ideas about growth, homeostasis and decay into the study of politics. We can clarify these terms:

- **inter-disciplinary** – blanket term covering all the others
- **multi-disciplinary** – separate disciplines working together
- **trans-disciplinary** – differences between disciplines dissolved
- **cross-disciplinary** – one discipline interpreted in terms of another

Try replacing the word 'disciplinary' with 'cultural' – are there any further insights that can be reached through pushing the metaphor further?

History suggests that the founding of an interdisciplinary subject is not easy. Initially, authorities will have to come from more established subjects and authors may find it difficult to get articles published in traditional journals. Often, new disciplines of this nature are held in great suspicion for being motivated by ideology rather than an objective love of knowledge. Such might be the case for attempts to found disciplines based on feminist or post-colonialist perspectives.

Disciplines – boundaries and distinctions

Let's look again at the prescribed essay title:

God may have separated the heavens from the earth. He did not separate astronomy from marine biology.

Jonathan Levy

To what extent are the classifications separating Areas of Knowledge justified?
© International Baccalaureate Organisation 2002

We could, perhaps, think of disciplines as shading into one another, either in terms of contents or methods. This might lead to a linear arrangement:

| mathematics | natural sciences | human sciences | history | the arts | ethics |

We can think of disciplines shading into one another.

Exercise

- On what basis could this arrangement be justified?
- What are the other possibilities? Try to find one and justify it. You might consider, for example, a hierarchical approach.
- To what extent do you think that the criteria used to create these classifications make hidden value judgements or assumptions about different kinds of knowledge?

Notice the position of the human sciences in the spectrum given above. In a follow-up to his original lecture in 1959, C.P. Snow suggested that he had not paid enough attention to these disciplines and their role in bridging the divide between his 'two cultures'. Would you agree that they provide such a useful bridge between the sciences and the humanities? Perhaps the concept of the 'two cultures' is itself a topic for the human sciences to explore.

Even if the boundaries between disciplines are moveable but not entirely arbitrary, perhaps there is a more fundamental split in our modes of thinking. The American psychologist Jerome Bruner has written about the following suggested dichotomy:

A: Model/map	B: Story
<ul><li>concerned with abstraction</li><li>general</li><li>allows repetition and testing</li><li>more about explaining</li><li>predictive</li><li>asking 'how'</li></ul>	<ul><li>concerned with lived experience</li><li>particular</li><li>deals with the unique</li><li>more about understanding</li><li>non-predictive</li><li>asking 'why'</li></ul>

The most reliable knowledge is map-like: 'If you do this, then that will always follow.' But such knowledge carries little if any inherent human meaning. Most meaningful is story-like knowledge, which teaches about morals and values; but about that, agreement cannot be forced by demonstration. Failure to distinguish between the meaningfulness and the reliability of knowledge helps to make arguments intractable. It would be very useful always to ask about a bit of claimed knowledge, 'Is this more like a story or more like a map?'

Henry Bauer in *Journal of Scientific Exploration*, Volume 9

Exercise

Consider the following subject disciplines and try to decide whether each is described best by A or B or both:

- biology
- chemistry
- computer science
- economics
- ethics
- geography
- history

- music
- physics
- psychology
- literature
- visual arts
- others…?

Look at your results.
- Do they suggest a dichotomy or a spectrum?
- Did you find both modes within the same discipline? If so, which?
- What is your response to Bauer's explanation above?

It seems almost as if we have found our way back to Snow's 'two cultures' again. Maybe the disciplinary divide to which he drew attention has been fuelled by two contrasting modes of thought. But, as has been repeatedly pointed out, these two modes are not exclusive alternatives; they complement each other – both within and across disciplines. As a scholar who is familiar with both, the Greek mathematician and novelist Apostolos Doxiadis claims:

A theory is a map. A story is a path. But you cannot have the map without the paths. And if the area in which you are travelling is particularly tricky, as life often is, no map is as useful as an abundance of knowledge of good paths.

Turning briefly to literature, in a massive book that apparently took 35 years from inception to completion (*The Seven Basic Plots: Why We Tell Stories*), the British writer Christopher Booker has tried to distill the stories that we find from novels to drama to opera into just seven categories, as follows:

1 **Overcoming the monster** – the 'call', initial success, confrontation and setback, final success
2 **Rags to riches** – wretchedness, out into world, crisis, eventual independence, fulfilment
3 **The quest** – the 'call', journey and setbacks, arrival, central ordeal, goal attained
4 **Voyage and return** – anticipation, fascination, frustration, thrilling escape and return
5 **Comedy** – systematic misunderstanding, encroaching darkness, dispelling of shadows
6 **Tragedy** – hope for gratification, commitment to action, final destruction
7 **Rebirth** – dark shadow, threat recedes, subsequent crisis, eventual redemption

Do you think there is a danger of too much classification (maps) of the (path-like) arts? In India, for example, it is said that there are only three plots in Bollywood movies (perhaps so that 37 language groups can understand them!). Maybe the seven stories could be condensed into one, such as, 'a problem arose and eventually it got solved'! What has been lost here?

Knowledge, society and global development

What is the relationship between new knowledge being created by scholars and knowledge learned in school? Is there a fundamental difference between 'knowledge production' (research) and 'knowledge replication' (curriculum)? In your school career, you might have experienced teachers telling you 'the truth' about something, only to tell you a different account when you reach a more advanced level class – what was your reaction to this?

Do teaching and research *reflect* society or do they *drive* society? C.P. Snow believed strongly in the power of education for change. Indeed, his primary motivation for his lecture was not a dry concern with the nature of disciplines but a commitment to harnessing their power in the service of exploited and impoverished people in the world. (He even reflected that he might better have called his lecture 'The Rich and the Poor'.) You might like to think about how academic knowledge can have a place in CAS activities. How have *you* brought (or do you intend to bring) *your* scholarly experience to bear in this part of the IB diploma?

At the same time, Snow was influenced, as we all are, by the society to which he belonged. Think about the following:

And as we saw when reviewing the history of disciplines on pages 116–7, ideas about knowledge are a product of their time as well as their cultural origin.

Today's world: the discipline wars

Differences of perspective between practitioners in different disciplines can and do have real and serious repercussions in the world. According to an article 'Never the Twain Shall Meet' published in *The Economist* in 2002, '[a]cademic disciplines are often separated by gulfs of mutual incomprehension, but the deepest and widest may be the one that separates most economists from most environmentalists… What underlies this is not so much disagreements about facts as disagreement about how to think.' Look at the following table for a simplified summary of some of the differences and assumptions:

Ecologist	Economist
The economy is part of the environment.	The environment is part of the economy.
Ethical values are irreducible.	Ethical values can be reduced to economic ones.
Natural resources cannot be substituted.	Natural resources can be substituted by other natural resources, or by manufactured ones.
Natural resources count as capital.	Natural resources count as income.
'We can't afford to wait for more evidence of environmental damage, as the consequences of it would be so severe.'	'We should wait for harder evidence before concluding there is serious environmental damage, in order to avoid misplaced priorities.'
Ecosystems are fragile.	Ecosystems are robust.
Links with the political left.	Links with the political right.
'We are correct!'	'We are correct!'

If you study biology and/or economics, does anything you have learned in these subjects seem to relate to this dichotomy?

One prominent thinker who has stirred up this particular dispute is the Danish statistician, Bjørn Lomborg, who over the years has moved from left to right as depicted in the table above – a study of his views might be an interesting starting point for developing a presentation on the knowledge issues arising from the conflicts between Areas of Knowledge. The ways in which we organize our knowledge have direct connections to the global problems we have to confront.

As informed citizens, what can we do when confronted with these apparently conflicting points of view? It would seem that environmental issues are too important for us simply to stand on the sidelines – but if we are not experts, how should we respond?

Ideal knower

Stephen Jay Gould, 1941–2002

If genius has any common denominator, I would propose breadth of interest and the ability to construct fruitful analogies between fields.

Stephen Jay Gould

Born in New York, Stephen Jay Gould was an eminent figure in the discipline of palaeontology (the study of fossils). He is well-known for promoting a version of evolution in which it is claimed that periods of rapid change are interspersed with those in which little seems to occur. This is known as *punctuated equilibrium* and you may have heard of it already if you are following a Biology HL course – particularly if you are studying Option D.

As a prolific writer of essays, Gould succeeded in bringing his massive scholarship to a wide audience. Although many of his writings concern his professional engagement with fossils, they show how knowledge of a variety of disciplines can enrich the understanding of all of them, and create new insights. In this sense, Gould was a brilliant multi-disciplinary champion.

Perhaps a discipline like palaeontology is likely to attract such a person – knowledge issues in history (for example, those to do with missing evidence and the accidents of time) must be reconciled with the traditional methods of the natural sciences (experiments and predictions, etc.). In other words, palaeontologists must be comfortable with both maps and stories! Palaeontologists also frequently consult other disciplines. Writing about past extinctions (and echoing Rumsfeld's contribution about unknown and known unknowns), Gould states:

When a problem has proved intractable for more than one hundred years, it is not likely to yield to more data recorded in the old way and under the old rubric. Theoretical ecology allowed [palaeontologists] to ask the right questions and plate tectonics provided the right earth upon which to pose them.

From *The Richness of Life: the Essential Stephen Jay Gould* by Stephen Jay Gould

There is an interesting parallel between Gould's ideas about the evolution of living things and of academic disciplines: namely that the development of each is dependent upon sudden and unforeseeable chance events. To him, the complexities of life and of human scholarship were grounds for awe and wonder – the present is precious because if we were to re-wind the clock the result would never be the same.

In contrast to many voices in recent years, Gould maintained that there was no fundamental reason for conflict between science and religion (Areas of Knowledge he called 'magisteria' after the Latin term for 'teacher'):

> The net of science covers the empirical realm: what is the universe made of (fact) and why does it work this way (theory). The net of religion extends over questions of moral meaning and value. These two magisteria do not overlap, nor do they encompass all inquiry (consider, for starters, the magisterium of art and the meaning of beauty), to cite the usual clichés, we get the age of rocks, and religion retains the rock of ages, we study how the heavens go, and they determine how to go to heaven.

On the topic of disciplines and their relation to human nature, Gould wrote as follows:

> Our propensity for thinking in dichotomies may lie deeply within human nature itself. In his Lives and Opinions of Eminent Philosophers (written circa AD 200), Diogenes Laertius quotes a much older maxim of Protagoras: 'there are two sides to every question, exactly opposite to each other'. But we can also utilize another basic trait of our common humanity – our mental flexibility, and our consequent potential for overcoming such innate limitations by education.

> Our tendency to parse complex nature into pairings of 'us versus them' should not only be judged as false in our universe of shadings and continua, but also (and often) harmful, given another propensity for judgement – so that 'us versus them' easily becomes 'good versus bad'…

> The contingent and largely arbitrary nature of disciplinary boundaries has unfortunately been reinforced, even made to seem 'natural', by our drive to construct dichotomies – with science versus art as perhaps the most widely accepted of all… this false division becomes magnified as the two, largely non-communicating, sides then develop cultural traditions that evoke mutual stereotyping and even ridicule.

Diagnosed with an unusual form of cancer in 1982, Gould discovered that the condition had an eight-month median survival period. He used this piece of apparently catastrophic personal news as the basis for an essay on the misunderstandings often associated with the interpretation of statistics ('The Median isn't the Message'), and demonstrated that he had a much higher survival chance than it appeared. Having defeated the condition, he lived, wrote and continued to shine his intellect upon the disciplines until his death in May 2002.

Student presentation

1 Can consistent criteria be put forward for judging the value of various Areas of Knowledge? A variant of the 'balloon game' is used as a role play, in which a group member represents an individual Area and makes a case for it to be retained within the overloaded sinking hot-air balloon, while others try to eject it on the grounds that it is 'dead weight' knowledge.

2 Carry out an investigation into human pre-history from the perspectives of an archaeologist and a psychologist. The archaeologist is a historical scientist who looks for knowledge in historical evidence (dead, sparse, but 'real'); the psychologist is an experimental scientist who uses knowledge of modern humans to investigate the past (living, prolific, but 'simulated'). Is one of these approaches 'better', or are they complementary?

Essay questions

Two recent Prescribed Titles (PTs) include:

1 Is it possible to justify a hierarchy of disciplines? If so, on what basis?

©International Baccalaureate Organization 1997

2 *This rubber tree won't yield latex – the biologist blames the sapling, the geologist blames the soil, the contractor blames the unskilled labourer and the owner says it is fighting back at being controlled.*

Amitav Ghosh

If different Ways of Knowing or Areas of Knowledge yield contradictory statements about the world, on what basis do we choose among them?

©International Baccalaureate Organization 2003

Mathematical knowledge

Mathematics: out of the ivory tower and into the real world

… Two brothers are arguing over a piece of chocolate cake. The older brother wants it all; the younger wails that this isn't fair – the cake should be split 50–50. The mother enters and makes them compromise. She gives three-fourths of the cake to the older brother and one-fourth to the younger.

From A *Mathematician Reads the Newspaper* by John Allen Paulos,
Perseus Books Group

Rightly or wrongly, we live in a world where personal judgements are made about each of us based upon some form of statistical or mathematical connection. This mathematical presence hits home to a majority of IB students when a number is assigned to results. If Alfredo scores 28 and Beth scores 42, then what exactly does this mean? Universities in certain national systems may slam the door in the face of the conscientious, well-organised, ethical, hard working, physically fit, intelligent and charismatic student who does not acquire the appropriate number total.

At the personal level, will people think differently of them because of these numbers? Are their futures somehow altered because of this numerical tag that comes with the diploma? Will Alfredo be less of a good brother or chemist or tailor or will Beth be a better student or accountant or be healthier? And that's not all. Try watching the 6 o'clock news or sorting through the BBC blogs without being able to make sense of the diagrams, percentages or correlations. News headlines like 'Use of Cell Phones tied to Ovarian Cancer' or 'Afghanistan Death Count Unknown' have significant mathematical connections, which you may or may not recognise, but the social and economic repercussions are out there.

Political judgements wait on the doorstep too, and they are relevant. We might think, for example, that in a democratic society a *fair* election is one where the majority of individual votes decide the winner. But Al Gore and his Democratic Party were only left to wonder what might have been after the US presidential election of November 2000. Simple vote counting was never more complicated. Gore indeed won the popular vote majority but nonetheless lost the election. Did the concept of 'majority rules' somehow become lost in the electoral process?

The mathematical analysis of this system is worthy of consideration. Winner of the 1972 Nobel Prize in Economics, Dr Kenneth Arrow, reasoned that ranked voting methods are not necessarily fair. He also showed the world how seemingly simple issues of social choice can be very problematic. The quote at the beginning of this chapter concerning the mother's diplomacy must surely make most of us want to scream out, 'Hey, that's not fair!' Mathematician and author, John Paulos, suggests that national powers like those in NATO (the mother) have applied this sort of diplomacy to Serbia (the older brother) and Bosnia (the younger).

The IB values mathematical knowledge and hence requires that diploma students must include a mathematics course as part of their six subjects. Mathematics is not simply about computation or finding *x*. It represents an open window to the natural world as well as a way of philosophical thinking. It offers an aesthetic experience along with the thrill of an intellectual game. The very characteristics of mathematics as an Area of Knowledge provide reinforcement for the support and justification of knowledge claims.

If you are to be labelled as a knower in the true sense, then you must be prepared to deal with the objectivity, reliability, validity and precision that are necessary components of an appropriate justification. Mathematics provides a means for the knower to add these qualities to the analysis of what is perceived in nature. It provides a means to form answers to questions like, 'How do I build a more fuel-efficient car engine?' or 'How do I know what causes little Fernando's bad behaviour?' And these answers may not simply be of a 'right or wrong' variety.

> *In the book of life, the answers aren't in the back.*
>
> Charlie Brown (Charles Schulz)

Mathematics in the school context

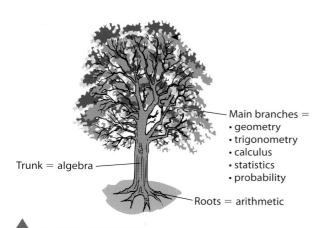

Main branches =
• geometry
• trigonometry
• calculus
• statistics
• probability

Trunk = algebra

Roots = arithmetic

A student's tree sketch depicting the growth of mathematical knowledge

The majority of IB students have already experienced the best part of nine or ten years of rather formal mathematical study at school. Hence, your outlook on mathematical knowledge has already taken some shape and direction. This outlook was seen in a certain TOK class where students were given the task to represent their perception of the growth of mathematical knowledge by sketching a tree. Odd as that task may seem (and you might find quite a few tasks within the TOK class odd!), figures were consistently constructed. The result shown opposite was typical, and provides a starting point for a reflection upon your own mathematical knowledge to date.

By and large students in this class view individual knowledge growth as a function of personal experiences brought about by a carefully planned school curriculum. And within this scheme it is not difficult to start generating a number of mathematical knowledge claims.

- $1 + 1 = 2$
- The sum of the interior angles of a triangle is 180°.
- There are infinitely many prime numbers.
- Parallel lines never intersect.
- If C and D are two independent events, then $P(C \cap D) = P(C) \times P(D)$.

But what is it exactly that allows us to make these claims? Does '$1 + 1 = 2$' come from our personal experience of the real world? The properties of the triangle as defined in a geometry lesson gave us the claim about the sum of the interior angles. A teacher may have asked you to justify this claim by physically cutting out the angles of a triangle drawn on a piece of paper and placing them side-by-side with a common vertex (see the diagram below). The result is that the exterior sides of the joined up angles magically form a straight line, which is measured to be 180°.

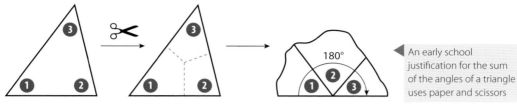

An early school justification for the sum of the angles of a triangle uses paper and scissors

This method of justification was perhaps one of many that were used to help lower school pupils develop an understanding of this triangle property. As students progress through mathematics they are exposed to various methods of justification. Some of the justifications ultimately become less intuitive. More formalised thinking relies on a collection of self-evident truths or axioms and a series of statements that flow from one to another in a logically rigorous manner (think back to the coherence truth test from Chapter 2: What is knowledge?). The conclusion at the end of the chain of reasoning provides the finishing touch. 'There are infinitely many prime numbers' is a proposition that may or may not be intuitive, but the result is undeniable and is shown by the rigorous **mathematical proof** of Euclid. It is a classic mathematical claim, solid as a rock and as aesthetically pleasing as a fine work of art. Or so the majority of mathematicians would claim.

And sooner or later, for all students of mathematics, come the formidable problems... *If a train is leaving Waterloo Station at 10 a.m. travelling at 120 km/h, and a second train leaves Brussels at 10:30 a.m. travelling at 140 km/h...* All of a sudden the IB student finds himself sitting in SL Mathematical Studies looking for the elusive solution that will guarantee a result of 5 or better and hence admission to the University of Some Place South of Watford. And then it's on to the TOK lesson where the teacher asks, 'Is mathematics better defined by its method or by its subject matter?' Good question, and the answer is not in the back of the book.

> ... *Columbus did not invent America, nor did Beethoven discover the Ninth Symphony.*
>
> From 'Philosophical Problems of Mathematics in the Light of Evolutionary Epistemology' by Yehuda Rav (published in *Eighteen Unconventional Essays on the Nature of Mathematics* edited by Reuben Hersh)

The formation of mathematical knowledge

As you reflect upon personal mathematical growth and development, you should soon realise that mathematical knowledge stems from a multitude of means and methods. Personal experience clearly plays a role. Developing the understanding of a topic within a teacher-led secondary mathematics class is not simply dependent upon rote memory. IB students are trained to explore and learn mathematics by taking personal ownership of concepts. Many a Mathematical Studies project or Extended Essay in Mathematics has been developed and structured from problem to data collection, to conjecture, to proof, to consideration of a new problem extension and algorithm, etc. The same could be said of student portfolio work at the SL and HL levels. Think back to the process that your pre-IB mathematics class used to understand the concept of solving quadratic equations. Does the process on the next page look familiar?

Mathematical proof This is usually a collection of logically valid steps or demonstrations that form an argument which serves as a justification of a mathematical claim. Steps within the argument normally make use of definitions, axioms, properties and previous claims that are consistent.

Solving quadratic equations – a typical in-school approach

Solve: a $x^2 = 4$
          b $3x^2 + 2 = 29$
          c $5x^2 - 15x = 0$
          d $x^2 - 5x + 6 = 0$ (by factoring)
          e $2x^2 + 5x - 3 = 0$ (by completing the square)

> Simple examples are first considered. More complex techniques are usually then provided.

Conjecture: The general solution for the solution
              of $ax^2 + bx + c = 0$ is …?

Prove: If $ax^2 + bx + c = 0$ where $a, b,$
         and $c \in R$, then

$$x = \frac{-b \pm \sqrt{b^2 - 4ac}}{2a}$$

> In this case forming the conjecture and establishing the proof go hand in hand. Students most likely go directly to the proof by completing the square on the general equation.

Solving Applications:

Mr Chang wants to build a rectangular fenced-in area next to his house. He has 32 m of fencing to use and wants to have an area of 128 m². What dimensions should be used for this enclosed area?

> Applications are often considered at the end of this unit after the technical skills of equation solving are understood.

Learning a pre-determined collection of knowledge claims in a descriptive manner (i.e. with a teacher's help) and *establishing* a knowledge claim through personal exploration not guided by a teacher are closely related, but nonetheless different. Scholars have put forward models to explain the formation of mathematical knowledge and one such model that is worthy of consideration is outlined below.

Buchberger's model

Dr Bruno Buchberger (of Johannes Kepler University in Linz, Austria) contends that mathematical discovery, and hence the formation of mathematical knowledge, takes place in stages. Buchberger contends that this knowledge spiral is made up of three phases. In the initial phase the mathematician starts with a particular problem and develops an algorithm or step-by-step procedure for the solution. This solution leads to other related problems and solutions. Eventually the data from these examples can be used to form a conjecture. This initial phase is known as the *phase of experimentation*. During the second phase, or *phase of exactification*, conjectures are turned into theorems through the method of proof. After proof is established, then an extension of problem solving ideas is formed and is further implemented. During the third phase, or *phase of application*, new algorithms or problem solving procedures are applied to real or fictitious data.

At the heart of the model exists a given problem along with a method of the problem's solution (i.e. algorithm). Further examples are considered and eventually generalisations of properties are made from the results. In a stage of development called *observation*, these generalisations are assembled to make way for a conjecture. The formal structure of mathematical knowledge comes about with the proof of the **conjecture**. This *proof* stage of development exists as a function of well-defined terms and mathematical axioms or assumed truths put together in a logical manner. This process of proof yields a theorem or justified knowledge claim. In return each theorem produces usable knowledge which can be implemented to form yet other new algorithms. This constitutes an *implementation* stage. New algorithms are thus applied to new data, yielding new examples, which lead to new observations, and so on to form an *application* stage.

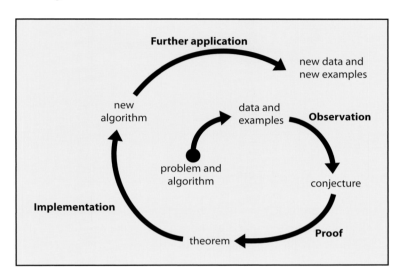

Conjecture
A conclusion made from a reasonable number of individual cases which are nonetheless insufficient to form substantial proof.

 Buchberger's model of the formation of mathematical knowledge.

Consideration of the implications of Buchberger's model is relevant to the TOK student. Indeed, this process hints that mathematical knowledge is formed in a **quasi-empirical** manner. Would a model of the formation of scientific knowledge share similar characteristics? Does mathematics simply serve as a tool that the sciences use to describe the natural world? Some will argue that mathematics not only provides a means to explain the elements of the natural world, but actually exists as an integral part of the natural world and is there waiting to be discovered. A note concerning this idea is worth considering and follows on pages 142–5.

The questions below will help you to form a comparison of the formation of mathematical knowledge claims to those from science or from any other area of knowledge.

Quasi-empirical
Having a likeness to a scientific method which requires careful observation and a gathering of relevant factual support.

Exercise

- What constitutes mathematical proof? Is mathematical proof formed through inductive or deductive reasoning?
- Do other Areas of Knowledge (e.g. science) provide proofs in the same way as mathematics?
- Is a mathematical proof final?
- Could the accumulation of additional mathematical knowledge possibly falsify an existing claim? Is this the case in other Areas of Knowledge?

It should be noted that Dr Buchberger and his colleagues became interested in this model as part of their investigation into the teaching and learning of mathematics with respect to technology and in particular computer algebraic systems. Of course, the IB Group 5 subjects are clearly on board with respect to the use of graphic display calculator technology. One of the plus points of the technology-based learning of mathematics is that the learner is able to develop a fuller understanding of concepts by working through the various stages of the knowledge acquisition cycle. The 'algorithm-data collection-conjecture' process is not simply a mechanical method, but more importantly a true handle of how things (both abstract and real world) behave.

Other models for the formation of knowledge (e.g. science, history etc.) exist, and it may be of interest to you to use the models to contrast and compare the individual qualities and characteristics of knowledge claims.

One,	1
ten,	1
add on	2
zeros more.	3
Infinity waits,	5
but can we find a proof for it?	8
	Fibonacci Poem

Conjecture and proof

Gathering data from a particular problem allows you to look for a pattern or process that in turn might allow you to generalise about an expected outcome. In daily life outside the classroom, people make generalisations constantly, often without thinking about the process itself.

Consider the day that Eamon decided to cross a busy street. When he started to take his first step, he paused to see if a car was travelling towards him. Indeed a car was coming, but Eamon noted that the car began to slow down. Eamon made eye contact with the driver of the car as the vehicle continued to slow down. At that point Eamon then determined that the car would come to a complete stop, and thus he decided to walk across the street in front of the car's path. Most people have made such a generalization without thinking about the consequences that could result in a life-threatening predicament. What if the driver of the car suddenly decided to speed up when Eamon was in the middle of the street?

Fortunately, making generalisations in a maths class is not life threatening. Yet, we exercise a similar inductive process frequently in our mathematical thinking. Consider the following exercise.

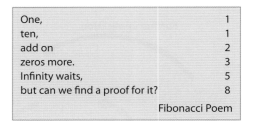

Identify the next three numbers or figures:

i 2   5   8   11   14 ...

ii ○◆○   ○◆◆○   ○◆◆◆○   ○◆◆◆◆○ ...

iii 2   4   6 ...

People may generally answer numbers 1 and 2 consistently, but what about the responses to example 3? Why might a person say that the next three terms in this example are 8 and 10 and 12? What if you gave the next three terms as 10 and 16 and 26? Who is correct? Even within a mathematical context, it is clearly important to have a satisfactory number of results before a generalisation or mathematical conjecture can be made.

Consider yet another mathematical example where careful thought must be applied.

Step 1: Draw a circle and then indicate a point on a circle as shown below.

How many regions are shown within this circle? *Answer = 1*

Step 2: Draw a similar circle and then indicate any two distinct points on the circle as shown. Then connect the two points with a line.

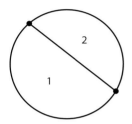

How many regions are shown within this circle? *Answer = 2*

Step 3: Draw yet another circle and indicate any three distinct points on the circle. Connect the three points to each other .

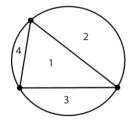

How many regions are shown within this circle? *Answer = 4*

Step 4: Add yet another point to the circle, thus making for a total of four. Connect the four points to each other.

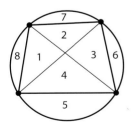

How many regions are shown within this circle? *Answer = 8*

It should become clear that as one increases the number of distinct points on the circle that the number of distinct regions formed within the circle is growing. Is there a clear pattern to this growth?

A table of data can be constructed as shown:

Number of points on circle	1	2	3	4	5	6
Number of regions in circle	1	2	4	8		

At this point, how many regions would you expect with a circle having five distinct points on the circle? What would you expect to happen in a circle with six distinct points? Now go to the figures below and make a count.

You might be surprised by the outcome. After all, aren't the mathematical examples straightforward and predictable, almost to the point of being boring? The results of this example must make you think. If a seemingly obvious conjecture or generalization cannot be made after five circles worth of evidence, then what are the implications concerning conjectures you could make within other real life contexts? (Mathematics aside… how many observations of male behaviour do you need to make a conjecture, 'Men always… '? The danger of making hasty generalizations about gender, sexuality, race or religion quickly becomes a concern.) The strength of any mathematical conjecture will, however, soon have to face a final judgement of sorts. That judgement consists of a formal proof.

> *I remember the time when I was kidnapped, and they sent a piece of my finger to my father. He said he wanted more proof.*
>
> Rodney Dangerfield (1920–2004)

The proof of the pudding

With respect to the notion of proof, mathematics exists in a special category. This is largely because the justification that leads to the proof exists in an artificial context. In contrast, a knowledge claim in natural science may be formed through empirical evidence that is gathered by observing real phenomena. The scientific evidence, when carefully constructed, virtually 'fails to falsify' a well thought out hypothesis. Some philosophers of science (e.g. Karl Popper) insist that science does not prove, but can only falsify a particular idea. Furthermore, a knowledge claim in history may be constructed through careful use of primary and secondary sources in such a way that when collected, analysed and justified by the historian, a clear thesis or position is put forward.

However, claims of knowledge in science and history may well leave the door open for further argument and analysis. Limitations with respect to details of evidence can result in claims that may eventually fall short of knowledge status. For example, in 1989 two well-known chemists, Stanley Pons and Martin Fleischmann, claimed that they had successfully performed nuclear fusion at room temperature. After much debate within the scientific community, this knowledge claim was dismissed.

The structuring of a formal proof is the core of the process that serves as the basis for knowledge claims in mathematics. The formation of a proof is largely dependent upon reasoning and language. A mathematical claim ultimately stems from the conclusion of proof. The structure of proof itself is built upon well-defined terminology, a system of axioms or assumed truths and a lock-tight system of formal reasoning. These ingredients may indeed have little to do with the real world.

Mathematical proof is the essence of what generally makes mathematics a unique knowledge form. This type of proof comes with distinct characteristics. First and foremost, mathematical proof is non-observational and hence does not rely upon your perception of events in nature. Secondly, mathematical proof is a deductive process. Even the 'proof by induction' taught in the IB Higher Level course is not to be confused with inductive reasoning. At its very core is deductive reasoning. Finally, conclusions arrived through mathematical proof are certain.

This is not to say that mathematical claims are not subject to a serious peer review just as they are in science or history. However, debate arising from any controversy will normally be settled to the point of final agreement. Such is the strength of the deductive process used in mathematical proof. Once the community of knowers accepts the formal mathematical proof, then the knowledge claim stands. Euclid's proof that there are infinitely many prime numbers is final. It has existed for over 2000 years, and as long as the grounds for the formation of the proof are accepted, then the claim stands.

It is interesting to consider the well-publicized proof of Fermat's Last Theorem by Andrew Wiles in 1993. Wiles spent the best part of seven years constructing the proof, but errors within its construction were found. Eventually, the complex pieces of the reasoning puzzle were properly fitted and the issues were resolved. Wiles was given full credit for the establishment of the proof of a statement that had existed only as conjecture for over 300 years.

> *How can it be that mathematics, being after all a product of human thought independent of experience, is so admirably adapted to the objects of reality?*
>
> Albert Einstein

Discovered or invented?

What is the true nature of mathematics as a knowledge form? Having an answer to this question will not necessarily help the mathematician to build a better bridge. It is, however, a question appropriate to any serious review of this knowledge area. The implications with respect to understanding the concept of truth will become relevant. Is mathematics invented or does it exist in the natural world waiting to be discovered?

There is little doubt that young students of mathematics (e.g. six-year-olds in primary school) develop mathematical ideas and concepts through use of the environment in their natural worlds. Simple addition, for example, is understood through the manipulation of objects. In this manner, mathematics and mathematical concepts are discovered. In yet another Area of Knowledge like natural science, phenomena are also discovered. Consider the recent astronomical findings concerning stars capable of sustaining solar systems similar to ours. These types of stars are physical objects in our universe. To find them the astronomer draws on other conceptual phenomena like gravity and the behaviour of visible light (redshift). Thus, when you consider a mathematical concept like addition as an 'object of nature', you must exercise care. Addition exists as a 'conceptual entity' (i.e. operator in this case) and not as a physical object. A child's development of mathematical understanding stems largely from the personal discovery of abstract concepts.

You do not have to look very far to gather even more formidable evidence that mathematics exists in the natural world. There is no getting away from the elegant symmetry that exists in the leaf of a tree or from the exquisite pattern formed by the statistical distribution of heights and weights of a population (i.e. the normal or Gaussian distribution).

It has been asserted that mathematics exists as a language used by nature. Hence, elements in nature are represented through mathematical symbols (i.e. numbers, graphs, etc.) and can be interpreted and understood accordingly. The role of the mathematician is to search for the numbers, patterns, graphs and models that can be found virtually everywhere. A special sequence of numbers, the Fibonacci sequence, is worthy of explanation.

The Fibonacci sequence and the golden section

Fibonacci was the nickname of the Italian mathematician Leonardo de Pisa (AD 1170–1250). The sequence, which bears his name, begins with the numbers 1 and 1. Adding the two previous numbers forms each following number. The first ten terms of this sequence thus become:

$$1, 1, 2, 3, 5, 8, 13, 21, 34, 55, \dots$$

Various aspects of nature's behaviour connect directly to this sequence. An investigation of the family tree of a male bee is one such example. Male bees hatch from eggs, which have not been fertilized, while female bees hatch from fertilized eggs. Consequently, a male bee has only one parent, his mother.

Part of a family tree for a male bee is shown below. The male bee has one parent and two grandparents, three great grandparents, etc. The numbers of bees per generation clearly form the Fibonacci sequence.

Part of the family tree for a male bee

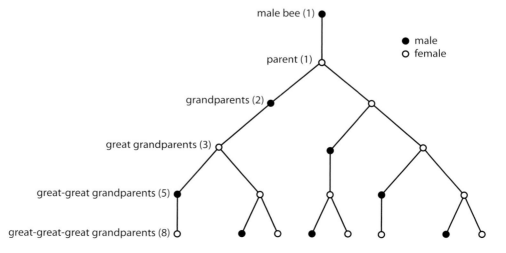

A further example of the Fibonacci sequence can be found in nature's construction of a nautilus shell. The results of such a finding can be mathematically modelled as shown below.

The Fibonacci spiral is formed from a series of quarter-circle arcs. The first arc is drawn using a unit square (1 × 1). See Figure A below:

Figure A

A second unit square is joined to the first and a second arc is drawn as shown in Figure B. This arc joins up with the first to form a semi-circle.

Figure B

A third square is formed to fit this figure. This new square must now be of a size 2 × 2. The arc is drawn as a continuation of the existing semi-circle. See Figure C below.

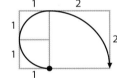

Figure C

This process continues the arc construction by adding on a 3 × 3 square, followed by a 5 × 5 as shown in Figures D and E below:

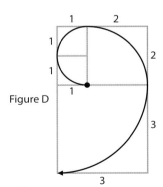

Figure D

Figure E

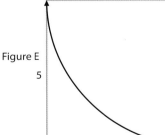

The spiral figure clearly grows within the diagram. This growth is based upon the sequence of squares used having dimensions that come directly from the Fibonacci sequence.

The series of figures A through E describes the geometric construction of a Fibonacci spiral

It is also interesting to consider the ratios formed using the successive terms within the Fibonacci sequence. These ratios are shown in the following table.

n	$(n + 1)$th term	nth term	ratio $(n + 1)$th to nth	Value of the ratio (6 d.p.)
1	1	1	1 : 1	1.000000
2	2	1	2 : 1	2.000000
3	3	2	3 : 2	1.500000
4	5	3	5 : 3	1.666667
5	8	5	8 : 5	1.600000
6	13	8	13 : 8	1.625000
7	21	13	21 : 13	1.615385
8	34	21	34 : 21	1.619048
9	55	34	55 : 34	1.617647
10	89	55	89 : 55	1.618182
11	144	89	144 : 89	1.617978
12	233	144	233 : 144	1.618056

Note that the calculated value of the ratio converges to a constant value of:

$$\frac{(1 + \sqrt{5})}{2} \ (\approx 1.618)$$

This value is known as the golden section or ratio and the Greek letter phi (ϕ) is used to represent it. While this numerical value may seem abstract, consider that the Fibonacci numbers and the golden section are found throughout nature, art and architecture. For example, think of:

- the number of petals on a flower
- spiral patterns seen on Romanesque broccoli
- the design of the Parthenon in Athens and the United Nations buildings in New York
- the artwork of Leonardo Da Vinci and Albrecht Dürer
- the violin construction of Stradivari.

This evidence supports the view that mathematics exists in the natural world and that we discover this marvellous phenomenon rather than invent it.

Contrary philosophical positions view this differently; mathematics is not waiting to be discovered but instead exists as a 'product of human thought, independent of experience' (Einstein).

An example of this view is seen in the history of geometry. Euclid's geometry is primarily that which you learn in secondary school. Claims that exist in this area include, 'the sum of three angles of a triangle is 180°', and 'parallel lines never intersect'. These ideas should not be new to you. They have been formally taught in schools for centuries. Euclid formulated this geometry in his book, the *Elements* (circa 300 BCE). The basis for the knowledge claims established in the *Elements* was a set of axioms or postulates. What had not been established at the time of Euclid was a discipline concerning the use of such axioms. The study of axiomatics came about years later. By the nineteenth century it became clear that axiom sets could be structured in different ways, and hence the mathematical knowledge developed from these sets could take on a different form. Indeed, a single axiom could be shown to be independent of a particular set of axioms to which it belongs.

The clever use of axiomatics by the Hungarian, János Bolyai, and the Russian, Nikolai Lobachevsky, allowed for the construction of a new geometry. Their results came about because they were able to show that one of Euclid's initial axioms was independent from the others. That is to say that the axiom (Euclid's Fifth Postulate, also known as the Parallel Postulate) could be removed from the original collection of axioms, and the remaining axiom set would still serve as a consistent basis for further claims. Consequently, Bolyai-Lobachevsky's geometry flourished into a collection of findings that varied from Euclid's.

> *If a line segment intersects two straight lines forming two interior angles on the same side that sum to less than two right angles, then the two lines, if extended indefinitely, meet on that side on which the angles sum to less than two right angles.*
>
> Euclid's Fifth Postulate

Less than 30 years later, Bernhard Riemann published further work leading to yet other conclusions and claims still different from Euclid's and Lobachevshy's.

Mathematics and reality – comparing geometries

The table shown below (taken from Davis and Hersh's book *The Mathematical Experience*) helps us to compare knowledge claims made by Euclidean and non-Euclidean geometries:

	Euclidean	Lobachevskian	Riemannian	
Given line L and point P not on L, there exist	one and only one line	at least two lines	no lines	through P parallel to L
A line	is	is	is not	separated into two parts by a point
Parallel lines	are equidistant	are never equidistant	do not exist	
The angle sum of a triangle is	equal to	less than	greater than	180°

With different constructs coming out of geometry it became clear that mathematics was somehow dependent upon the mathematician himself. A manipulation of simple assumed truths led to the formation of ideas that were different in appearance but were seemingly consistent within their own systems.

After being exposed to non-Euclidean geometries for the first time, many a student becomes perplexed (or downright annoyed), and may demand to know the *truth* of the matter, 'Do parallel lines intersect or not?' The truth in this case clearly becomes dependent upon a consistent set of coherent rules. Time will eventually tell whether a single geometry best describes the natural world.

Forming knowledge claims with an axiom set

How exactly does the creation of mathematical knowledge work? Can one simply make up a set of axioms and proceed to generate any fancied claims? It's not quite that easy!

A system of axioms must be workable, i.e. consistent. A particular postulate is said to be independent of the other members of its postulate set if it can be falsified and the remaining postulates can be shown to be consistent. As we shall see in the illustration below, 'pulling a postulate out of its set' can give rise to different conclusions. It was the liberation from Euclid's Fifth Postulate that eventually led to the formation of the non-Euclidean geometries of Lobachevsky and Riemann.

Consider the following exercise taken from *An Introduction to the History of Mathematics, Sixth Edition* by Howard Eves.

Exercise

Bees and hives

Consider the following postulate set, in which *bee* and *hive* are primitive terms:

P1: Every hive is a collection of bees.

P2: Any 2 distinct hives have 1 and only 1 bee in common.

P3: Every bee belongs to 2 and only 2 hives.

P4: There are exactly 4 hives.

a Show that this set of postulates is absolutely consistent.

b Show that postulates P2 and P3 are independent.

c What are some possible theorems that might be deduced?

Hint: *Identify each bee by using a letter of the alphabet (a, b, c etc.). At the same time, start numbering each hive that you use. Proceed by placing each bee in a particular hive until you've satisfied each postulate.*

Possible solutions to this exercise are shown on page 309 in the Appendix.

> *The mathematician is fascinated with the marvellous beauty of the forms he constructs, and in their beauty he finds everlasting truth.*
>
> J.B. Shaw

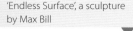
'Endless Surface', a sculpture by Max Bill

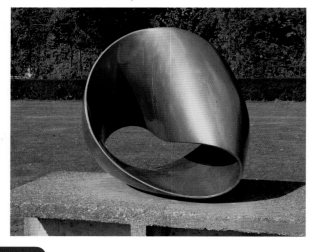

Mathematics, art and culture: knowledge makes strange bedfellows

There is an unlikely yet provocative relationship between mathematics and art. Mathematics opens a window to unique views of the natural world, and artists take advantage of that view. Artists have clearly used mathematics as a theme, as a message and as a focal point of thought. Nickolas Andrew's poem 'Mathematical Thoughts' provides a unique connection between the study of mathematics and TOK (see next page).

Mathematical Thoughts

Degrees become radians,
constructing angles,
but sine law leaves me
two answer tangles.

Proof by induction
steps 1, 2, 3.
3rd step deduction?
You're kidding me!

My dear calculator
all reason removed,
logic eludes me,
what have I proved?

Linear systems
in columns and rows,
matrix solutions
on fingers and toes.

One rabbit plus one rabbit
can make more than two,
goodbye addition
I thought I once knew.

Two drops of water
fall in my hand,
I grasp at the truth,
can I understand?

Rabbits and water,
reshape what I know,
in beauty and truth
new thoughts may now grow.

By Nickolas Andrew

Mathematicians themselves sometimes view their field as an art form. In 1988 David Wells sent a questionnaire to the readers of *The Mathematical Intelligencer* which asked professional mathematicians to rank 24 well-known mathematical knowledge claims according to their aesthetic qualities. The top three results were as follows:

1 $e^{\pi i} = -1$

2 Euler's formula for a polyhedron: $V + F = E + 2$ where $V =$ the number of vertices, $F =$ the number of faces and $E =$ the number of edges.

3 Euclid's proof that the number of primes is infinite.

The aesthetic qualities of a mathematical statement might not be so obvious to the non-mathematician. But then again the wisdom shown in Holbein's painting 'The Ambassadors' or the passion of a poem such as Pablo Neruda's 'If You Forget Me' are usually acquired after skilled teaching and through careful reflection. A recognition of the beauty of a mathematical creation is generally not promoted in the way that conventional artistic appreciation is.

It is argued that mathematical truths are created by people in much the same way that artistic truths are formed. The mathematical process is indeed creative. Refined thought is required and respect for all aspects of nature must be given. Mathematical models and equations are established through the harmonious use of number and pattern. They add structure to the chaos of the world in which we live. Imagination runs deep in mathematics and art, and the resulting messages formed by each represent ideas that could not otherwise be stated.

Philosopher, historian, mathematician and Nobel Prize winner, Bertrand Russell, may have best noted the special qualities of mathematics as art:

> *Mathematics, rightly viewed, possesses not only truth, but supreme beauty – a beauty cold and austere, like that of sculpture, without appeal to any part of our weaker nature, without the gorgeous trappings of painting or music, yet sublimely pure, and capable of a stern perfection such as only the greatest art can show. The true spirit of delight, the exaltation, the sense of being more than Man, which is the touchstone of the highest excellence, is to be found in mathematics as surely as poetry.*
>
> 'The Study of Mathematics' in *Mysticism and Logic, and Other Essays*

You, as the TOK student, must consider the history and richness of different cultures. It comes with the turf of an international education. Mathematics and art are a part of the cultural complexities and intellectual growth that exists for all. This includes everyone from the scholarly Jewish Rabbi to the Vietnamese schoolgirl keen to get her mathematics homework right. Cultures are partially defined by the way they connect to and make use of Areas of Knowledge like mathematics and art. Yet the human understanding from these areas transcends political boundaries, ethnic differences and gender. You will be left to judge the merit of statements like that by Sardar and Ravetz who claim in *Understanding Mathematics* that ethnomathematics is 'the mathematics of all those people who have been excluded from knowledge and cultural production.'

Standard Hebrew Gematria

Gematria is the study of the numerical value of letters and words.

Example: shalom = שלום

שׁ = 300
ל = 30
ו = 6
ם = 40

Value of shalom =
300 + 30 + 6 + 40 = 376

Vietnamese 'Checking the Product'

problem:

16 **a**
× 3 **b**
48 **d**

(1) sum of digits from **a**
1 + 6 = 7

(4) product of (1) and (2)
3 × 7 = 21
and 2 + 1 = **3**

(3) sum of digits from **d**
4 + 8 = 12
and 1 + 2 = **3**

(2) sum of digits from **b** = 3

Assume that your answer is correct when parts (3) and (4) are equal. In this case 3 = 3!

> *Mathematics is a more powerful instrument of knowledge than any other that has been bequeathed to us by human agency.*
>
> René Descartes

Mathematics: the abstract language

It has been argued that mathematics, like the various art forms, exists as a language and serves as a system of symbols and diagrams that can be used to represent ideas not easily expressed by conventional written or spoken words. You are quite familiar with the written numeral '3', and you can easily use it within a mathematical context. But what exactly does 3 mean? Is it important that we understand what the numeral represents?

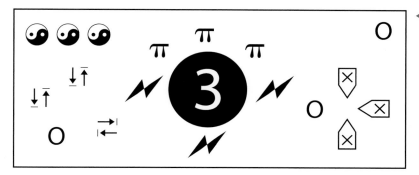

Is the number the common quality of each set of like objects?

A relatively simple mathematical concept can be expressed and used to communicate other ideas with the use of appropriate language. You use common mathematical speak in your day-to-day language in a matter-of-fact sort of way. Simple things like the cost of your MP3 player or the number of CAS hours needed for service can be easily expressed. A pie chart is shown to the Business Management class and a discussion of the per cent of this month's budget spent on food is understood by all.

An abstract concept, albeit as basic as 'the number 1', is common to you and is expressed with clear notation. But the language of mathematics has expanded over time and for many it may appear to become detached from day-to-day common usage. The concept behind the number 1 is abstract but the number itself no doubt has a meaning for you. You use this number on a daily basis and you understand it. On the other hand, the number i is defined to the mathematician as $\sqrt{-1}$, and it may not readily correspond to any particular object or idea in the world external to that of the mathematician's thought process.

However, abstract language is necessary for the mathemetician. In actuality numbers like i, $\pi (\approx 3.1415)$ and $e (\approx 2.7183)$ are not more abstract than the commonly used numbers 0 and 1. They appear in mathematical context and allow the mathematician to think, to communicate, to perform manipulations and to express results in simple and elegant ways. Consequently, abstract thinking does have a way of reducing to simple and strikingly beautiful forms. Consider the truly aesthetic result: $e^{\pi i} = -1$. Reflections on abstract thinking should make you wonder where the knowledge exists.

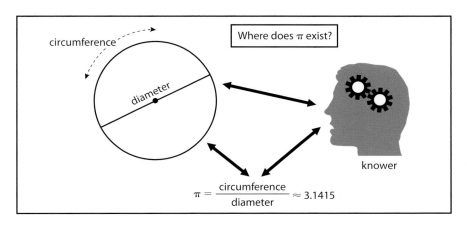

The concept, the symbols and the knower… where is the knowledge of π?

The death of one man is a tragedy. The death of millions is a statistic.
Josef Stalin's comment to Churchill at Potsdam, 1945

Today's world: mathematics and statistics

Various knowledge issues can come into play at practically every level of statistical analysis. Our perception of how information is presented within a context can easily be manipulated by clever use of a diagram scale. Consider the example shown below where two different diagrams represent the growth of earnings made by the Acme Oil Company over a one-year period.

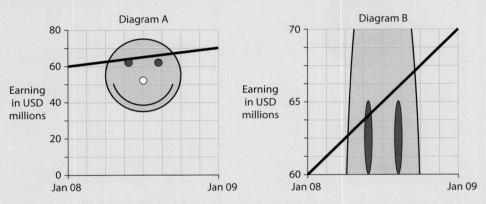

If the Managing Director of Acme Oil shares information concerning growth earnings to his Board of Directors, then which graph might he want to use? What might be his selection if he was to address company customers who complained about recent increases in the price of oil products?

Mathematical terms and concepts can be used to control the way a person thinks about a particular situation. Consider the Fun Sports Shoe Manufacturers who have a payroll consisting of the following:

Fun Sports Shoes – annual salaries:	
Chief Executive Officer (1)	£250,000
Director of Sales and Marketing (1)	£80,000
Director of Distribution (1)	£60,000
Manufacturing Management (2)	£40,000
Manufacturing Labour (20)	£8000

What is the average salary of employees working for Fun Sports Shoes? Average might normally mean the statistical mean, and in this case that would be £25,200 per employee. But it might also refer to one of two other measures of central tendency as well. The median, i.e. the middle score, or the mode, the most frequently occurring score, could also be used as an 'average'. Each of those central tendencies is calculated to be £8000 per employee.

Consider the Healthy Living Drug Company who answered the complaints of male customers worried about the negative side-effects of using a hair-loss treatment. Mr Jones asked the Healthy Living Director, 'How many of your customers aged 30 to 45 have experienced stomach disorders after using the hair-loss treatment?' The Director of the company answered that only 18 customers out of 10000 or 0.18% now using the drug had experienced some problems. Should Mr Jones be concerned? What if it is known that a random selection of 10,000 men aged 30 to 45 would normally experience a mean value of 6.5 stomach disorders (with a standard deviation of 1.2)?

A good TOK class long won't take long to form a list of other statistical methods that could be manipulative. The important point to keep in mind is that any presentation of information, be it mathematical or otherwise, must be carefully examined. A few basic questions should always be kept in mind.

- Who is presenting the information? Does this person or group have any particular motive or bias?
- How has the information been gathered? Has a truly random sample of data or opinion been used?
- Has information been withheld? Does this person or group stand to benefit by not telling 'the whole truth'?
- Has the information been compared to what is normally expected?

Ideal knower

Lord Robert May, Mathematical Biologist and Royal Society Research Professor, Oxford and Imperial College London

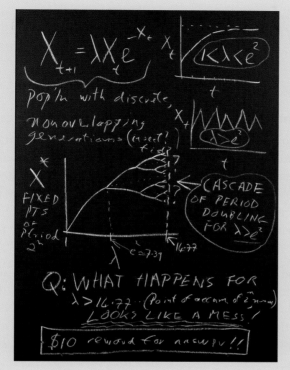

Lord Robert May's blackboard in Sydney University, 1972

Scientists have always struggled to predict the unpredictable. Now a new mathematics shows that we may not be governed by laws of order at all but by rules and patterns of disorder. When we see very complicated behaviour – an insect population fluctuating from year to year or an unpredictable crash in the stock market or wild excursions in the weather as a hurricane blows all the trees down. We tend to think that such complicated phenomena must be the outcome of very complicated causes. We are beginning to learn that very simple laws and equations can generate astonishingly complicated dynamic behaviour – apparently random behaviour which we call *chaos*…

Our world is full of examples – from the flow of a river, the turbulent turning of the atmosphere, the aerodynamic patterns of jet flight… Chaos has even been discovered in space in the strange patterns in Jupiter's atmosphere and the tumbling motion of moons and asteroids. There is chaos in oscillation of electrical circuits, the irregular beating of a transplanted heart, and even in the rigidly determined motion of a simple pendulum.

The bad news is that for all that we may be able to understand patterns that lurk within the apparent randomness, we nonetheless have a barrier to predictability. We have seen that arbitrarily close starting points can lead to trajectories – can lead to behaviour that diverges widely in quite a short time. We can have a simple rule. We can have a simple law. We can have nothing random within the system. Everything is known, and yet we cannot make long term predictions about the future because the fluttering of a butterfly's wings can disturb the initial conditions.

I feel very strongly that the intuition we take away from high school, where we study simple equations that do simple things is a crippling intuition to bring into the world of biology, social sciences, economics… Worlds where the very simplest laws are nonetheless nonlinear. Where two and two do not as it were make four, and where the consequence of those non-linearities are that simple systems behave chaotically. That's an intuition that we need to be armed with.

Lord Robert May speaking in 1988 on the programme *Chaos*,
part of the BBC TV production 'Antenna'

As a TOK student you have the luxury of selecting a topic for your presentation or essay. The unique characteristics of mathematical knowledge can lead you down an interesting road of contrasts and comparisons. Don't hesitate to take such a path.

> *One day Alice came to a fork in the road and saw a Cheshire cat in a tree. 'Which road do I take?' she asked. 'Where do you want to go?' was his response. 'I don't know,' Alice answered. 'Then,' said the cat, 'it doesn't matter.'*
>
> From *Alice's Adventures in Wonderland* by Lewis Carroll

Student presentation

1 **Knowledge claims, mathematics and the world of what's normal** – statistical support for claims made in natural or human science may be based upon the analysis of a data collection that is normally distributed. Such analysis requires the consideration of 'degrees of confidence'. What are the implications of such support? The 'rock solid' reputation of mathematical justification comes into question. What do the mathematicians have to say about the scientist who fails to reject a null hypothesis that is indeed false?

2 **Technology and modelling the natural world mathematically** – an analysis of the role that graphic calculator technology (now required in all IB mathematics courses) plays in modelling natural phenomena. A close look at linear regression analysis and correlation coefficient provides a platform to discuss key TOK terms. What is the validity of the process? Do correlations close to $+1$ or -1 imply causality?

Essay questions

Two recent Prescribed Titles (PTs) include:

1 Is knowledge in mathematics and other Areas of Knowledge dependent on culture to the same degree and in the same ways?

© International Baccalaureate Organization 2004

2 *'... mathematics may be defined as the subject in which we never know what we are talking about, nor whether what we are saying is true'*

From *Mathematics and the Metaphysicians* by B. Russell

Critically assess this assertion. What does it mean? If this is the case, how does mathematics differ from other forms of knowledge?

© International Baccalaureate Organization 1999

Natural science
How is science important?

Science is a tribute to what we can know although we are fallible.

Jacob Bronowksi

Science is much closer to myth than scientific philosophy is prepared to admit.

Paul Feyerabend

You have grown up in an environment that has led you to believe that modern science is the only sensible way to understand the workings of nature. Or have you? Have you grown up at a time when science is losing credibility as a way of understanding our world? Would your answer depend on which part of the world you have grown up in? Would you have written the same response some years ago, as you would today to the TOK question, 'Do you believe that science is the supreme form of knowledge?' How would you go about answering such a question?

We will examine opposing views about these issues later in the chapter. However, the IB and all national educational systems take the view that it is important to study science; but to what purpose? Is it to build up a store of knowledge about the world and a set of useful explanations for what happens in the physical and natural world or, in a small number of cases, to prepare you to become a scientist? The creators of the TOK course believed that this is not sufficient. It is more important that you can make critical judgements about the extent to which you can rely on what scientists tell you. Look at the extract in the box below from the United Nations Environment Programme.

> Climate change is one of the most critical global challenges of our time. Recent events have emphatically demonstrated our growing vulnerability to climate change. Climate change impacts will range from affecting agriculture, further endangering food security, sea-level rise and the accelerated erosion of coastal zones, increasing intensity of natural disasters, species extinction and the spread of vector-borne diseases.

This is a very strong scientific statement; notice that it tells you that recent events have 'emphatically demonstrated' and that it makes important predictions about the future that will have a very significant impact on the quality of your life in the years ahead. But, on what evidence is this statement made and how do the predictions follow from the evidence? If you are to believe the statement and, perhaps, to decide what actions you should take as a result of your belief, do you need to do more than simply accept this as the truth? Do you need to understand the process at work here, the way the evidence was gathered and the bases upon which the evidence was used to make predictions about the impact of climate change? If you do not, how do you make sense of issues such as the one that the following BBC headline raises?

> **Climate science: sceptical about bias**
>
> Of all the accusations made by the vociferous community of climate sceptics, surely the most damaging is that science itself is biased against them.
>
> Richard Black, BBC, 14 November 2007

> **Exercise**
>
> What message is the BBC correspondent giving here? What does he mean when he says that an allegation made against science is that science itself is biased? Can science, as an Area of Knowledge be biased? Does he mean that those scientists who present evidence for climate change are biased?

We have looked briefly at a contemporary issue in which science and, of course, scientists, are involved. It raises issues that are not remote nor academic; instead, they concern matters that are of considerable relevance to our lives. In order to understand the reliability of the predictions made about climate change, do you need an insight into the way science works? Do you need to clarify what a scientist means when he or she says something is a 'fact'; that the evidence upon which an explanation is based is reliable and the extent to which you can trust a scientific explanation?

Should a science be compulsory in the IB?

Read the extract below which argues why science should be taught effectively in British schools. Think about your own science classes and ask yourself whether the way you are learning science will make you less gullible, particularly to the claims of advertisers.

Should a science be compulsory in your IB?

Whenever you read a newspaper, watch television or walk past a billboard, you cannot escape advertising. You are told that this cream will remove teenage pimples, that this oil will clean the engine of a motorbike or that these tablets will reduce the stress as you study hard for your final examinations and that you can be sure that there will be no harmful side-effects. You will certainly be able to think of many more examples and as you do, ask yourself what was it about the advertising that made you buy a certain product. In fact, did you even stop to think about what was being claimed or did you just accept the claim?

But what has this to do with learning science? Well, ask yourself: What sort of questions should I ask before I accept the claims made by the advertisement? How can I be reasonably sure that the product will be effective and what, for example, might the harmful side-effects be? Think about your own science classes and ask yourself whether the way you are learning science will make it less easy for you to be misled, particularly by the claims of advertisers. Do you agree that at least one science subject should be part of your own IB programme?

Is this a sufficient argument for requiring that you take at least one science subject as part of your own IB programme?

Exercise

What do you think science is?

Look at the list of statements below. For each one state whether you agree, disagree or whether you are not sure about the statement. As you move on through the chapter, you can then check what you think now against what you read. Ask yourself at each stage whether what you are reading confirms what you think now, whether it clarifies what you think or whether you disagree with what you are reading.

Statement	Agree	Disagree	Not sure
1 Scientific knowledge is based solely on observation.			
2 As scientific knowledge progresses, it gets nearer to the truth.			
3 A subject is not a science unless you can do experiments in it.			
4 Science is about making explanations of the world around us.			

Statement	Agree	Disagree	Not sure
5 There is no such thing as scientific proof.			
6 Science is about finding out things that have not been known before.			
7 There is such a thing as 'the scientific method'.			
8 Biology, chemistry and physics are separate subjects.			
9 Scientific thinking is more about deduction than induction.			
10 No one can be both scientific and religious.			
11 Copernicus showed that Ptolemy was wrong.			
12 The theory of evolution by natural selection is 'just a theory'.			
13 Economics is a science.			
14 Language is not very important to scientific knowledge.			
15 Einstein proved that Newton was wrong.			
16 Scientific thinking is a kind of thinking that occurs in all cultures around the world.			
17 Scientists should not be held responsible for the uses to which their discoveries are put.			
18 The methods of the scientist are totally different to those of the mathematician.			
19 A scientist is under no obligation to share his knowledge with the public.			
20 History is not a science.			
21 There is nothing in common between the methods of the scientist and those of the artist.			
22 All technology is based on science.			

How does science work?

Science: organised, systematic enterprise that gathers knowledge about the world and condenses the knowledge into testable laws.

Edward O. Wilson, Professor in Entomology at Harvard University

Anyone who has listened to a small child knows that 'What?' and 'Why?' are among the first words that people use as they begin to speak. 'Man', says Daniel Boorstin, 'is the asking animal.' Whatever culture we grow up in, and whichever language environment we live in, we all seem to be questioners from an early age. Curiosity and the need to verbalise our questions seem to be human instincts. We observe the world around us and ask the question, Why is it like that? When we do, do we ever add a second question, Why is it like what? If you do this, you have taken a step from casual to more systematic **observation**. Systematic observation reveals facts that our curiosity seeks to explain, or evidence that might support an explanation that we already accept.

 Observation An observation is a scientific fact when, under the same set of conditions, anyone, anywhere and at any time ,will record it in the same way.

Curiosity does not end with a collection of observations. Why not? Why do we require an explanation for what we observe? Can you list the number of different ways in which you try to explain what you see of the world around you and what is happening? Do you consider any of them to count as a scientific explanation; on what grounds? Try to apply what you think makes an explanation scientific to the way that the Greek philosopher, Thales of Miletus, accounted for the regular movement of the stars across the night sky over 2500 years ago.

Thales's explanation for the regular movement of the stars across the night sky. Do you think that this qualifies as a scientific explanation or what we can call a scientific hypothesis?

Scientific hypothesis
Fits the observed facts *and* enables testable predictions to be made.

The eternal fire that burns beyond the bowl of night and day.

The bowl of night and day that holds in place the seas surrounding the land.

'Windows' in the bowl of night and day through which you see glimpses of the eternal fire.

Certainly, Thales's idea of an unseen hand turning the bowl of night and day seems far from what we expect of such an explanation. There is one feature, however, that does match a modern requirement of a **scientific hypothesis**: we can put it to the test. We can ask whether or not it fits the observed facts. When we do, we find that, for most of the pinpoints of light that appear to move across the night sky, it certainly fits the facts. However, careful and systematic observation reveals new facts: a small number of pinpoints of light that do not move in great circles, night after night. The ancient world knew of this and the Greeks called them 'wanderers', *planetos*, from which the word 'planet' derives. These objects, looking to the naked eye like all the other lights, follow a quite different motion that Thales's hypothesis simply cannot account for.

November 1 / July 1 / June 1 / Ecliptic / Aquarius / October 1 / Capricornus / August 1 / September 1 / Pisces Austrinus / Microscopium

What is it about the observed path of Mars across the night sky over a six month period that Thales's explanation cannot account for?

Whatever other reasons we might have for not accepting Thales's explanation as scientific, it fails the most basic test: it does not fit the observed facts. But is this all that is expected from a scientific hypothesis: that it provides a reasonable explanation of the observed facts? Of equal, and practical, importance is the ability to predict the outcome of future action on the basis of the hypothesis. We will examine this in more detail in the next section.

© International Baccalaureate Organization

What do you really observe?

You also make observations when you carry out experiments and you record data; but what do you actually see? When you are measuring a temperature or recording the value of an electric current, ask yourself, What am I really seeing and recording? How does this correspond to what is actually happening in the experiment? What comparisons can you make with the extract from an article called 'In the Mind's Eye' in the box on the next page?

I am continually amazed at the confidence with which physicists claim to 'see' particles that effervesce into existence for a mere billionth of a second, or quasars teetering 12 billion light-years away at the very brink of space and time. I know, for a fact, that they have seen no such thing. At best, they have seen a bump on a curve plotting the ratio of various kinds of particles produced in a nuclear collision; more often, their sightings are conclusions laboriously drawn from long hours of computer calculations and long chains of assumptions and inferences. Hardly the sort of thing to inspire an exultant 'Eureka!' (or even 'Land, Ho!'). Sometimes the things scientists see are so far removed from actual quarks or quasars that one wonders if they (or we) should believe their eyes.

Of course, the way we go about seeing things in our everyday lives is scarcely more direct. I see my typewriter because rapidly oscillating electrons in the filament of the light bulb overhead are sending out streams of photons, some of which collide (as in an atom smasher) with the molecules on the surface of the typewriter and are rapidly re-emitted in the direction of my eyes. Those that penetrate the pupil are focused onto a light-sensitive screen (the retina), which passes along information about their energies, frequencies, and trajectories to the brain in the form of electrical signals. On the basis of laborious calculations and long chains of inferences and assumptions, the brain concludes that the light patterns represent something hard and cool and heavy and solid that translates passing thoughts into printed words.

From 'In the Mind's Eye' by K.C. Cole, published in *Discover*, April 1985

Exercise

• Try to set up your own model of the scientific method as a flow chart. Consider the following key words and phrases that relate to the formation of scientific knowledge. Cite a particular example from your experience with IB science that makes use of this model.

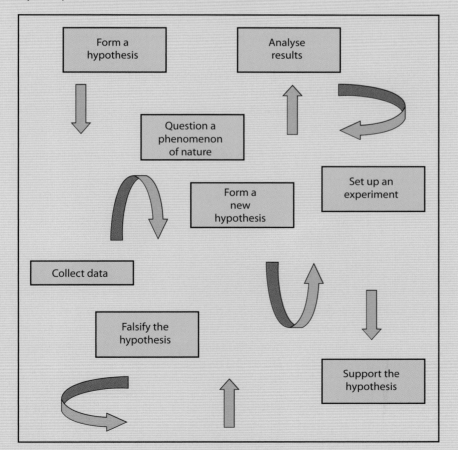

Elements used in a model of the formation of scientific knowledge

• Keep a copy of your model so that you can compare it with the other models that you will encounter as you continue in this chapter.

What are scientific laws?

What do you understand by a law? Is it a rule that you are required to follow? This type of law is the one you encounter in daily life. However, unlike the laws of the land, scientific laws are not rules to be obeyed. Look at the two scientific laws in the box below; you may have come across these in physics. Ask yourself what they are telling you and then compare your own ideas with the paragraph after the box.

Boyle's Law

The volume (V) of a fixed mass of gas is inversely proportional to the pressure (P) exerted on it when the temperature of the gas remains constant.

$$V = \frac{k}{P} \text{ where } k \text{ is a constant}$$

Newton's Second Law

The acceleration (a) of an object of fixed mass moves in proportion to the unbalanced force (F) acting on it and inversely in proportion to its mass (m) for the same unbalanced force.

$$a \propto \frac{F}{m}$$

Notice that in both cases, the 'law' is a precise mathematical description of the relationship between quantities such as volume, pressure, force, mass and acceleration that can be measured with considerable precision and that can be defined clearly. Notice, also, that in both cases, the conditions under which the relationship exists are set out. Do you think that this law gives an explanation of how gravity acts? Think how you would explain to a friend why the pen that you are holding falls towards the ground when you let it go; imagine that your friend has never heard about the law of gravitation.

Look at the next box, which is a statement of Newton's Universal Law of Gravitation.

Newton's Universal Law of Gravitation

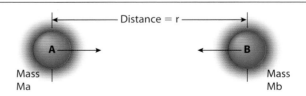

Newton's Universal Law of Gravitation describes the force acting between any two objects A and B in the diagram above. If A has a mass Ma and B has a mass Mb and their centres of mass are a distance, 'r', apart, then there is a mutual force of attraction between them that is proportional to the product of the two masses and inversely proportional to the square of the distance between them.

This force, called 'gravity', keeps us firmly on the surface of the Earth and is the same force that keeps the Earth in its orbit around the Sun, so we have an explanation of both these observations. Or do we? Look at how Newton himself expressed this:

> *Hitherto we have explained the phenomena of the heavens and of our sea by the power of gravity, but have not yet assigned the cause of this power.*

How does your explanation sit against this statement? Did you simply use the term 'force of gravity' to explain why the pen fell? By giving a name to an observed force, have you explained how the force of gravity acts? In fact, you may have used a classic circular argument in your explanation:

Question: What made the pen fall?

Answer: Gravity.

Question: So what is gravity?

Answer: It's what the made the pen fall!

Newton's Law of Universal Gravitation tells us with mathematical precision how the various quantities are connected, but it has not explained the mechanism by which the force of gravity acts. Nonetheless, physical laws such as the law of gravitation are so reliable and precise that they enabled scientists and engineers to design the equipment that landed men on the Moon and brought them safely back to Earth again.

What is a scientific theory?

After talking about hypotheses as scientific explanations that fit the observed facts and that enable predictions to be made, you will have noticed in the previous section that the word 'theory' was introduced. So what is it, if anything, that distinguishes a scientific theory from a scientific hypothesis? The simplest distinction is that a theory is simply a well-tested hypothesis. Usually, however, when an explanation takes on the status of a theory, it does so because it explains a wide range of phenomena on the basis of a small number of key ideas. This type of explanation is very common in science. The next box gives a very good example of a well-known theory that uses **reductionist thinking**. Before you go onto the following paragraph ask yourself what is the key to this sort of explanation.

Reductionist thinking
A form of explanation based on the belief that a complex system can be understood by reducing it to combinations of simpler systems. The atomic theory is a good example of a reductionist explanation.

Atomic theory

The chemical properties of all of the known elements are accounted for by the theory that they are all made up of atoms and that their atoms are themselves made up of different combinations of just three particles: the proton, the neutron and the electron.

In the atomic theory, the incredible variety of the elements is reduced to the different combinations of the three particles that make up their atoms. This is, in fact, a further reduction of the way that chemistry explains the amazing complexity and variety of all of the materials: living or non-living; solid, liquid or gas, that make up our natural world. This multitude of different substances is reduced to the various combinations of the 93 naturally-occurring elements. It is known as 'reductionist thinking' and it will be examined in more detail later in the chapter. However, before we do that, look carefully at the following case study. Consider how your own model of scientific enquiry matches the ways in which the search for the cause of the problem was conducted. Do any of them match your own model?

The scientific method in action: a case study

As a simple illustration of some important aspects of scientific enquiry, let us consider Ignaz Semmelweis's work on childbed fever. He was a physician on the staff of the Vienna General Hospital from 1844 to 1848 and was disturbed to find that a large number of women were dying of puerperal, or 'childbed' fever. Oddly enough, the majority of cases were confined to the First Maternity Division where the death rate was 11.4 per cent of the patients. In the adjacent Second Division, the mortality rate was much lower: 2.7 per cent. In a book he wrote later on the causes and prevention of the illness, Semmelweis describes his efforts to resolve the dreadful puzzle.

He began by considering various explanations that were current at the time. Some of these he rejected out of hand; others he subjected to specific tests.

One widely accepted view held that the fever was due to 'epidemic influences' which were vaguely described as spreading over the whole city. But how, Semmelweis reasoned, could such influences have plagued the First Division for years and yet spared the Second? How could the fever rage in the hospital while hardly a case occurred elsewhere in Vienna or its surroundings? A genuine epidemic such as cholera would not be so selective.

In addition, Semmelweis noted that some of the women admitted to the First Division who lived far from the hospital had been overcome by labour on their way and had given birth in the street. Yet, despite these unsanitary and adverse conditions, the death rate for the 'street births' was lower than the average for the First Division.

Another view held that overcrowding could be the cause of the high incidence of mortality. However, Semmelweis pointed out that, in fact, the crowding was heavier in the Second Division; partly because patients were so desperate to avoid the notorious First Division. He also rejected two similar conjectures that were current by observing that there were no differences between the two Divisions with regard to diet or general care of the patients.

He next investigated the charges that the illness and deaths were due to injuries from rough examinations by the medical students, all of whom received their training in the First Division. Semmelweis noted that: (a) the injuries as a result of examinations were far less than those resulting from the natural process of birth itself and (b) the midwives who received their training in the Second Division examined their patients in much the same manner but without ill effect. Nevertheless, even when the number of examinations by medical students was reduced to a minimum, the mortality rate did not decrease.

Various psychological explanations were now attempted. One of them noted that the First Division was so arranged that a priest bearing the last sacraments to a dying woman had to pass through the First Division before reaching the sickroom beyond. The appearance of the priest accompanied by the attendant's bell-ringing was said to either 'scare women to death', or make them more likely victims of the fever. In the Second Division, this factor was absent. Semmelweis decided to test this conjecture. He persuaded the priest to come by another route and without ringing the bell, but the mortality in the First Division did not decrease.

A new idea was suggested to Semmelweis by the observation that, in the First Division, the women were delivered lying on their backs; in the Second, on their sides. Though he thought it unlikely, he decided to test whether this difference was significant. He introduced the lateral position in the First Division, but again the mortality remained unaffected.

At last, early in 1847, an accident gave Semmelweis the decisive clue for his solution to the problem. A colleague of his, Jakob Kolletschka, received a puncture wound in the finger from the scalpel of a student with whom he was performing an autopsy. Kolletschka died after an agonizing illness during which he displayed the same symptoms that had been observed in the victims of childbed fever. Although at the time the role of micro-organisms, 'germs', in such infections had not yet been recognised, Semmelweis realised that 'cadaveric matter' from the scalpel had entered Kolletschka's bloodstream and caused his death. The similarities between the course of Kolletschka's disease and that of the women in his clinic led Semmelweis to conclude that his patients had died of the same kind of blood poisoning. He, his colleagues and the medical students had been carriers of the infectious material for they used to come to the wards directly from performing dissections in the autopsy room. Their normal routine was to examine the women in labour only after a superficial washing of their hands.

Again, Semmelweis put his idea to a test. He reasoned that, if he were right, then childbed fever could be prevented by chemically destroying the infectious material which clung to their hands. He issued an order requiring all medical students to wash their hands in a solution of chlorinated lime before making an examination. The mortality from childbed fever promptly began to decrease and, for the year 1848, it fell to 1.27 per cent in the First Division compared to 1.33 per cent in the Second.

In further support of this hypothesis, Semmelweis noted that it accounted for the fact that the mortality in the Second Division consistently was so much lower; midwives whose work did not include performing autopsies attended the patients there.

The hypothesis also explained the lower mortality among 'street births'. Women who arrived with babies in their arms were rarely examined after admission and thus had a better chance of escaping infection.

Similarly, the hypothesis accounted for the fact that the newborn babies who died of the fever were all among those whose mothers had contracted the disease during labour. For then, the infection could be transmitted to the baby before birth through the common bloodstream of mother and child, whereas this was impossible when the mother remained healthy.

So far, the hypothesis fitted the known facts, but further clinical experience soon led Semmelweis to broaden his hypothesis. On one occasion, for example, he and his associates, having carefully disinfected their hands, examined a woman in labour who was suffering from a festering cervical cancer. They then proceeded to examine 12 other women in the same room after only casual washing. Eleven of the 12 patients died of the fever. Semmelweis concluded that childbed fever can be caused not only by cadaveric material, but also by 'putrid' matter from living organisms.

Testing the hypothesis

We have seen how, in his search for the cause of the fever, Semmelweis examined various hypotheses that had been suggested as possible answers. How such hypotheses are arrived at in the first place is an intriguing question which we shall consider later. First, however, let us examine how a hypothesis, once proposed, is tested.

Sometimes, the procedure is quite direct. For instance, in the case study above, the difference in diet, crowding or general care could be easily and directly measured. Since there were no differences between the divisions, the hypotheses were rejected as false. No further experimentation was required.

However, usually, the test will be less simple and straightforward. Take the hypothesis about the priest and his attendant. The intensity of that fear and its effect upon the patients were not so clear. Thus, an experiment was set up. Semmelweis reasoned that, if the hypothesis were true, then a change in the priest's route should be followed by a decline in fatalities. He checked this implication and found it false and so rejected the hypothesis. Similarly, to test the idea about the lateral delivery position, he reasoned if this hypothesis were true, then a change in position of delivery would reduce mortality. Again, this was not borne out by the experiment and the idea was discarded.

In the last two cases, the tests are based on the argument that, if the hypothesis (H) is true, then certain events (I) will follow. These events are called 'test implications' of the (H) and are implied by or inferred from (H). Briefly, if (H) is true, then so is (I). In the last two examples, the (I) did not follow, so the (H) was rejected. The reasoning that led to the rejection may be schematised as follows:

If (H) is true, then so is (I).	$p \rightarrow q$
But, as evidence shows, (I) is not true.	not q
Therefore, (H) is not true.	therefore not p

Any argument of this form (called 'modus tollens') is valid. That is, when the premises are true, then the conclusion must be true also. The first premise asserts that it is never the case that (H) occurs and (I) does not follow. Thus, if the premises are properly established, the (H) being tested must be rejected, because (I) does not follow. As a premise, it is false.

Next, let us look at the hypothesis when the test implication *is* borne out. From the (H) that childbed fever is produced by cadaveric matter, Semmelweis inferred (I) that strong antiseptic measures would reduce the fatalities from the disease. This time, the (I) is shown to occur. Mortality declines. What does this mean with regard to the (H)? Does this make (H) true? Not necessarily, for the underlying argument would have this form:

If (H) is true, then so is (I).	$p \rightarrow q$
As the evidence shows, (I) is true.	q
Therefore, (H) is true.	therefore p

So far so good, but this mode of reasoning is deductively invalid. It commits the fallacy of the converse. This means that the conclusion may be false even if the premises are true. This is, in fact, exactly what happened to Semmelweis. The original version of his (H) assumed that cadaveric matter was the one and only source of the fever. He was right in reasoning that if this (H) should be true, then (I) would be true and the test confirmed it. So, both premises were true. However, the (H) as envisioned was false, for, as he later discovered, putrid material from living organisms could also cause childbed fever.

To make the point clear with reference to the fallacy, consider the following example. Suppose you make the conditional statement, 'If I lose weight, then my mother will worry'. If (H), then (I). Sure enough, when I lose weight, my mother does worry. It is true as a matter of fact and the argument is valid. However, here I have affirmed the antecedent, not the consequent.

If (H), then (I)	$p \rightarrow q$
(H)	p
(I)	q

Suppose I affirm the consequent and say, 'It's true, my mother is worrying'. Can you then say that since my mother is worrying, I must be losing weight? How many things, however, cause my mother to worry: failing exams, being late for lunch, watching too much television, etc. Any number of (H)s could lead to the same (I) and, conversely, (I) may occur even if none of the conditions of (H) are met.

Thus, the favourable outcome of a test does not prove the hypothesis to be true. Even if many (I)s have been borne out by careful testing, the (H) is not conclusive. It may still be false.

However, we should not be led to think that we are no better off than if we had not tested at all. We learn something either way – no matter what the outcome. Suppose from a test we obtain 'unfavourable' results. That might force us to reject the hypothesis. We learn from our failures as well as from our successes and the only way to know is to test.

On the other hand, when we obtain 'favourable' results, we are encouraged to continue our investigation along those lines even if those results do not give final and complete 'proof'. They, at least, provide some support and partial confirmation for an idea. How much support and to what degree often depend on how the hypothesis and the testing are set up. However, that is another problem!

Exercise

What counts as worthy of scientific investigation? Read the account below about the science of umbrellaology. Take a stance on this: you do not accept that umbrellaology should be accepted as a science. As you read the article, jot down the reasons that you think disqualify umbrellaology from being regarded as a science. How would you respond, as the editor of a reputable science magazine, to each of the arguments that the writer puts forward? Why do you regard the study of umbrella use as not worth investigating?

For the past 18 years, assisted by a few faithful disciples, I have been collecting materials on a subject hitherto almost wholly neglected by scientists – the umbrella. The results of my investigations to date are embodied in the nine volumes which I am sending to you under a separate cover. Pending their receipt, let me describe to you briefly the nature of their contents and the method I pursued in compiling them. I began in the borough of Islington. Proceeding street by street, house by house, family by family, and individual by individual, I ascertained:

1 the number of umbrellas possessed
2 their size
3 their weight
4 their colour.

Having covered Islington after many years, I eventually extended the survey to the other boroughs of London, and at length completed the entire city. Thus I was ready to carry forward the work to the rest of England and indeed the rest of the UK and the whole known world.

It was at this point that I approached my erstwhile friend. I am a modest man, but I felt I had the right to be recognized as the creator of a new science. He, on the other hand, claimed that umbrellaology was not a science at all. First, he said, it was silly to investigate umbrellas. Now this argument is false, because science scorns not to deal with any object, however humble and lowly, even to the 'hind leg of a flea.' Then why not umbrellas? Next, he said that umbrellaology could not be recognized as a science because it was of no use or benefit to mankind. But is not the truth the most precious thing in life? Are not my nine volumes filled with the truth about my subject? Every word in them is true. Every sentence contains a hard, cold fact. When he asked me what was the object of umbrellaology I was proud to say, 'To see and discover the truth is object enough for me.' I am a pure scientist; I have no ulterior motives. Hence it follows that I am satisfied with truth alone. Next he said my truths were dated and that any one of my findings might cease to be true tomorrow.

From 'Umbrellaology' by J. Sommerville

Has science remained the same throughout history?

What now satisfies our curiosity and so counts as a good, scientific explanation has not been the same throughout history. In some cases, what is seen to be a problem by today's scientists was not thought to be a problem in past times. It is often firmly held views that are simply assumed to be true (and, because of this, that are not questioned) which determine the questions that are asked and the way in which answers are sought. In ancient Greece, for example, it was possible to hold two contradictory accounts of the motions of the planets. One fitted the observed facts but made no physical explanation; the other provided a physical explanation for the way things appeared to behave but did not fit the observed facts. For example, the Greek philosopher Aristotle sought to provide a physical explanation of the way the physical world works, but never considered it important to put this to any sort of experimental test. He believed that thought alone was the way to the truth about the world. On the other hand, the Alexandrian astronomer, Claudius Ptolemy, devised geometrical descriptions of the motion of the planets that fitted the observed facts, but did not give any physical explanation for why his model worked.

Moreover, Aristotle's physical explanation is at odds with what we now regard as common sense. We take it for granted that there is only one set of explanations and that only one set of scientific laws operates throughout the universe. Aristotle did not do this. He divided the universe as he knew it into two zones: the earthly zone and the heavenly zone. The orbit of the moon separated the universe into two realms, the celestial and the terrestrial. In the two regions, the properties of substances were different. Ask yourself, 'To what extent are my assumptions about what counts for a good scientific explanation based on the way I am taught about the workings of science today?'

The way Aristotle explained the natural world raises another issue. The facts have not changed, yet our explanations of them have and the assumptions that are made in order to make these explanations have certainly changed.

Can science escape from history? Are scientific explanations rather more linked to the nature of the society that we, and of course scientists, live in? Look at the quote below by a theoretical physicist called Lee Smolin who is now working at the frontier of research. He is talking about the scientific ideas of Isaac Newton and René Descartes, two of the most eminent scientists, and of John Locke and Hobbes, two equally eminent philosophers of the sixteenth and early seventeenth centuries and whose thinking has had a major impact on the way we think today.

> *It cannot be a coincidence that the view of the universe invented by Newton and Descartes resembled to a remarkable degree the ideal society as envisaged by Locke and Hobbes; atoms moving individually, their properties defined by their relationship to a fixed and absolute structure that is identified with God via absolute and immutable laws that apply equally to all.*
>
> From *The Life of the Cosmos* by Lee Smolin

Lee Smolin, a theoretical physicist working at the frontier of research

At that time, some 300 to 400 years ago, the ideal for European society bore a close resemblance to this view. It is called a *deistic view* and it states that, in the beginning, God created matter, space and time and the unchanging laws by which all observed changes take place. Once set into motion, the whole future of the universe is set; its original state determines its entire future.

At the dawn of time was written what the last day of reckoning shall read.

From the Rubaiyat of Omar Khayyam, translated by Edward Fitzgerald

In this sort of universe, human society mirrors the behaviour of the physical world. People move individually but according to properties defined by their relationship to God. Lee Smolin contrasts this view of society to that of the rigid hierarchical feudal society it replaced. In doing so, he similarly contrasts the universe of Descartes and Newton with that of Aristotle and the mediaeval thinkers, each a mirror of its own society. The quote below from *The Life of the Cosmos* states his argument clearly.

Both medieval and Aristotelian cosmologies were based on a hierarchical view of a fixed and finite universe, with different layers composed of different essences governed by different laws, with the Earth at its centre and the highest levels connected directly to God.

Exercise

To what extent do your own attempts to make sense of your life depend on your personal experience of the world around you? Do you think that scientists are equally captives of their own times? To what extent do contemporary scientists generalise their own experience of today's society? Can scientists escape from only carrying out experiments in the direction that current theory directs them? To what extent is currently accepted theory an expression of the state of present human society?

What role do assumptions play?

When you try to explain something, where do you begin? Remember the way that explanations of the movement of objects in the night sky changed between the time of Thales and that of Ptolemy. You may need to look back at page 156 to check this. Ask yourself what was taken for granted, or assumed, in each of the explanations. Do you have to make assumptions or do you simply take certain things for granted when you make any explanation? Could it be that in certain cases you do not even know what you are assuming?

As a case study, look at the dispute between two great natural philosophers of the seventeenth century, Isaac Newton and Gottfried Leibniz, about the nature of space. Newton's view is the one that is easiest for us to understand. This is because it is what we have been taught, formally and informally, since early childhood. In this view, space exists independently of us as observers. Objects, from the very smallest to the very largest, are located in space and this is empty and absolutely at rest. After all, if space is nothing, then it cannot have any properties such as movement. Even as Newton proposed this idea, it was challenged by Leibniz who argued that space cannot be something in itself if it cannot be observed. He put forward the notion that it does not make sense to invent something that is not needed to provide an explanation. This is known as **the principle of sufficient reason**. All we can observe, said Leibniz, are objects and the effects that they have on one another. Our explanations should be based only on what can be observed.

The principle of sufficient reason This states that anything that happens does so for a definite reason.

These two views, the absolute of Newton and the relational of Leibniz, are central to efforts to make sense of the world and they provide different outcomes. In the Newtonian view, the universe is made up of very many identical objects, the fundamental particles. These objects have had their properties since the dawn of time,

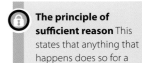

or in a modern view, since shortly after the Big Bang. The properties do not change with time. The particles move in empty space, and it is in the many ways in which the particles are arranged that the universe is given its complex structure. According to the relational view put forward by Leibniz, the complexity of the universe arises from the fact that it is the interaction between the particles that is fundamental. The universe is a vast, interconnected system of relations.

There is a serious problem, in fact, in ascribing fixed properties to the fundamental particles. It arises from the very nature of the explanation that the world is built up of different combinations of a few different basic particles that themselves have no constituent parts. As we have seen, this type of explanation is called reductionism, and it is very successful. Think of the way modern chemistry is able to explain the enormous variety of natural substances in terms of the combination of just 93 naturally occurring elements and to explain these elements in terms of the combination of just three particles which make up their constituent atoms. The problem is that, when you explain the properties of anything in terms of its constituent parts, how do you explain the properties of the fundamental particles that have no constituent parts? The question then becomes, 'From where did these particles acquire their properties, and why do they have the values that they have?' As yet, there is no answer to these questions.

How does science progress?

Despite the fact that scientific theories may well reflect the society around them, science does make progress. You have only to step back for a moment and look at the achievements of science over the past 100 years to see how much has been accomplished. It is difficult to imagine that, just over 100 years ago, the great Austrian physicist Ludwig Boltzmann committed suicide while on holiday in a small north Italian seaside village that now hosts an IB school; he did so because his ideas about the atomic theory were not accepted by his colleagues.

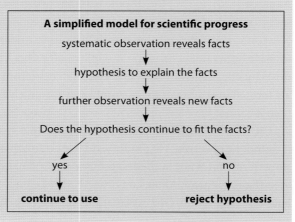

Exercise

- In the last 100 years, much progress has been made by science – but in what manner? Is it possible for us to develop a model to describe the progress of science?

- Look at the simple model opposite and compare it with the model that you have already developed. What are the similarities and what are the differences between them? Do either of them account for scientific progress or do they both raise more questions than they answer?

- List the issues that you think both models raise. You should compare these with the different explanations of scientific progress that you will meet later in this chapter.

A simplified model for scientific progress

systematic observation reveals facts
↓
hypothesis to explain the facts
↓
further observation reveals new facts
↓
Does the hypothesis continue to fit the facts?

yes / no

continue to use / **reject hypothesis**

Let us look at just one aspect of the simple model above, 'Does the hypothesis fit the facts?' and ask, first of all, What if it does not? What comes next – is the old hypothesis simply thrown out of the window?

If you look back at attempts to explain the motions of objects moving through the night sky, we can see what happens. Remember that Thales's model could not account for the observed motions of the planets. Over the centuries that followed, several increasingly successful attempts were made, culminating in the work of Ptolemy over 2000 years ago.

A simple diagrammatic representation of Ptolemy's model is shown below. Look at it carefully and compare it with Thales's model on page 156. Ask yourself, What has changed and what remains the same? Compare your answers with those given in the next paragraph.

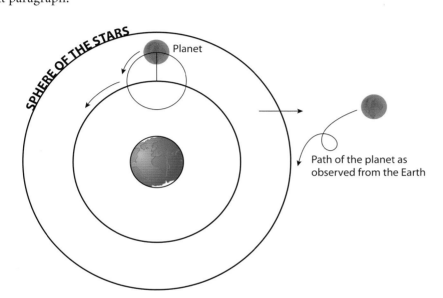

Ptolemy's description of the observed motion of a planet through the night sky

In both cases, you will see that the Earth remains at the centre of the universe, all heavenly motions follow circular paths and the universe is of finite size bounded by the sphere of stars. The details have changed and a much closer fit has been made for the wandering motion of the planets but certain basic assumptions remain unchanged and unchallenged. Much of scientific activity has always occurred in this way and it still does. Thomas Kuhn, the American philosopher of science whose ideas we will meet shortly, calls it 'normal science'.

The search for simplicity

Does science always progress by keeping the same set of often-unchallenged assumptions, simply making modifications to the basic design? Obviously not, because we do not share with past ages the same assumptions about the universe or about the nature of matter nor of what counts as a scientific explanation. What else has been a motive for change? Perhaps you might get an insight into this from the quotation below. This was made in the twelfth century by Alphonse the Wise, who was then King of Castile, and it is about the Ptolemaic explanation of the motion of the planets.

> *If God had asked me before he built the Universe, I would have suggested something simpler.*

Perhaps this was in Copernicus's mind in 1513 when he took a different step forward in science by challenging one of the basic assumptions upon which all previous attempts to explain the movement of objects through the night sky had been based. He shifted the point of view from an Earth-centred to a Sun-centred universe. He did not do so lightly, for Copernicus himself was a great admirer of Ptolemy. His need for elegance and simplicity of explanation must have outweighed not only this but major physical considerations as well. If the Earth moves, how is it, for example, that objects fall vertically to the Earth's surface?

The fact that objects fall straight towards the Earth and that birds and other flying objects are not left behind seemed at odds with the idea of a moving Earth. In fact, have you ever wondered why, when you are in a fast-moving car, the fly that keeps buzzing around your head keeps up with the car when it is not attached to it? Most importantly, however, Copernicus did not have a physical theory to replace that of Aristotle and this was a major problem. If the Earth moved, then it was simply another planet and this implied that the Earth and the other planets were made of the same material. Yet the heart of Aristotle's explanation of the behaviour of objects on Earth and those beyond the Moon's orbit was that they are made up of different materials. This challenge to the accepted framework of explanation is what Thomas Kuhn called, in a highly influential book written in 1962 called *The Structure of Scientific Revolutions*, 'the onset of a scientific revolution'.

Earth does not move and the weight falls on the man.

Earth moves so the weight falls behind the man.

▲ One of the reasons for believing that the Earth did not move was the observed behaviour of falling objects

Thomas Kuhn and paradigm shifts

You may recall the description on pages 121–2 of Thomas Kuhn's theory of the way science can change through revolutionary shifts in the basic concepts that underpin a whole set of explanations. In the extract below, Kuhn's own words set out very clearly his view of the importance of a scientific revolution on the scientific community.

> … the historian of science may be tempted to exclaim that when paradigms change, the world itself changes with them. Led by a new paradigm, scientists adopt new instruments and look in new places. Even more important, during revolutions scientists see new and different things when looking with familiar instruments in places they have looked before. It is rather as if the professional community had been suddenly transported to a different planet where familiar objects are seen in a different light…
>
> From *The Structure of Scientific Revolutions* by Thomas Kuhn

The social impact of a paradigm shift

Think about the implications of Charles Darwin's publication of *On The Origin of Species* as an example of a paradigm shift. Before Darwin, the prevailing view was that all living things had been created in the form in which they were presently observed. Even if you disregard the religious aspect of this, think of the implications of Darwin's idea of natural selection and the impact that this must have had, not only on his fellow scientists, but also on the way people everywhere thought.

Darwin's *On The Origin of Species* sold out on the first day of its publication in 1859. When it was first published, the book was extremely controversial – and still is today.

The wife of the Bishop of Worcester remarked, 'Descended from apes? My dear, let us hope that it is not true, but if it is, then let us pray that it will not become generally known.' Whether they agreed or not, what most disturbed those who argued against Darwin was the belief that evolution meant human beings were descended from monkeys.

This cartoon from the time of Darwin satirises the idea of evolution. What does this tell you about the fears that people had about his ideas?

At the core of the revolution that Darwin initiated was the issue of whether species could evolve, that is change after time, or whether they had always held the form in which they were presently observed. In the quote below from Darwin, the words 'mutable' and 'immutable' are used and mean that species do change or do not change.

Darwin's critics tried to ridicule his ideas

Why, it may be asked, have all the most eminent living naturalists and geologists rejected this view of the mutability of species? … The belief that species were immutable productions was almost unavoidable as long as the history of the world was thought to be of short duration… but the chief cause… is that we are always slow in admitting any great change of which we do not see the immediate steps. … The mind cannot possibly grasp the full meaning of the term of a hundred million years; it cannot add up and perceive the full effect of the slight variations, accumulated during an almost infinite number of generations.

From *On The Origin of Species* by Charles Darwin

At the heart of the paradigm shift

Darwin's book has been called 'the most fundamental of all intellectual revolutions in the history of mankind'. It changed people's attitudes towards God and to what it meant to be human. Politicians, imperialists and anarchists used it to justify their actions.

Darwin's ideas are still controversial, provoking fundamentalist Christians to push for the teaching of evolution to be removed from the schools' curricula or to be matched by the teaching of a unique creation of all species. The basic issue is the role that natural selection gives to chance; and hence the role it denies to design.

In Kuhn's terms, it is the role of chance that is responsible for the paradigm shift. The current scientific paradigm of the mid-nineteenth century was Newton's mechanistic universe; in the beginning, God created the universe and the unchanging laws by which it operated. There was no role for chance to play a part in bringing about change; as things were first designed, so they continued.

The mechanistic world view

This is the deterministic explanation of the universe that derived from Newton's thinking. Basic to Newton's explanation were ideas about the nature of matter, space and time:

- space is absolutely empty and so is at rest
- it separates matter which is the material from which all things are made
- time goes by independently and uniformly
- the laws by which all observed change takes place are unchanging so that the present state of the world will determine its future.

> **Mechanistic world view** This is the belief that the universe is made up wholly of matter in motion controlled by an unchanging set of laws.

Is this your own commonsense understanding of the way the universe works? If it is, then you will see what a major impact new knowledge has on the scientists who are responsible for it. Below is an exploration of such an impact on Albert Einstein, one of the key scientific figures responsible for the downfall of the mechanistic world view.

The impact on the scientist responsible for a paradigm shift

Sometimes the impact of a paradigm shift is evident in what the scientists themselves say about the effect of the new explanation. Look at Einstein's comment after his explanation of the photoelectric effect in 1903. This gives a clear indication of what the new ideas meant to him.

> *When I realised what this new kind of knowledge meant, it was as if the ground had been pulled from under me and I had no place left to stand.*
>
> Albert Einstein

This was a dramatic statement and it is worth taking a little time to understand why he made such a strong declaration as it gives a very good idea of what Kuhn meant by a paradigm shift. It all concerns the nature of light and it begins in the seventeenth century with two rival theories; one proposed by Isaac Newton, the other by Christian Huygens. According to Newton, light travelled as a stream of particles and according to Huygens, it travelled as a wave motion. Look at the diagram below; the properties of waves and particles are mutually exclusive – if something is a wave, it cannot be a particle and vice versa.

> The properties of waves and particles are mutually exclusive

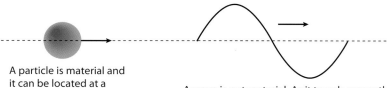

A particle is material and it can be located at a definite position in space.

A wave is not material. As it travels across the surface of water, for example, none of the water moves along with the wave; the water simply moves up and down.

By the middle of the nineteenth century, it had been shown that, if light behaves as a wave motion, it fits all the observed facts, whereas if it behaves as a stream of moving particles, it does not. Remember, a simple model for accepting a scientific hypothesis: if it does not fit the observed facts, it is not a scientific hypothesis. The idea that light behaves like a stream of particles had therefore been rejected.

The discovery of the photoelectric effect late in the nineteenth century caused a problem. If light travelled as a wave motion, it could not explain this phenomenon.

Nowadays, you are used to the photoelectric effect; it is used in automatic cameras to adjust the size of the aperture according to the amount of light and to operate the mechanism that automatically opens a door as you walk towards it.

In 1903, Einstein explained how the photoelectric effect worked. But, here is the strange fact that explains his comment. In order to fit the observed facts and so to count as a scientific explanation, light had to travel as a stream of particles. So now can you see Einstein's problem and why he made such a strong statement? If light has to behave like a wave motion to explain some observed facts and like a particle to explain others, and behaving like a particle and a wave are completely contradictory, we have a problem.

How can you be sure that an explanation is 'really' scientific?

Do you ever look at your horoscope and wonder whether or not there is any truth in it? Is it attempting to do what a scientific hypothesis seeks to do (to predict the future)? You may ask yourself if there is any simple way that you can distinguish between a scientific explanation and any other sort of explanation; the difference, for example, between astronomy and astrology? As you can see below, the philosopher of science, Karl Popper, writing in the 1940s, believed that there is a clear way to make such a distinction.

> But I shall certainly admit a system as Empirical or Scientific only if it is capable of being tested by Experience. These considerations suggest that not the verifiability but the falsifiability of a system is to be taken as the criterion of demarcation. In other words: I shall not require of a scientific system that it shall be singled out, once and for all, in a positive sense: but I shall require that its logical form shall be such that it can be singled out, by means of Empirical tests, in a negative sense: it must be possible for an Empirical scientific system to be refuted by Experience.
>
> From *Conjectures and Refutations: The Growth of Scientific Knowledge* by Karl Popper

Popper is saying that if you cannot show by experience or experiment that an explanation or prediction is wrong, then it is not a scientific hypothesis.

Exercise

Try putting this to the test with astrology. Read the prediction that an astrologist makes in your local newspaper for you for the coming week. Wait for a week to see if the predictions match with what happened to you. If they match, look at the predictions again. Are they sufficiently clearly formed that there is any way that what happens to you could show that they were wrong? What role do you think that chance or coincidence plays in this?

If the predictions made by the astrologist are always so vague that you can never prove them wrong, then astrology is simply not a science by Popper's demarcation.

The debate, principally in the US, about whether creation should be taught in schools alongside, or in some cases, instead of evolution, highlights the importance of having some way of distinguishing between what counts and what does not count as a scientific explanation. The issue is not simply whether one explanation is true and the other is false, it is also about whether there are different forms of explanation, different ways that you can make sense of the world in which you live. If there are different forms of explanation then, as a TOK student, you need to know the different criteria for accepting one or more than one of them.

Putting Popper's demarcation to a test: creation versus evolution

In the IB Biology programme you are taught evolution but not creation. Why is that? Examine the evidence upon which creation and evolution rest and you will see that they are different. The source of evidence for the creationist view is the belief in the literal truth of the Bible; the source of evidence for the evolutionary view is in observation of the natural world. Before you read on, stop for a moment and jot down the key differences between these two forms of explanation.

The crucial difference is that:

- **Evolution** is an explanation that is based on observation of the real world, for example, the fossil record and the diversity of animal populations. It may be tested and retested by future observations.

- **Creation** is the explanation given in the Bible; central to any sacred text such as the Bible is that this is the revealed truth and, as it is a matter of faith, experimental testing is simply not relevant as a means of establishing its truth.

If you apply Popper's demarcation, then creation is not a scientific explanation. Several of the court cases in the US that have involved attempts to have creation taught in schools as a scientific explanation have been judged against the issue of what counts as science. However, some judgements have been made in favour of allowing the teaching of creation *alongside* evolution and the debate goes on.

Exercise

Compare the two cases given in the box below and ask yourself how you, as a TOK student, stand on this issue.

McLean versus Arkansas Board Of Education

An act was signed into Law in the State of Arkanas in 1981 requiring public schools to give equal treatment to creation science and evolution science. This was contested in the case 'McLean versus the Arkansas Board of Education' just two months later. The judgement of the court was against the act on a number of grounds. Central to the judgement, however, were two issues:

1 Creation science, by its own definition, does not present its theory in such a way that it can be tested against evidence and hence it is not a science.

2 Evolutionary science does not put forward an explanation for the creation of life – it assumes that life existed and is concerned with how life evolved after it had originated.

*****

No-one was present when life first appeared on Earth. Therefore any statement about life's origin should be considered a theory not a fact.

Washington State Senate Bill 6058

Induction This is the reasoning process by which a general conclusion is drawn from a number of separate observations.

The problem of induction

The demarcation between a scientific explanation and one that is not scientific grew out of Popper's concern about the use of a form of reasoning called **induction**. This is used in the process of developing a scientific hypothesis.

You know and you regularly use this form of reasoning in everyday situations. You have a new friend who again and again turns up 15 minutes late every time you are going out together. After some weeks, you buy tickets for a concert and you know that the doors will close at a certain time and after that no one will be admitted. What do you do? You reason that, because your friend has always been late in the past, he will be late again, so you say that you must meet 15 minutes earlier than you need to. You have assumed that, because something has happened in a certain way in the past, it will continue to do so in the same way in the future. You have drawn a conclusion from a series of separate observations about the same event.

The problem in drawing a conclusion from this sort of reasoning is obvious. You can never be sure that you have made every relevant observation nor can you be sure that, in the future, what you have observed will continue to behave in the way that it has in the past. However, you can be pretty sure, and we normally live our everyday lives on the assumption that certain things will happen. You do not test every chair before you sit on it; you believe that, because chairs have always supported your weight, the next one you sit on will do the same. Logically, however, you cannot be sure.

The traditional view of science dates back almost 400 years to the English philosopher and scientist Francis Bacon. An outline of this view is set out below. Notice that this relies on the process of induction, which Karl Popper attacked strongly.

Step 1: Make a number of observations.
Step 2: Through induction, develop a hypothesis that explains the observations.
Step 3: Confirm the hypothesis by further observations and tests.

Compare this with your own model for the way that science works. Does any part of this match with the traditional view above? Ask yourself what is wrong with this. Do you just look around at random and then come up with an explanation of what you see?

It goes back to our original thinking about curiosity as the starting point of the need for any form of explanation. You must direct your observations at something so that you do not simply ask 'Why?' but 'Why what?' Popper explained this by saying that you need a hypothesis to guide what you are looking for. If you do not, you have no way of deciding which of your observations are relevant and which are not. Science, therefore, progresses by testing the predictions made by scientific hypotheses in an attempt to falsify them. A good hypothesis is one that has withstood many attempts at falsification. It does not, however, become something that has been proven; it is a form of knowledge, according to Popper, that remains hypothetical and subject to future falsification.

Science as a passion

At the heart of Popper's view is the rationality of science and scientific practitioners. The philosopher of science, Michael Polanyi, took a different approach to the way that science progresses. As you read about Polanyi's ideas, compare them with your own model, with Thomas Kuhn's idea of paradigm shifts and with Karl Popper's demarcation by falsification. Are these complementary to one another or do they make different assumptions about the nature of science?

Central to Michael Polanyi's thinking was the belief that creative acts (especially acts of discovery) are shot-through or charged with strong personal feelings and commitments (hence the title of his most famous work *Personal Knowledge*). Arguing against the then dominant position that science was somehow value-free, Michael Polanyi sought to bring into creative tension a concern with reasoned and critical interrogation with other, more 'tacit', forms of knowing.

Polanyi's argument was that the informed guesses, hunches and imaginings that are part of exploratory acts are motivated by what he describes as 'passions'. They might well be aimed at discovering 'truth', but they are not necessarily in a form that can be stated in propositional or formal terms.

Exercise

Is the story of Archimedes in his bath, leaping out and shouting *Eureka!*, a good example of what Polanyi is saying about scientific discovery?

When is an error really an error?

If falsification is the test of a scientific hypothesis, it raises the question, How do you know when an observation has falsified a hypothesis? How do you distinguish between experimental error and a genuine falsification? In theory, you come across this problem every time you carry out an experiment and your readings do not agree with what they should be according to accepted theory. Why do you not claim to have falsified the theory and accept that you are in error?

In practice, it is not as easy as it may seem and it raises the important issue of the relationship between theory and observations. Look at the box below; this describes a situation in which an observation that was thought to be an error and hence disregarded in one experiment, because there was no theory to explain it, became the stimulus for another experiment when there was a theory to explain the observation.

In 1921, Robert Millikan at the University of Chicago measured the charge carried by an electron. It was a painstaking experiment that involved him in measuring the charge carried by thousands of oil drops. What he found was that the charges on the oil drops were all multiples of a very small unit of charge. He concluded that this charge was the smallest possible unit of charge and hence was the charge on the electron. The fact that the oil drops had different charges was simply due to the fact that they had been charged up with different numbers of extra electrons.

Millikan was an excellent experimental scientist but it seems that he did not record the fact that on a very small number of occasions he had measured a charge of one third of his smallest charge. There were so few of these measurements that he simply regarded them as errors. Over 40 years later, when the idea of a quark had been proposed, and that one of its properties was that it carried one third of the charge of the electron, Millikan's experiment was revisited. This time, a theory existed: that of the quark, a particle that, according to the theory, carried a charge of one third that of the electron. This made sense of what Millikan had ignored because he felt it was an experimental error.

Put this into the context of your extended essay. How did you decide on your research question if you chose a scientific topic? Did your question come from what you had previously learned in class? Did you change the question once you began to collect your data?

Which comes first – theory or observation?

You may now be wondering whether observations are the source and stimulus for scientific explanations or whether theories are needed to direct the search for data. Two philosophers of science, Thomas Kuhn, whose ideas you have already come across, and Paul Feyerabend, argue that all observation is dependent on holding a theory. Is this the same as saying what you see depends on what you believe? The answer is more complicated than you might imagine at first sight.

> Observation statements are as fallible as the theories they presuppose and therefore do not constitute a completely secure basis on which to build scientific laws and theories.
>
> From *What Is This Thing Called Science?* by Alan Chalmers

As you saw in Chapter 4: Sense perception, one of the problems of observation is the nature of perception. Many experiments have been carried out that show clearly that what we see is not the same as our visual experience. What we see is the image formed on the retina, what we experience depends on the way this information is processed in the brain and this depends on past experience, on our knowledge and on what we expect to see. A good example of this is when people are shown playing cards one by one and asked to name them. If the pack contains 'false' cards such as a black ace of diamonds, this is reported either as a normal ace of spades or as a normal ace of diamonds. You experience what you expect to see. Kuhn takes this idea further with his idea of a paradigm; think about the implications of the extract below.

> In Kuhn's view, scientists don't discover the nature of reality; they create it. There is no way the world is, for each paradigm makes its own world. It's easy to see why such views raise questions about the end of science. If there is not truth with a capital 'T', then, of course, it makes no sense to say that scientists have a monopoly on it.
>
> From 'The End of Science' by Theodore Schick Jr, published in *The Skeptical Inquirer*

Does this imply, however, that observation or experiment has no use in science? Of course not, but what it does imply is that it is wrong to take the naïve view that observation provides the facts upon which scientific hypotheses are developed.

A very clear example, and one that involves political decisions as enormous sums of money are involved, is the construction of huge synchrotrons. These are machines which accelerate particles such as electrons to velocities approaching the speed of light and smash them into other sub-atomic particles. The object is to study what particles are produced by the collision. This sort of experimental research is driven by the theory that all of matter is built up from a small number of building blocks. However, if you think about this, what is being done is the setting up of an experiment that can only provide evidence to support the theory that is held, that particles such as protons are further divisible. In this case, the observations that can be made are actually limited by the theory held.

Exercise

- Throughout the last few pages, you have looked at a number of different interpretations of the way that science works and how it has developed. Study carefully the following six graphic interpretations put forward by six different scientists about the growth of scientific knowledge.
- You should discuss each one with a small group of your fellow TOK students and select the one that you think is most appropriate. What are the arguments in favour of your choice? How would you present your choice to other TOK students?

1 Scientist A demonstrated that scientific knowledge growth has occurred purely and simply in linear fashion as shown below.

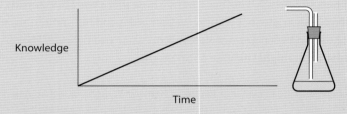

2 Scientist B showed that the knowledge claims have not grown in linear fashion but rather in 'curved' growth. Note that the curve represents an accelerated growth in the earlier days of recorded knowledge, while more modern claims appear to occur less and less.

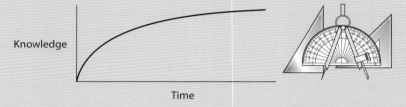

3 Scientist C stated that he agreed with Scientist B's 'curve' interpretation but that he disagreed with the way the curve has been drawn. Scientist C stated that the acceleration of growth has occurred not at the beginning of recorded knowledge but rather at the end, as shown below.

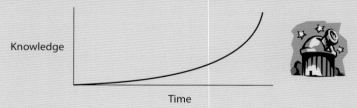

4 Scientist D stated that the growth of scientific claims has come neither in a strictly linear fashion nor in a curved style, but rather in a 'piece-wise linear' manner. He argued that the steps or break points in the curve represent major claims (e.g. electricity, laws of motion, atomic energy, etc.).

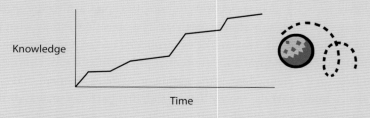

5 Scientist E agreed with the spurt growth of knowledge described by Scientist D, but he added yet another point to consider. He stated that once a major claim of knowledge has come to light, that other prior claims may indeed become false. Therefore we see that after a major 'stair-step' jump, we have a slight drop off in total claims still considered to be true.

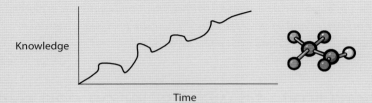

6 Scientist F had to disagree with all the others. He stated that the growth of scientific knowledge is all relative to what we know at a particular time. He asserted that science has actually raised more questions than it has answered. Indeed his 'curved' graph shows a decrease in knowledge (i.e. relative to the amount of knowledge that humans actually thought they knew at a particular time). As Socrates said, 'The more I think I know, the less I really know.'

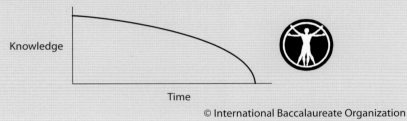

Is there a single scientific method?

The oldest description for the way science works is that observation is the fundamental source of scientific knowledge. This view is no longer held by many working scientists; they believe that the theories held by scientists direct their search for data in so far as they determine the kinds of experiments that are carried out. Karl Popper's attempts to avoid this problem led to his belief that falsification is the only test of a scientific theory.

Thomas Kuhn objected to the notion that falsification can establish objective scientific knowledge because the data that might be used to falsify a scientific hypothesis is dependent on the theory held by the scientist. Instead, he argued that science is essentially puzzle-solving. Michael Polanyi believed that scientists are driven by the urge to discover and that creativity, guesses and imagination play a major role in this. If you were to write a TOK essay now on how science works and why it changes, what approach would you take?

However, if you turn your attention from what science is to what research scientists do, and from what you do when you carry out experiments in the science laboratory, do you find that there is, in practice, a single scientific method? Or do you find that all of the descriptions of the scientific methods set out in the paragraphs above are used? Do you find that some researchers do develop a specific hypothesis that they set out to verify or falsify while others ask vague questions, and then collect data that sometimes changes the nature of the questions that they originally sought to answer? This is not surprising; scientists are not all cast in the same mould, as the quotation from Sir Peter Medawar, a Nobel prize winner for his work in medical research, shows.

> *Scientists are people of very dissimilar temperaments doing different things in very different ways. Among scientists are collectors, classifiers and compulsive tidiers-up; many are detectives by temperament and many are explorers; some are artists and some are artisans. There are poet-scientists and philosopher-scientists and even a few mystics.*
>
> Peter Medawar

Are there limits to what science can explain?

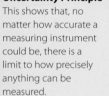

Uncertainty Principle
This shows that, no matter how accurate a measuring instrument could be, there is a limit to how precisely anything can be measured.

Of all the assumptions that scientists have to make about our universe, the most basic one is that it can be explained. Look at the statement that Sheldon Glashow, a Nobel prize-winning physicist, makes.

> *We believe that the world is knowable, and that there are simple rules governing the behaviour of matter and the evolution of the universe. … This statement I cannot prove, this statement I cannot justify. This is my faith.*
>
> Sheldon Glashow

Even if the world is knowable fully as Glashow says, are there limits to how precisely we can know it? According to the Quantum Theory, there are such limits and the **Uncertainty Principle** describes these limits.

The problem arises because, in order to observe anything, you have to interact with it. For example, in order to see anything, light has to have been reflected from it and then the light must enter your eye. You might then wonder, if the light hits an object and bounces off it, does it change the object? Is what you see not the way the object was before the light (with which you see it) interacted with the object? Fortunately, the energy that a light beam carries is so low that we can assume that its impact on any object (which is large enough for us to see with the naked eye) makes no noticeable change.

But what happens when the object to be observed is very small indeed? For example, what happens when scientists try to observe sub-atomic particles? This is where the problem starts because, at this level, the interaction between the object to be observed, and the particle or wave that is needed by the observer to interact with the object, changes the object under observation.

Jacob Bronowski argued that calling this the Uncertainty Principle did not convey a correct understanding of what was happening. He thought of the effect of limiting the precision with which we could finally know anything and widened the idea to encompass all quests for knowledge.

> Yet the Principle of Uncertainty is a bad name. In science or outside it, we are not uncertain; our knowledge is merely confined within a certain tolerance. We should call it the Principle of Tolerance… All knowledge, all information between human beings can only be exchanged within a play of tolerance.
>
> From *The Ascent of Man: A Personal View* by J. Bronowski

This idea, in the more general sense that an observer cannot stand outside the system that is being observed, undermines one of the cornerstones of the mechanistic world view. The observer does not affect in any way that which is being observed.

The limits to which we can know fully the nature of the universe became a major issue through attempts to make sense of the Quantum Theory in the first half of the last century. We looked at this earlier in the chapter when the impact of Einstein's explanation of the photoelectric effect was discussed. How was it possible for light to behave as a particle in order to explain certain observations and as a wave in order to explain other observations? This, and other equally strange outcomes of Quantum Theory, led to a dispute between the physicist Niels Bohr and Albert Einstein about the extent to which the universe is fully knowable.

Niels Bohr, who was one of the major influences on the development of Quantum Theory, believed that it is complete in that it describes reality as it is. This means that built into the nature of reality itself is a degree of 'unknowability'. No matter how precise scientists' measurements become in the future, we will never have an absolutely certain knowledge of the universe.

Albert Einstein disagreed with this and his famous comment 'God does not play dice' refers precisely to this issue. His own view was that Quantum Theory is incomplete and it does not give a full description of the nature of reality. It is, thought Einstein, possible to have full knowledge of the real world once we have the right theory. This view of the nature of the universe is built into both the special and general theories of relativity, Einstein's greatest contribution to our understanding of the universe.

You may wonder whether this issue is of importance. Does it matter that we know the absolute truth about the nature of the universe? Is the job of science more modest; to give us an explanation that makes sense in the light of observation and to serve the very practical goal of benefiting our lives through its application in technology? The fact that language places limitations on the way that an electron is 'pictured' does not, however, imply that electrons do not really exist. The remarkable power of science to make extremely accurate and testable predictions is strong evidence for the real existence of, not only electrons, but the many other entities that are not directly observable but form a part of the network of explanations used by scientists.

Think of the limitations that human language also places on what we can know. In part, understanding the nature of light is one of language. When scientists describe the nature of things that cannot be directly perceived, they have to use the language of things that can be perceived; they use analogy. So, when light is said to behave like a wave motion, it does not mean that light is a wave motion – simply that its observed behaviour in certain situations is the same as that of observable wave motions such as water waves. Similarly, when it is said to behave like a stream of particles, an analogy is being drawn because a stream of observable particles behaves in these conditions in the same way.

Relating effects to causes

In everyday situations you expect a scientific explanation to provide you with a reliable link between what you see happening, an effect, and what made this happen, a cause. It is not always an easy task to make a clear relationship; think of the present problems in linking climate change directly to carbon emission levels. The attempt made in the last century to make a direct link between smoking cigarettes and lung cancer provides a good example of this.

Until the last century, lung cancer was a very rare disease. The incidence of the disease only began to increase noticeably after the First World War. It then continued to rise at an increasing rate as the century went by. As a result, members of the medical profession began to seek an explanation for this observation. A wide range of possibilities were initially proposed, of which the increase in cigarette smoking was just one.

During the 1950s, evidence linking cigarette smoking with lung cancer began to accumulate. At the same time, the major cigarette companies founded the Tobacco Industry Research Commission to look at the evidence. This group found insufficient evidence to make a link, blaming other factors such as air pollution.

Around the same time more detailed information became available about cancer rates among smokers. Longer-term studies were set up. One such study, carried out in Britain between 1951 and 1994, revealed that the death rate for smokers from lung cancer was about three times that of non-smokers for men over 35. However, cigarette companies continued to argue that the causal connection had not been made. During this period, they fought and won several court cases on the grounds that the relationships found in the studies were coincidental not causal. Simply because there existed a high correlation, the causal connection could not be established definitely as no linking explanation was available. This was not helped by the fact that the tobacco companies continued to fund university research.

It was not until 1998 that scientists discovered a chemical explanation for the link. It was that tars in tobacco release a chemical into the smoke that, when drawn into the lungs, produces mutations in the cells that line the wall of the lungs and that these induce cancer. Only after this evidence was presented did the tobacco companies abandon their claim that cigarette smoking is not related to lung cancer. Look at the quotation below by the Director General of the World Health Organisation as she defines a cigarette to see how much has changed in attitudes towards smoking in the last decade.

> *A cigarette is a euphemism for a cleverly crafted product that delivers just the right amount of nicotine to keep its user addicted for life before killing the person.*
>
> Gro Harlem Brundtland

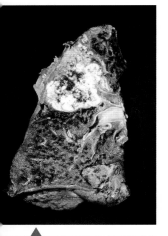

A human lung damaged by smoking

Exercise

Did the claim that 'cigarettes kill' only get a scientific sanction after a direct cause-effect relationship was found in 1998? Or was a strong correlation enough? What is the status of meteorology in this respect as it may never get beyond correlative predictions? Does this make weather forecasting unscientific?

Explanation across the sciences

So far, we have talked only of science in general terms, but do scientific explanations have the same meanings across all the sciences; from physics and chemistry to biology, ecology and geology, for example? Which science or sciences are you studying? Discuss the similarities and differences between what one of you is doing in biology from what someone else is doing in physics. What are the major differences when you carry out an experiment in the two subjects?

Do you find that in the former there are many less variables to consider and control in an experimental observation than in the latter? For example, when you are studying the behaviour of a gas subjected to different external pressures, what are the factors that you have to consider and to control in setting up the experiment? Compare this with an experiment in biology, for example, the growth rate of peas under different conditions. What are the differences? Compare these with those set out in the following box.

Comparing the variables in the physical and human sciences

Physical sciences:
- There are few variables to control in any experimental situation.
- The variables are easy to specify.
- The variables are easy to control.

Human sciences:
- There are usually many variables to control.
- The variables are often difficult to identify.
- The variables are seldom easy to control.

This makes it much more difficult for scientists working with living organisms to formulate precise mathematical relationships between the observed quantities. The scientific laws described earlier in the chapter were examples from the physical sciences. If you look again at the box, you may see why there are many laws in physics and in chemistry but few in biology. The living world is much more complex than the non-living world as the next box shows.

The nature of the subject material

The non-living world:
- The variables can be isolated.
- Identical samples can be obtained on many occasions.
- The subject material can be measured with precision.
- The subject material has no past history.

The living world:
- The subject material is often directly observable but is multi-variable.
- The variables cannot be isolated.
- The past history of the subject material influences the present and may often determine it.

This means that when explanations are made, hypotheses about the non-living world have a different status than those about the living world. In the former, a hypothesis will predict future behaviour of the system without exception. Hypotheses about the behaviour of the living world, however, are statistical in nature. They indicate an overall trend but they cannot predict individual outcomes.

Scientists and social responsibility

On 6 August 1945, the Japanese city of Hiroshima was bombed using a nuclear weapon. The decision was taken by the then President of the US, Harry S. Truman. It is estimated that, before the end of 1945, around 140,000 people had died in Hiroshima as a result of the bombing.

The decision to use an atomic bomb and, a few days later, a second atomic bomb on a second Japanese city, Nagasaki, was a political one. It was taken to avoid a potentially even bloodier end to the Second World War if a land invasion of Japan was made.

The issue here, however, is not with the political decision to use the atomic bomb; it is with the responsibility of the scientists who developed the bomb. It raised (and in other contexts it continues to raise) the question of whether scientists carry a responsibility for the way their inventions are used.

The physicist Józef Rotblat, who was the only scientist to resign from the project team that developed the atomic bomb, held a very strong view on this. Rotblat dedicated much of his later life to making scientists accountable for the way science is used. In 1955, along with ten other eminent scientists including Albert Einstein, he issued a statement that scientists must take responsibility for what they create, including (but not limited to) nuclear weapons.

In July 1957, the first Pugwash conference on science and world affairs was organised by Józef Rotblat. It took place in the town of Pugwash in Novia Scotia. In 1995, the Pugwash conferences and Józef Rotblat were jointly awarded the Nobel Peace Prize.

However, there is an alternative view that insists that scientists are not responsible for the way their creations are used. This view holds that scientific enquiry is always objective, neutral and value-free. Therefore, in itself, science cannot be wrong, only its applications can be judged in a moral sense. This view also holds that, whatever your view on the social responsibility of science, it is inevitable that science will continue to progress.

Where do you stand in this respect? We will examine briefly the issues in the context of genetic engineering. At one extreme is the view that research in genetic engineering is driven by nothing more than a profit motive. In her book on genetic engineering, Dr Mac-Wan Ho of the Open University argues that 'the moral responsibility of science is absolute and cannot be abdicated in the name of profit or value-freedom'. She details the potential dangers of interfering with natural processes and the possible impact of mutant strains should they escape from research laboratories. Set against this view is the one that, without genetic engineering, particularly with respect to the production of disease-free and pest-resistant crops, the world will be increasingly unable to feed itself.

Exercise

How do you apply your own knowledge of science in this context? What criteria do you use to make a judgement in this situation? Some people are in such extreme opposition to certain aspects of scientific research that they take the law into their own hands. Look at the box below containing a recent report by the BBC about the jailing of an animal rights activist. What do you feel are the key issues at stake here?

Animal protester jailed for attacks

An animal rights extremist who caused £40,000 of damage in 'military style' attacks on cars of Huntingdon Life Sciences employees has been jailed for six-and-a-half years. Sarah Gisborne carried out a shocking campaign of hate against people linked to animal experiments, a court was told. ... Judge Nicholas Coleman said: 'It seems to me a deterrent sentence is required.' He said statements from victims of the attacks made 'chilling' reading. ... Timothy Greene, for Gisborne said 'She very strongly believes it is wrong for human beings to cause suffering to animals, however good the motives.'

Cambridge News, 26 February 2005

The issue of whether scientists should be held responsible for the way their discoveries are used opens up a related matter. This is whether a line of scientific research is morally right or wrong in itself, irrespective of the way that it is put to use. Look at the following quotes from a number of recent BBC reports; this time, about embryonic stem cell research.

> It crosses a moral boundary that our decent society needs to respect...'
>> George W. Bush, President of the USA

> We are in favour of progress but this is unethical.
>> Dr Michael Jarnulowicz of the Guild of Catholic Directors

> They would be cannibalising embryos.
>> Mike Nichols from Movement Against Human Cloning

> Using embryo clones is not ethically acceptable.
>> Dr Liam Fox, British MP and Shadow Health Secretary

These are powerful statements and represent just a few of the attacks on embryonic stem cell research on moral grounds. How do you react to them? Do you, like most people, not understand what embryonic stem cells are, or how they were discovered, or the motives of the scientists who carried out the research that led to their discovery and potential for use? If you do not, are you justified in taking a moral stance, for or against, this form of research? In this situation, is your knowledge of the way science works essential before you can make a moral judgement?

Your answers to the questions in the paragraph above are important because science has an impact on almost every aspect of your life. In fact, the whole workings of modern society would be quite impossible without science and its application through technology. But has this made people more likely to turn to scientific explanations for solutions to many of the problems that are faced in everyday life? Certainly religious faith remains as important as ever for most of the world's population and modern day superstitions such as those expressed in the so-called New Age thinking are common.

This chapter began by asking whether science is losing its appeal as a way of understanding our world by a significant proportion of the world's population. At the same time, our way of life depends more than ever on the practical application of scientific knowledge. What is at the root of this apparently contradictory situation? The ongoing debate about the use of genetic engineering highlights the two sides of this issue. On the one hand there is the argument which highlights the benefits, including greater food production and the potential for the cure of diseases. While on the other hand, there are moral concerns that science has begun to tamper with the natural order of things.

Before we look at the nature of scientific truth, look again at the paragraph above. Does progress in science mean that we are coming closer to a true understanding of the universe of which we are all a part? If so, why do you think that we seem to live in a time that demands progress based on scientific discovery yet grows more suspicious of the process and the motives that drive such progress?

What is a scientific truth?

We have looked at different models for the way that science works and at how it has progressed historically. We have also examined limitations to what science can explain.

As you have done so, have you asked yourself a basic TOK-type question? Does this mean that a scientific theory is true?

Try to apply what you now understand about science to what is called the standard theory of matter. This theory holds that the whole of the matter throughout the entire universe is made up of just four types of subatomic particles:

- two types of quark that make up the protons and neutrons in the nucleus
- two further particles: the electrons surrounding the nucleus and neutrinos that emerge from nuclear reactions.

This, then, is accepted nowadays by almost all of the community of working scientists, so presumably they accept it as true. But what does this mean?

Ask yourself first if anyone has ever directly observed any of these entities. If they have not been directly observed, then what makes scientists believe that they do exist? If you cannot observe something directly, what is it that you do to justify your belief in the fact that it exists?

Does progress in science mean that we are coming closer to a true understanding of the universe?

Exercise

Look at the two approaches that scientists typically use and ask yourself if one or the other, or either of them, matches your own justification for belief. Jot down your reasons.

- **The instrumentalist view** holds that it does not matter whether the non-observable particles from which the theory says all matter is built really exist. What matters is that the theory is useful in that it enables accurate predictions to be made. In Chapter 2: What is knowledge? you came across different theories of truth. What theory of truth is this?
- **The realist view** holds that the basic particles really do exist. The fact that we cannot directly observe them is an outcome of the limitations of our sense perception. They are indirectly observed through technological extension to our own senses. If they did not exist, then we could not make accurate predictions about the world using the standard theory of matter. What theory of truth is this?

Do scientists always tell the truth?

As you have read in this chapter, for an explanation to be regarded as science, it must fit the facts and it must be based on experimental evidence. This is a great strength, because it means that the reliability of such evidence can be cross-checked by other scientists. This makes it difficult for individual scientists to cheat, and overwhelmingly scientists are honest. Recently, however, as some of the following extracts suggest, this is not always the case. What is the impact on the laymen's trust in science of well publicised frauds?

Look at the 'facts' on the next page about scientists who have cheated. Do you believe them? What do you need to know before you can decide?

- Claudius Ptolemy, the 'greatest astronomer of antiquity', did not make the observations of the stars he claimed he did, but plagiarized the work of another astronomer.

- Galileo Galilei said his theories were based on experiments he had conducted, but today many doubt he ever carried out these experiments.

- John Dalton, the great nineteenth century chemist who proved the existence of different types of atoms, published results that chemists now believe were fabricated.

- Gregor Mendel, the founder of modern genetics, recorded experimental results during the 1800s that are too perfect to be true: they had to have been made up.

- Cyril Burt, the British psychologist credited with the theory that IQ is inherited, fabricated the data on which his theory is based throughout 1943 to 1966.

From *Betrayers of the Truth: Fraud and Deceit in the Halls of Science* by William Broad and Nicholas Wade

---

Exercise

Read the three case studies below about René Blondlot, Trofim Lysenko and Boris Derjaguin. When you have done this ask yourself what, if anything, they share in common.

René Blondlot: N-rays

René Prosper Blondlot (1849–1930) was a French physicist who claimed to have discovered a new type of radiation, shortly after Roentgen had discovered X-rays. He called it the N-ray, after Nancy, the name of the town and the university where he lived and worked. Blondlot was trying to polarize X-rays when he claimed to have discovered his new form of radiation. Dozens of other scientists confirmed the existence of N-rays in their own laboratories.

In 1903, Blondlot claimed he had generated N-rays using a hot wire inside an iron tube. The rays were detected by a calcium sulfide thread that glowed slightly in the dark when the rays were refracted through a 60° angle prism of aluminium. According to Blondlot, a narrow stream of N-rays was refracted through the prism and produced a spectrum on a field. The N-rays were reported to be invisible, except when viewed as they hit the treated thread. Blondlot moved the thread across the gap where the N-rays were thought to come through and when the thread was illuminated it was said to be due to N-rays.

Nature magazine was sceptical of Blondlot's claims because laboratories in England and Germany had not been able to replicate the Frenchman's results. *Nature* sent American physicist Robert W. Wood of Johns Hopkins University to investigate Blondlot's discovery. Wood suspected that N-rays were a delusion. To demonstrate such, he removed the prism from the N-ray detection device, unbeknownst to Blondlot or his assistant. Without the prism, the machine could not work. Yet, when Blondlot's assistant conducted the next experiment he found N-rays. Wood then tried to surreptitiously replace the prism but the assistant saw him and thought he was

Go to www.heinemann.co.uk/hotlinks and insert the express code 4327P to find the source of this article about René Blondlot.

removing the prism. The next time he tried the experiment, the assistant swore he could not see any N-rays. But he should have, since the equipment was in full working order. Wood's exposure of Blondlot may have led to the French scientist's madness and death.

Trofim Lysenko: Vernalization

Lysenko was [portrayed in the Soviet Union as] a 'barefoot scientist' – an embodiment of the mythical Soviet peasant genius. Lysenko's 'science' was practically nonexistent. When he had any clearly formed theories, they were generally a mishmash of Lamarckism and various confused forms of Darwinism; the majority of Lysenko's work consisted of 'practical directions' for agriculture, such as cooling grain before it was planted. Lysenko's primary procedure was a mixture of so-called 'vernalization' (by which Lysenko generally meant anything he did to plant seeds and tubers) as well as hybridization. During one period, for example, he picked a spring wheat with a short 'stage of vernalization' but a long 'light stage' which he crossed with another variety of wheat with a long 'stage of vernalization' and a short 'light stage'. He did not explain what was meant by these stages. Lysenko then concluded on the basis of his stage theory that he knew in advance that the cross would produce offspring that would ripen sooner and as such yield more than their parents and thus did not have to test many plants through their generations. Though scientifically unsound on a number of levels, Soviet journalists and agricultural officials were delighted with Lysenko's claims, as they sped up laboratory work and cheapened it considerably. Lysenko was given his own journal, *Vernalization*, in 1935, with which he generally bragged about forthcoming successes.

The Soviet press reported great successes from Lysenko's early initiatives, though in the end they would almost all result in failure. What most caught the Soviet government's eye with Lysenko was his success at motivating peasants, however. Soviet agriculture was deeply damaged by the mandatory collectivization movement in the early 1930s, and many peasants were at best unenthusiastic and at worst prone to destroy their grain to keep it away from the Soviet government. Lysenko energized the enthusiasm of the peasants, making them feel truly in control and participants in the great Soviet revolutionary experiment. By the late 1920s, the Soviet political bosses had given their support to Lysenko. Lysenko himself spent much time decrying academic scientists and geneticists, claiming that their isolated laboratory work was not helping the Soviet people.

In 1962, three of the most prominent Soviet physicists, Yakov Borisovich Zel'dovich, Vitaly Ginzburg, and Pyotr Kapitsa, set out the case against Lysenko, his false science and his policy of political extermination of scientific opponents. This happened as a part of a greater trend of combating the ideological influence that had held such sway in Soviet society and science. In 1964, physicist Andrei Sakharov spoke out against Lysenko in the General Assembly of the Academy of Sciences.

The Soviet press was soon filled with anti-Lysenkoite articles and appeals for the restoration of scientific methods to all fields of biology and agricultural science. Lysenko was removed from his post as Director of the Institute of Genetics at the

Academy of Sciences and restricted to an experimental farm in the Lenin Hills, near Moscow (the Institute itself was soon dissolved). After the dismissal of Khrushchev in 1965, the president of the Academy of Sciences declared that Lysenko's immunity to criticism had officially ended and an expert commission was sent to Lysenko's experimental farm. A few months later, a devastating critique became public and Lysenko's reputation was completely destroyed in the Soviet Union, though it would continue to have effect in China for many years. Lysenko died in 1976.

Trofim Lysenko, (n.d.), Wikipedia, retrieved 30 April 2008

W Go to www.heinemann.co.uk/hotlinks and insert the express code 4327P to find the source of this article about Trofim Lysenko.

Boris Derjaguin: Polywater

In 1966 the Soviet scientist Boris Valdimirovich Derjaguin lectured in England on a new form of water that he claimed had been discovered by another Soviet scientist, N.N. Fedyakin. Formed by heating water and letting it condense in quartz capillaries, this 'anomalous water', as it was originally called, had a density higher than normal water, a viscosity 15 times that of normal water, a boiling point higher than 100°C, and a freezing point lower than 0°.

Over the next several years, hundreds of papers appeared in the scientific literature describing the properties of what soon came to be known as polywater. Theorists developed models, supported by some experimental measurements, in which strong hydrogen bonds were causing water to polymerize. Some even warned that if polywater escaped from the laboratory, it could autocatalytically polymerize all of the world's water.

Then the case for polywater began to crumble. Because polywater could only be formed in minuscule capillaries, very little was available for analysis. When small samples were analysed, polywater proved to be contaminated with a variety of other substances, from silicon to phospholipids. Electron microscopy revealed that polywater actually consisted of finely divided particulate matter suspended in ordinary water.

Gradually, the scientists who had described the properties of polywater admitted that it did not exist. They had been misled by poorly controlled experiments and problems with experimental procedures. As the problems were resolved and experiments gained better controls, evidence for the existence of polywater disappeared.

Reprinted with permission from the National Academic Press,
© 1995, National Academy of Sciences

Today's world: creating a synthetic bacterium

A synthetic chromosome has been created by a team of scientists that includes Craig Venter. The team plan to transplant this into the neucleoid of a cell to produce a bacterium that will be able to replicate itself with its man-made DNA. Venter's aim is to create and patent the first man-made life form.

In issue No. 2626 of *New Scientist* (2007), he was asked, 'Assuming you can make synthetic bacteria, what will you do with them?'

Venter replied, 'Over the next 20 years, synthetic genomics is going to be the standard for making anything. The chemical industry will depend on it. Hopefully, a large part of the energy industry will depend on it. We really need to find an alternative to taking carbon out of the ground, burning it, and putting it into the atmosphere. That is the single biggest contribution I could make.'

Ideal knower

Richard Feynman (1918–88)

Richard Feynman worked in many areas of physics and was jointly awarded the 1965 Nobel Prize in Physics for his work in developing a pictorial representation for the mathematical expressions that described the behaviour of subatomic particles. His series of lectures, given in 1959 at Caltech to undergraduates, show him to be not only an eminent scientist but also a great teacher, passionate that others should share his own delight in seeking to understand the nature of our world. James Gleick, his biographer, writes of him:

Richard Feynman

> So many of his witnesses observed the utter freedom of his flights of thought, yet when Feynman talked about his own methods not freedom, but constraint… For Feynman the evidence of scientific imagination was a powerful and almost painful rule. What scientists create must match reality. It must match reality. It must match what is already known. Scientific creativity, he said, is imagination in a straitjacket… The rules of harmonic progression made for Mozart as unyielding as the sonnet did for Shakespeare.
>
> From *Genius: The Life and Science of Richard Feynman* by James Gleick

In order to see why Feynman seems to be 'an ideal knower', look at the extracts below from a speech that he gave at a teachers' conference in 1966.

What is science? Of course you all must know, if you teach it. That's common sense. What can I say? If you don't know, every teacher's edition of every textbook gives a complete discussion of the subject. There is some kind of distorted distillation and watered-down and mixed-up words of Francis Bacon from some centuries ago, words which then were supposed to be the deep philosophy of science. But one of the greatest experimental scientists of the time who was really doing something, William Harvey, said that what Bacon said science was, was the science that a lord-chancellor would do. He [Bacon] spoke of making observations, but omitted the vital factor of judgement about what to observe and what to pay attention to.

And so what science is, is not what the philosophers have said it is, and certainly not what the teacher editions say it is. What it is, is a problem which I set for myself after I said I would give this talk.

*****

Another of the qualities of science is that it teaches the value of rational thought as well as the importance of freedom of thought; the positive results that come from doubting that the lessons are all true.

When someone says, 'Science teaches such and such,' he is using the word incorrectly. Science doesn't teach anything; experience teaches it. If they say to you, 'Science has shown such and such' you might ask, 'How does science show it? How did the scientists find out? How? What? Where?'

It should not be 'science has shown' but 'this experiment, this effect, has shown'. And you have as much right as anyone else, upon hearing about the experiments – but be patient and listen to all the evidence – to judge whether a sensible conclusion has been arrived at.

Presented by Richard Feynman at the fifteenth annual meeting of the National Science Teachers Association, 1966 in New York City, and reprinted from *The Physics Teacher* Vol. 7, issue 6, 1968

As this chapter on science comes to an end, you may feel a little frustrated that you have not been provided with a clear blueprint for the way that science works. The selection of arguments put forward by some of the foremost philosophers of science of the past centuries show that there is, in fact, no shared consensus about the nature of science. The final extract on the next page reflects in science itself a continuing challenge to understand nature just as those seeking to understand the working of science face a similar challenge.

There is concern that research, if left to itself, driven by its implacable reductionism, will quickly penetrate all the great mysteries and we will be left with nothing to contemplate but the nasty little details of a monstrous machine. There is a genuine apprehension that science may be taking the meaning out of life.

But if you concentrate on science, it is in real life not like this at all. We are nowhere near comprehension. The greatest achievements in the science of this century are themselves the sources of more puzzlement than human beings have ever experienced. Indeed, it is likely that the twentieth century will be looked back at as a time when science provided the first close glimpse of the profundity of human ignorance. We have not reached the solutions; we have only begun to discover how to ask questions.

Science is founded on uncertainty. Each time we learn something new and surprising, the astonishment comes with the realisation that we were wrong before. The body of science is not, as it is sometimes thought, a huge coherent mass of facts, neatly arranged in sequence, each one attached to the next by a logical string.

From 'On Science and Uncertainty' by Lewis Thomas

Student presentation

1 Today's news reports the successful cloning of cells from a Rhesus monkey bringing the possibility of the cloning of human cells one stage nearer. If scientists have developed such techniques and they have potential medical benefit, then it is unethical to do other than support the scientists in their endeavours.

2 Is research into climate change biased so that the results can be used to support the alarmists?

Essay questions

Two recent Prescribed Titles (PTs) include:

1 For some people science is the supreme form of all knowledge. Is this view reasonable or does it involve a misunderstanding of science or knowledge?

© International Baccalaureate Organization 2005

2 To what extent may the subjective nature of perception be regarded as an advantage for artists but an obstacle to be overcome for scientists?

© International Baccalaureate Organization 2005

Human sciences
Understanding human sciences

Human (or social) sciences Any discipline that deals with human behaviour in its social and cultural aspects. These mainly include: anthropology, sociology, psychology, political science and economics. Their main feature is that they study the behaviour of individuals in groups.

Imagine the following situation…

It is 8 a.m. on the first Monday of term and you have just arrived at your new school, chosen because it is an IB World School. In some cases it may be just down the road, in others in a part of the world almost totally unfamiliar to you. Because we can imagine situations before having experienced them, you have probably been picturing what sort of reception you might receive – how other students who have their established groups of friends will react to you.

Most people, whether teachers or students, use their imagination in this way and assume that what they predict is accurate to some degree. But ask yourself, how is this possible? Or to put it another way, what sort of knowledge do you rely on to see into the future so that you can anticipate the behaviour of others?

How will other students, with their established groups of friends, react towards you?

In science you might point to a general law, such as the law of gravity, that would allow you to predict an event, but that doesn't seem possible here. Any expectations you have don't seem to be tied to general certainties such as those in the natural sciences, do they?

But if we widen the definition of 'predict' (increase its 'margin of tolerance' if you like) is it not likely that you will feel the day went pretty much as you expected? Is this feeling strange? How is it that we can have a fairly good idea of what we might face? What sort of knowledge is this that we have about other people? Is it because of personal acquaintance with other people your age as well as with adults that you have come across in other schools? Would you feel equally at ease if your move were to an international school with students from many different cultures? Or to a national school in a culture you knew nothing about, including not knowing the language?

On the other hand, your first day could have been a big surprise. You may have been wildly optimistic and then bitterly disappointed, or have had low expectations only to return home glowing from all the unexpected attention! So when we make predictions about human behaviour we may often be right, but we have nothing approaching the sort of certainty that allows us to put a man on the moon. However, what we do know about human behaviour seems knowledge enough to allow us to get about in the world more or less successfully.

Exercise

Think about those people who do not seem to get along well with others. Is it because of a lack of knowledge, the wrong kind of knowledge, or some other reason?

Understanding nature and understanding society

As part of your IB programme, you may have come into contact with subjects which are traditionally considered part of the human sciences, for example, economics or **social anthropology**. If you chose psychology you may have thought of it as something closer to the 'hard sciences'; yet others would not agree.

In fact, you may well have had opinions like these when choosing *your* subjects, such as, 'I much prefer the right answers in maths or science to the woolly thinking about why people behave in one way or another…' and so on. Yet students who favour the human sciences sometimes make similarly negative judgements in relation to maths and science.

Things don't get any easier if you have chosen philosophy or history. How much 'knowledge' can we really claim to have in these subjects when compared to other disciplines, and is it knowledge of the same sort? These are the kinds of issues we will be considering in this chapter. In doing so we will be asking ourselves questions such as:

- How is the study of human individuals or groups similar to the study of natural phenomena, or *things*? Can we (and should we?) use the same methods to study social behaviour that we use to study nature?

- Can we speak of *facts* in the human sciences, or only of *opinions*?

- Why might the study of human conduct not be considered a legitimate area of scientific research?

- Do we worry that if someone can explain our behaviour it shows that we are not really free?

- Can researchers place the appropriate distance between themselves and what they are studying, or are they always *involved* in ways that do not occur in science?

- Are we happy to describe and explain nature as it *is* but harbour dreams of what we think social life *should be* (more or less fair to all, more or less permissive or free)?

- Do our own experiences get in the way of what we are trying to achieve, or are these experiences a fundamental key to understanding human reality? Does this mark a significant shift in what we *mean* by knowledge?

 Anthropology The word 'anthropology' is derived from Greek and means 'the study of man'. Historically, anthropologists examined traditional, non-western peoples, often tribal. Today, studies of contemporary western and non-western societies have become common.

Social anthropology Social anthropology developed in the early twentieth century, under the influence of French sociological theory and the fieldwork methodologies of the Polish–British anthropologist Bronislaw Malinowski.

What are the differences between social and natural realities?

The prodigious achievement of natural science in the direction of the knowledge of things contrasts brutally with the collapse of this same natural science when faced with the strictly human element. The human element escapes physico-mathematical reason as water runs from a sieve.

✶✶✶✶✶

Man, in a word, has no nature; what he has is… history

From *History as a System* by José Ortega y Gasset

Ever since the first attempts at a scientific explanation of human behaviour were made in the nineteenth century, the question of whether such an explanation is possible has been a bone of contention. And the contention, both within and outside the human sciences, is simply that you cannot explain the behaviour of conscious living beings using the same methods and approaches that are used in the natural sciences. The debate can be as narrow as whether these disciplines can be regarded as sciences, or viewed from the broader and more sceptical question of whether *any* knowledge, in the strong sense of the term knowledge, is possible of human behaviour.

Human beings seem to be the only species that seeks to explain the world that surrounds them. The highly sophisticated language that we have developed has allowed us to build systems such as the great ancient myths, as well as the scientific theories looked at in Chapter 10: Natural science. It is, in part, because of this capacity for language that the world exists in ways that are meaningful for us. Thus, human beings develop what we might term an emotional investment in the way things are – that is, we *care* about the world! And nowhere is this more true than in our dealings with each other.

This capacity to care comes naturally to us, so what is the problem? The problem, as some see it, is that it makes it impossible to apply a strictly scientific approach to the understanding of human behaviour. Planets and electrons do not care about the world, so there is nothing we need to explain their behaviour other than the behaviour itself. But what would you think of someone trying to explain *your* behaviour, who couldn't care less about what *you* thought you were doing, or what your action meant to *you*! We think of our actions as purposeful, as based on reasons or motives; we are also likely to think that we know our reasons better than anyone else. And even if we don't know our reasons better than anyone else, even if we delude ourselves constantly, we would still think that our reasons were an important element in explaining our actions, wouldn't we?

Exercise

Has someone explained your behaviour by just looking at you without asking you what were doing or were trying to do? What did you think of this kind of interpretation that did not include your input?

The question about the meaningful nature of social action is at the centre of the debate regarding the scientific status of this field of study. Some have argued that only when social behaviour can be stripped of meaning will we be able to speak of the human sciences as sciences, and be able to apply the methods of science. In simplest terms, if I have an idea in my head about what I want to do, but you cannot see that idea, then you cannot study my behaviour scientifically. Others contend that it is only when we pay attention to, or seek to discover, the meaning that people attach to their behaviour (what *they* think they are doing) will we be able to interpret what is going on and understand this behaviour.

What do you make of the fact that most theoretical concepts (for example, 'force of gravity' or 'natural selection') are not observable either, yet we do not ascribe meaning to them! Consider the following extracts:

> Suppose now we bring someone into a room and place a glass of water before him. Will he drink? There appear to be only two possibilities: either he will or he will not… It is of no help to be told that… 'he drinks because he is thirsty…' If it means that he drinks because of a state of inner thirst, an inner causal event is invoked (and) it cannot serve as an explanation.
>
> B.F. Skinner
>
> *****
>
> There is a man and a glass of wine. Either he drinks or he does not. If he drinks, this act might be (among many) an expression of politeness, a show of loyalty or honour, a religious observance, a gesture of despair, an act of pleasure, a taste test, an attempt to seduce, corrupt, summon up courage, and so on. Any of these possibilities can be accepted as a good explanation, but to find the meaning of the action we may have to know the reason for its performance. That is, perhaps the action can be explained only in terms of someone's intention, or by reference to social norms and conventions, or some combination of the two.
>
> A.J. Ayer

The first extract represents the most radical attempt to eliminate any reference to what we might call purpose or what is going on *inside* someone. In this account, all non-observables must be eliminated according to a strictly scientific approach. Yet, as the second quote shows, the scientific approach may well miss the point of the act by confusing *movement* (the merely physical observable movement) with *social action* (movement that means something) – an important distinction in human behaviour.

Exercise

Consider the following events and discuss whether you think description of movement is enough, or whether something else, such as the purpose or the motive, is necessary to understand what is going on.

- A crowd cheering at 22 men or women chasing and kicking a soft spherical object on a rectangular patch of grass.
- A young man with a bag standing by the side of the road with his arm outstretched and his thumb pointing up.
- A man in a white coat looking at smudges on glass through a black apparatus.
- People mumbling with their heads bowed as a box is lowered into the ground.
- Men with painted faces engaged in strange rhythmic motion around a fire.
- People moving about aisles in a large building pushing carts with wheels and occasionally taking things from the shelves and putting them in the carts.

Think of similar examples you can suggest for discussion!

To further clarify some of the concepts central to the human sciences, the examples in this chapter will be taken mainly from sociology. Sociology is the reference, not because it can claim a special status in the human sciences, but because it is the discipline that most clearly set itself up to study and explain social behaviour over a century ago.

Durkheim and suicide: the quest for objectivity

Suppose you wanted to find out why suicide rates were increasing in certain areas, or amongst people of a particular age range? How would you go about it? Would you interview friends and colleagues or next-of-kin to find out why they felt their loved one had taken such a drastic decision? Would you study suicide notes, diaries, emails, chat room conversations and other sources that might give you a hint of what the person was going through?

Emile Durkheim, one of the founding fathers of modern sociology

This kind of investigation would make sense if you wanted to reconstruct an individual's frame of mind. But, in order to explain the more general (or objective) phenomenon (the increase in the suicide rate) you might look for common elements in the different cases, such as unemployment or post-traumatic stress, etc. (It is important to note that when we are explaining human behaviour, we need to distinguish whether we are talking about a single person or a group's behaviour.)

A different analysis can be found in the classical study of suicide conducted by Emile Durkheim (one of the founding fathers of sociology) and published in 1897. Durkheim examined current trends in suicide, but instead of looking into someone's mind or trying to figure out their intentions, he set about looking at the phenomenon in an entirely different way, an objective way. He combed through mountains of death certificates noting:

- age
- gender
- marital status
- religion
- number of children
- address (i.e. rural or urban settings)
- day of the week and season, etc.

However, he did so with no reference at all to what was going through the minds of those who actually took their own lives or tried to commit suicide. He didn't interview people, he didn't enquire as to the meaning or purpose they gave to what they were about to do; he simply looked at the data. This was a radical departure from previous styles of explanations.

Once he tabulated his findings, Durkheim came up with some quite remarkable data. One explanation of this data concerned what happens when someone moves from a rural to an urban setting. Durkheim called this move a shift in social integration. That is to say, the experience of moving from a tightly integrated community to a fast growing urban area was often accompanied by a feeling of *anomie*, of not knowing what was expected, or of not having a guiding framework for one's life. In short, a kind of confusion that brought about an anguish of spirit. Suicide sometimes followed.

The significance of Durkheim's findings is that he was able to provide an explanation for suicide rates that was grounded in what he termed 'social facts', and why the rates differed across different communities and social circumstances.

> When each people is seen to have its own suicide-rate, more constant than that of general mortality, that its growth is in accordance with a coefficient of acceleration characteristic of each society; when it appears that the variations through which it passes at different times of the day, month, year, merely reflect the rhythm of social life; and that marriage, divorce, the family, religious society, the army, etc., affect it in accordance with definite laws, some of which may even be numerically expressed, these states and institutions will no longer be regarded simply as characterless, ineffective ideological arrangements. Rather they will be felt to be real, living, active forces which, because of the way they determine the individual, prove their independence of him; which, if the individual enters as an element in the combination whence these forces ensue, at least control him once they are formed. Thus it will appear more clearly why sociology can and must be objective, since it deals with realities as definite and substantial as those of the psychologist or the biologist.
>
> From *Suicide: A Study in Sociology* by E. Durkheim

Weber and capitalism: meaning and *social* action

A different perspective to Durkheim's was developed by German sociologist, Max Weber (1864–1920) who thought that the most relevant feature of any kind of social action was that it was purposeful. In a word, such action, any kind of human behaviour, had meaning. He also believed that to interpret the meaning of human behaviour for those involved was the key to understanding any kind of social action.

> In 'action' is included all human behaviour when and insofar as the acting individual attaches a subjective meaning to it… the specific task of sociological analysis or of that of the other sciences of action… is the interpretation of action in terms of its subjective meaning.
>
> From *The Theory of Social and Economic Organization* by Max Weber

Weber's most famous work, *The Protestant Ethic and the Spirit of Capitalism,* is where he put forward the theory that capitalism prospered in the unique conditions that it found in the protestant communities of North America and Europe.

The question of why particular social changes take root more quickly in some settings than in others, rather than develop at similar speeds, is one that has vexed social theorists and economic historians, so let us briefly consider Weber's idea.

Take for example the author of this chapter who was born and bred in Santiago, Chile, and other than periods studying in the UK and Canada, this has always been home. A question that often arises in Latin America is why, given the proximity of the dates of wars and later declarations of independence to those of the US, Latin America did not take off in terms of economic development the way the US did. Even closer to the present, Australia, Canada and Argentina had very similar stages of economic development in the first half of the twentieth century but have very different levels today. A motion that was put to the author during a school debate back in the 1960s was, 'If Admiral Popham had won the Battle of Buenos Aires in 1806, Latin America would be a developed continent.' What do you make of this motion?

Weber asked himself a similar question in seeking to answer the question of why capitalism developed as quickly as it did in some parts of Europe, and in North America. His answer, in a nutshell, was that Protestantism, and more specifically Calvinism, was the ideal breeding ground for the budding social forces of capitalism. The idea that a devotion to work was the way in which you carried out the Lord's will in this life, and that your success in worldly affairs was proof that you were doing the right thing, was a powerful incentive. Even though salvation was not guaranteed by what you had done in your life, it was felt likely that leading a good life could tip the Lord's grace in your direction, whereas slothfulness would clearly lead you to damnation.

Note that Weber is not saying that Protestantism is the *cause* of capitalism, in the sense in which we might seek for a cause in physics (one billiard ball bumping into another and causing its movement). Nor is he arguing that we can infer greater and greater degrees of generalization… Weber's argument is simply that if you want to understand the process of capitalist development, and its uneven speeds of development in geographic terms, you must look to the meaning that people attach to what they are doing (or what they are refraining from doing).

The emphasis that Calvinist protestantism placed on rugged individualism, hard work, austerity and worldly success as a sign that one was indeed carrying out the Lord's work, was ideally suited to the developing capitalist societies, as compared to the older emphasis on community or rigid social hierarchy. It was a marriage made in heaven! Or rather, to use Weber's concept, the two had an **elective affinity** for each other, which means more or less the same thing.

What might Durkheim have suggested, or how might he have gone about looking at this same phenomenon? Perhaps he would have simply noted the coincidence of rates of development with the dominance of certain religious beliefs, that is, capitalism developed more quickly in countries with a largely protestant population. The coincidence can be established as an objective fact, and explained with reference to the beliefs of a particular religion, but certainly *not* by trying to establish what the individuals involved might think of what they were doing.

Max Weber, a German sociologist

Elective affinity A term used to describe how any two things, capitalism and Protestantism, (or even people) seemed made for each other, or, how there was 'good chemistry' between them.

Exercise

How do you square these two sociologists against each other? Are you more Durkheimian or Weberian? Do you feel they both make good points?

What do you think Durkheim and Weber might make of the piece below about chemistry in the dating game? One of the companies that offers the matchmaking service estimates they are responsible for about 2 per cent of marriages in the US per year! Could matchmaking be a legitimate human science?

Hitting it off, thanks to algorithms of love

Pasadena, California

The two students in Southern California had just been introduced during an experiment to test their 'interpersonal chemistry'. The man, a graduate student, dutifully asked the undergraduate woman what her major was.

'Spanish and sociology,' she said.

'Interesting,' he said. 'I was a sociology major. What are you going to do with that?'

'You are just full of questions.'

'It's true.'

…

Bogart and Bacall it was not. But Gian Gonzaga, a social psychologist, could see possibilities for this couple as he watched their recorded chat on a television screen.

They were nodding and smiling in unison, and the woman stroked her hair and briefly licked her lips – positive signs of chemistry that would be duly recorded in this experiment at the new eHarmony Labs here. By comparing these results with the couple's answers to hundreds of other questions, the researchers hoped to draw closer to a new and extremely lucrative grail – making the right match.

Once upon a time, finding a mate was considered too important to be entrusted to people under the influence of raging hormones. Their parents, sometimes assisted by astrologers and matchmakers, supervised courtship until customs changed in the West because of what was called the Romeo and Juliet revolution…

But now some social scientists have rediscovered the appeal of adult supervision – provided the adults have doctorates and vast caches of psychometric data. Online matchmaking has become a boom industry as rival scientists test their algorithms for finding love.

From *The New York Times*, nytimes.com, by John Tierney, 29 January 2008

Clearly the matchmakers are not concerned with the inner thoughts or subjective meanings attached to what is going on with the couple involved – simultaneous laughter and the licking of lips are far more meaningful (for the researchers, that is). Would Weber or Durkheim even think of this matchmaking as human science?

The different approaches between Weber and Durkheim led to a difference in methodology for human scientists: the top-down approach associated with Durkheim gave rise to what was termed **holism**, while Weber's emphasis on meaning led to the label of **methodological individualism**.

▲ Matchmaking – a social science?

Holism The properties of a given system (biological, chemical, social, economic, mental, linguistic, etc.) cannot be explained by its parts alone; the system as a whole determines how the parts behave.

Methodological individualism This is a method aimed at explaining and understanding broad society-wide developments as the sum total of decisions by individuals. In the most extreme version, the 'whole' is nothing but the 'sum of its parts' (atomism). It has also been described as 'reductionism', a reduction of the explanation of all large entities by reference to smaller ones.

Exercise

Find out more about holism and methodological individualism by visiting the Stanford Encyclopedia of Philosophy.

Go to www.heinemann.co.uk/hotlinks and insert the express code 4327P to access the Stanford Encyclopedia of Philosophy.

Human thought and dichotomies (either/or polar opposites)

We have seen how our authors have approached society from two opposing angles. One (Durkheim) argues that the whole structure or system determines how the parts relate, while the other (Weber) sees the whole as emerging from the individual parts (*top-down* versus *bottom up* analysis, or *holistic* versus *methodological individualism*). One prefers to examine social *facts* without recourse to the meaning that individuals attach to their actions, while the other feels that this misses the point of what is distinctly human about social action (*outside* versus *inside*). A question that we could ask about human knowledge is whether these dichotomies are ways in which we simplify reality in order to deal with it more easily, or features of the reality itself.

Social science, values and objective knowledge

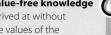

Value-free knowledge
Arrived at without the values of the researcher influencing the result. Often called 'objective' knowledge (in contrast to 'subjective' knowledge).

The question of how **value-free** knowledge can be (or ought to be) is not an issue that only applies to human sciences. However, in human affairs we are not only interested in knowing how things *are* (although this can be of great importance) but we care about how we would *like them to be*.

Human scientists and philosophers have hotly debated whether it is possible to have a value-free human science. Some scholars, known as 'naturalists', argue that you *can* apply the methods of the natural sciences to the study of social behaviour, and that the analysis of social behaviour can be just as objective as that of a natural science. Others, known as 'interpretivists', contend that the goal of this kind of objectivity is an impossible (and undesirable) goal since human sciences are by nature interpretive disciplines.

Weber was amongst the interpretivists. He would have been shocked to think that anyone would argue in favour of a value-free human science, since he believed that it was precisely our values, that is to say, our *caring* about what we were doing, that made something an interesting problem to analyse.

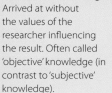

Objective knowledge
Knowledge of things as they *really are*, rather than as the observer believes them to be.
Subjective knowledge
Knowledge in which the observer's beliefs colour the reality perceived.

Interpretation is often contrasted with *description*. With description, people are supposedly told how things *really are*, while interpretation goes beyond, or adds a slant to, the description. This is often used as a way of establishing a difference between human and natural sciences, but one might well ask whether it is that easy to separate factual description from interpretation.

Another way of thinking of this difference would be to ask yourself whether all knowledge has *degrees* of **objectivity** and **subjectivity**, rather than the clear-cut separation that is often suggested among different areas of knowledge.

However, there is still another important difference between the human and natural sciences. In the natural sciences the *observer* is not *like* what is being observed (a person is not a stone or a planet), whereas in the human sciences, people are observing people, their own kind. So there is not a hard and fast line between what is observed and what is said about the behaviour of others.

The following example may help to clarify your thoughts on the questions above.

Think about the owner of a chain of supermarkets who wants to know the best way to organize his products in the store. He is not very much interested in *why* certain events occur, since his goal is to predict regular patterns of behaviour in order to gain maximum sales. While working on his product placement, the owner will draw on personal experience to some extent since he is a shopper himself. Obviously near the check-out is a prime spot for some items, but there are other considerations that come into play, for example, eye-level position, etc. Let's presume, however, that deciding on the most effective shop-floor layout can best be approached by studying what people actually *do*, that is, *how* they actually shop. This approach comes close to what can be called 'the study of regularities', that is, describing what actually happens in the store as a basis for making predictions.

By contrast to a description of what is taking place in any defined and observable situation, take the presidential primaries in the US. Enormous amounts of money are spent on what can be called 'public opinion'. Much of this money is spent recording the perceptions or intentions of possible voters. But a great deal of time is also devoted to finding out what gives rise to or causes these perceptions or voting intentions amongst the various segments of voters defined by age, gender, ethnicity, social background, etc.

Is it possible that we could choose different methods depending on what we are looking at, and what we are seeking to do?

> '*Some people believe that psychology is just being replaced by brain imaging, but I don't think that's the case at all,' Dehaene said. 'We need psychology to refine our idea of what the imagery is going to show us. That's why we do behavioral experiments, see patients.* **It's the confrontation of all these different methods that creates knowledge.'**
>
> 'Numbers guy: are our brains wired for math?' by Jim Holt, published in
> *The New Yorker*, 3 March 2008

(Look back to page 123 and the discussion on 'black boxes' and the levels of explanation.)

Might it not be the case that in the human sciences in general, and perhaps in other areas, the combination of different methods is what will create knowledge?

A plurality of disciplines

As we said before, you might have had personal experience of a human science as part of your IB programme. This is because the IB's *Individuals and Societies* requirement also includes subjects that would not normally come under that heading, such as philosophy or history (though some might argue that they should).

The main feature distinctive of the human sciences is not just that they study human behaviour, but that they concentrate on *social* behaviour. That is, the behaviour of individuals in groups. Even so, the collection of disciplines that are normally included seem to exhibit important differences amongst them including sociology, anthropology, economics and political science.

Think of the variety of names that you could attach to yourself, names that sociologists would call 'roles' (much like in a play). You are a student, a son or daughter, an IB Diploma candidate, a member of a particular religion, ethnic group, etc. See how many you can think of, both for yourself and for your parents or maybe your TOK teacher. In each of these roles you are expected to follow certain rules, or rather, there are accepted patterns of behaviour to which you are expected to conform, at least to some degree. How do people that belong to groups such as families, government bureaucracies, religious groups, armies, civic and political associations behave when they are members of them? How are societies divided into groups according to income and status, and how does this affect their behaviour? These are the sorts of questions sociologists ask themselves. And anthropologists, particularly social or cultural anthropologists, ask themselves similar questions, but usually in relation to earlier or pre-literate societies. However, as mentioned, this is changing more and more to include contemporary society.

How many roles do you have?

Economists often think that of all the human sciences they have the biggest claim to being scientific because they use modelling and hypothesis testing, etc. It is probably also true to say that economics is the discipline in which mathematics is used most extensively. In addition, most economists would like to think that their subject is one in which it is easier to isolate variables, or to stipulate conditions under which we could know how these variables might behave. Of course there are some areas, such as the stock market, that are often used as examples of chaotic systems, where the system can just as easily go haywire.

Political science is probably the discipline that is most obviously a mixture of description and evaluation, formed in order to put forward remedies that could improve political arrangements. It would seem that an obvious goal of research in this field is to understand so that we can make improvements.

This is why John Rawls has described political theory as realistically utopian when he says:

> Our hope for the future of our society rests on the belief that the social world allows at least a decent political order…
>
> From *Justice as Fairness: a Restatement* by J. Rawls

This is what was meant earlier when the question was raised whether you could have a science concerned with how things *ought to be*!

Social research methods

Diverging opinions about methodology amongst human scientists are reflected by the methods they prefer. This is not surprising.

Those who favour a *naturalist* or *positivist* view, namely, that human sciences are in essence no different from the natural sciences, tend to favour an approach where *quantitative* methods are dominant. Those who have this outlook are therefore concerned to gather data for analysis using techniques such as surveys, questionnaires, secondary statistical data, analysis of the behaviour of key indicators, etc. An important objective for researchers in this tradition is to be able to limit the variables involved in order to generalize their conclusions as much as possible.

By contrast, others favour *qualitative* analysis, where the research offers detailed descriptions of phenomena (case studies, ethnographies, etc.). Here quantification might have little to offer regarding attitudes related to God or religion, the workplace experience of a woman in an all-male environment, or growing up under Mao's Cultural Revolution.

Go to www.heinemann. co.uk/hotlinks and insert the express code 4327P to visit a useful website on research methods.

Exercise

How might a human scientist determine the truth of the following generalisations?
- Gender behaviour is learned, not inherited.
- Children who are raised in a violent manner become violent adults.
- Powerlessness breeds apathy.
- Private management is always more efficient than public management.

Exercise

1 Take sociology, anthropology, economics and political science and ask yourself which you consider to be *most scientific* and *why*.

Typical features for considering something to be a science include a unique method involving:
- the capacity for experiment or controlled observation
- the capacity to isolate variables
- testable hypotheses
- the generation of Laws
- predictability
- explanatory power
- the importance of mathematics
- theoretical agreement
- consensus amongst practitioners
- others you may think of…

2 Rank the subjects from *most* to *least scientific*, and compare notes with others. Finally, ask yourself if, as a result, you can consider some of them to provide *better* knowledge than others.

The ethics of research in social science

When we talk about our knowledge of social behaviour, and whether it is scientific or not, many of the questions raised about the ethics of natural scientific research are seen as relevant to the human sciences. What are the moral boundaries that must be observed in human science research? Suppose we wanted to know how a particular group might react if it knew that one of its members was being tortured in the room next door. Is it ethically acceptable to subject an experimental group to simulated screams in order to study their reactions to the supposed torture? Are there situations where a research study violates what we consider to be the limits of human dignity? When human beings, not sticks or stones, are the subjects of research, should extra or different limits be in place?

For example, a well-known project, the Milgram experiment, was conducted to test the obedience of people to authority. Participants were asked by an authority figure, a supposed experimental scientist, to apply an electric shock to a person who was in the next room. Those who were administering the shock treatment had no knowledge that it was actually an actor who was simulating the pain – they thought it was really happening. Yet most of the participants applying the shock continued to obey instructions even when the subject could be heard suffering as the voltage increased. This behaviour would clearly have been unacceptable to them in their day-to-day affairs. Is this kind of experiment legitimate? Clearly there is at least a problem of *informed consent*. Is this kind of deceit acceptable in the name of research?

As background information, the experiment was devised at the time that Eichmann was being tried in Jerusalem for the wholesale slaughter of millions of people in the Holocaust. Milgram may well have thought it more important to understand *why* people might have behaved as they did in Nazi Germany (i.e. the compliance with immoral orders) than to consider the rights of the participants in the experiment. What do you think?

A more detailed account of the Milgram experiment can be found at www.heinemann.co.uk/hotlinks and by using the express code 4327P.

Exercise

How do you feel about the ethical questions that might be raised by this sort of experiment?
- Go to www.heinemann.co.uk/hotlinks and insert the express code 4327P to find a more detailed account of the Milgram experiment.
- On the same website, you will find a link which takes you to a website showing Derren Brown's modern day re-enactment of the experiment.

You may also want to consider this topic (ethical dilemmas of social research) for your TOK presentation.

For related experiments in the human sciences, go to www.heinemann.co.uk/hotlinks and insert the express code 4327P. There you will find two links. The first takes you to an explanation of the Stanford experiment and the second will take you to a description of Asch's Conformity experiment.

The lack of consensus in human science

The natural sciences seem to achieve a high degree of agreement with regard to their accepted theories and methods. By contrast, there seems to be far more controversy and competing viewpoints in the human sciences, thus much less agreement. Do you recall the earlier discussions related to the idea of paradigms?

In Thomas Kuhn's view, the human sciences are at a 'pre-paradigmatic' stage – that is they have not matured to the level where consensus reigns throughout the community. (Look back to page 121 for more information on Kuhn.) You would not expect to find the sort of methodological differences (subjective versus objective) that we saw between Durkheim and Weber in the natural sciences. (However, it is possible to make too much of the level of agreement in the natural sciences, as the closer one moves to cutting edge science, the more controversies arise.)

In the human sciences, however, controversy can run so deep that it becomes impossible to mediate between the positions, or to find a way of deciding what the *facts* are. (A typical result, for Kuhn, of the lack of an agreed paradigm.) These differences are often built into the language used by each camp, as you can see in the following story or parable. Such differences may not seem too significant until we see groups torn apart by the profound divisions that opposing camps represent. As far as knowledge is concerned, if we can't arbitrate between the two, how can we decide which one offers us the 'better' knowledge?

The story of A-town and B-ville

Once upon a time, said the Professor, there were two small communities, spiritually as well as geographically situated at a considerable distance from each other. They had, however, these problems in common: both were hard hit by a recession, so that in each of the towns there were about one hundred heads of families unemployed.

The city fathers of A-town, the first community, were substantial and sound-thinking businessmen. The unemployed tried hard, as unemployed people usually do, to find jobs; but the situation did not improve. The city fathers had been brought up to believe that there is always enough work for everyone, if you only look for it hard enough. Comforting themselves with this doctrine, the city fathers could have shrugged their shoulders and turned their backs on the problem, except for the fact that they were genuinely kind-hearted men. They could not bear to see the unemployed men and their wives and children starving. In order to prevent hardship, they felt that they had to provide these people with some means of sustenance. Their principles told them, nevertheless, that if people were given something for nothing, it would demoralize their character. Naturally this made the city fathers even more unhappy, because they were faced with the horrible choice of (1) letting the unemployed starve, or (2) destroying their moral character.

The solution they finally hit upon, after much debate and soul-searching, was this. They decided to give the unemployed families 'relief payments' of two hundred dollars a month. (They considered using the English term 'dole,' but with their characteristic American penchant for euphemism, they decided on the less offensive term.) To make sure that the unemployed would not take their unearned payments too much for granted, however, they decided that the 'relief' was to be accompanied by a moral lesson; to wit: the obtaining of the assistance would be made so difficult, humiliating, and disagreeable that there would be no temptation for anyone to go through the process unless it was absolutely necessary; the moral disapproval of the community would be turned upon the recipients of the money at all times in such a way that they would try hard to get 'off relief' and 'regain their self-respect.' Some even proposed that people on relief be denied the vote, so that the moral lesson would be more deeply impressed upon them. Others suggested that their names be published at regular intervals in the newspapers. The city fathers had enough faith in the goodness of human nature to expect that the recipients would be grateful, since they were getting something for nothing, something which they hadn't worked for.

When the plan was put into operation, however, the recipients of the relief cheques proved to be an ungrateful, ugly bunch. They seemed to resent the cross-examinations and inspections at the hands of the 'relief investigators,' who, they said, took advantage of a man's misery to snoop into every detail of his private life. In spite of uplifting editorials in A-town Tribune telling them how grateful they ought to be, the recipients of the relief refused to learn any moral lessons, declaring that they were 'just as good as anybody else.' When, for example, they permitted themselves the rare luxury of a movie or an evening of bingo, their neighbours looked at them sourly as if to say, 'I work hard and pay my taxes just in order to support loafers like you in idleness and pleasure.'

This attitude, which was fairly characteristic of those members of the community who still had jobs, further embittered the relief recipients, so that they showed even less gratitude as time went on and were constantly on the lookout for insults, real or imaginary, from people who might think that they weren't as good as anybody else. A number of them took to moping all day long; one or two even committed suicide. Others, feeling that they had failed to provide, found it hard to look their wives and children in the face. Children whose parents were 'on relief' felt inferior to classmates whose parents were not 'public charges.' Some of these children developed inferiority complexes which affected not only their grades at school, but their careers after graduation. Finally, several relief recipients felt they could stand their loss of self-respect no longer and decided, after many efforts to gain honest jobs, that they would earn money by their own efforts even if they had to rob. They did so and were caught and sent to the state penitentiary.

The depression, therefore, hit A-town very hard. The relief policy had averted starvation, no doubt, but suicide, personal quarrels, unhappy homes, the weakening of social organizations, the maladjustment of children, and, finally, crime, had resulted. The town was divided in two, the 'haves' and the 'have-nots,' so that there was class hatred. People shook their heads sadly and declared that it all went to prove over again what they had known from the beginning, that giving people something for nothing inevitably demoralizes their character. The citizens of A-town gloomily waited for prosperity to return, with less and less hope as time went on.

The story of the other community, B-ville, was entirely different. B-ville was a relatively isolated town, too far out of the way to be reached by Rotary Club speakers and other dispensers of conventional wisdom. One of the aldermen, however, who was something of an economist, explained to his fellow aldermen that unemployment, like sickness, accident, fire, tornado, or death, hits unexpectedly in modem society, irrespective of the victim's merits or deserts. He went on to say that B-ville's homes, parks, streets, industries, and everything else B-ville was proud of, had been built in part by the work of these same people who were now unemployed. He then proposed to apply a principle of insurance: if the work these unemployed people had previously done for the community could be regarded as a form of 'premium' paid to the community against a time of misfortune, payments now made to them to prevent their starvation could be regarded as 'insurance claims.'

He therefore proposed that all men of good repute who had worked in the community in some line of useful endeavour, whether as machinists, clerks, or bank managers, be regarded as 'citizen policyholders,' having 'claims' against the city in the case of unemployment for two hundred dollars a month until such time as they might again be employed.

Naturally, he had to talk very slowly and patiently, since the idea was entirely new to his fellow aldermen. But he described his plan as a 'straight business proposition,' and finally they were persuaded. They worked out in detail, to everyone's satisfaction, the conditions under which citizens should be regarded as policy-holders in the city's social insurance plan, and decided to give cheques for two hundred dollars a month to the heads of each of B-ville's indigent families.

B-ville's 'claim adjusters', whose duty it was to investigate the claims of the citizen 'policyholders', had a much better time than A-town's 'relief investigators'. While the latter had been resentfully regarded as snoopers, the former, having no moral lesson to teach but simply a business transaction to carry out, treated their clients with businesslike courtesy and got the same amount of information as the relief investigators had, with considerably less difficulty. There were no hard feelings. It further happened, fortunately, that news of B-ville's plans reached a liberal newspaper editor in the big city at the other end of the state. This writer described the plan in a leading feature story headed 'B-VILLE LOOKS AHEAD'. Adventure in Social Pioneering Launched by Upper Valley Community.' As a result of this publicity, inquiries about the plan began to come to the city hall even before the first cheques were mailed out. This led, naturally, to a considerable feeling of pride on the part of the aldermen, who, being boosters, felt that this was a wonderful opportunity to put B-ville on the map.

A-town

B-ville

Accordingly, the aldermen decided that instead of simply mailing out the cheques as they had originally intended, they would publicly present the first cheques at a monster civic ceremony. They invited the governor of the state, who was glad to come to bolster his none-too-enthusiastic support in that locality, the president of the state university, the senator from their district, and other functionaries. They decorated the National Guard armoury with flags and got out the American Legion Fife and Drum Corps, the Boy Scouts, and other civic organizations. At the big celebration, each family to receive a 'social insurance cheque' was marched up to the platform to receive it, and the governor and the mayor shook hands with each of them as they came trooping up in their best clothes. Fine speeches were made; there was much cheering and shouting; pictures of the event showing the recipients of the checks shaking hands with the mayor, and the governor patting the heads of the children, were published not only in the local papers but also in several metropolitan picture sections.

Every recipient of these insurance cheques had a feeling, therefore, that he had been personally honoured, that he lived in a wonderful little town, and that he could face his unemployment with greater courage and assurance, since his community was behind him. The men and women found themselves being kidded in a friendly way by their acquaintances for having been 'up there with the big shots', shaking hands with the governor, and so on. The children at school found themselves envied for having had their pictures in the papers. All in all, B-ville's unemployed did not commit suicide, were not haunted by a sense of failure, did not turn to crime, did not manifest personal maladjustments, did not develop class hatred, as the result of their two hundred dollars a month…

At the conclusion of the Professor's story, the discussion began:

'That just goes to show,' said the Advertising Man, who was known among his friends as a realistic thinker, 'what good promotional work can do. B-ville's city council had real advertising sense, and that civic ceremony was a masterpiece… made everyone happy… put over the scheme in a big way. Reminds me of the way we do things in our business: as soon as we called horse, mackerel tuna-fish, we developed a big market for it. I suppose if you called relief "insurance", you could actually get people to like it, couldn't you?'

'What do you mean, "calling" it insurance?' asked the Social Worker. 'B-ville's scheme wasn't relief at all. It was insurance.'

'Good grief, man! Do you realize what you're saying?' cried the Advertising Man in surprise. 'Are you implying that those people had any right to that money? All I said was that it's a good idea to disguise relief as insurance if it's going to make people any happier. But it's still relief, no matter what you call it. It's alright to kid the public along to reduce discontent, but we don't need to kid ourselves as well!'

From *Language in Thought and Action* by S.I. Hayakawa

Imagine after reading this story that someone says to you that the facts are clearly the same in both cases and the difference is only one of interpretation. What would the facts be without the interpretation? Recession? Unemployment? Monthly payments? But do even these terms mean the same to the different communities? Can you really separate the facts from what they mean to the people involved? Or rather, is meaning not really a central and inseparable part of the *social fact*?

Exercise

Imagine for a minute that the argument is not taking place between the advertising man and a social worker. Instead, there is a third city, 'ABCity', where half the city council agrees with A-town and half agree with B-ville! How would they sort their differences out and arrive at a solution for the unemployment crisis?

A tale of two perspectives

You have already considered the question of sense perception, including how our expectations, prior experiences and viewpoints influence what we perceive. This phenomenon also occurs in the natural sciences, which is why Popper thought falsification was the way to guarantee intellectual honesty (see Chapter 10: Natural science). In short, it is easier to find confirmation for your hypothesis than to try to falsify it.

Although originating in the previous century, these two opposing viewpoints divide the human sciences, in a sense, into two camps. The camps can best be described as asking two diametrically opposed questions:

- What are the forces that bind societies together?
- What are the forces that tear them apart?

These two perspectives also start from different basic assumptions that lead into different interpretations of society.

- Societies, though they occasionally exhibit signs of conflict, are basically systems that tend towards equilibrium.
- Societies have internal tensions that explain their historical development: these explain their periods of apparent stability, social breakdown and change.

What are the forces that bind societies together?

What are the forces that tear societies apart?

Exercise

- To get a feel for the differences, brainstorm answers to both of the questions posed by the photographs above and list them in two columns. A couple of examples have been given to get you started.

Forces that bind societies together	Forces that generate conflict
A shared legal system	Unequal distribution of resources

- This exercise is more effective if carried out and discussed in class, or if you at least compare your notes with other people's.

As already said, most human scientists are as interested in changing or improving society as they are in understanding it, and in this equilibrium/conflict debate it was no different. Equilibrium-oriented theories tried to understand the institutions of *successful* societies usually in the *developed* world. They then compared the successful societies to those that were less developed, that is, those societies with weaker institutions and seemingly permanent conflict. These thinkers felt that it would be a good thing if the less developed societies could move towards the more modern values of those that were more developed (think of today's efforts to *spread* democracy). Conflict theory thinkers tended to believe that conflict was the result of social injustice, and that only a collapse of the existing system would allow the liberation of the oppressed. As a result, revolutionary change was sought.

Imagine trying to find a common ground between these two schools of thought... And if we cannot find common ground, could we somehow argue that one of these views is true, or more true than the other, or that there are other grounds for preferring one over the other (arguing that one produces better results, for instance)?

In order to understand the contemporary relevance of these two divergent ways of thinking, take a common example, such as industrial action and striking workers. At the risk of oversimplification, a conflict view might see a strike as the natural resistance of workers to an unfair social arrangement in which they have drawn the short straw. However, another approach could interpret the strike as an example of disaffection, of insufficient socialisation into the norms and values of the community, etc.

Would you agree that all perspectives have basic built-in assumptions or core beliefs about what the world is like that are seldom spelled out explicitly? The assumptions mentioned above, about the nature of society as tending toward equilibrium or conflict, are this sort of belief. As a result, could we claim that all knowledge is built on some unquestioned basic beliefs? If so, that might seem to provide a shaky foundation for knowledge but, at the same time, it may be an inevitable feature of human knowing.

The Greek explanation for flames rising was that they wanted to be in their natural place, which they believed was the Sun (a wonderful explanation if in your world things can have desires). Newton's reference to the force of gravity stemmed from the belief that nothing moves unless there is a force applied to it (something that is part of our experience).

In the natural sciences, the existence of assumptions is less obvious because the natural scientists can generate widespread consensus and, when everyone agrees, assumptions simply look like obvious truths! However, in the case of the human sciences, as in A-town and B-ville, it is easier to see that they start from different assumptions. As a result, it can be very difficult to get the different positions to agree on what the facts of the matter *are*, and even more difficult to get them to agree on a common explanation.

Exercise

- Go back over the A-town and B-ville extract on pages 203–5 and try to pick out the assumptions made there, including those of the final dialogue.
- Alternatively, choose a common hypothesis (it could be your Extended Essay) and try to make all its assumptions explicit.

Some other complications

There are other problems or difficulties to be faced when trying to gain knowledge of social affairs. One is the *complexity* of the variables in social realities, for example, trying to be precise about subjective meaning or dispositions such as consumer confidence or social mood. Added to this is the difficulty of isolating these variables so that we can have a clear idea of what is affecting what or what causes what. In the natural sciences, there are techniques which allow us to factor out the influences of certain variables so that we can see the effect of one variable on another. In the human sciences, with some minor exceptions, it is extremely difficult to identify the variables, isolate them for experimental study and then explore their causal relationship to one another.

This is because of:
- the size of the chunks that are being analysed
- the interaction of variables from many of the different subsystems that are the domain of different social sciences (the economy, the political system and other social institutions).

Another knowledge issue arises from the fact that we are trying to explain conscious beings who are (sometimes) aware of the fact that they are being studied, or aware of the statements that are being made about them. As a result, there can be problems of honesty (people not telling the truth when replying to surveys), or of people behaving in ways that might not be the norm if the observer were not present. And, if predictions are made about social behaviour, it is possible that this very fact could cause people to deliberately act otherwise. It could even become a self-fulfilling prophecy, causing people to act in a way they would not have done if the prediction had not been made. Imagine a Chancellor of the Exchequer predicting a run on the banks during the evening news, or a Health Minister saying she expects huge queues at vaccination centres given the appearance of a deadly virus. It is highly likely that both these things will occur, not because they would have anyway, but simply because the prediction was publicly made.

There is also the question of rationality. It has often been an assumption in the human sciences that human beings are essentially rational creatures. Indeed, the hallmark of intelligent action has reason in firm control of the emotions. This has proved to be unwarranted, and it has now been shown that the emotions play an enormous part in what we call intelligent behaviour. Hence in more contemporary research there is a current emphasis on 'soft skills' as important personal attributes. Of course, there is nothing wrong with this new emphasis, except for the additional difficulty it poses for human scientists. The assumption of rationality may be wrong (at least in many circumstances) but it certainly made research easier when we believed it to be right.

Exercise

See what you can find out about intelligent behaviour as linked to emotions by looking up the following authors:
- Robert Solomon
- Ronald de Souza
- Martha Nussbaum
- Antonio Damasio
- Daniel Goleman.

Today's world: Internet galaxy

An interesting analysis of today's world can be found in the work of Manuel Castells, a Catalan sociologist and city planner. His work on the effects of technology (ICT) on social structures, and the emergence of the 'networked society', is particularly fascinating. This is a society:

> … *where the key social structures and activities are organized around electronically processed information networks.*
>
> From 'Conversations with History' interviews conducted
> by the Institute of International Studies at UC Berkeley

The global character of these networks, which allows simultaneity in ways that were not possible before, creates situations of inclusion, but also an important element of exclusion. Those who do not feel part of the system or its values can also avail themselves of the technology to make themselves heard, whether it be minorities, anti-globalization movements, ecological organizations, NGOs or guerilla movements. There are others who cannot avail themselves of the technology and struggle to assert their identity by negating the validity of these global forces. They counter with their own religious or ethnic identities which they perceive as superior to the crass values of the global economy. For Castells, the networking and the struggle for identity are key interacting forces.

British sociologist, Anthony Giddens, has also taken an important look at our contemporary reality, and the forces unleashed with the processes of globalization; it is telling that one of his most recent publications has the title *Runaway World*.

Finally, it is worth mentioning the emergence of forms of work that were unheard of until quite recently. For example, not merely the capacity to work together at a distance on a document, but the free exchange of ideas and products, open-source software, universities publishing their entire curriculum online, etc. These collaborative efforts seem to suggest that the view that human beings are essentially selfish beings is really a caricature.

Ideal knower

Zygmunt Bauman (1925–), the 'hopeful pessimist'

Zygmunt Bauman (born in Poznan, Poland) is widely regarded as one of the most profound and original voices in contemporary social thought. His work deftly interweaves issues of ethics, culture and politics, with the express intention of interpreting society in a way that challenges and provokes us to aspire towards something better. Bauman's reflections on consumerism and poverty, uncertainty and insecurity, political disengagement and moral indifference, should give us pause for thought…

> From 'Searching for politics in an uncertain world: an interview with
> Zygmunt Bauman' by D. Leighton

Zygmunt Bauman

A key notion in Bauman's work is that the axis in modern society has shifted from the producer to the consumer. Freedom was once understood as a social and political good that endowed us with rights and duties in our social relations, and towards the community as a whole. But in modern society, the dominant view of freedom is 'freedom to choose', a very personal and private idea which shifts the focus from 'me and my community' very decisively to 'me'. The result, in Bauman's view, is both political apathy and moral indifference. The 'common good' (an important view of what politics was all about in past times) is no longer something that engages our interest, and morality is something you tailor to your own interests, rather than tacitly agreed ways of acting towards and treating our equals – *chacun à son goût*! (It's a matter of individual taste.)

While it might be thought that Bauman is nostalgic, yearning for past times, he is really trying to tell us that in moving forward we must overcome some of the ideological discussions that are central to our time (state versus market, individual versus community). Freedom and community cannot be viewed as ideas that stand opposed to each other if we are to construct more satisfactory ways of living together.

His notion of *liquid modernity* is a powerful metaphor in understanding the fluid nature of contemporary society.

Student presentation

1 Choose a social problem which you would like to research and ask yourself how you would go about it. What methods would you use to better understand or explain what is going on and, more importantly, what sort of knowledge or expertise would you need? Imagine you had to put together a team of six researchers. What sort of people would you choose, and why?

2 A common debate about human beings is the extent to which we are the product of our environment as opposed to that of our biological make-up (nature versus nurture). Schools are often thought to be a major influence, either through teaching or via playground peers. How might you research this, and how confident would you be of the results?

Essay questions

1 This is a recent Prescribed Title (PT). Discuss the implications of the statement below for the knowledge that might be obtained in social sciences, and contrast with other Areas of Knowledge.

> We know ourselves as individuals but we also know that what goes on inside ourselves is almost exactly what goes on inside everybody else... We recognize the whole of the human race within ourselves.

> J. Bronowski
> ©International Baccalaureate Organization 1996

2 *In the art of living, man is both the artist and the object of his art, the sculptor and his marble, both doctor and patient...* (Erich Fromm). Does this dimension restrict our capacity to know ourselves in ways that are not present in other areas of knowledge?

History

Part 1: the contested past

Living history: the Japanese textbook controversy

In 2001, a committee of Japanese historians wrote *A New History Textbook* (this was the actual title) for Japanese students. It offered a revised account of the invasion and occupation of East and South-East Asia by Imperial Japan between 1937 and 1945. The traditional account, supported by every available piece of evidence and thousands of witnesses, painted a picture of one of the most brutal invasions of the Second World War. When the Chinese port of Nanjing was invaded, the Japanese Army was allowed to run amok, brutalising the population for days. War records show that there were about 300,000 deaths in only two weeks. *A New History Textbook* denied this account and claimed that 'perhaps only 2000 died in war conditions'.

The ten countries of South-East Asia protested strongly. But the East Asian countries of China, North Korea and South Korea, where Japanese military occupation was the longest and most bloody, staged protests at the United Nations and at every Japanese embassy across the world, to highlight what they called 'historic distortion'. Within Japan, teachers and intellectuals filed a court case that brought the textbook controversy to the attention of the world media.

Now examine the following perspectives of China, Japan, North Korea and South Korea to *A New History Textbook*. The source is 'Ghosts from the Past', a research paper by three young historians, Tim Beal, Jian Yang and Yoshiko Nozaki.

Chinese views

Assumption: China is traditionally fearful of Japanese nationalism.

The Chinese accused *A New History Textbook* of portraying Japan's former imperialism and aggressive war stance as a force to help free Asian countries from European and American colonial rule. The Chinese state-run newspaper (*People's Daily*) noted that:

> It [the textbook] shamelessly justifies Japan's invasion of South-East Asia as 'Japanese victories over the Western powers that allowed countries in the region to achieve post-war independence'.

What angered the Chinese most, perhaps, is the description of the Nanjing Massacre. The draft of the textbook claimed that even if there had been some killings, they were not in the same category as the Jewish Holocaust. The final version of the textbook was approved by the Ministry of Education in Tokyo.

North Korean views

Assumption: North Korea needs financial compensation more than an apology.

Korea's reaction to the textbook is largely affected by the different relationships the two Korean states have with Japan, and the current state of inter-Korean relations. North Korea has hostile relations with Japan and is partitioned from South Korea. They see the textbook controversy only as part of their call for compensation.

South Korean views

Assumption: South Korea will not sacrifice her trade relations with Japan.

It is vitally important that South Korea's attitude towards Japan is positive – politically, economically, socially and culturally – and yet there is wide, deep-felt and continuing animosity towards Japan. Nonetheless, the importance of trade between Japan and South Korea allows protest against the textbook, but also compromise, so that trade is not endangered.

Japanese views

Assumption: Japan was defeated in the Second World War.

Japan itself is deeply divided over the textbook controversy. In the late 1980s, the Nationalist political party established the Committee for the Examination of History. The committee agreed to launch a campaign promoting views of history that held the Asia-Pacific War to be justifiable, and that denied the existence of the Nanjing Massacre and other wartime events.

History and the nature of knowledge

History offers a record, both of the growth of knowledge and, perhaps more significantly, the changes in knowledge. It constructs a context for the understanding of events and topics and thus contains multiple knowledge issues. When context shifts, the nature of knowledge is affected.

Exercise
What knowledge issues can you find in each of the passages above? Take into consideration the assumption of each country:

  1 Chinese
    Example: The Chinese fear that actual events would be erased by this textbook and others that follow.

  2 North Korean

  3 South Korean

  4 Japanese

Each of the countries on page 212 had, by 2001, shifted their historical paradigms from 1945 and the end of the Second World War. Each one's historical paradigm now has a different intent or purpose.

What is the nature of truth in history?
- Truth is based on historical fact.
- Truth can be approached from multiple perspectives.
- Truth in history cannot claim to be absolute except in terms of historical facts.
- Truth in history is sensitive to **paradigm** shifts and interpretations.

Creating the knower's perspective

In the introduction to Chapter 3: Ways of Knowing on page 31, you looked at an exercise called *A snapshot of history*. You were invited to trace the stages of the writing of a history book starting from an actual incident to the reader's final judgement of its telling. Now try taking an event or incident your class is studying and reverse the process. Start from the textbook and move through the stages to the original event.

Here are the steps in reverse for you to follow:
- You read the account in your text and liked it/didn't like it.
- The teacher chose the book and taught it.
- The IB Coordinator read the catalogue and chose the book for the library.
- A critic compared it to other books on the topic and selected it for a prize.
- The publisher read the script, liked it and printed it.
- An academic read it and passed it to a publisher.
- A historian pieced the story together.
- The colleague read more and researched further.
- Her friend heard about it and asked questions.
- Another person was fascinated by the tale.
- A citizen read it and told a friend.
- A scribe wrote it down.
- An eyewitness saw it.
- An incident happened.

 Paradigm This is used here in the sense of a template of values and judgements that dominates a period in history. Often the paradigms of one generation are replaced by the paradigms that emerge from subsequent generations. For example, the era of traditional paradigms in the Cold War was replaced by the era of revisionist values in the next generation of historians.

> **Exercise**
>
> - Which Ways of Knowing did you use?
> - Did your perspective shift as you followed the development of the book from judgement to interpretation to fact?

What, then, is history?
- History is what actually happened in the past.
- History deals with the accounts of past realities or what is called historiography. This is what TOK is most concerned with!
- It is the formal study of selected areas of history.
- It is an historical reproduction, whether it is in literature, the visual arts, theatre, music or film.

History and the IBO

Although history is not a compulsory course in the diploma programme, the IBO has given history a special place in the TOK curriculum. In the exercise that follows you will explore some of the reasons why history could be given this particular attention.

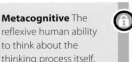

Metacognitive The reflexive human ability to think about the thinking process itself. TOK, by definition, is a course in metacognition.

Exercise
Choose from the reasons suggested below why you think the IB has given history separate attention. <ul><li>Because all knowledge is historical knowledge (in the sense that it lay in the past).</li><li>Because historical knowledge serves as a check on other Areas of Knowledge, in so far as they are rooted by origin and cause in the past.</li><li>Because the history of humankind is the history of knowledge-development.</li><li>Because humans are **metacognitive** or self-analytic.</li><li>Because humans construct collective identity through the past.</li><li>Any other?</li></ul>

Through our Ways of Knowing, history offers us a release from our own lives, time periods and locations. History extends an invitation to enter the lives of others, in the times and places where they lived and the events they experienced. It is also among the most internationally minded of the IB disciplines.

Multiple perspectives in history

Consider the following (hypothetical) statements that could apply to several conflict zones in the world today. Each of them is rooted in their understanding of history.

- An area which has been ours for the last 500 years, and yours for the last 50 years, must be returned to us – you are the occupiers.
  Example: Palestinian claims to the Gaza
- An area that has been yours for 500 years, and ours for 50 years, must continue to belong to us – the integrity of all borders must be respected.
- An area that has been yours for 500 years, but ours before that time, must be given back to us – it is our historic cradle.
- An area where our people are a majority must belong to us – the majority has to decide.
- An area where our people are a minority must belong to us – the minority has to be protected.
- Our great dream is historic justice – yours is chauvinist and fascist.

The Gaza strip ▶

Now look at historical facts and perspectives again. This time, let's use the actual example of the Balkans Conflict.

The Balkans Conflict, 1914

This is often taken as the root cause of the First World War. It offers a sound example of:

- simplicity of facts
- the range of perspectives on the facts
- the implications or deductions that can be drawn from the facts.

In 1914, Europe was heading towards war. One major cause was a rise in national feelings among small countries such as Serbia and Bosnia (part of the Balkans) who wished to be free of the Austrian Empire. The other major cause was the Alliance System by which Germany would have to go to war with Russia if Russia attacked Austria, which was Germany's ally. Also because of the Alliance System, Russia was committed to defend Serbia against Austria.

Exercise

1 Below are some historical facts or indisputable events. What implications or outcomes would follow logically from the fact given?

- **Fact 1** Crown Prince Franz Ferdinand, heir to the Austrian throne, was shot and killed by Bosnian nationalists in Sarajevo, Serbia on 28 June 1914.

  Implication or outcome?

  Example: Austria would now go to war with Serbia to avenge the death of the Prince and to stop the nationalists.

- **Fact 2** On 5 July 1914, Kaiser Wilhelm of Germany sent a 'blank cheque' or 'blood bond' to Austria, which offered unconditional military support.

  Implication or outcome?

- **Fact 3** On 28 July 1914, Austria attacked Serbia.

  Implication or outcome?

- **Fact 4** On 3 August 1914, Germany attacked Russia.

  Implication or outcome?

2 Therefore, which country was most responsible for the outbreak of the First World War? Did fact or interpretation lead you to your concliusion?

Conclusions we can reach are:

- An historical fact has little worth without interpretation.
- History should aim to be objective, but not sterile or value-free.

History and the Ways of Knowing

In TOK, what we study as history is not the reality of the past but the historiographies of the past. These are representations created by historians out of selected evidence and presented as a whole picture that we examine. The nature of historical understanding relies on the Ways of Knowing the historian deploys and on the intent, or purpose, of the historian. The Ways of Knowing overlap in their functions but it is interesting to examine them in isolation for a moment.

Sense perception and the role of fact in history

History uses the available facts selectively. Facts don't select themselves – they are chosen to serve the intent, purpose or expectation of the historian. Perception directs the selection, or de-selection of facts. The perception of the historian is directed by what he or she thinks happened, and what he or she thinks we should know. The biases and perception of the historian are part of the selection process.

There are important philosophical questions we should ask:
- Can a fact exist outside of a context?
- Do historical facts have any worth, without a context?

The selection of a fact gives it historical worth or merit. For example:

Japan bombed the American Naval Base at Pearl Harbour on 7 December 1941.

This is an historical fact. Its worth is measured in terms of what caused it and what the outcomes or effects were. An historical fact carries a similar weight to a scientific fact.

Historical knowledge, as in the human sciences, exists only within a given context. So it is the context that gives it meaning. History is dynamic and fluid by nature. History is continually rewriting itself.

In the selection and de-selection of facts, the historian may omit the evidence of certain groups. Many such groups claim today that their history has never been told.

You might like to go to www.heinemann.co.uk/hotlinks and enter the express code 4327P to read an interview with historian Judith Zinsser which is relevant to this point.

Exercise

In writing an account of American slavery called *'Let the Trumpets Call'*, American historian, Stephen Alter, examines historical sources from the slave traders themselves and from the slave owners. He notes that the narratives of the slaves themselves were excluded.
- Can you give **two** reasons why their view was omitted?

Emotion and the nature of historical interpretation

Emotion serves that aspect of history that makes a fact into an interpretation, by placing the fact in the framework of a context. This is the art of the historian.

- Emotion offers the imaginative interpretation of historical fact and it gives meaning to the contexts of historical fact. Thus history creates realities.

The historian's reality is rooted in the time period and prevailing paradigms. The historian's paradigms guide his or her interests and his or her interpretation of the facts.

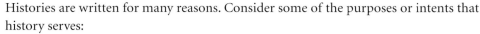

Histories are written for many reasons. Consider some of the purposes or intents that history serves:

- Celebration – many history textbooks celebrate achievements.
- Condemnation – some histories condemn the practices of the time.
- Causations – some histories are scientific in their interest in cause and effect.
- Regret/revision – some histories are written as apologias.
- Explanation/justification – some histories offer explanations of actions.
- Collective memory – some histories are written to provide a group identity.

The historian R.G. Collingwood claims:

> *Each man can only write from his cultural paradigm and from his interest. No man is a 'tabula rasa' [blank slate].*

Reason and the tools of historical representation

The evidence, data or tools of historical inquiry lie everywhere but they are neither even nor whole. In the end, these pieces of data can tell only a selected tale. The selection, classification and use of historical facts are made credible and coherent through reason.

Reason is a valuable part of the historical toolbox. It:

- constructs historical facts into a framework of knowledge
- filters out the illogical
- places the structure of validity upon the historian's selection of facts.

Methods of classification and categorization of historical facts are based on reason and logic. The facility of reason is what makes a history transferable across time and culture and varying empathies.

Historians have developed a method of categorization that groups evidence as a **primary source** or as a **secondary source**. Even this categorization of sources depends on what is being researched.

Primary sources

Primary sources are from the accounts of people who lived at the time of the event or movement. An example would be the series of cables sent between Czar Nicholas II and Kaiser Wilhelm of Germany just before the First World War. These accounts have the advantage of authenticity and reality. Yet this does not always mean that they are reliable. Other primary sources include important memoirs, such as those of Bismarck, Chancellor of modern Germany.

In the dialogue on the next page, the noted Indonesian historian and politician, Wimar Witoelar, offers comments on the nature and purpose of the memoir as an 'historical source'.

Wimar Witoelar was the Chief Spokesman for President Gus Dur of Indonesia, who won the first democratic election after the 32-year dictatorship of President Suharto. Witoelar's book, *No Regrets*, is one of the few primary sources of this time period. *The New York Times* featured Gus Dur in 1998 as one of the top ten 'Globalutionaries'.

Primary sources The accounts of people who lived at the time of the actual event or movement.

Secondary sources These are written much later and are based upon selected primary sources.

History in the making: a brief interview with Wimar Witoelar

Q: How is a memoir different from a history?

A: A memoir consists of personal recollections with no factual formality. This does not mean that historical facts are not treated with respect.

Q: As a historian, how did you select and deselect your facts?

A: By starting from my personal intent and selecting the events that formed the base.

Q: Whom did you seek to write for? For example, this generation? Future generations?

A: Mainly for this generation to avoid charting the future based on inaccurate assumptions.

Q: You are perhaps the only spokesperson who has written about this era. What was your responsibility?

A: My responsibility was to provide the context and the background for the President's sayings, and building up public confidence to think independently.

Q: Finally, how did you deal with your own biases?

A: By bringing them to the surface and presenting them alongside my convictions.

Wimar Witoelar

Secondary sources

Secondary sources are written much later and are based upon selected primary sources. This is the art of piecing evidence together to produce a representation.

But history is not like a jigsaw where the number of pieces is given all at once and where the picture is preconceived and will turn out the same no matter who assembles it. Evidence may continue to emerge. And thus history is continually being rewritten. Good history should use deduction in its reconstruction of reality.

You can find sources of evidence in many forms:

- writings – texts, documents of state, official papers, private writings, memoirs, letters and diaries
- arts – paintings, sculpture, music, opera, plays, photographs, cinema, video, cartoons
- mathematics – the use of figures and statistics
- geography – in maps and charts and plan sheets.

Like a map that can represent only one aspect at a time, history tells only one tale at a time, or offers one interpretation at a time. The TOK knower accommodates multiple perspectives and seeks counter sources to reach an historical judgement. This judgement is derived from the values of the historian and of the audience.

While there are other perspectives, history is often written and judged from the vantage point of the historian and the audience. Both are products of their time. Reason, thus, is a crucial part of the historical process. It assures the reader or viewer of the historian's credibility and of the coherence of his or her narrative.

Language and representation in history

The use of language in history has a particular power. Language not only frames thought but gives it status and strength. Since history has traditionally been written or preserved by the powerful, the educated, the court, the church, mosque or synagogue and the winners of conflict, it has often been portrayed as a series of triumphs by the state or as injustices inflicted upon the state.

Many histories are now being offered that re-examine and re-evaluate events from the viewpoint of groups without power. Of course this brings to history a difference in language. Language is a doorway into another way of thinking. The language of triumphalism (or the history of the victors) creates an attitude and strengthens the values of conquest and achievement. The new revolutionary histories often use the language of oppression and anger and vengeance. This too creates the attitudes of revolution. Karl Marx's famous line 'Religion is the opium of the masses' is an example of how language creates new thoughts and how language itself is a metacognitive tool.

Historical language has traditionally relied upon euphemisms to create pride, triumph and glory. Counter-language has emerged to balance this. Some of it bears the label 'political correctness' i.e. language that is neutral. Some historians argue that history cannot use objective language. Look at the terms below and note the duality of attitudes they convey:

- freedom-fighter/terrorist
- fell bravely/died
- killed by your own troops/friendly fire
- massacre/ethnic cleansing
- pacification/deaths of civilians.

There are several historical articles and books written on the topic of language and the power of myth-making in history. A distinct terminology also serves history. Here are some terms that are indispensable for the historian.

- **Bias** – shows the intent of the historian. It may take several forms from the selection of the event, to the type of evidence, to the omission of evidence. It may also reflect the framework of attitudes and intent of the historian.
- **Reliability** – focuses on the relevance, appropriateness and worth of the source of evidence.
- **Primary source** – evidence from the time of the event. This has the advantage of authenticity but that does not necessarily mean it is unbiased.
- **Secondary source** – evidence and analysis by historians after the time of the event and selected by intent.
- **Intent** – the purpose or preconceptions from which the historian approaches history.
- **Schools of thought** – the various established and new frameworks of historical thought that are recognized (for example, traditional, revisionist, Marxist).

Exercise

How then can we rely on the language of history to be objective? Discuss this question as a group.

Knowledge issues in history
The nature of history – conflicting views

Just as with historical claims made by different groups or individuals, a similar diversity of opinions and viewpoints emerges in the study of history among historians.

> *Historical study is not the study of the past but the study of present traces of the past. If people have said, thought, done or suffered anything of which nothing no longer exists, those things are as though they had never been.*
>
> G.R. Elton

> *My first answer… to the question 'What is history?' is that it is a continuous interaction between the historian and his facts, an unending dialogue between the present and the past.*
>
> E.H. Carr

History and method

Is history a science or an art?

History is always written wrong, and so always needs to be rewritten.

George Santayana

All history is a combination of fact and interpretation. Facts are selected from what is available and this immediately impacts on the approach of the historian. Interpretation arises from the intent of the historian and reflects the prevailing values of his or her society. One can debate whether these cycles of historical values are progressive or reactionary. History does both. History can also produce an original voice, for example, Judith Zinsser, one of the first historians of women's history (see page 224) and also Stephen Alter, one of the first writers of slave history (see page 216). More discussion about this shift in prevailing paradigms follows in the section on historical process on page 221.

Every historian is a product of his or her cultural paradigm. The events are judged through the lens of the audience (readers or viewers). They, again, may be products of yet another time and paradigm.

History is like no other science and like no other art. It relies on scrupulous historical methods to construct a rational reality and then breathes the life of historical imagination into it. There is a relationship between the paradigms of:
• the era of the events
• the era of the historian
• the era of the audience.

The diagram below shows the continual and dynamic relationship between the cultural paradigms of the people in the events of history, the people in the time of the historian and the people in the time of the audience. It signals why we seek the explanations offered by knowledge of our past, which is quite distinct from the explanations given by the natural sciences or of the measurement offered by mathematics. History lets us relive the past, and seeking knowledge of the past is part of the human experience.

The continual and dynamic relationship between the eras of the events, the historian and the audience

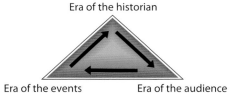

Era of the historian

Era of the events   Era of the audience

The goals of a scrupulous historical process include:
• objectivity
• freedom from bias
• an incorruptible approach.

However, history, by definition, is dynamic and as such reflects the values of the time. Historians have some constraints upon their methods:

- Historians cannot run or rerun experiments.
- Historians do not come to the task as a *tabula rasa* or 'blank slate'.
- Historical evidence is in continuous renewal.
- History without judgement is sterile.

The informed judgement of the historian is what instructs the interpretation.

Exercise

Is history then merely the invention of historians? Is that why it is continually rewritten?

Historical process

Historical patterns are sought, and after a while they might yield to a newly established school of thought. New evidence or a change in attitudes may cause such a shift.

The Battle of Gallipoli is an example of a shift in attitude. Gallipoli is a peninsula that lies in the Black Sea. Australian and New Zealand troops (called ANZACs) were sent there to help the English troops fight the Turks in the First World War. They were under the command of English officers, who sent them out in batches to take the fire from Turkish guns so that English soldiers could land safely. The ANZAC troops, who were in low land, were picked off easily by the Turks who were in the hills above. The death toll among the ANZAC troops was enormous. In the years immediately after the First World War, the great number of ANZAC troops who died at Gallipoli was held up as a patriotic sacrifice for Mother England. But new evidence, which revealed the English commanders' carelessness with colonial troops, caused a shift in attitudes of loyalty to attitudes of nationalism; it came to be seen as a massacre.

> *Gallipoli was the field in which the seeds of Australian nationalism were planted.*
>
> Mahatma Gandhi

The comparison to Kuhn's scientific revolutions and paradigm shifts (which you examined in Chapter 10: Science) arises easily. Note that Kuhn uses the language of history (for example, 'revolution') to describe changes in scientific thought.

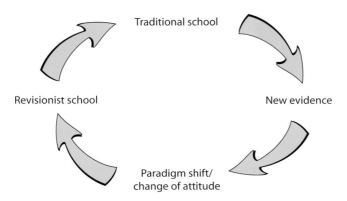

Traditional school

New evidence

Paradigm shift/ change of attitude

Revisionist school

◄ Kuhn's model applied to history

The role of the individual versus groups in history

One of the continuing controversies in history is between the 'great person' theory and the 'great movement' theory. A popular justification for this controversy is that individual leaders offer a symbolic oneness that can bring about a paradigm shift. But great social movements, like communism, can also make a claim.

The history of the world is but the biography of great men.

Thomas Carlyle

The mutual relations between the two sexes seem to us to be at least as important as the mutual relations of any two governments in the world.

Lord Macaulay

The history of all hitherto existing society is the history of class struggles.

Karl Marx

The idea of historical dualities

History appears to works in dualities of concept. Can you provide examples for the pairs below?
- Change and continuity
  Example: First World War – Balkan nationalism, colonialism – tribalism
- Fact and interpretation
- Certainty and uncertainty
- Great men and great movements
- Celebration and mourning

Looking at the power of individuals in history, we can see the dualities again. Each individual symbolises an ideology or a movement. It is when ideologies or positions clash that history is made. The moral knowledge issue arises, often, not when right and wrong clash, but when two 'rights' clash.

Mao Ze Dong and Chiang Kai Shek

Fidel Castro and Fulgencio Batista

Nelson Mandela and Frederik de Klerk

Nelson Mandela

Frederik de Klerk

Mahatma Gandhi and Muhammad Ali Jinnah

Elizabeth I of England and Phillip II of Spain

Napoleon and the Duke of Wellington

Is all history the history of human thought?

One of the major knowledge issues we have been looking at in the last few pages is whether or not facts have any significance outside of human interpretation. The quotations below illustrate the point that historical facts are important but static (or unchanging). It is the nature of human causes and human responses that we are seeking. Causes and responses are dynamic (or shifting) according to the lens of the historical thought that examines it.

We are fascinated by conquest, revolution, insurgency and repression. Connect this again to Kuhn's scientific revolutions and you might notice that science has borrowed the language of history to describe scientific movements.

> *The facts themselves may be interesting, but hardly useful. It is the study of causes that makes history fruitful.*
>
> Polybius

> *The historian makes a distinction between what may be called the outside and the inside of an event. The outside means everything belonging to it which can be described in terms of bodies and their movements (e.g. Caesar's crossing of the Rubicon or his assassination in Rome). The inside means that in it which can only be described in terms of thought (e.g. what did Brutus think which made him decide to stab Caesar?). The cause of the event means the thought in the mind of the person by whose agency the event came about… All history is then the history of thought.*
>
> From *The Idea of History* by R.G. Collingwood
> by permission of Oxford University Press

Patterns in history

Most eras claim that there are historical patterns and that history is fundamentally progressive.

> *Men wiser and more learned than I have discerned in history a plot, a rhythm, a predetermined pattern. These harmonies are concealed (hidden) from me. I can see only one emergency following another as wave follows upon wave, only one great fact with respect to which, since it is unique, there can be no*

generalizations, only one safe rule for the historian: that he should recognize in the development of human destinies the play of the contingent and the unforeseen…

H.A.L. Fisher

The twentieth-century experience does seem to teach us one thing: if you misrepresent civilization as progressive, you are bound to disappoint people… The civilized and the barbarous are usually thought of as mutually exclusive categories, but every society is a mixture of both. So is almost every individual.

Felipe Fernandez-Armesto

Exercise

- Both Fisher and Fernandez-Armesto reject the idea of a 'pattern' or predictable outcomes in history. Do you agree with them? Why or why not?
- Do you agree with Fernandez-Armesto that we 'misrepresent civilization as progressive'? Are there examples of 'progress' in history that you would strongly defend?

Exercise

Truth in history

- Given the ambiguities and fluidity you have been discussing and reading about, what kind of truth can be found in history?
- Are there truth tests that can be applied?
- By what standards can we claim an historical account to be true?

An online visit to a working historian

Judith P. Zinsser is an exemplar of a teacher, academic and historian. She taught for several years in the IB programme at the UN School in New York. She has written several books on women's history including:

- *A History of Their Own: Women in Europe from Prehistory to the Present* (Volumes 1 and 2)
- *La Dame D' Esprit: A Biography of the Marquise du Châtelet*
- *History and Feminism: A Glass Half Full*

Dr Zinsser has been the President of the World History Association and has served as consultant to various other associations, journals and encyclopedias. She teaches history at Miami University, in Oxford, Ohio. Below is an interview with Dr Zinsser about knowledge issues in history.

Q: Why have you chosen women's history as your specialty?

A: Women's history chose me. A high-school friend said, 'How would you like to write a narrative history of European women with me?' So, I said yes, and ten years later we had the two volumes of *A History of Their Own* which remains *the* only narrative history from prehistory to the present, and is in its second edition. It became a mission to give women back their history. And it was the late 1970s and early 1980s, so many women were engaged in this endeavour. After that, anything I seemed to be interested in writing about had to do with women or feminism: the United Nations Decade for Women from 1975–85; the effects of feminism on history and the historical profession; and then Emilie du Châtelet, another ten-year project.

Q: What were some of the historical issues in writing the history of women?

A: The 'issue' was the absence of women from history, just half of humanity wiped out. Then there was the search for an explanation for this omission and the search for a way to put women into the history. The key to the mystery and to the solution was the same: history was a story of men and what had been considered significant in their lives. The feminist historian, Gerda Lerner, explained the sequence by which women historians offered an alternative story. The first efforts in women's history chronicled what elite women had done, women who acted like men: such as queens. Then came 'the contributors,' women reformers such as Florence Nightingale and Jane Addams who led the social movements of their day. But, women were still being valued by male measures of significance and placed in a men's chronology. It took a radical revisioning of the past to see that you could not tell women's history by simply inserting them into the men's narrative and using male criteria of significance.

Q: In the prologue to *A History of Their Own,* a massive work done in two volumes, you speak about the myths about women regarding history. Can you comment further?

A: Women's historians realized that they would have to create new measures of significance, new ways of ordering the past that looked at history from women's perspectives. For example, in *A History of Their Own,* Bonnie Anderson and I borrowed from anthropology and sociology and identified European women across time by 'place' and 'function': peasant women of the fields; women of the churches; women of the courts; women of the salons and parlours, and so on. There is agreement that the history of women is not the same as the history of men.

A word about 'deconstruction'. Feminist historians were 'deconstructionists' before the word was popular. We questioned the old construction of history, the use of gendered language, found ways to make the 'subaltern' speak, valued new kinds of sources and learned to 'read between the lines'. To tell women's history, that is what you have to do – take apart the old history, describe its flaws, identify its biases, formulate new approaches, find and value different sources, construct the story of those who had apparently been silenced.

Q: Can you address some of the 'new knowledge' that shifts perspectives?

A: The principal myths would be that women did nothing of 'significance' unless they did what a man did. At best, the woman was a 'prodigy,' an exception. To shift perspectives, women's historians have endeavoured to prove that what women did was significant. For example, enslaved women in the Americas, peasant women in Europe, maintained families against incredible odds. They birthed babies, raised generations, preserved and passed on language, culture and knowledge. Then, women's historians proved that women did achieve in male categories, but they also expanded those categories to prove women's unique contributions. There were 'great' women artists in the male sense of 'painter,' 'sculptor', but more important, women created their own kinds of art: quilts, embroidery, lace, stencilling, delicate botanical drawings for a children's book. The list is endless when you move to other regions of the world; for example, the delicate designs of the 'lotus slippers' which seventeenth and eighteenth century Chinese women sewed for their bound feet.

The story of Emilie du Châtelet is indicative of how the truisms of women's history traditionally worked. She was lost to history for two reasons. First, the kind of 'science' she presented fell out of fashion in the progressive male-dominated trajectory created from Newton to Einstein, in the rejection of any search for the metaphysical and causative explanations of natural phenomena. Second, she fell into the shadow of her companion, Voltaire. Subsequently, her writings were ignored or attributed to others, and her life became the story of their love affair. Her biographies had titles such as *The Divine Mistress* and *Voltaire in Love*. Need I say more? [See the Ideal knower on page 40.]

Q: How do you deal with your own biases in your selection of evidence?

A: Women's historians, and feminist historians particularly, accept that they have a bias. We want to give women their history and to prove their lives were of value. Personally, I have discovered more biases in my actions than I could ever have imagined. But that is the only recourse, to identify and admit a bias and to make it clear how it affects your choices. The problem with modern historians (mostly males, but some females, as well) is that for a century or so, they insisted that they were telling the 'truth', that there was no bias in a history that ignored three-quarters of the world

Dr Judith Zinsser

I know I write about women and only include men when I have to. So, I say what I'm doing – writing women's history – and then I do just that. I don't pretend that I'm writing 'the human story' and then really write about only a part of humanity. I look forward to a time when *all* historians (many do now) will begin their books by trying to identify their biases and how these attitudes influenced their choice of subject and the way they wrote about it. For example, imagine a book that begins: 'I am going to write about men in World War I'.

Q: In the prologue to *Biography of the Marquise du Châtelet*, you say the following:

'Three possible introductions to the Marquise du Châtelet. Each is a "true" "real" account of her last months. All are based on sources, on facts that make up the historical record, the official memory of her life. As her biographer, I can choose the time, the place, when and where to begin the narrative.'

Is history therefore more of an art than a science?

A: I divide the creation/construction of history into two parts: historian's problems and writer's problems. Getting the 'facts', finding the information, all of that is in the first category and comes as close to 'science' as history gets. We study an era, we formulate a question, we make hypotheses, we test them against the most certain facts, in the context of an era, and then we formulate an answer. That is like science. What we do with those facts and that answer is the art, both intellectual and literary. I tried to show this artistic process in the prologue of the biography. You can introduce du Châtelet as the translator of Newton or as Voltaire's mistress. The historian decides what she wants to highlight in the biography, the woman's mind or her body. You can arrange du Châtelet's letters to Saint-Lambert in ways that make her look like an hysteric, or like an experienced courtier. The historian decides which seems more in character with the rest of du Châtelet's life and her other relations with men.

Previous biographers, and some who write on her today, refuse to give up the idea that du Châtelet was a sex-starved eccentric, with multiple partners, including those who tutored her in mathematics. I chose to show that her love of mathematics was more than enough explanation for her desire to spend long hours over calculations with the men who taught her analytical geometry and calculus.

Q: You have been an IB teacher for many years. Can you comment on the impact of the Ways of Knowing (sense perception, reason, emotion and language) on your own historical portrayals? For example:
- reconstructing the marquise's emotions
- representing her use of language – especially in the translation of *Principia*
- developing her logic as it was seen in her work
- portraying her sensory awareness of life.

A: I am having a hard time separating out the four Ways of Knowing. They seem to be part of the process in so many interrelated ways that I can't say when one begins and ends. In a biography this is especially true because you are always trying to understand why a single person did something at a particular time, in a particular place and in a particular manner. For example, take the translation of the *Principia*. Du Châtelet, as the two historians, Antoinette Emch-Dériaz and Gérard Emch, have explained, chose to translate Newton's work literally, but there are obscure passages where the translator has to guess at his meaning, and places where he 'fudges' the data. Du Châtelet made choices: clarifying some, leaving others. But then in her commentary, she dealt with all such problems and added the most up-to-date information relating to Newton's text, including those discoveries that proved him wrong. These insights come from pure study of language and reasoning by historians who know both Newton's original and her translation very well.

To explain why du Châtelet chose to handle the *Principia* that way, and to show what her life was like as she was doing it, draw on perception and emotion, in the sense that the historian perceives her motivation and plays on emotional responses from readers to create the images of the marquise at this time in her career. The three alternate openings to the biography described in the Prologue exemplify this process: her motivation for finishing the project is suggested, she is shown in Lunéville and Paris in that summer of 1749. To give her life, I drew on my own memories of the two sites – my photograph from a window in Lunéville is one of the illustrations in the book – and of my own pregnancy in a different summer. Yet my knowledge of, for example, her letters, her possessions, Voltaire's writings, were integral to the reasoned reconstruction of the imagined scenes.

One last thought on 'language'. I purposely included many French words in the text. Somehow the French made the story more real to me, and I hope to readers. Words like *esprit* have no equivalent in English and seem to convey so much more of the time and the culture than a weak translation. Also, one of my goals in the biography was to introduce France, to make readers want to go there and to know more of its history, perhaps even to learn the language – the truest lens through which to perceive another people's world.

Q: Did you come to the work with a prior intention?

A: Yes, and I believe all historians are bound by their own circumstances and their own preconceptions. A biographer chooses a subject for rational and irrational reasons. I simply found du Châtelet fascinating, amusing, exciting. And her life meant the challenge of: learning French, trying to understand complex mathematics, returning to physics which I almost failed in high school. The biography form proved a challenge for me as a writer. As a women's historian, I now had a mission. That's intentionality!

Q: Would you say that there is a feminist impact on historiography?

A: Actually, I wrote a whole book about the 'feminist impact on history and historians'. The answer is still, 'yes and no'. Women's history and the feminist perspective have created whole new research and writing fields with positions in universities for their experts, journals, prizes and organizations devoted to promoting their discoveries. Since the late 1980s, hundreds of books have been written and thousands of articles about women and the significance of gender in the history of all regions of the world. Still, however, when you go to a history conference, or into a book store, you would not find many works that integrate women's and men's history. Usually, the stories of women and men's pasts remain on separate shelves, in different places on the programme. And too many people still ask why we study women's history at all. How, for example, does it change my understanding of the French Revolution? Of the Cold War?

What I can say is that if you do not include the feminist perspective and women's history in a curriculum, in an examining system, you rob half of humanity of its special heritage. That's one injustice that does not need to be perpetuated.

Part 2: knowledge as history – the knower's common inheritance

Sir Isaac Newton, acknowledging the debt that he owed to thinkers who went before him, is reputed to have said that he 'stood on the shoulders of giants'. This holds for us all as knowers.

Karen Armstrong the religio-political historian, points to the first great inspirational period, which the German philosopher Karl Jaspers called the 'Axial Age', from about 900 to 200 BCE, since:

> … *it was pivotal to the spiritual development of humanity… one of the most seminal periods of intellectual, psychological, philosophical, and religious change in recorded history.*

> From *The Great Transformation* by Karen Armstrong

The insights of the 'Axial Age' emerged at four great centres of ancient civilization: China, India, Israel and Greece.

Confucianism: the cultivation of the 'gentleman' or the superior learner

◀ The Confucianism sign

The following extracts form part of the 'Analects' of K'ung-fu-tzu, or Confucius, the Chinese sage of the sixth century BCE. His teachings have influenced East and South-East Asian societies, and by extension other cultures, in a continual thread to the present:

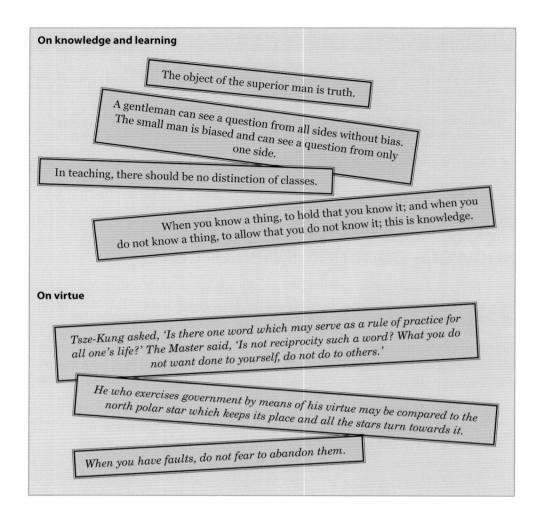

On knowledge and learning

The object of the superior man is truth.

A gentleman can see a question from all sides without bias. The small man is biased and can see a question from only one side.

In teaching, there should be no distinction of classes.

When you know a thing, to hold that you know it; and when you do not know a thing, to allow that you do not know it; this is knowledge.

On virtue

Tsze-Kung asked, 'Is there one word which may serve as a rule of practice for all one's life?' The Master said, 'Is not reciprocity such a word? What you do not want done to yourself, do not do to others.'

He who exercises government by means of his virtue may be compared to the north polar star which keeps its place and all the stars turn towards it.

When you have faults, do not fear to abandon them.

Exercise

- Which of the quotes above best describes the TOK goal of open-minded thinking and tolerance of multiple perspectives? Why is this goal important for a TOK knower?
- Why does Confucius emphasize virtue and ethical goodness as vital elements of the 'superior man'?
- The passage on 'reciprocity' is also called the 'Golden Rule' of ethical behaviour. Using examples, explain why it is considered the basis of a good society in multiple cultures. Is this a TOK value?
- Why do Confucius's ideas have a powerful influence in many societies today? Is tradition a good basis for knowledge?

Buddhism: India, South/East-Asia – the cultivation of wisdom and compassion

Siddhartha, or the Buddha, lived and taught in India in the same era as Confucius. His ideas radiated outwards, influencing civilizations near and far and shaping the life experiences of countless knowers since. The following are extracts from the Buddha's teaching and from the *Dhammapada* (a Buddhist text which means the 'path of Dharma', the universal law).

On the mind and wisdom

> There is no impurity greater than ignorance. Remove that through wisdom and you will be pure.

> All created things are transitory [impermanent, changing]; those who realize this are freed from suffering. This is the path that leads to pure wisdom.

> The cause of human suffering, called 'trishna' or 'thirst', includes not only desire for, and attachment to, sense pleasures, wealth, and power, but also desire for and attachment to ideas and ideals, views, opinions, theories, conceptions, and beliefs.
>
> Walpola Rahula, Buddhist scholar

On goodness and compassion

> The scent of flowers or sandalwood cannot travel against the wind; but the fragrance of the good spreads everywhere. Neither sandalwood nor the lotus nor jasmine, can come near the fragrance of the good.

> Just as a mother with her own life
> Protects her child, her only child, from harm,
> So within yourself let grow
> A boundless love for all creatures.
> Let your love flow outward through the universe,
> To its height, its depth, its broad extent,
> A limitless love, without hatred or enmity.

Exercise

- The teachings of Buddhism are also called 'the middle way', a balance of wisdom and compassion, of knowledge and goodness. How does TOK reflect this balance?
- The quotation from Rahula mentions the dangers of attachment to opinions, theories and assumptions. To what extent does personal or ideological bias influence knowledge claims in the study of history?
- What is the significance for TOK of the Buddhist idea of 'impermanence' or change? By what stages does the knower revise his or her opinion or assumptions about a historical event or historical personality?

 Monotheism Belief in one god or supreme power.

The Israelites: Jewish teachings – monotheism and the cultivation of justice

The Jewish tradition of Israel bequeathed a vision of **monotheism** allied to ethical behaviour and social justice, a powerful combination that greatly influenced the ideas and practices of the later religions of Christianity and Islam, touching a considerable proportion of humanity.

Yahweh was the word that represented the name of an omnipresent and mysterious God. It was thought that names have power, and therefore you should not pronounce the name of God. Yahweh became the sound of God. (In Hinduism there is a similar

The nine-branched hannukiah derives from the seven-branched menorah; both are symbols of the Jewish faith

belief system surrounding *om* (the sound that represents the name of God). In re-establishing the power of this God, it becomes the first religion to call for social justice and ethical behaviour.

The Om symbol

> Yahweh stands up in the divine assembly,
> Among the gods he dispenses justice
> 'No more mockery of justice,
> No more favouring the wicked!
> Let the weak and the orphan have justice,
> Be fair to the wretched and the destitute;
> Rescue the weak and needy,
> Save them from the clutches of the wicked!'
> Rise, Yahweh, dispense justice throughout the world,
> Since no nation is excluded from your ownership.
> Psalm 82
>
> *****
>
> Without good ethical behaviour… ritual alone was worthless. Religion should not be used to inflate communal pride and self-esteem, but to encourage the abandonment of egotism.
>
> *****
>
> … Before Abraham, history had been a succession of disasters; humanity seemed caught in a downward spiral of rebellion, sin, and punishment, but Abraham had reversed this grim trend. The covenant with Abraham had been the turning point of history.
> From *The Great Transformation* by Karen Armstrong

Exercise

- What is the significance of monotheism in world history? How have the monotheistic religions shaped the lives and ethical outlook of believers?
- How far has Yahweh's call for social justice been followed in the course of human history? Why or why not? (Offer some examples.)
- In your opinion, is there a 'deeper significance of events' in history? Explain some of the purposes of history.

Eudaimonia The growth and flourishing of the human mind.

Open discussion was how rationalism was promulgated

Greece: the cultivation of rationalism and 'eudaimonia'

The Greek thinkers and dramatists of the 'Axial Age' are credited with constructing the foundations of some of humanity's great historical achievements, including political democracy, rational debate and inquiry, the scientific method, and aesthetic catharsis. These endeavours arose from a faith in the capacity of human reasoning and a commitment to **eudaimonia** or a flourishing of the human body and soul.

The first relativist, Heraclitus, argued that everything depended on context; seawater was good for fish, but potentially fatal for men… [he] believed that even though the cosmos seemed stable, it was in fact in constant flux and a battlefield of warring elements… Yet beneath this cosmic turbulence, there was unity. Flux and stability, which seemed antithetical, were one and the same; night and day were two sides of a single coin… [note the dualities]

You could not rely on the evidence of your senses, but must look deeper to find the *logos*, the ruling principle of nature. And that also applied to human beings.

*****

By the fifth century, [the plays] showed the well-known characters of myth – Agamemnon, Oedipus, Ajax or Heracles – making an interior journey, struggling with complex choices, and facing up to the consequences… In tragedy there was neither a simple answer nor a single viewpoint… neither the hero nor the chorus expressed the 'correct' view. The audience had to weigh one insight against another, just as they did in council… Tragedy taught the Athenians to project themselves towards the 'other', and to include within their sympathies those whose assumptions differed markedly from their own.

*****

Protagoras taught his students to question everything. They must accept nothing on hearsay or at second hand, but test all truth against their own judgement and experience… 'The measure of all things is man', he wrote in his epistemological treatise.

*****

[Socrates] understood just how little he knew, and was not ashamed to encounter the limitations of his thought again and again.

*****

The discovery of the psyche was one of the most important achievements of Socrates and Plato… It enabled human beings to reason and inspired them to seek goodness. The cultivation of the soul was the most important human task, far more crucial than the achievement of worldly success.

From *The Great Transformation* by Karen Armstrong

Exercise

- Compare Heraclitus's insights to the ideas of the 'uncertainty principle' in contemporary science. Is there a 'ruling principle of nature'?
- Among the important elements in TOK inquiry are the acknowledgement of the counter-argument or the 'other point of view', and the development of the 'voice of the knower'. How do the perspectives of Greek tragedy and Protagoras illustrate these aspects?
- Why did Socrates and Plato emphasize the seeking of 'goodness', similar to other Axial Age thinkers? Is this part of a TOK search as well?
- Do you agree with Socrates' view on the limitations of human knowledge? How might this inform the study of history?

Exercise

Having looked at the ideas of the 'Axial Age' thinkers, debate the following assertion:
'Human history can be best understood as a search for goodness and wisdom'.

We can conclude with the following quote:

All the human facilities exist but to serve the Truth.

Mahabharata

Today's world: cultural paradigm shifts and history

Sometimes school history portrays the nature of history to be a series of triumphant wars, invasions and conquests interspersed with a few peace treaties and an occasional revolution.

But recently Australian Prime Minister, Kevin Rudd, apologized for the earlier behaviours of the white Australian governments towards Aboriginal peoples.

Australian PM apologises to Aborigines for mistreatment in the past

Aborigines Accept Australia's Apology

The Australian Prime Minister has offered a formal apology for mistreatment of Aborigines in the past. Kevin Rudd's apology was accepted. Kevin Rudd told the country's parliament that past policies of assimilation, under which Aborigine children were taken from their families to be brought up in white households, were a stain on the nation's soul.

'Today, the parliament has come together to right a great wrong,' Mr Rudd said.

'We apologise for the laws and policies of successive parliaments and governments that have inflicted profound grief, suffering and loss on these our fellow Australians. A great stain has been washed from a nation's soul.'

A major report published 11 years ago found that between one in three and one in 10 Aborigine children had been taken from their families between 1910 and 1970.

The report called for a national apology to those affected, known as the Stolen Generations, but the then Conservative government under Prime Minister John Howard rejected the finding and offered only a statement of regret.

Extract from *Sky News*, 12 March 2008

Ideal knower

Xuan Zang, China, 602–664 CE

One of the two giant statues of the Buddha in the Bamiyan valley of central Afghanistan

Xuan Zang was born to an important family of conservative Confucian scholars. When he was 11 years old he decided to study Theravada and Mahayana Buddhism. He ordained as a monk as this was the route of a scholar in those days. He also shocked his teachers by studying Sanskrit, the language of Indian writings.

Xuan Zang decided to walk overland to India to discover the original monastries and archives of Indian Buddhism. For 17 years he travelled towards Nalanda, the great university of Ancient India and of Indian Buddhism. He went through the wars that the Tang Dynasty was waging and came out safely. Kings heard of him and assisted in his journey.

He travelled through the steppes of Krygyzstan and Uzbekistan and Afghanistan. He lived among the cave monastries and meditated under the two giant Bamiyan statues of Buddha (now destroyed by the Taliban).

In India he met Hindus for the first time. Along the journey he noted how Buddhism had modified itself to the influences and needs of the places it spread through. He began translations of Buddhist texts from Sanskrit into Chinese and developed the skill of debate, which is part of Buddhist education. In Nalanda he decided that to think for himself he must study logic and reason and scientific method. Xuan Zang went on to:

- document and write historical commentaries using the path of Buddhism from India to China as his framework
- share knowledge of one culture and religion with several other countries
- set up a translation bureau (he translated 1,335 facsimiles of documents into Chinese)
- write one of the definitive histories of King Harsha of India
- introduce into the university system in China doctrines of logic and reason, perception, consciousness, spirituality and scientific method using evidence
- complete his history of several countries (at the Emperor's request) in 646. It was called *Journey to the West* (India was seen as the West).

Student presentation

1 Imagine that you are the Minister of Tourism in your country. The UN Secretary-General and important press people are coming on a visit. What single monument or site will you choose to show them?

- Select the monument or site.
- Describe what it commemorates – categorise it – military, massacre, freedoms, other?
- Why do you want the world to know this about your country?

Ask each student to present the site they have chosen.

- What range of choices did the class make?
- What Ways of Knowing dominated the decision-making? Perception? Reason? Emotion?
- How did language develop the concept?

2 Describe and analyse the nature of a memoir. The key TOK questions to address are:

- What epistemologies are at work in a memoir?
- What is the nature of interpretation in a memoir?
- What is the nature of truth in a memoir?

To help you prepare, consider what Tim O'Brien tells us in the extract below about the selection and de-selection of facts and the nature of interpretation.

> *In many cases a true war story cannot be believed. If you believe it, be skeptical. It's a question of credibility. Often the crazy stuff is true and the normal stuff isn't because the normal stuff is necessary to make you believe the truly incredible craziness. In other cases you can't even tell a true war story. Sometimes it's just beyond telling.*
>
> *From* 'How to tell a True War Story' by Tim O'Brien

To find about more about O'Brien's ideas, go to www.heinemann.co.uk/hotlinks and insert the express code 4327P.

Essay questions

Two recent Prescribed Titles (PTs) include:

1 'A historian must combine the rigour of the scientist with the imagination of the artist'. To what extent, then, can the historian be confident about his or her conclusions?

© International Baccalaureate Organization 2001

2 'History is part myth, part hope, and part reality.' Critically evaluate this claim, and consider the extent to which it might also be true of other disciplines.

© International Baccalaureate Organization 1997

Ethics
How do morals matter?

Strictly speaking, ethics is the philosophical study of morality. However, the terms are commonly interchanged, e.g. Einstein's ethics and/or Einstein's morality, and this chapter will use *morals* and *ethics* interchangeably.

With the advent of the Internet, people of all ages are turning to online matchmaking services to find friends and lovers, husbands and wives, even university house mates.

Because people are particular about what they want in a companion, the house mate search, to take only one example, usually has a long list of 'nos'! No smoking, no dogs, no hip-hop, no parties – with cleanliness a must. Other sites are more focused on the romantic quest and may sound like this:

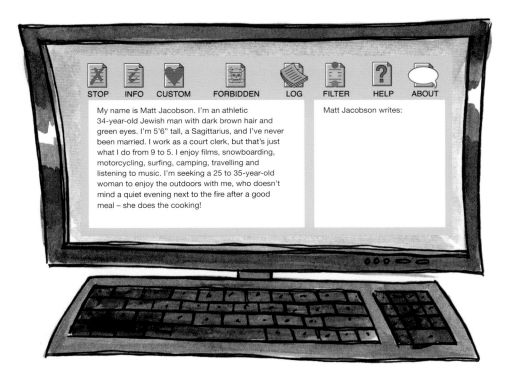

Some Internet sites are more focused on the romantic quest

While the posting above is value-laden in the sense of likes and dislikes, such values are usually lifestyle ones, not moral ones. Yet, whatever the attraction between two people, or the reason for getting together, when a break-up occurs, the separation more often than not *is* over a moral issue. He or she was unfaithful, abusive or selfish, broke promises, stole from or lied to the other one, or cheated in some way. So given that moral values can make or break a professional or personal human arrangement, you might ask, why not put these value judgements in the advertisement in the first place?

Two reasons come to mind. First, there is an accepted style to such writing, but of much greater importance, people by and large take for granted the trustworthiness of others in their groups. Just try composing an advertisement for yourself that lists your seven deadly sins and your seven shining virtues. How many responses would you get? Meeting a new person at a party is more than an exchange of names; there is a tacit understanding, a kind of *social contract* that says I can be trusted, I do not lie, steal, cheat, rape or pillage. It is a gift we give one another. It is an understanding that community depends on a common moral base, maybe not in all things, but in enough to ensure cohesion. If this were not so, then life would indeed be, 'a war of all against all'. As Thomas Hobbes (an English philosopher who lived from 1588 to1679) says, 'solitary, poor, nasty, brutish and short'. Where values are not shared there are quarrels, disputes, strife, tension, a lack of peace and a lack of pleasure. It is in our self-interest to make such moral compacts with others, to keep the ethical norms of those values and to be able to articulate them to ourselves and others.

Jean Jacques Rousseau, 1712–82

Have you heard of the *social contract*? A Frenchman, Jean Jacques Rousseau, is usually linked to the political idea that people give up some of their natural rights to an authority in exchange for peace and protection. On the personal level, people get along with one another by a set of rules not always spelled out that is a give and take arrangement among members. You give up some freedom for the benefit of belonging to the group. Such a contract depends on the spoken or unspoken value of *reciprocity*.

Exercise	
• What are your *social contracts*? • With what groups? • What is your exchange of autonomy for the safety of belonging? • What does *reciprocity* mean to you?	

Jean Jacques Rousseau

Can we ever agree on moral values?

The subject matter of ethics and one of its central questions, Why should I be moral? has a personal and a high stakes dimension to it. Reputations are gained, and sometimes ruined, based on morality or immorality. Laws are created to preserve the good and violators are punished. Nearly all religions have codes of conduct, most schools have written and unwritten ethical rules, and families and couples may promote values of a highly specific nature to ensure their togetherness.

And while many ancient documents such as the *Code of Hammurabi,* the Confucian *Analects*, the Koran and the Bible all express virtues similar to one another, as does the more modern *Universal Declaration of Human Rights*, disputes about right and wrong are commonplace. Students are fond of saying, 'We're all different so we all have different values'; and while such a statement may have a ring of plausibility, surely we could not have families and friends, clubs and teams, cultures and societies if everyone had a value system different from everyone else. Suppose you ask, 'How many people believe that we are all different, therefore we all have different values?' and everyone raises their hands? What has just happened? Everyone has agreed that everyone is different. Logically, something weird is going on, and in this case it is called a self-refuting proposition. In other words, it contradicts itself.

Pondering self-refuting statements is good mental exercise. For example, consider the puzzle called *The Liars Paradox* from the sixth-century Cretan, Epimenides, who proclaimed, 'All Cretans are liars'. What he says cannot be true. If Cretans are always liars, and he is a Cretan, then he must be lying, in which case his statement is true. Or is it?

Yet, agreement about values is not easy and these two quotes from Bertrand Russell deserve some thought:

> *I can only say that while my own opinions as to ethics do not satisfy me, other people's satisfy me even less.*

> *I can't believe that the only thing wrong with wanton cruelty is that I don't like it.*

Russell's first statement shows that there may be shades of moral differences even among like-minded people of goodwill and that if a person is honest with himself, he will recognize that the moral landscape is sometimes (but perhaps not always) one of shifting ground depending on context or circumstances. Russell's view also expresses how ethical statements are usually open to interpretation because language is ambiguous and we are often dealing with concepts, not matters of fact. We'll go on to look at these statements again later in the chapter.

One message from this cartoon is, if we can't define what *cheating* means in general, how can we decide in any individual case if something is an act of *cheating*? We are simply left hanging. Consequently, disagreement about moral judgements in individual cases might be a disagreement about language and examples, and not one about whether *cheating* is right or wrong in principle.

In a similar vein, look at the exercise in the box on the next page about *stealing*. The items suggested range from the *prime* example of taking something from someone by force, for example, a bank robbery, to something as far-fetched as robbing people of their time by keeping them waiting. There is usually more agreement with prime examples as compared to the far-fetched (also known as a *limiting case*) examples, whose meanings often produce argument and dissension. The prime examples seem to hit the bull's eye, while the limiting case examples are stretching the point.

Exercise

On a scale of 1–10, rank the following as *stealing* where 'holding up a bank' would be 1 and 'keeping your friend waiting' would be 10. Reasons can be given later.

1 Holding up a bank   _____

2 Taking your mum's money without asking   _____

3 Taking a car from the street   _____

4 Pinching books from the library   _____

5 A doctor overcharging a patient   _____

6 Hiding goods from customs   _____

7 Underpaying workers   _____

8 Charging for repairs that are never made   _____

9 Mugging a woman for her jewellery   _____

10 Weighing your thumb along with the meat   _____

11 Keeping your friend waiting   _____

12 Copying answers from your neighbour's test   _____

13 Running away with your best friend's wife   _____

Try adding five more examples across the entire range from the *prime* to the *limiting cases* and note the ease or difficulty of reaching consensus. Or make a ten-item list for another moral term, such as *cheating* with the same ranking of 1–10 and discuss your agreement or disagreement with others.

Concept analysis

Concept analysis
This is an attempt to get at the heart of an idea or concept by looking at what the concept is, what it is not, its synonyms and antonyms, and the most telling example of the idea that can be described.

This kind of exercise is a form of what is called **concept analysis**, a good skill to acquire in order to sort out the meaning of any term, ethical or otherwise. Such an analysis involves trying to get at the meaning of concepts or vague terms by giving:

- definitions
- synonyms
- examples
- counter-examples

or by asking questions of the concept.

In its simplest form, the beginnings of a concept analysis of *stealing* might look like this:
- **definition** – taking what does not belong to you without the owner's consent
- **synonyms** – thieving, pilfering, pinching
- **example** – a person goes into a shop and intentionally takes a chocolate bar and does not pay for it
- **counter-example** – a person takes an item in a shop and pays the agreed price without coercion
- **asking questions of the concept** – Does stealing always include force? Can stealing occur without inflicting harm on another person? Does stealing imply accepting the idea of private property?

The kinds of questions that go with concept analysis often occur in discussions that begin with, 'It all depends on what you mean by *stealing, cheating, lying, killing* etc.' These are discussions that help us think about where the definition of a moral term begins and ends. Again, disagreement about what does and does not count as examples of cheating or stealing may not be a disagreement about values, but about examples of that value. The same goes for almost any moral principle or moral term.

Belonging to a moral community

The following exercise is a stimulus to make you think about ethical concepts of cheating and stealing within the context of your school or college life, as well as to make you think about your school as a moral community. Give the appropriate answer for YOU, then match your responses with others and discuss your differences. Are some of the disagreements tied to language, definitions, principles or examples? How important is it that the school community agrees on what is right and wrong and the consequences of observing (or not) a moral code?

Exercise

Answer 'yes' or 'no' to the questions below, then match your responses with others and discuss your differences. Are some of the disagreements tied to language, definition, principles or examples? How important is it that the school or college community agrees on what is right and wrong and the consequences of observing (or not) a moral code?

Question	Yes or no?
1 Is there an unwritten rule in school against cheating?	
2 Is there an unwritten rule in school that accepts cheating as long as you don't get caught?	
3 Is there an unwritten rule in school against stealing?	
4 Is there a written rule in school against stealing?	
5 If you saw someone doing something wrong, would you report them to someone in authority?	
6 Does your answer to question 5 depend on the action?	
7 Does your answer to question 5 depend on the person?	
8 Is there an unwritten rule in school against reporting people?	
9 Is there an unwritten rule in school against snitching on friends?	
10 Would your answer to question 6 or question 7 depend on the circumstances?	
11 Would your answer to questions 5–8 depend on whether anyone knew that you reported someone?	

Is there a written or unwritten rule in your school against stealing?

It's fairly clear that most people could not give an overly simplistic 'yes' or 'no' answer without some sort of concept analysis going on even privately in their own minds. And it is also usually the case that we have strong feelings about what is right and wrong for ourselves and others, even if we have never had to put our feelings into so many words or justify those feelings through rational argument. In fact, studies of pre-school age children suggest that moral intuitions, or the immediate response to a situation, around issues of fairness in the sharing of food, toys and attention show up long before the ability to reason things out or put feelings into words. Can you recall your earliest awareness of right and wrong?

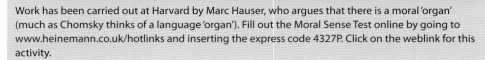

Exercise

Work has been carried out at Harvard by Marc Hauser, who argues that there is a moral 'organ' (much as Chomsky thinks of a language 'organ'). Fill out the Moral Sense Test online by going to www.heinemann.co.uk/hotlinks and inserting the express code 4327P. Click on the weblink for this activity.

To find the Moral Sense Test go to www.heinemann.co.uk/hotlinks and insert express code 4327P.

Subjectivity and relativity

Let us revisit Russell's second statement on page 239.

> *I can't believe that the only thing wrong with wanton cruelty is that I don't like it.*

This quotation speaks about the **subjectivity** or **relativity** of moral judgements. Like Russell, we may think that everyone has the right to make his or her own moral judgements, but when we stop to think about the meaning of Russell's words, we might realize that there could be something disturbing about everything being totally *subjective* or individualistic. *Subjective* here means something like 'goodness is in the eye of the beholder'. In other words, if I say that something is right or wrong, true or false, then it *is* right or wrong or true or false. It is up to the subject, namely me, to make that judgement and its truth is relative to me, not to any objective standard outside of my own opinion.

Subjectivity Based in the individual's outlook or opinion.

Relativity Depending on something else for its value rather than standing on its own.

Some critics have called this relativistic way of thinking the 'Boo! Hooray!' theory of morality, which means that moral approval or disapproval is not much more than an attitude or an expression of feelings on the part of the speaker. And by extension, since moral statements cannot be judged true or false in any objective way, they are matters of opinion, not matters of self-evident truths or matters of fact. In short, there is no one right way to act morally. For a presentation topic in this area, carry out a search on the Internet on *emotivism within ethics* or *moral philosophy*.

Of course, this sort of *relativism* can take different forms. While *moral relativism* in modern culture usually refers to the individual's personal set of morals as being right or wrong relative to that person, ethical judgements could be relative to a society, a culture, a nation or even the whole human race at a particular time in history. It is important to remember that any form of *ethical relativism* denies that there are universal or objective moral values that we can verify. And, if this is so, if there are no moral standards independent of human beings, then, indeed, it may be that 'Man is the measure of all things', to quote Protagoras.

Yet, Russell's quote makes us think again. Could there be something real, something *objective*, in an action that gives us the 'moral shudders', a kind of moral repugnance? Perhaps burning a baby to atone for the sins of an adulterous mother is an example, to use Russell's words, of 'wanton cruelty' in so far as this act is wrong in and of itself. This means there is something *objectively immoral* in the situation and my response to this act – what Stephen Pinker of Harvard University calls 'the moral shudders' – is a response to the inherent cruelty imposed upon an innocent being. You, then, would be responding to the situation in a way that doesn't only depend on your feelings or opinions about it. This position of *moral objectivity* stands in total opposition to the Boo/Hooray theory of *moral subjectivity* or *moral relativism*.

The resolution to the *subjective/objective* debate will not be settled in this chapter but Russell's statement points up the fact that he is not alone in his repugnance for wanton cruelty despite our possible disagreement over its meaning or its examples.

But whether moral values are objective or subjective, written or unwritten, more often than not, within any society or culture etc., what is deemed right or wrong is usually observed as the norm by the majority of its members. To do otherwise is to risk being ostracized or punished by the law or the group you offended.

Reasons and emotions in moral judgements

One of the tensions in moral judgements is concerned with the role of reason and emotion (Ways of Knowing) in decision-making. To look at a different kind of questionnaire, go to the Morality Play via www.heinemann.co.uk/hotlinks, enter the

Find the Morality Play at www.heinemann.co.uk/ hotlinks using express code 4327P.

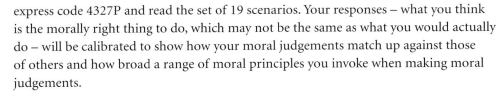

express code 4327P and read the set of 19 scenarios. Your responses – what you think is the morally right thing to do, which may not be the same as what you would actually do – will be calibrated to show how your moral judgements match up against those of others and how broad a range of moral principles you invoke when making moral judgements.

Your responses result in your *moral quotient* although at no time will your responses be labelled correct or incorrect. The Morality Play by Julian Baggini and Jeremy Stangroom is part of *The Philosophers' Magazine*, an online magazine based in the UK, a site serious enough to attract scholars of rank to its discussions. Here is a sample question:

Question 1

You pass someone in the street who is in severe need and you are able to help them at little cost to yourself. Are you morally obliged to do so?

- Strongly obliged
- Weakly obliged
- Not obliged

Julian Baggini and Jeremy Stangroom

This activity, apart from its connection with ethical reflection, is good practice in careful reading and thinking before jumping to a conclusion. For instance, several questions talk about moral obligation without specifying that the Golden Rule or its variations might be implicit in any item. In this questionnaire, to say you are morally obliged to do something means that in order to behave morally, you *must* do that thing. When the moral obligation is strong, this means not doing what is obliged of you is a serious wrongdoing; when the obligation is weak, failing to do what is obliged of you is still a wrongdoing, but not a serious one. What do you think of this distinction of degrees of morality where things are not strictly, and always, right and wrong?

Sometimes there is an advantage to removing yourself from the situation and looking at the same kind of question from another perspective. Take the instance of a murder that occurred in New York City in 1963: a young woman named Kitty Genovese was walking home at night down a residential street when she was attacked and killed, seemingly in full view of witnesses safe in their apartment buildings, who could have called the police without further involving themselves. The question still haunts thoughtful people, What would I have done? What should I have done? What was my obligation, if any? What would you have done?

Question 2

You have a brother. You know that someone has been seriously injured as a result of criminal activity undertaken by him. You live in a country where the police are generally trustworthy. Are you morally obliged to inform them about your brother's crime?

- Strongly obliged
- Weakly obliged
- Not obliged

Julian Baggini and Jeremy Stangroom

In the second question of the Morality Play, the introduction of a family member changes the picture for many people. It prompts the question, How wide do we cast our ethical net? How far should we cast it? What is the extent of our responsibility to others? Does it extend to everyone or only to morally significant others? Remember the question asks us what we *ought* to do, not what we probably would do. How might the situation change for you if your brother were the victim of the crime and not the accused?

One of the interesting features of the Morality Play is the revelation about oneself from what is implied in certain responses. This author was told that her answers indicated that she held the view that an act can be wrong even if it is entirely private and no one, not even the person doing the act, is harmed by it; that she is more permissive than average; not likely to recommend societal intervention in moral issues and less likely than average to see moral wrongdoing in universal terms as far as the 19 scenarios are concerned.

It seems that people who have very strong emotional responses to the scenarios of the Morality Play find it difficult to provide a justification for what they are feeling and for their choices the extent that, when they have to explain or justify them to someone else, they may become clumsy and tongue-tied. According to Steven Pinker, who wrote *The Blank Slate: The Modern Denial of Human Nature,* this is because:

> People have gut feelings that give them emphatic moral convictions, and they struggle to rationalize them after the fact.

That is, moral convictions are rooted in feelings, not in reason. Pinker thinks this biological basis – these gut feelings – arise from the neurobiological and evolutionary design of the organs we call **moral emotions**.

Moral emotions The feelings of right and wrong.

Exercise

You may have heard of a best-selling book called *Emotional Intelligence* by Daniel Goleman, but did you ever think that, in addition to having emotional intelligence – if you know what this means – that you might also have something called 'organs of moral emotions'? What could this mean? Do the words explain anything to you?

What could be the consequences of linking moral attitudes to emotions? Feeling strongly in a negative way about something – what Pinker calls 'the Yuk factor' – might make us condemn something solely because of powerful feelings. For example, Pinker says, most issues of racism or religious hatred are just that, feelings of disgust toward another group of people with no good reasons to support the prejudice.

According to Pinker most issues of racism or religious hatred are feelings of disgust toward another group of people with no good reasons to support the prejudice

For instance, to take just one example from one country, consider the fate of the untouchables in the Indian caste system. They were not allowed to touch people from the higher castes; they were not allowed to drink from the same wells; on public occasions, they had to sit at a distance from everybody else; and in some regions, even contact with the shadow of an untouchable person was seen as polluting and required a cleansing ritual. While this situation might have improved in recent times, discrimination still exists. Such prohibitions may be stirred by raw sentiment but are difficult to justify in the light of reason.

On the other hand, emotions may have some role to play in moral judgement, since caring or indifference can lead to a wide variety of actions or no action at all. In fact, empathy, or the sympathetic imagination of another person's situation, may be an essential part of a good moral framework. And, indeed, some have argued that the atrocities throughout history were possible only because people's moral emotions had been switched off and they could not imagine themselves in the position of their victims. What act would it be impossible for you to do because of empathy? As a TOK student, you need to think about both sides of an issue, no matter which one appeals to you, consequently what could be said for or against rooting moral judgements in emotions, biologically or otherwise?

In *The Blank Slate: The Modern Denial of Human Nature*, Pinker puts it like this:

> *The difference between a defensible moral position and an atavistic gut feeling is that with the former we can give reasons why our conviction is valid. We can explain why torture and murder and rape are wrong, or why we should oppose discrimination and injustice. … And the good reasons for a moral position are not pulled out of thin air; they always have to do with what makes people better or worse off, and are grounded in the logic that we have to treat people in the way that we demand they treat us.*

What could 'grounded in the logic' mean?

You might want to remember this question when you read the interview with the Harvard University law student on page 254. Her response contains the notion that rightness is somehow linked to human nature and the successful operation of the universe. Others, including the professors Steven Pinker and Robert Wright of Harvard University, have given academic voice to the related view that a 'reciprocal altruism' has emerged through natural selection and should be included in any serious thinking about the natural basis of human ethical theory. It is important for you to begin to try to understand these fairly recent thoughts and to form an opinion as your thinking matures.

Another seminal thinker is Marc Hauser who has written what critics declare to be a groundbreaking book: *Moral Minds: The Nature of Right and Wrong.*

The publisher's notes proclaim that, in his thesis, Dr Hauser has put:

> *… forth a revolutionary new theory that humans have evolved a universal moral instinct, unconsciously propelling us to deliver judgements of right and wrong independent of gender, education, and religion. Combining his cutting-edge research with the latest findings in cognitive psychology, linguistics, neuroscience, evolutionary biology, economics, and anthropology, Hauser explores the startling implications of his provocative theory vis-à-vis contemporary bioethics, religion, the law and our everyday lives.*

The material in this book and related publications is rich in possibilities for your TOK presentations. Also, you might want to note the number of disciplines or fields of study that Dr Hauser draws on as you think about the features of each distinctive discipline, yet, at the same time, how in their own evolution they merge into one another. As an example, consider the title of Dr Hauser who is a professor of Psychology, Organismic and Evolutionary Biology, and Biological Anthropology at Harvard University, where he is director of the Cognitive Evolution Laboratory and co-director of the Mind, Brain and Behaviour Program. A similar richness of crossover in disciplines is expressed by the Ideal knower, Martha Nussbaum (see page 76).

A related idea for discussion is how and why one university, or one locale, collects or generates original thinking in a particular field.

Judging moral behaviour

> ### Exercise
>
> Although the following may be over-simplified, in order to begin thinking about the foundations of moral judgements, you need to consider the following:
>
> > A young man is doing poorly in school. He has the opportunity to *borrow* the work of another student and he does so as if invisible. Only he knows. His marks improve. He is happy; so are the teacher, his parents and the football coach (because he will be able to stay on the team).
>
> Using this example as a case study, ask yourself honestly, what is wrong here, if anything? You might want to refer back to the cartoon on page 239 ('When you say "no cheating", what do you exactly mean?') and begin a concept analysis of the term 'cheating' within this situation (or concept).

Generally it helps to distinguish between *rightness* and *wrongness* and *goodness* and *badness*. For the most part, actions are said to be *right* and *wrong*, and people and their motives, and the consequences of their actions, are called *good* or *bad*.

The scenario in the exercise above can be paraphrased a dozen different ways, one of which is Plato's parable of *The Ring of Gyges* (350 BCE) where Gyges the shepherd finds a magic ring, puts it on and becomes, in effect, capable of doing anything without fear of consequences. You may not, as Gyges did, choose to ravish the queen, murder the king and plunder the castle, but the moral of the story asks you to consider, what difference would it make to your behaviour if you knew you would not get caught?

Glaucon, in Plato's *The Republic,* insists that no man is so virtuous that he could resist the temptation of being able to steal (or cheat) at will by the ring's power of invisibility. Glaucon also states that morality, in such cases, is no more than the desire for a good reputation. Thus, if the sanction were removed, moral character would evaporate. That there is no easy answer is proven by the tale repeated in various forms down through the centuries including the *Lord of the Rings* (in which the ring corrupts the character of those who possess it), to situations today within our own lives.

Two classical ethical theories

Without getting too technical, let's look at two widely different ethical theories of judgement:

- **deontological**, which deals with principles, the intrinsic right and wrong of an action itself, and the intention to act and the concept of universalizability
- **consequentialism**, which considers the good or bad consequences of any action.

Deontological principles Rules of behaviour which are claimed to be right or wrong, regardless of the consequences.

Consequentialist principles These involve weighing up the consequenses to work out the right action.

In short, deontological theory judges an action by moral *rules*, while consequentialism, or utilitarianism, judges an action by its good or bad *results*. Another relevant difference is that the first, the deontological, looks backward, so to speak, to the rules, or the right thing to do come what may, while the second, the consequentialist, looks forward to what will happen in terms of the happiness produced by an action, or its usefulness.

Deontological	**Consequentialist**
Rules	Results
Principles	Pragmatic
Categorical imperative	Utilitarian
The RIGHT thing to do	The GOOD brought about
Duties and obligations	Justified by effects

This framework suggests that within the deontological theory the student (see previous page) is wrong regardless of the good or bad consequences if he violates, or intends to violate, such moral codes as doing his own work and not taking what does not belong to him. In the same vein, he is wrong if he has violated the written or honour code of his school or classroom or an agreement among peers. As you will often hear, 'It is the principle of the thing'. Where these principles or moral codes comes from will be addressed below. Yet, in contrast, according to the consequentialist theory, if nothing bad happened, and happiness for all concerned has increased, another judgement might be much less harsh.

> **Exercise**
>
> Which of the following contain the premises of the deontological and of utilitarianism?
> - The end justifies the means.
> - Let the chips fall where they may.
> - The road to hell is paved with good intentions.
> - The greatest good for the greatest number.
> - The Confucian principles of *Li, Jen* and *Chun-Tzu*.
> - Do unto others as you would have them do to you.

Although it is not the goal of TOK to master philosophers' thoughts, in the interests of intellectual honesty, it seems right to cite two of the major thinkers, Immanuel Kant and John Stuart Mill who are associated with the two theories of ethical judgement: the deontological and utilitarianism. Below is a brief summary of their positions.

Immanuel Kant (1724–1804) – deontological

Kant claimed that a free will and a rational mind (not feelings) are assumed in all moral judgements, and that all genuine moral behaviour comes from the concept of duty. If any moral agent wanted to commit an act from feeling or inclination, then the moral element could not be identified since he or she wanted to do it anyway. Moreover, that duty, the **categorical imperative**, is absolutely binding on all people. The method by which we come to know our duties – what we should or should not do – is not easy to understand but it is worth mulling over. First, apply the **universal principle** by asking yourself, what kind of world would it be if everyone did this or that? Kant does not mean, How many people would your action help? Or would the world be a better or worse place in terms of happiness or chaos? Rather, he means, use your head and think it through. Is it even a possible world?

Take, for example, lying, cheating, stealing or killing, and ask, what if everyone lied, cheated, stole or killed? In the case of lying, if everyone lied, there would be no truth; thus it is an incoherent notion and not a possible world. The same with killing – if killing were allowed, then there would be no one left to kill or be killed; as with cheating, if everyone borrowed everyone else's homework, there would be no homework to borrow. You would have created an incomprehensible world, logically, and thus the immorality of cheating is revealed and should be avoided at all costs. At a simpler level, take for example jumping the queue. This action, of course, would destroy the queue, the thing you are morally concerned about. So the rationality involved in discovering our moral duties should be clear – moral actions are those that can and should be universalized.

Why the emphasis on logic and reason? Kant might answer that if a person were to know the good, it would be through some human quality and he ruled out the gut, the heart, etc., as well as all feelings, as too unreliable and indefensible. And reason, being the defining feature of the human species, gained pride of place. Thus, if right and wrong were to be revealed to us, it would be through the light of reason and the power of logical thought.

▲ Immanuel Kant

Exercise

In addition to the universal principle of 'What if everyone did it?', Kant also believed in the maxim that you should always act in such a way that you never treat people simply as a means only, but always as an end. In other words, *don't use people*. Can you even imagine what kind of world this would be if this maxim were the only ethical duty that everyone, including rulers of government, abided by?

Do you think the IB Learner profile is an example of student or teacher qualities that could or should be universalized to everyone? (See page ix.)

John Stuart Mill (1806–73) – utilitarian

John Stuart Mill is most closely linked to the utilitarian maxim, 'the greatest good for the greatest number' when judging whether any action is right or wrong. At a common sense level, it seems that this kind of thinking (the ability to look ahead and consider the results of our actions) is what many people want from their government or from their family and friends (or even from their own behaviour). They ask themselves, what if I do this or that? How many people will be harmed or helped?) However, the problem is, what is the greatest good and how can it be measured? Furthermore, even if the greatest good is defined as happiness, how is the minority protected from something that benefits most people?

For some people, it is a moral intuition that others should not be sacrificed for the greater good if another's happiness involves someone else's unhappiness. This notion can be seen in the situation described in Ursula Le Guin's *The Ones Who Walk Away From Omelas*. In this modern fable, the improbable situation is that a prosperous and happy group comes to realize that their good fortune depends absolutely upon a child being kept in a dark cell underground . The title of the story is taken from those who walk away after seeing the pitiful creature. What then is the moral status of those who

▲ John Stuart Mill

refuse the condition of their supposed well being? Utilitarianism does not seem to be able to address this conundrum, since there is no other moral scale available than the actions of those who produce the greatest good? So does this mean that the people who stay are the better ones?

If you wish to delve more deeply into the utilitarian ethic and to evaluate its strengths and weaknesses, it is good to remember that in modern times, the greatest good for the greatest number, in this global society, might imply the entire world.

For instance, a Pakistani journalist at the United Nations once criticized the Japanese government for dumping rice into the ocean instead of sharing it with the world's needy. His position was that if we moved our thinking to a higher level we could see that human benevolence should not stop at geo-political borders. The question then arises, do you really mean the greatest good for the greatest number of people in the world or only the greatest good for the greatest number of people like us? Addressing this question brings forward the notion that rice-dumping or giving rice to poorer populations both have their own economic consequenses to be considered as a good.

In short, if utilitarianism depends on how many people will be affected by any action, how can anyone ever assign moral worth to the consequences, if no one knows how many heads there are to be counted as the consequences are spread around?

One moral issue: lying

Although students are often asked to consider the moral judgements linked to abortion, capital punishment, genocide and euthanasia – important and complicated issues – this next section will elaborate on the more everyday example of lying. It will call on the skills of concept analysis, use surveys of the attitudes in your school or college community and set out what some writers have thought about this moral issue.

But first a question: could you go one day without lying? The question is meant to be provocative. It is introduced with an example from the author's experience as a teacher when, after a class discussion about lying and what its prevalence might signify, the teacher and some students returned to the office to continue the conversation. Just then the telephone rang. The call was for the teacher who said, 'Tell them, I am not here'. It took a couple of seconds for the teacher to realize the irony of the situation while the students never noticed. What is the significance of this story?

At the very least, it connects with something Monica Lewinsky said in an interview after her affair with US President, Bill Clinton:

> *I was brought up with lies all the time… that's how you got along… I have lied my entire life.*

This cynicism regarding truth telling and its opposite, the lie (if there is a simple opposite) is addressed in Sissela Bok's book *Lying: Moral Choice in Public and Private Life*. In it, she says that discussions about lying by moral philosophers, particularly contemporary ones, have generally been:

> *… brief and peremptory. The major works of moral philosophy over the past hundred years or so are silent on this subject. For instance, the index to the eight-volume* Encyclopedia of Philosophy *contains not one reference to lying or to deception, much less an entire article devoted the issue.*

Bok goes on to wonder if there is a theory of moral choice which can help in quandaries of truth-telling and lying. To stimulate our thinking, she poses these questions:

- Should doctors lie to dying patients so as to delay the fear and anxiety which the truth might bring them?
- Should teachers exaggerate the excellence of their students on recommendations in order to give them a better chance in the competition for college and university placement?
- Should parents conceal from children that they have been adopted?
- Should social scientists masquerade as patients to doctors in order to find out if there are racial or sexual biases in diagnosis and treatment?

In her research, Sissela Bok found the following worthy of our attention.

From St Augustine there is a taxonomy of lies from the ruthless to the harmless:
1 The deadly lie, one to be shunned since it distorts the teaching of religion.
2 The lie that injures someone unjustly and helps no one.
3 The lie that benefits one person but harms another.
4 The lie told solely for the pleasure of deceiving.

Others follow: the lie that smoothes conversation and so on until the eighth rank where lies harm no one (except perhaps the teller) – what we might today call 'the white lie'.

Exercise

Why do you think the concept of 'the white lie' might be important? Could you give examples of each of these lies that St Augustine describes? Is it helpful to distinguish between different kinds of lies?

St Augustine's distinctions are in stark contrast to those of Immanuel Kant whose categorical imperative demands that you never lie, no matter what, and whoever tells a lie, for whatever good reason, must be ready to face the consequences. The Kantian rigidity comes from the view that truthfulness is a duty which must be regarded as inviolate. That is, truthfulness is the bedrock of all goodness and all contracts between people, and no exception can be admitted.

From the view of how lying functions in the personal realm, Dietrich Bonhoeffeer advises that we should think about:
- the various meanings of words
- how meaning can be obliterated in the lie
- how, when different words are no longer clearly felt or understood because of the lie, then the personal bond between two people is destroyed.

What is the advantage to you, he asks, of 'letting go of the truth'? Inevitably, no one will want to talk to you, because you cannot be trusted. And if you don't mean what you say, you will turn out to be boring because you will say anything, and that is not interesting. For Bonhoeffeer, our moral duty then is to find the right words. Could the teacher in the earlier story about the telephone caller have, with a little more care and thought, found the *right words*?

Exercise

Think about how what Bonhoeffeer says coincides with St Augustine's words:

> *When regard for truth has been broken down or even slightly weakened, all things will remain doubtful.*

How would it be possible to survive or have peace of mind in a world where everything was doubtful?

Confucius

While not cited in Bok's book, the teachings of Confucius extend the notion of how morality and the use of language are intertwined when he talks about the relationship between language and action.

> *If language is not correct, then what is said is not what is meant; if what is said is not what is meant, then what must be done remains undone; if what must be done remains undone, the rites and arts will deteriorate; if the rites and arts deteriorate, justice goes astray; and if justice goes astray, the people will stand about in helpless confusion. Hence there must be no arbitrariness in what is said. This matters above everything.*
>
> *Analects of Confucius*, XIII, 3

Confucius certainly would not have approved of many present-day leaders, or even some of us, who deliberately misuse words to hide our true intentions.

Exercise

Consider the following in relation to your own life with the view to reaching a decision about whether truth-telling or lying matters, and how *the rectification of names* or the use of language can matter in a moral sense.

Question	Yes or no?
1 Do you feel guilty when you lie?	
2 Do you always know when you are lying?	
3 Is lying a fairly common practice in school/college and/or elsewhere?	
4 Do you think people lie because others will get angry if the truth is told?	
5 Do you think that people lie because the other person will have their feelings hurt if the truth is told?	
6 Do you get angry when you find that someone has lied to you?	
7 Do you think that it is OK to lie to others, but not to be lied to yourself?	
8 Do you think that the end justifies the means?	

Thinking once more about Plato's view of morality, he held the belief that it was better to be the injured party, than to injure another; namely, that it was better to be lied to than to lie to someone else because of the corrupting effect of the lie on the teller. Certainly, this perspective is central to several of the plays of the Nigerian Nobel Prize winner, Woyle Soyinka, where rulers become so corrupted by power that the distinction between what is and what is not true no longer matters to them one way or the other. This indifference eventually blinds them to the point that they can no longer see the world clearly. Thus they cannot make accurate statements about the world even if they wanted to fool others, so their downfall is inevitable. Do you agree that your views about truth-telling and falsehoods could affect your perceptions of the world?

In less dramatic terms, but just as seriously, consider what Lewis Thomas has to say in his essay, 'The Lie Detector', about how the human body is linked to telling the truth:

> *As I understand it, a human being cannot tell a lie, even a small one, without setting off a kind of smoke alarm somewhere deep in a dark lobule of the brain, resulting in the sudden discharge of nerve impulses... The outcome, recorded by lie-detector gadgetry, is a highly reproducible cascade of changes in the electrical conductivity of the skin, the heart rate and the manner of breathing, similar to the responses to various kinds of stress.*
>
> From *Late Night Thoughts on Listening to Mahler's Ninth Symphony* by
> Lewis Thomas

Lying is stressful even when we do it for protection, or relief, or escape, or profit, or just for the pure pleasure of lying and getting away with it.

> *Lying, then, is in a pure physiological sense, an unnatural act.*

In an American comic book of the 1940s, *Wonder Woman*, the sexy, Amazonian superhero, wields a golden 'lasso of truth'. Anybody she captures is rendered temporarily incapable of lying. Like the golden lasso, the polygraph or the lie detector, compels the body to reveal the mind's secrets. The artist of Wonder Woman, himself one of the inventors of the lie detector, believed that the conscious mind could be circumvented and the truth uncovered through the measurement of bodily signals.

Can it actually be true that human beings are hard-wired in some way to be truth-tellers? Lewis Thomas goes on to say that truth-telling makes a sort of shrewd biological sense. Of course, as an eminent scientist himself, Lewis knows that good science depends on truth-telling but he is saying something more profound, namely that we 'as a species have evolved beyond mendacity, except under extraordinary conditions, and that it is amazing to think that we cannot tell even a plain untruth, betray a trust, without scarring some part of our own brains or perhaps our own soul.

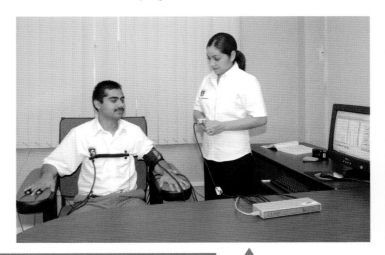

A lie detector in use

Exercise

- How do Lewis Thomas's thoughts connect with those of Steven Pinker who talks about the biological basis – the gut feelings – of making moral decisions?
- Do you think that there is something to the idea that it is good for the human species to be good?
- Would a biological basis for truth-telling affect the view of moral relativism where right and wrong are tied to different cultures?

Today's world: a different voice

There is no doubt that advances in brain research will stimulate new thinking about right and wrong, good and bad, and how we make and justify those decisions. In addition, new perspectives in gender studies have tried to show that women tend to follow a different path of moral development to that of men. Rather than thinking through moral dilemmas in terms of justice and rights, or interpreting moral behaviour within the deontological or utilitarian framework, Carol Gilligan, a psychologist and author of *In a Different Voice: Psychological Theory and Women's Development*, tries to build a theory about *ethics of care*. This new way of looking at morality claims that women tend towards a philosophy that emphasizes the importance of relationships and accommodating the needs of others. Her views about gender differences in moral reasoning have not gained widespread acceptance, except in the medical field, but for TOK students, her writing offers an alternative that can be explored for presentations or for greater substance in their TOK essay. And as the cartoon opposite shows, the question still remains, how do we know right from wrong and how can we make the best judgements about right and wrong actions and good and bad people?

"WITH ALL I'VE LEARNED ABOUT PSYCHOLOGY RECENTLY, ESTABLISHING WHO'S NAUGHTY AND WHO'S NICE IS NOT AS SIMPLE AS IT USED TO BE."

At the very least, we can continue to give important issues our best thinking and one way to do this is to continue to ask questions of ourselves and reflect on our thoughts thereby revising, rejecting or reaffirming our own moral views. The following questions may help:

Question	Yes or no?
1 If you lived alone on earth, would it be possible for you to do anything wrong?	
2 If you follow your own ethical code, is it possible for you to do anything wrong?	
3 Do you have a set of ethical principles or an ethical code?	
4 Can you explain them to someone else clearly?	
5 Do they guide your behaviour?	
6 If you answered 'yes' to question 3, are these principles the same or similar to your parents?	
7 If you answered 'yes' to question 3, are these principles the same or similar to your best friends?	
8 Could you be friends with someone who did not share your ethical values?	
9 Could you marry someone who did not share your ethical values?	
10 Does it matter if you are a good person?	
11 Does it matter if others think of you as a good person?	
12 Can you define what it means to be a good person?	
13 Do you know anyone who is a really good person?	
14 Is it possible for a bad man to write a good book?	

Finally, to understand how a young person can reflect on his or her own moral development, consider this interview with a 25-year-old law student at Harvard University who described her conception of morality as follows:

Q: Is there really some correct solution to moral problems or is everybody's opinion equally right?

A: No, I don't think everybody's opinion is equally right. I think that in some situations there may be opinions that are equally valid and someone could conscientiously adopt one of several courses of action. But there are other situations to which I think there are right and wrong answers, that sort of belong to the nature of existence, of all individuals here who need to live with each other. We need to depend on each other and hopefully it is not only a physical need but a need of fulfillment in ourselves, that a person's life is enriched by cooperating with other people and striving to live in harmony with everybody else, and to that end, there are right and wrong, there are things which promote that end and that move away from it, and in that way, it is possible to choose in certain cases among different courses of action, that obviously promote or harm that goal.

Q: Is there a time in the past when you would have thought about these things differently?

A: Oh, yeah. I think that I went through a time when I thought that things were pretty relative, that I can't tell you what to do and you can't tell me what to do, because you've got your conscience and I've got mine …

Q: When was that?

A: When I was in high school, I guess it just sort of dawned on me that my own ideas changed, I felt I couldn't judge another person's judgement, but now I think even when it is only the person himself who is going to be affected, I say it is wrong to the extent it doesn't cohere with what I know about human nature and what I know about you, and just from what I think is true about the operation of the universe, I could say I think you are making a mistake.

Q: What led you to change, do you think?

A: Just seeing more of life, just recognizing that there are an awful lot of things that are common among people. There are certain things that you come to learn that promote a better life and better relationships and more personal fulfillment than other things that tend to do the opposite, and the things that promote these things, you would call morally right.

Q: How do you describe yourself today as a moral person?

A: Well, I have a very strong sense of being responsible to people I am tied to and of being responsible to the world as well. I want to have a good time, but I can't just live for my enjoyment, since just the fact of being in the world gives me an obligation to do what I can to make the world a better place. I think I can do this and I think I should do it. It makes me feel good and it seems like the right thing to do.

From Woman's Place in a Man's Life Cycle, *Harvard Educational Review*,
Vol 49, No 4, November 1979, pp. 431–46
by Carol Gilligan

Ideal knower: Dalai Lama

Ethics for the new millennium

Of course, both as a Tibetan and a monk, I have been brought up according to, and educated in, the principles, the precepts, and the practice of Buddhism. I cannot, therefore, deny that my whole thinking is shaped by my understanding of what it means to be a follower of the Buddha. However, my concern in this book is to try to reach beyond the formal boundaries of my faith. I want to show that there are indeed some universal ethical principles which could help everyone to achieve the happiness we all aspire to.

▲ The Dalai Lama

I believe there is an important distinction to be made between religion and spirituality. Religion I take to be concerned with faith in the claims to salvation of one faith tradition or another, an aspect of which is acceptance of some form of metaphysical or supernatural reality, including perhaps an idea of heaven or *nirvana*. Connected with this are religious teachings or dogmas, ritual and so on. Spirituality I take to be concerned with those qualities of the human spirit – such as love and compassion, patience, tolerance, forgiveness, contentment, a sense of responsibility, a sense of harmony – which bring happiness to both self and others. While ritual and prayer, along with the questions of nirvana and salvation, are directly connected to religious faith, these inner qualities need not be, however. There is thus no reason why the individual should not develop them, even to a high degree, without recourse to any religious or metaphysical belief system. This is why I sometimes say that religion is something we can perhaps do without. What we cannot do without are these basic spiritual qualities. Those who practise religion would, of course, be right to say that such qualities, or virtues, are fruits of genuine religious endeavour and that religion therefore has everything to do with developing them and with what may be called spiritual practice. But let us be clear on this point. Religious faith demands spiritual practice. Yet it seems there is much confusion, as often among religious believers or among nonbelievers, concerning what this actually consists in. The unifying characteristic of the qualities I have described as 'spiritual' may be said to be some level of concern for others' well being. In Tibetan we speak of *shen pen kyi sem* meaning 'the thought to be of help to others'. And when we think about them, we see that each of the qualities noted is defined by an implicit concern for others' well being. Moreover, the one who is compassionate, loving, patient, tolerant, forgiving and so on to some extent recognizes the potential impact of their actions on others and orders their conduct accordingly. Thus spiritual practice according to this description involves, on the one hand, acting out of concern for others' well being. On the other, it entails transforming ourselves so that we become more readily disposed to do so. To speak of spiritual practice in any terms other than these is meaningless.

My call for a spiritual revolution is thus not a call for a religious revolution. Nor is it a reference to a way of life that is somehow otherworldly, still less to something magical or mysterious. Rather it is a call for a radical reorientation away from our habitual preoccupation with self. It is a call to turn toward the wider community of being with whom we are connected, and for conduct, which recognizes others' interests alongside our own.

From *Ethics for the New Millennium* by the Dalai Lama

Student presentation

1 Consider the list of vices that Pope Gregory the Great drew up in the sixth century, known today as 'the seven deadly sins':

- lust
- anger
- envy
- gluttony
- sloth
- pride
- greed

a How did he make his selection?

b What would be their corresponding virtues?

c How does this list compare to that of the Dalai Lama's?

d If you were to make a list of vices or virtues more fitting to today's world, what might they be?

Look out for the series published by Oxford University Press which is concerned with the modern relevance of the seven deadly sins. For instance, Professor Simon Blackburn of Cambridge University argues that lust has been wrongly condemned as a vice for centuries and should be 'reclaimed for humanity' as a life-affirming virtue. By analogy, he says, thirst is not criticized although it can lead to drunkenness and in the same way lust should not be condemned just because it can get out of hand.

2 Compare and contrast the various meanings of 'good' using a concept analysis technique, such as:

a giving a standard definition of what 'good' is in each of the following cases:

- a good teacher
- a good student
- a good book
- a good game
- a good person
- a good deed

b trying to show its opposite

c giving an example from real life or literature.

Essay questions

Question 1 is a recent Prescribed Title (PT).

1 'Doing the right thing starts with knowing the right things.' In what ways does responsible action depend on sound critical thinking?

© International Baccalaureate Organization 2005

2 'Why should I not be selfish? Why should I be moral?' How might this chapter help you put together your response?

Art

It's just a question of taste…

So we, holding Art in our hands, self-confidently consider ourselves its owners, brashly give it aim, renovate it, re-form it, make manifestos of it, sell it for cash, play up to the powerful with it, and turn it around at times for entertainment, even in vaudeville songs and in nightclubs, and at times – using stopper or stick, whichever comes first – for transitory political or limited social needs. But Art is not profaned by our attempts, does not because of them lose touch with its source, each time and by each use it yields us a part of its mysterious inner light.

© The Nobel Foundation 1970

You enjoy a piece of music; another fails to move you. You find beauty in one painting and are repelled by another. One poem inspires you; another has no meaning for you. You appreciate the skill and craftsmanship in one sculpture, yet look at another and say that you could have done that yourself. You could say that this is quite obvious, for art is just a matter of personal taste, or to quote an old saying that first appeared in the third century BCE: 'Beauty lies in the eye of the beholder'. But, look again at the contrasts that have been made in the statements above. Do they all relate to one sort of reaction to works of art or do they cover a range of reactions: aesthetic, intellectual and emotional?

Exercise

Are there standards by which you judge a piece of art, in whatever form, or are there criteria that go beyond the personal? If there are, what might they be? Which of the following extracts from various poems do you like best? Make your choice immediately after you have read them and before you read on:

1 In spite of all the love I gave
   She wanted me to be her slave
   She was not young, not nice, not rich
   But still she saw a man with which…

2 So I am stuck here in this world,
   Which is not really real.
   You might think it genuine;
   That's not the way I feel.

3 Wishing me like to one more rich in hope,
   Featured like him, like him with friends possess'd,
   Desiring this man's art and that man's scope,
   With what I most enjoy contented least;

4 When we two parted in silence and tears,
   Half broken hearted to sever for years,
   Pale grew thy cheek and cold, colder the kiss;
   Truly that hour foretold sorrow to this.

Each is an extract and deliberately taken out of context, but did you have any difficulty in making a decision? If you did, what was the basis for your difficulty? If you made a choice, on what grounds did you do so; would you be able to explain the choice to someone else? Finally, if you had known in advance the author, would this have made any difference to your choice?

The first extract was written by three teenagers in just 14 minutes as part of a classroom exercise. The second is from the poem 'Reality' and is written by a contemporary British poet called Robert Muir. The third, you probably guessed, is from a Shakespeare sonnet called 'When a disgrace with fortune and men's eyes'. The final extract was written about 200 years ago by the English poet, Lord Byron.

Did any of the extracts have any meaning for you? If any one of them had no meaning for you, would you classify it as a piece of art? Would any of the extracts be chosen for study in an IB literature programme? What would the criteria be for either inclusion or rejection? Returning to the statement that introduced this section, is the appreciation and the meaning of art simply a question of subjective taste? Is this perhaps why, with the exception of literature, you do not have to take an aesthetic subject when you must study at least one of the other main Ways of Knowing?

As you consider these questions, you are facing the issue of whether or not there are qualities in a piece of art that are not in your own response to it, but are actually in the work itself. The issue is whether aesthetic values are subjective or objective. If you take the view that what matters when you listen to a piece of music, read a poem or a novel, look at a painting or sculpture or any other work of art is simply that you like it, whatever that means, then you are taking a **subjectivist view**. On the other hand, if you feel that there are qualities in the work of art itself that determine your response, then you are taking an **objectivist view**.

There is, in fact, no general agreement about whether or not there are objective standards by which a work of art can be judged; this chapter will present a variety of issues that may help you to clarify your own position. At the outset, however, you should bear in mind that, whenever you encounter a work of art, you are taking part in a triangular relationship.

This relationship looks straightforward, but does it make certain assumptions? Does, for example, your response to a work of art mean that you necessarily have a relationship with its creator and if it does, then in what manner? Before we can answer the questions raised here, we should consider whether criteria can be established by which works of art can be identified and distinguished from all other creations of humankind, for example, mathematical theorems, historical accounts or scientific hypotheses.

Subjectivist view There is nothing intrinsic in a work of art that determines whether an observer thinks it good or bad – it is simply a matter of whether the observer likes or dislikes it.

Objectivist view There are qualities in the work of art itself, irrespective of the observer, which determine whether it is seen as good or bad art.

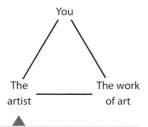

The relationship between the individual, the artist and the work of art

What counts as art?

Before we look in more depth at the nature of art, at what knowledge or truth it may give you, can you draw a dividing line between what counts as art and what does not? Would you, for example, consider a comic strip to be art? In the same context, what do you think of the new genre 'graphic novels'?

Look at the six photographs below. Using your own judgement, rank them on a scale from 1 to 6, according to what you consider to be the least to the most aesthetically pleasing.

The photographs from the top, left-hand corner are: a rose, a student's sculpture, a dinner plate, a pair of binoculars, an outdoor sculpture made by a student and a flower arrangement.

What criteria did you use to put these pictures into order from least to most pleasing? Compare your order with those of other members of your class. How do you account for any similarities or differences between the orders? What criteria did you use? Is there a cut-off point at which you would not consider the object a work of art or is the rank at which you placed an object independent of whether or not you consider it to be a work of art? Does the fact that the objects have been photographed change their status with respect to being ranked or regarded as works of art? If you had seen the objects, could or would this have made a difference to the way you ranked them?

One way of deciding whether or not an object is a work of art is to ask if it has any practical purpose. This distinction, it has been argued, determines the attitude we have when, for example, looking at the binoculars; these have an obvious practical use compared to the sculpture which has clearly been created as a piece of art. The difference in attitude when looking at the work of art is based on the fact that the object has no practical interest to us, such as the way that we might use it. In the case of the work of art, we look at it, listen to it or read it simply for the thing in itself. When you look back at the decisions you made with respect to the objects, does this argument make sense to you?

Exercise

Now look at this short extract from a play. Can you apply the same form of judgement to the play that you did when you ranked the photographs of the objects? Do you find the extract pleasing, or is this not an appropriate question to ask? Does a piece of art have to be pleasing for that matter?

Goldberg:	When did you come to this place?
Stanley:	Last year.
Goldberg:	Where did you come from?
Stanley:	Somewhere else.
Goldberg:	Why did you come here?
Stanley:	My feet hurt!
Goldberg:	Why did you stay?
Stanley:	I had a headache!
Goldberg:	Did you take anything for it?
Stanley:	Yes.
Goldberg:	What?
Stanley:	Fruit salts!
Goldberg:	Enos or Andrews?
Stanley:	En – An
Goldberg:	Did you stir properly? Did they fizz?
Stanley:	Now, now, wait, you….
Goldberg:	Did they fizz? Did they fizz? You don't know. When did you last have a bath?
Stanley:	I have one every…
Goldberg:	Don't lie.

This extract is taken from a play called *The Birthday Party* and it was written by Harold Pinter. Does it count as art, according to the criteria which you used to judge the photographs? Can you use the same criteria from one art form to judge another? In the case of the extract from the play, for example, what other factors would you need to take into consideration before making your judgements?

Artists and philosophers have sometimes set out their own criteria with which to define what counts as a work of art. Look at the two extracts below, written by the art critic Clive Bell:

A work of art is an object beautiful, or significant, in itself, no wise dependent for its value on the outside world, capable by itself of provoking in us that emotion which we call aesthetic. Agreed. But people do not create things unconsciously and without effort, as they breathe in their sleep. On the contrary, for their production are required special energies and a peculiar state of mind. A work of art, like a rose, is the result of a string of causes…

*****

The artistic problem is the problem of making a match between an emotional experience and a form that has been conceived but not created.

From 'The Artistic Problem', in *Art*, by Clive Bell

The first extract sets out the view that works of art are human creations and they are made intentionally and that they cause an emotional response. Does this view match your own when you decided which of the objects in the photographs you considered to be works of art? The second extract raises different issues; that the artist is making a match between the emotional experience and the work of art that will be created. What does this have to say about whether or not your own judgement can be a purely subjective one?

How do you judge a work of art?

Is it possible to talk about judging any work of art without first considering the impact of culture on art? It can be argued that art reveals social values and meanings more clearly than any other cultural product of a society. Read the passage below. Do you agree with the author in arguing that even the physical environment of a society has a determining impact on the nature of the art that it produces?

> … the influence of the desert, the Nile, and the prevalence of bright sunshine is seen in the simplicity and massive solidarity of Egyptian art as well as on its infrequent use of bas relief. The dense, subtropical vegetation of India is reflected in its crowded and 'eye filling' sculptures and paintings…
>
> From *The Social Function of Art* by Radhakamal Mukherjee

This chapter began by asking you to think about whether you believe that your own judgements of works of art, in whatever form, are purely subjective. We now need to examine the evaluation of artistic beauty in more depth and, to do so, we must begin by asking whether the very idea of subjectivity with respect to artistic judgement is common to all cultures.

The extract below is from an early Indian text called the Citralaksana of Nagnajit. It sets out clearly the rules for artistic representation of the human face in a work of art. Notice that it is not concerned with exact representation; instead its concern is with the beauty of representation.

> The face should be divided into three parts, forehead, nose and chin, each of which should measure four digits. The width of the face is given as the total of 14 digits; the upper and lower parts of the face amount to 12 digits in width; on the grounds of this measurement, the length of the face is taken to be 12 digits.

This clearly sets out the dimensions that must be used if the sculpture of a face is to be regarded as beautiful and it leaves no room for subjectivity. Another example of an art form that leaves little room for subjectivity is the creation or copying of religious icons in the tradition of the Eastern Orthodox Christian church.

The purpose of an icon was to convey specific information about the person or the event that it portrayed. There is generally a prescribed method for the manner in which a person should be portrayed and it is common for icons to be copied from older models. Does this mean that a perfectly copied icon should not be regarded as a work of art? If you feel that it should not, are you simply expressing a cultural belief about the need for individual creativity before something can be considered to be a work of art? Might you ask the same question about photography, on the grounds that a photograph is a perfect copy of the original?

Are the issues of cultural background and subjectivity at odds when you make a judgement about a work of art? In fact, it is difficult to find evidence for the belief in subjective judgement of a work of art before the middle of the nineteenth century.

A religious icon from a church in Crete

The influence of the German philosopher Nietzsche was important in this respect. He argued that the value of art lies in the fact that it is not true; instead, that all art is an illusion. This strips away a sense of objectivity from art. You may ask yourself if the idea that artistic judgement is purely subjective derives from the ideas that Nietzsche proposed. In seeking to answer this, we should continue our exploration of the nature of beauty in a cross-cultural context.

Is the appreciation of beauty universal?

Do all cultures recognise the same form of beauty or is the notion of beauty relative to the culture? In fact, is it possible to apply the same concept of beauty across all art forms and, if it is, what is the common linking notion of 'the beautiful'? Is it possible, for example, to recognise something of the same quality when reading the following two poems? They are both in translation, the first from Japanese and the second from Anglo-Saxon:

> The line of the cherry
> Fades too quickly from sight
> All for nothing
> This body of mine grows old –
> Spring rain falling.
>
> 'Ono no Komachi' translated by Jon Lacure

> The wisdom of age is worthless to him.
> Morning after morning, he wakes to remember
> That his child has gone; he has no interest
> In living on until another heir
> Is born in the hall...'
>
> From *Beowulf* translated by Seamus Heaney

Can you make a comparison on the basis of the words alone and the fact that they are in translation? Is there something that reaches through the different contexts so that, over 1000 years since both were written, they have an aesthetic appeal? Is it necessary to know the context of each and the background of the poet before you can make a judgement? If the poems are from the same era and the same cultural background, as in the next two examples, does this make a difference?

> **When you are old**
>
> When you are old and gray and full of sleep
> And nodding by the fire, take down this book,
> And slowly read, and dream of the soft look
> Your eyes had once, and of their shadows deep;
>
> How many loved your moments of glad grace,
> And loved your beauty with love false or true;
> But one man loved the pilgrim soul in you,
> And loved the sorrows of your changing face.
>
> And bending down beside the glowing bars,
> Murmur, a little sadly, how love fled
> And paced upon the mountains overhead,
> And hid his face amid a crowd of stars.
>
> W.B. Yeats

When I am old

When I am old and grey
And full of death,
Caress me still,
And with your breath
Assure me that I live.

Despite all proof of imminent collapse
Contrive to bring relief,
Through your belief
In permanence of a kind, perhaps.

When winter's light pales down
To dark and cold and void,
Let us be gay in living
What we can't avoid.

Let death be sure
We will not let him gloat,
But rather stuff his message
Down his throat!

A. Maley

Different languages have different expectations of their poetry. In its original form, Japanese poetry relied on subtlety of meaning expressed usually through the use of characters in addition to a clear set of rules. The Haiku, for example, had to convey the message in 17 syllables, usually in the form of 5, 7, 5 per line for a total of 3 lines and it somehow had to have a word to indicate a relationship with the weather. One of the lines had a definite break from the other two, either the first or the last; these needed a form of punctuation to indicate this.

The Anglo-Saxon poem stressed alliteration, with the repetition of the same consonant sound at the beginning of two or more words. On the other hand, the two modern poems above, like poems in most European languages, have a sense of rhythm and, quite often, of rhyme. But are there common themes? If there are, can you apply them when you search for a common sense of beauty in the sculptures below that are chosen from different cultures and historical periods?

Fang sculpture from Gabon, date unknown

'The Fountain of the Neptune' Rome, 1574

'The Thinker' by Rodin, Paris, early 1900s

A statue from the Meiji period (1868–1912), Japan

Celestial nymph, circa 1440, Rajasthan, India

Beauty and the beholder

If there is a universal sense of what is beauty, then how might it apply to the human body? Look at the extract below from an article called 'The Biology of Beauty' that appeared in 1996 in the magazine *Newsweek*.

> It's widely assumed that ideals of beauty vary from era to era and from culture to culture. But a harvest of new research is confounding that idea. And though no one knows how our minds translate the sight of a face or a body into rapture, new studies suggest that we judge each other by rules we are not even aware of. We may consciously admire Kate Moss's legs or Arnold's biceps, but we're also viscerally attuned to small variations in the size and symmetry of facial bones and the placement of weight on the body. …One key to physical attractiveness is symmetry; humans, like other species, show a strong preference for individuals whose right and left sides are well matched.
>
> From 'The Biology of Beauty' by G. Cowley

Does this suggest that the appreciation of beauty has a biological basis when judgements are made about human beings? If so, to what purpose? You may like to consider this in the case of natural selection.

In the context of art, however, to what extent are considerations such as symmetry, or harmony, also applied to different art forms? We will look at this in the next section.

Exercise

Look at some paintings by Picasso in which he has deliberately altered the symmetry of a face. What impact does this make? Can such paintings be considered 'beautiful' and, if so, in what sense?

Is the distortion of the face a deliberate attempt to make it appear ugly? The following extract by Louis Arnaud Reid, a professor of education, argues that we are all able to make the distinction.

> What is the difference, if any, between beautiful and ugly? That there is a difference, common sense would urge, and although it may be difficult to make correct and certain judgements about what is ugly, because aesthetic taste is so much disputed and is so liable to be prejudiced by fashion, yet the common opinion that there is a difference is very convincing, and at least we may say that the onus of proving it wrong rests on the opponents of the common sense view.
>
> From 'Intellectual Analysis and Aesthetic Appreciation' in the *Journal of Philosophical Studies*

In music there may seem, at first hearing, to be very different standards for what counts as 'beautiful' across different cultures. In the following extract, however, Benedict Clark argues that present differences between the music from different parts of the world are a result of the different foci that these cultures have placed on harmony and rhythm historically.

> The paradoxical turn of the European Medieval mind took pleasure in trying out the juxtaposition of separate melodies at once and it was a conceit of the Renaissance to explore their combination with permutations such as a retrograde and contrary motion. This art of 'counterpoint' became extremely refined and advanced before it came to underpin the strongly determined, yet richly flexible, 'western' sense of harmonic progression. The feeling of one rhythmic meter simultaneous with another is a form of musical tension traditionally less examined in European music than in the music of other places. African, South American and some East Asian music explored, by contrast, a rhythmic counterpoint of short repeating cells and it is still amazing to the European ear how detailed can be the intrigue in a conversation between two voices with only two notes and two words each (and how very challenging such music can be to perform). This counterpoint is neither less profound nor fundamentally less intelligent than the other, but it is very different in focus. It is an example of music as widely divergent Ways of Knowing.
>
> Benedict Clark, Head of Aesthetics at the Mahindra United World College of India

Are there objective standards of beauty?

The German philosopher Immanuel Kant thought that if you believe that something is beautiful, then you will want everyone to agree with you. But does this get us anywhere in questioning whether or not there are objective reasons for believing that something is beautiful, beyond the suggestion above that symmetry in living organisms is regarded as attractive?

The Golden Ratio

The theory of the Golden Ratio, which is over 2000 years old, is perhaps the best example of what might be considered an objective standard. This is the division of the length of the object into two parts, such that the ratio of the larger to the smaller part is approximately 1.62. The Greeks based much of their art and architecture on this proportion without, it seems, knowing its mathematical basis; simply that it pleased the eye.

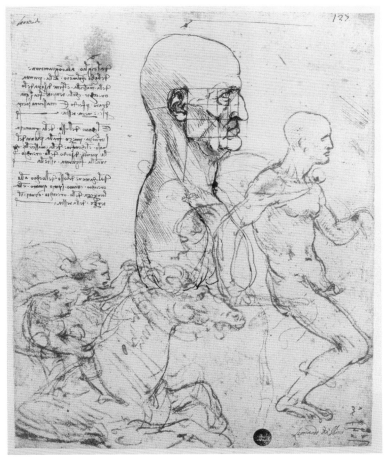

'Study of a Man in Profile and Soldiers on Horseback' by Leonardo da Vinci

In nature, the same ratio is found in many biological structures such as the cluster of seeds in the centre of a sunflower, in the chambered nautilus shell, in claws and in many other plants and animals (see Chapter 9: Mathematical knowledge). Does this suggest that an appreciation of beauty in the creation of humans derives from an appreciation of beauty in the natural world? Many works of art make use of this as you can see in the sketch of an old man by Leonardo da Vinci.

Beauty and harmony

It is interesting that in much musical harmony, what is aesthetically pleasing is also a mathematical relationship. The note emitted from a stretched string or wire produces a pleasing harmony with the note emitted from a stretched string or wire which is of the same material and half its length (and again when the string or wire is one third of the length). It is interesting that not only balance, harmony and proportion seem to be important to give a feeling of beauty but that it is also the way the parts are organised so that they give a sense of order to the whole. This is true whether it be in music, a poem or a piece of visual art. The feeling that something is ugly is stimulated when the whole may have variety but lacks a sense of order.

A poll carried out in the 1990s across 15 countries by two Russian artists, Alexander Melamid and Vitaly Komar, revealed a surprising level of agreement about what people do and don't like in a painting. Overwhelmingly, irrespective of country, people expressed a liking for paintings in which the colour blue dominated rather than when red was predominant; there was also a preference for a pastoral landscape, rather than an abstract painting.

The passage below from *Art* by Clive Bell expresses the view that, without being able to put it into words, we are all clearly capable of appreciating beauty.

> I do not disbelieve in absolute beauty any more than I disbelieve in absolute truth. On the contrary, I gladly suppose that the proposition – this object must either be beautiful or not beautiful – is absolutely true. Only, can we recognise it? Certainly, at moments we belive we can… Every now and then the beauty, the bald miracle, the 'significant' form… of a picture, a poem or a piece of music, springs from an unexpected quarter and lays us flat… When we have picked ourselves up we begin to suppose that such a state of mind must have been caused by something of which the… value was absolute. 'This', we say, 'is absolute beauty.' Perhaps it is.

Are these indications of the fact that all human beings share a common sense of what is aesthetically pleasing that is somehow genetic in origin? But, even if it does, how does the purpose for which a piece of art was created affect the way it is judged?

What is the purpose of art?

If the results of Melamid and Komar's survey (as summarised above) are a true reflection of people's aesthetic judgement, then one important function of art is simply to please. For many, that pleasure seems to be the evocation of the countryside. But is this all that art does?

What is your first thought about the purpose of art? For many, it is that art (whether it be as dance, theatre, music, drama, literature or painting) is the expression of emotion. But is this a western cultural assumption, and a recent one at that? Did the paintings of renaissance Italy, for example, express only emotion or did they have a spiritual purpose? The same could be asked of a Tibetan mandala.

Madonna with child by Lorenzo di Credi (circa 1500)

A Tibetan mandala

Art as 'teacher'

Throughout history, the arts have also served a social purpose; to teach or persuade. In ancient Greece, Aesop's fables taught lessons about human weaknesses such as pride or greed. The writer George Bernard Shaw once said: 'For art's sake alone I would not face the toil of writing a single word.' Think about the novels that you are reading as part of your language courses. For each one, can you discern the writer's main purpose? There are many such purposes: political commentary, social criticism and satire are simply a few examples.

The significance of art within world cultures

Art also plays a crucial role in giving significance to important events in the social life of many cultures.

Exercise

What major events in your own culture are celebrated with music or with dance; for example, weddings, birthdays and coming of age? What role do national anthems play in this respect and do they count as works of art? Can you regard flags as works of art?

Not only does art play an important role in the social life of a culture, it plays an equally significant role in giving expression to the spiritual or religious life of a society. In what form, for example, does music play a role in different religions, with different age groups or in different cultural settings?

Can graffiti, such as the work of **Banksy**, be considered as art? Is the purpose for which the work was produced irrelevant to the aesthetic judgement that is made about it? Can graffiti and propaganda be regarded along with conventional works of art as commentaries on life?

 Banksy A contemporary British graffiti artist. There is some uncertainty about his identity as he does not make this public. It is generally thought, however, that he was born in Bristol in 1974.

Art as propaganda

Art has been used, and continues to be used, for propaganda purposes. In totalitarian states such as the former Soviet Union, artists were often subsidised by the state. Such artists were expected to produce works of excellence that were sympathetic to the state and its ideals. Is there a contradiction in this? Can any work of art be judged excellent when constraints are placed on the freedom of the artist? Are works of art produced under these circumstances necessarily propaganda?

Exercise

Look at the recruiting poster on page 268. This was produced in the US to encourage enlistment in the armed forces in the First World War. This is, without doubt, a piece of propaganda, and produced with that clear purpose. As such, can the same standards of judgement be applied to it as to other works of art? In fact, can it be regarded as a work of art at all?

An American recruitment poster from the First World War

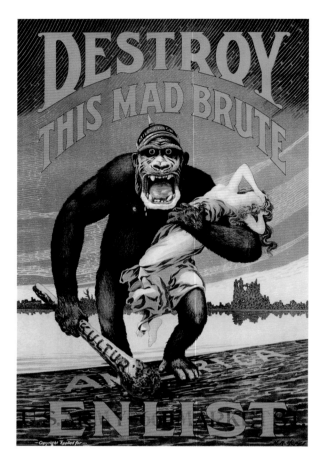

Art is also used (and has been throughout history) to represent reality. In the next section, we will look at the impact of both mathematics and technology on the way that art is able to represent reality.

The representation of reality through paintings

If you look back at the oldest paintings, like the example below, you find that they do not represent figures in a three-dimensional manner; the paintings are flat, two-dimensional representations and there is no sense of perspective.

A fragment of Egyptian papyrus

Read the extract below. The authors address the problem of how to represent the three-dimensional world on a two-dimensional canvas and, in doing so, they show how mathematics and art were linked.

> The person who is credited with the first correct formulation of linear perspective is Brunelleschi. He appears to have made the discovery in about 1413. He understood that there should be a single vanishing point to which all parallel lines in a plane, other than the plane of the canvas, converge. Also important was his understanding of scale, and he correctly computed the relationship between the actual length of an object and its length in the picture depending on its distance behind the plane of the canvas. Using these mathematical principles, he drew two demonstration pictures of Florence on wooden panels with correct perspective.
>
> From 'Mathematics and Art-perspective' by J. O'Connor and E. Robertson

The authors of the article go on to describe the way that a clear understanding of perspective was developed by artists in the fifteenth century. For example, by Piero della Francesca, who was not only one of the leading artists of his day, but also a leading mathematician.

> Della Francesca begins by establishing geometric theorems in the style of Euclid but, unlike Euclid, he also gives numerical examples to illustrate them. He then goes on to give theorems which relate to the perspective of plane figures. In the second of the three volumes Piero examines how to draw prisms in perspective. Although less interesting mathematically than the first volume, the examples he chooses to examine in the volume are clearly important to him since they appear frequently in his own paintings. The third volume deals with more complicated objects such as the human head, the decoration on the top of columns, and other 'more difficult shapes'. For this della Francesca uses a method which involves a very large amount of tedious calculation. He uses two rules, one to determine width, the other to determine height. In fact, he is using a co-ordinate system and computing the correct perspective position of many points of the 'difficult shape' from which the correct perspective of the whole can be filled in.

Look at the painting called 'The Flagellation' that della Francesca painted in circa 1459. You can see how he applied his geometrical ideas about perspective into a representation of reality. What his calculations enabled him to do was to construct those lines of the building that give the feeling of depth by appearing to come together at a distant point as if they were to be continued. In modern terms, we call this 'the vanishing point'.

'The Flagellation' by Piero della Francesca

Leonardo da Vinci and perspective

The work of Leonardo da Vinci took the notion of perspective into almost its modern form as you can see in the extract on the next page.

Not only did Leonardo study the geometry of perspective but he also studied the optical principles of the eye in his attempts to create reality as seen by the eye. By around 1490 Leonardo had moved forward in his thinking about perspective. He was one of the first people to study the converse problem of perspective: given a picture drawn in correct linear perspective, compute where the eye must be placed in order to see this correct perspective. Now he was led to realise that a picture painted in correct linear perspective only looked right if viewed from one exact location. Brunelleschi had been well aware of this when he arranged his demonstration of perspective through a hole. However, for a painting on a wall, say, many people would not view it from the correct position. Indeed for many paintings it would be impossible for someone viewing them to have their eye in this correct point, as it may have been well above their heads.

Leonardo distinguished two different types of perspective: artificial perspective which was the way that the painter projects onto a plane which itself may be seen foreshortened by an observer viewing at an angle; and natural perspective which reproduces faithfully the relative size of objects depending on their distance. In natural perspective, Leonardo correctly claims, objects will be the same size if they lie on a circle centred on the observer. Then Leonardo looked at compound perspective where the natural perspective is combined with a perspective produced by viewing at an angle. Perhaps in Leonardo, more than any other person we mention in this article, mathematics and art were fused in a single concept.

From 'Mathematics and Art-perspective' by J. O'Connor and E. Robertson

Technology and colour

Technology has also been a factor in determining the extent to which reality can be represented in a painting. The range of colours that any art student now takes for granted has not always been available to painters. In fact, until the Industrial Revolution in the early part of the nineteenth century, only a limited range of colours was available.

When the Spanish conquered the New World in the sixteenth century, they brought back to Europe pigments such as carmine that had never been seen by Europeans until that time. You can see the effect that this had by comparing the range of colours used in European paintings of the fifteenth century with that of a century later.

Exercise

With the information above, you should be able to place the two paintings below in the correct chronological order.

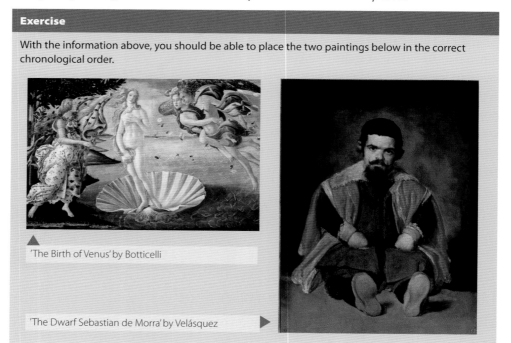

▲ 'The Birth of Venus' by Botticelli

'The Dwarf Sebastian de Morra' by Velásquez ▶

The impact of science on art

You have seen how the availability of new pigments and the discovery of perspective enabled painters to create an increasingly accurate representation of reality. However, the discovery of photography in the nineteenth century had a more profound effect. The following extracts are from an essay called 'The Impact of Photography on Painting' by Philippe Garner, a senior director of Sotheby's, the auction house in London.

When photography was invented and became public in 1839, painting was the domain of artists and artisans serving a variety of needs. Many of the artist's functions were practical and served a range of social duties, celebrating and building the prestige of eminent sitters, spreading information on the physical appearance of the world, its landscape, its wonders, its cities and architecture, commemorating events of local interest or of great historical importance, and providing images which implemented the psychological grip of religions and the hierarchies and structure of society. Painting also became the domain for the free expression of the imagination.

*****

The group of nineteenth century artists whose relationship with photography is perhaps most ambiguous is the Impressionists. Their approach to painting was diametrically opposed to the high 'photographic' realism of the Academy. They rejected the pursuit of fine detail such as could be recorded unselectively on light-sensitive plates. Their way of looking was concerned rather with the way in which the eye and intellect perceive things rather than the dispassionate way in which the camera records. Yet at the very basis of their approach was the analysis of the effects of light on their subject matter. The Impressionist intuition was an echo of the structured investigations of photo-scientists, both groups sharing an interest in chromatic analysis and in the qualities of light as it defines form.

*****

Perhaps the greatest contribution which the new technique of photography could make to painting was to liberate Art from its ties to realism, to factuality. There was, ultimately, no need for the artist's pencil or brush to labour intensively to depict and record people, occasions or things which the photographer could document through his lens with practical ease and speed. Art was freed on its path to abstraction.

Exercise

- In the extracts above, Phillipe Garner contrasts the way that a camera catches an image with that of the impressionist painters. Use the Internet to find the following impressionist paintings:
  - 'Sunrise' by Claude Monet
  - 'Moonlight over the Port of Boulogne' by Edouard Manet
  - 'Landscape at Chaponval' by Camille Pissaro
  - 'On the Racing Field' by Edgar Degas
  - 'The Meadow' by Auguste Renoir
- Can you see any similarities between the way in which the five artists have chosen to capture their scenes? If you can, what are they and why might these similarities be the reason that they are called impressionists?
- On the basis of these five paintings, would you agree with Phillipe Garner that they capture the scene in a different way to the camera?
- Do you feel that they give you a better or worse sense of what you might have seen if you had been looking over the artist's shoulder as he painted the scene?

You should consider a further interaction between scientific discovery and art. The article concludes by saying that the invention of photography was the stimulus that set artists on the path toward abstract painting. If we go forward to the start of the last century, we see the beginning of the revolution in science created by Quantum Theory and Relativity Theory. This was the period, led by artists such as Picasso, in which abstract art became the predominant school of painting. Is there a second or fundamental link here between art and science? Consider the fact that both Relativity Theory and Quantum Theory make predictions about the nature of our world that conflict with our direct and common sense view of reality.

Art and truth

Some people claim that all of the arts (literature, music, dance, drama, painting and sculpture) have a special responsibility to tell the truth. This is a claim that you should consider carefully. Can you find statements whether in written form, in music or in a visual form that are true in the sense that they are factual? This is, of course, possible; for art in its many forms can accurately reproduce reality. Is this, however, what is meant by the claim that art can, and should, tell the truth? If it is not, and a different or perhaps deeper meaning of the word 'truth' is implied, what does it mean? Look at the views expressed in the extract below and ask yourself what assumptions are made by the author.

> What is truth? Like everything in art, the concept of truth is completely subjective. People define their own truth. A person might wax eloquent on the truth embedded in Mondrian's simplicity. I, on the other hand, only see sterile intellectual concepts placed on canvas. We both believe that we are right.
>
> I view truth not simply as honesty, but as emotion or expression that has a deeper, more powerful effect on the viewer. Satire and deconstruction are objects of fashion; this kind of art is easily forgotten. Comments on the human condition have the strongest impact. The viewer can relate to the canvas, both today and – since the human condition stays consistent through the centuries regardless of how our environment changes – in the future. Truth about humanity does not need to focus solely on subject matter. Cezanne's and Basquiat's truth can be found in their paint handling. Their uncompromising passion leaps out of the canvas. Cezanne is more popular because he balanced the trinity of truth, beauty and innovation.
>
> From 'Truth in Painting' by Cliff Constable

This extract talks of a deeper sense of truth in art as an evocation of emotion in a social sense; but is this the extent of artistic truth? The following extract goes far beyond this. It is a second extract from the speech that Alexander Solzhenitsyn wrote for his acceptance of the 1970 Nobel Prize award for literature (the first extract opened this chapter on page 257). He was unable to accept the award in person because of his fear that he would not be allowed back into the Soviet Union if he left to collect the prize himself.

The speech is a powerful rationale for the crucial importance of art to the well-being of humanity. It takes its theme from a Russian proverb: 'One word of truth outweighs the whole world.' As you read it, look carefully at the way in which Solzhenitsyn relates the sense of value in a work of art to the sharing of human experience and, through that, to the creation of a common set of standards by which to judge what is good and what is bad.

Who will give mankind one single system for reading its instruments, both for wrongdoing and for doing good, for the intolerable and the tolerable as they are distinguished from each other today? Who will make clear for mankind what is really oppressive and unbearable and what, for being so near, rubs us raw – and thus direct our anger against what is in fact terrible and not merely near at hand? Who is capable of extending such an understanding across the boundaries of his own personal experience? Who has the skill to make a narrow, obstinate human being aware of others' far-off grief and joy, to make him understand dimensions and delusions he himself has never lived through? Propaganda, coercion, and scientific proofs are all powerless. But, happily, in our world there is a way. It is art, and it is literature.

There is a miracle which they can work: they can overcome man's unfortunate trait of learning only through his own experience, unaffected by that of others. From man to man, compensating for his brief time on earth, art communicates whole the burden of another's long life experience with all its hardships, colours, and vitality, re-creating in the flesh what another has experienced, and allowing it to be acquired as one's own.

© The Nobel Foundation, 1970

Is Solzhenitsyn saying that the truth of art lies, not in it being an exact representation of reality but that, instead, art opens up to us a truth that takes us beyond our own experience? The great artists, in whatever form they express their art, teach us how to experience the world in a different way from that of our everyday sensations, be they perceptions or emotions.

The art critic

Critics do not exist for artists any more than palaeontologists exist for fossils.

Clive Bell

What is the role of the critic in judging works of art? Does the existence of expert opinion imply that not only can objective valuations be made of a work of art but that some people are better able to make such judgements than others? It would certainly be a naive position to hold that all people are equally equipped to judge the worth of a work of art, but on what basis can this be justified?

There are two different, and sometimes complementary, ways of judging a work of art. One is to consider the internal or intrinsic features while the other is to examine the context in which the work was created, its relationship to other works by the same and other artists and its impact on society.

The **contextualists** often reject the view that what inspires an artist cannot be analysed, for it is personal and private and inspirational. Instead, they look at the historical context in which the artist worked and at the major events that were occurring during the time that the works were produced. For some, this results in an analysis of the intentions of the artist and the manner in which the techniques used by the artist reveal these intentions.

 Contextualist The contextualist theory of art holds that all art is integrated with life; it is set in a particular historical and cultural context. This is opposed to the isolationist theory that claims art is separate from the rest of life.

Exercise

Consider how the view of the contextualists relates to the issue of whether or not objective judgements can, or ought, to be made, of works of art.

On the other hand, other critics argue that in order to assess its value, a piece of art must be analysed in terms of its own internal structure. This view has, particularly with respect to literary criticism, focused attention on the work of art itself ignoring its context. Is it possible for there to be effective criticism if this view is held? You should look at recent book reviews or other published critics' views of plays or the works of art and try to work out what position the critic is taking.

Art and knowledge

What sort of knowledge does art give us? In Chapter 2: What is knowledge?, we examined the different ways that the word 'knowledge' is used. You should refresh your memory before we consider what is meant if we claim that art can give you knowledge; it will not be as easy to identify as, for example, scientific knowledge, which can be tested against reality and judged by whether or not it makes measurable predictions. This is very different from the meaning of knowledge expressed in the following lines from Keats's poem written nearly 200 years ago:

> *Beauty is truth, truth beauty, that is all*
> *Ye know on Earth, and all ye need to know.*
>
> From 'Ode to a Grecian Urn'

Exercise

Notice the link that Keats makes between beauty, truth and knowing. What does he mean? What is the link between beauty expressed through art, on the one hand, and truth and knowledge on the other?

As we have seen in the previous section, art takes us beyond a simple and direct representation of our own reality by enabling us to share the experience of the artist. Is it in this sense that it widens our knowledge by giving insight, unlike that of the experimental sciences, which cannot be repeated and therefore is unique? The following extract by Louis Arnaud Reid examines this idea:

In poetry the ability to use words, the greatest of all single human powers, can open up new perspectives of imagination and conception, new understanding of love, youth, age, mortality, the Greek hero pitted against fate, the Shropshire lad against the world and his inevitable end. Metaphysical ideas, religious adoration, the problem of pain, the evanescence and the eternity of love – these and the other human themes come into union with the flesh and blood of living words. Of drama all this is true too, to which are added the special opportunities of drama from Sophocles through Shakespeare to O'Neill, Ionesco, Fry, Pinter and Beckett.

From 'Art, Truth and Reality' published in *The British Journal of Aesthetics*

Is the writer of the above passage saying that an artist is representing only his experience or his emotion in his art? Ric Sims, a professional musician and TOK examiner, argues that this is not the case; that many works of art do not express the emotions of their creator.

Not all works of art are expressionist! There are countless examples to adduce in attacking this point of view. Being a composer, I often quote my own music as non-expressionist art: I know about my own emotional state when composing and can definitely rebut any suggestion that my music is in any way an expression of my emotions. Sure, it is in some sense an expression of my ideas, but this is hardly a controversial statement. Any act of mine originating from a cognitive process can be said to be an expression of my ideas; but my emotions, now that is a different matter.

From 'How poksy are the arts?' by Ric Sims, published in *Forum 45*

The difficulties in trying to clarify what sort of knowledge art gives are clear, the more so because the arts cover such a diversity of forms: music, dance, painting and sculpture, literature and poetry, film and drama. Yet certain themes do seem to apply across the arts. They do not seek to give us propositional knowledge or knowledge that is testable against the facts. However, is knowledge limited in this sense? For example, you know how to tie your shoelaces without having any logical sense of what you are doing. If you talk about science, then is what you say a part of science? Compare this with talking about any piece of art and ask yourself if this can ever be the same as the work of art itself. Art evokes feeling but it also stimulates an intellectual awareness; the knowledge it gives us is a direct awareness of the whole. In this sense is it a necessary complement to knowledge gained through scientific reductionism? The next extract draws an interesting connection between feeling and knowledge.

What has rarely been considered is the relation of feeling to knowledge. Knowing and feeling are thought to be polar opposites, and the dominating assumption of the prestige of propositional statements still holds sway. For talking animals thinking in language, expression in propositional language is always of great importance, but can our knowledge that mugging is wrong, or that our knowledge of Cezanne as a painter, or of a Beethoven sonata, or of the person of Mary Smith, count as knowledge only in the sense that we can say many true things about the objects of such knowledge? Are intuition and feeling just to be dismissed?

From 'The Arts, Knowledge and Education' by Louis Arnaud Reid, published in
The British Journal of Educational Studies

Art as systems of knowledge

There is a temptation to think of art as a purely individualistic endeavour or one that is only an expression of the individual artist's feelings. However, this ignores the fact that 'schools of thought' have existed and still exist in, for example, poetry, dance, music, painting, as well as in art criticism. These schools of thought are sometimes called 'movements'.

Exercise

Carry out your own research to identify at least one movement in poetry or in music. When you have done so, set out the key features by which this can be identified. What does this say about the collective nature of the arts?

Just like other systems of knowledge, the arts have their own vocabulary, their own history and traditions and common problems to solve. They have not remained static, nor has the change over time been haphazard. For example, the impact of the invention of photography on painting in the nineteenth century was profound. Can you draw a comparison between this and, for example, the impact of technology on science? Consider the way that the invention of the telescope changed physics.

Isaac Newton said that he had seen further than others only because he had stood on the shoulders of giants, for example, Gallileo and Kepler. Could the same be said of Picasso and other great artists whose work has built on the work of earlier artists? If we say that science is an evolving system of knowledge, can we not say the same for the arts? If this is the case, then do revolutions such as Cubism or the choreography of Balanchine count as paradigm shifts that change the framework within which a community of artists works?

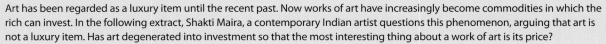

Today's world: art as a luxury?

Art has been regarded as a luxury item until the recent past. Now works of art have increasingly become commodities in which the rich can invest. In the following extract, Shakti Maira, a contemporary Indian artist questions this phenomenon, arguing that art is not a luxury item. Has art degenerated into investment so that the most interesting thing about a work of art is its price?

Modern Art has become a category of luxury consumption. But art is not a luxury item. It is what can make life feel more abundant no matter how poor we are. Luxury has become equated with wealth, though its root Latin word, *luxus*, means abundance. Luxury can be both an abundance of things and a state of mind. A state of mind where, no matter how much or little we have of things, we have the luxury of time to look at art, of being sensitive and responsive to beauty, and can happily make art, or purchase what we can afford from a craftsman at Dilli Haat (in New Delhi) and place it on our bare walls.

From 'Art: the Ultimate Luxury' by Shakti Maira, published in *Design Today*

Is this an indication that art has been taken away from the everyday experience of life and, instead, has become something that exists to be bought and sold?

In her book *Believing Is Seeing: Creating the Culture of Art*, Mary Anne Staniszewski, an American professor of art, says:

Art is the creation of an object of aesthetic beauty; separate from everyday life: something to be seen in galleries, preserved in museums, purchased by collectors, and reproduced within mass media.

If this view is correct, what impact does it have on you? There is a complete contradiction between this view and that of Alexander Solzhenitsyn quoted in the passage at the start of this chapter; that art has a life of its own and cannot be taken away from personal and everyday experience. Do you agree with this claim? If you do, on what grounds?

Perhaps such divergent views exist on the significance of art in today's world because of the way that art has itself diverged in its forms of expression, particularly since the 1960s. This phenomenon is described in the following passage by Michael Archer in the preface to his book, *Art Since 1960*. Archer marks the decade that followed as one that saw the breaking of all traditions in art, not only in the western world, but across the globe.

What is immediately noticeable about today's art, compared to even a few decades ago, is the unprecedented profusion of styles, forms, practices and agendas. From the outset, it appears that the more one sees, the less certain one can be about what allows works to be designated 'art' at all, at least from a traditional point of view. For one thing, there are no longer any particular materials that enjoy the privilege of being immediately recognizable as art media: recent art is made not only with oil paint, metal and stone, but also air, light, sound, words, people, food, refuse, multi-media installations and much else besides. There are few, if any, conventional techniques and methods of producing art nowadays that can guarantee the finished work being thought of as art. A traditionalist can do little to prevent the outcome of even the most mundane activities being considered art. That painting continues to be important has neither stemmed a rise in use of other means of representation, such as photography and video, nor halted the adoption of other less likely tactics in making art that include going for walks, shaking hands and cultivating plants.

From *Art Since 1960* by Michael Archer

Ideal knower

Susanne Langer (1895–1985)

Art is the creation of forms symbolic of human feeling.

Susanne K. Langer

Although not an artist herself, Susanne Langer expressed ideas about the meaning and nature of art with a unique clarity, one that may help you in framing your own thoughts about art.

Susanne Langer was born in New York in 1895 and throughout her long life was a profound and original thinker who made a significant contribution to our understanding of the nature of art. Her ideas are based on the belief that human beings are essentially users of symbols and hence that the capacity for symbolic thought is a fundamental part of what it means to be human.

Susanne Langer

Langer links art to emotion in a unique and profound way. Instead of viewing a work of art as the expression of the emotions of the artist who created it, she sees the essence of art in expressing a universal human experience of emotions. In this sense, a work of art becomes a symbol that distinguishes it from other works of human creativity that use different forms of symbolic representation. Her major work, *Philosophy in a New Key*, applies her ideas principally to music, but they are readily applicable across all forms of art.

Art may be defined as the practice of creating perceptible forms expressive of human feeling. I say 'perceptible' rather than 'sensuous' forms because some works of art are given to imagination rather than to the outward senses. A novel, for instance, usually is read silently with the eye, as a painting is; and though sound plays a vital part in poetry, words even in poetry are not essentially sonorous structures like music. Dance requires to be seen, but its appeal is to deeper centres of sensation. The difference between dance and mobile sculpture makes this immediately apparent. But all works of art are purely perceptual forms that seem to embody some sort of feeling.

From *Philosophical Sketches* by Susanne Langer

*****

'Feeling' as I am using it here covers much more than it does in the technical vocabulary of psychology, where it denotes only pleasure or pain, or even in the shifting limits of ordinary discourse, where it sometimes means sensation – sometimes emotion – or a directed emotion, – or even our general mental or physical condition. As I use the word, in defining art as the creation of perceptible forms expressive of human feeling, it takes in all those meanings; it applies to everything that may be felt.

From 'The Cultural Importance of the Arts' by Susanne Langer, published in *Aesthetic Form and Education* by M.F. Andrews

Student presentation

1 'What is it that distinguishes an ordinary bag of rubbish from a major work of art that just looks like a bag of rubbish?' Can anything be art – and, if so, what makes it art?

2 Why are people prepared to dismiss contemporary art without understanding much about it, while often blindly believing scientific claims?

Essay questions

Two recent Prescribed Titles (PTs) include:

1 If someone says, 'I know this music,' how can the claim be evaluated? Compare your answer with the evaluation of claims in Areas of Knowledge other than the arts.

© International Baccalaureate Organization 2004

2 'The arts deal with the particular, the individual and the personal while the sciences deal in the general, the universal and the collective.' To what extent does this statement obscure the nature of both Areas of Knowledge?

© International Baccalaureate Organization 2004

Assessment
Assessment as knowledge

But there are advantages to being President. The day after I was elected, I had my high school grades classified Top Secret.

Ronald Reagan

It would not be surprising if you have approached this chapter with mixed feelings. The word 'assessment' can cause a shiver of anxiety, for it implies making judgements about your work, and this may or may not be a pleasant prospect. At the same time, you will be used to the idea that assessment is an unavoidable and highly consequential part of your school experience, and so it makes sense to treat it seriously and make sure that you are fully prepared. You might actually relish the opportunity to display your knowledge and skills.

Exercise

How would you feel about enrolling on a course that was not going to be assessed. (Maybe in some contexts this has been the case?) Would you prefer this to what you find in your IB studies (remember that even CAS is assessed)? Why or why not?

In keeping with the TOK course, we should reflect on the nature of assessment. Broadly, we could think of it as a process that generates knowledge about your knowledge. This is not a simple matter. We need to be sure that we are assessing the knowledge we intend to assess. We must be confident that this knowledge actually can be reliably measured. We need to reflect on why we want to do this assessment in the first place, and for whom. We also need to think about who is going to do the assessing. The following diagram might help us to focus; we will modify it as we go along:

How assessment works ▶

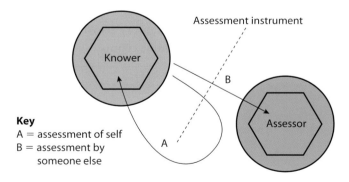

Key
A = assessment of self
B = assessment by someone else

Assessment: of what knowledge?

The IB diploma lays down guidelines about what is to be learned and assessed. These guidelines are called the formal curriculum and each course has a syllabus that is an attempt to specify the requirements as precisely as possible. Such information is found in the IB subject guides and the *Handbook of Procedures* and it might be interesting to compare the guides for different subjects. Why, for example, are some guides so much longer and more detailed than others? What do these differences have to do with the nature of knowledge in the various subject areas?

Remember the distinction between 'knowing that' and 'knowing how'? (See Chapter 2: What is knowledge?, page 18.) How do these differences relate to the tasks that you are set in the IB diploma? Some examples are given below. Think about the facts and skills that you are expected to acquire in each of your hexagon courses. Do you think the balance is appropriate in each case? Consider internally and externally assessed components. Is the emphasis different? If so, why would this be?

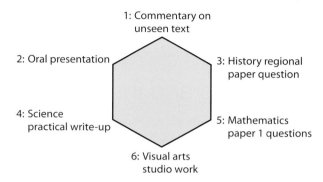

1: Commentary on unseen text
2: Oral presentation
3: History regional paper question
4: Science practical write-up
5: Mathematics paper 1 questions
6: Visual arts studio work

◀ Selected assessment requirements around the hexagon

The 'syllabus' for TOK is presented as a series of questions divided mostly into Ways of Knowing and Areas of Knowledge. It's perhaps rather easy to misconstrue this and think that either there are no definitive answers in TOK, or that any answers will do. It would be more accurate to say that the questions may require careful thought, that they may sometimes lead to alternative acceptable answers, but that some answers are certainly wrong!

Assessment: why and for whom?

At this stage, we can introduce another important distinction – concerning the purpose of assessment and the uses of the knowledge it produces.

Assessment can be:
- *of* learning: this is sometimes called **summative assessment** and its purpose is to measure the level of achievement at the end of a course or unit
- *for* learning: this is sometimes called **formative assessment** and its purpose is to measure ongoing progress and guide the process of learning.

Exercise

What are your experiences of these two types of assessment so far in your IB studies? Do you think that they are completely separable? Explain your answer to this.

Assessment: knowledge generated by whom?

Who is in the best position to assess you – your teacher or someone else? You can probably remember occasions where a teacher has encouraged you to evaluate your own work, or created a situation in which you and other students take a critical look at each other's material. It might be instructive to think about the circumstances in which each of these potential assessors would be most helpful. What would be the advantages and disadvantages if your work were assessed by each of the following? Some suggested answers are offered.

Summative assessment This is sometimes described as assessment *of* learning – to measure the level of achievement at the end of a course or unit.

Formative assessment Assessment *for* learning – to measure ongoing progress and to guide the process of learning.

Assessor	Advantage	Disadvantage
Teacher	Knows you well and understands the tasks set within the school	Makes too many allowances for your weaknesses and personal traits
Examiner	An impartial expert stranger	Doesn't grant any benefit of doubt about what you really meant!
Self	Less stressful	You can easily delude yourself
Peers	Understand the difficulties because they have had the same experiences	Not experts on the material

Assessment tasks and instruments

You might also think about the task you are set and the methods used to assess your response. Consider how the IB diploma includes:

Type	Examples
Formal examinations	Final IB examinations
Externally-assessed written tasks	Extended Essay, world literature assignments, TOK essay
Teacher-assessed written tasks	Portfolios, projects, practicals…
Teacher-assessed oral tasks	Language orals, TOK presentation
Self-assessed tasks	CAS self-evaluations, TOK presentation self-evaluation

Your responses to some of these tasks are assessed using strict mark schemes; others using assessment criteria with descriptor levels. The former are more effective when specific answers are expected; the latter when the task is more open-ended. Consider also how assignments are different sizes, and allow for varying amounts of freedom when choosing topics – on what basis would examiners make decisions about these variables? Let's now turn to the issue of assessment in the TOK course.

Assessment in Theory of Knowledge

The final summative assessment in TOK (i.e. the scores that contribute to your final IB mark or points) has two components:

	Presentation	Essay
Assessment by whom?	Teacher (internal)	Examiner (external)
Assessment instrument?	4 criteria	4 criteria
Maximum possible mark?	20 (1/3 of available marks)	40 (2/3 of available marks)
Size of task?	10 minutes per presenter	1200–1600 words
Origin of topic/title?	Free choice	From prescribed list

Now revisit the aspects of assessment discussed above. Why do you think that the IBO has arranged TOK assessment like this? Do you think it is a good arrangement?

The total score out of 60 is converted onto a scale of grades from A to E. This A to E scale is also used in the assessment of the Extended Essay. The grades for these two components are then combined in a manner that generates a score from 0 to 3. This score counts towards your total diploma score.

Exercise

You may have already had a discussion about TOK assessment with other students or with your teachers. Apart from the final summative ones, what assessment tasks or situations will take place during the course in your school? Who will be doing the assessing? What will the assessments be used for?

Consider the following comments made by students after they completed the TOK course:

> I think I'm entitled to my own opinion about things, just as everyone else is entitled to theirs. So I don't think it's right that TOK is assessed.

Akosua

> I found the TOK course interesting but I couldn't bring myself to take it as seriously as those other courses worth 7 points.

Karen

Frank

Nishant

> Personally, I think TOK is good but it should not be graded. We are being taught to be open to different approaches but how can we have set criteria for marking open-mindedness?

> TOK has been a wonderful experience for me. Too bad that most of the work I did during the course won't count for much of the final grade.

Remarks made by students who have finished their TOK course

Do you have sympathy with some of these points of view? Which ones? What is your view on assessment in TOK?

Now let's look more closely at these situations. As you read about each student in turn, imagine you are a 'best friend' to them. In this role, what responses could you offer to the questions posed?

Before she started the IB diploma, Akosua was looking forward to the TOK course as an opportunity to enter into heated debate on many interesting issues. In keeping with her combative character, she thought the general idea was to defend her own views and try to attack and 'beat' those of others. However, once the course began she quickly came to realize that this was not really what was expected of her. Becoming disillusioned with this, she found herself muttering to friends that 'there are no answers in this course', with everyone seemingly entitled to whatever view they find most attractive. If there are no answers that we can agree on (and seemingly no credit for winning debates), she thinks to herself, then there should be no assessment.

What would you say to try to convince Akosua that TOK assessment is legitimate?

Frank is a smart and pragmatic student who thinks that the amount of effort invested in something should be proportional to the reward directly available for it. In his life, he often finds himself calculating costs and benefits before making decisions. Consistent with this, he directs his workload while paying careful attention to the mark allocation for each component of the diploma. Sometimes, in discussions with his friends, he finds himself arguing further that the points or grade associated with courses and their components are accurate indicators of the intrinsic value of these things themselves, and thus that the designers of the IB diploma basically think along the same lines as he does.

What arguments or examples could you use to undermine the idea that the potential reward in TOK is always proportional to its value?

Karen is a very fair-minded and uncomplicated student who thinks that credit should go where credit is due. She normally performs quite well in her IB diploma work but sometimes she is frustrated and baffled when, despite all of her hard work, she fails to achieve the very top grade. She believes assessed tasks need always to be very clearly spelled out so that students can know exactly how to respond to them, and feels that sometimes this doesn't happen. Indeed, when she asks teachers for extra feedback on her work, they seem to be unable to tell her precisely what to do to improve it. For her, objective assessment is the only acceptable assessment.

What could you say to Karen that might persuade her that assessment is still worthwhile even if there is an element of doubt in the judgements made?

Nishant is a conscientious student who can always be counted upon to give all tasks his honest best. He feels he has made a lot of progress during the TOK course and is quietly proud of some of his contributions to class discussion, which other students have recognized as valuable. He is sure that, in one way or another, some of them have gained from his presence in the classroom. What worries him is that he gets nervous when deadlines approach and finds final assessment tasks rather stressful. He suspects that he will not perform so well under such circumstances.

How might you reassure Nishant and give him confidence?

Now reflect on what *you* think about these matters. Do you agree more with what the students thought or with the responses you suggested for them? You could discuss the issues raised here with other students in your class to get a feel for overall opinions.

Assessment and accuracy

It has been said that, because of the complexity of the tasks, there is no exact true score for a TOK presentation or essay; rather, there is an area of approximation within which an assessment must fall. Does this claim worry you? How much does it matter? Would you agree with it? Keep these questions in mind as you read on through this chapter.

Exercise

Why does the IB insist that the assessment of TOK presentations and essays be quantitative? Are numbers over-valued? Are they useful for formative or summative assessment, or both? Why does CAS assessment, alone within the IB diploma, not attract numbers? Should TOK be like this? There is the germ of a TOK presentation itself here!

Perhaps the most positive way of thinking about your forthcoming assessment tasks in TOK is to focus on the benefits they might bring you. The British computer programmer and essayist Paul Graham has likened the preparation of such work to the act of cleaning up one's room before inviting people over. If others are going to see it, your thinking should be respectable!

TOK presentations and essays

Some students find it easier to communicate orally, as opposed to writing an essay; others feel the opposite. Both situations involve important skills that we need to practise.

Remember – a TOK presentation is not the same as a TOK essay.

What are the similarities and differences between TOK presentations and TOK essays?

A common feature of both presentations and essays is that they are logically structured responses to titles. In an essay, the title must come from the prescribed list, while a presentation title is likely to be left open for you to choose. This is a freedom that you must take very seriously.

It might be helpful to think of essays as providing specific examples and arguments in support of more general claims, whereas presentations should be more concerned with a knowledge issue drawn from a real-life situation. As a rough rule of thumb:

- Essays: more general (prescribed title) → more specific (arguments and examples)
- Presentations: more specific (real-life situation) → more general (knowledge issue)

Presentations: speaking and conversation

It is sometimes said that TOK is a 'conversation course'. It is certainly true that the knowledge issues that are at the heart of the course can be examined effectively only if they are aired in the classroom and students are given the chance to contribute their opinions. Indeed, many of these knowledge issues have probably come up among inquisitive people for thousands of years. On the timescale of our species, writing is a relatively recent invention; oral conversation is a much older form of discourse. What goes on in the TOK classroom could be regarded as part of an ancient and venerable tradition!

Exercise

You may like to find out more about oral traditions and knowledge. You could search for:

- Confucius + discussion
- Buddha + group teaching
- Plato + dialogue
- Homer + poetry
- Jewish + Kabbalah
- African + storyteller

But what kind of conversation are we looking for in TOK? It has been suggested that 'five Ds' might be distinguished:

1 **dispute** (enslaves): minimal engagement between participants, uncompromising claims and demands

2 **debate** (divides): set positions adopted by participants, each 'side' plays to win

3 **discussion** (contracts): participants attempt to reach consensus, search for compromise

4 **dialogue** (expands): contributions from participants lead to new relationships between ideas

5 **dialectic** (enlightens): all participants enriched through the development of new insights arising out of their interactions

Exercise

In your experience of TOK to date, which of the 'five Ds' on the previous page seems closest to the spirit of the course you have been following? Is there a place for all of these in TOK? Explain.

The human brain starts working the moment you are born and never stops until you stand up to speak in public.

Sir George Jessel, a British judge

Conversations often need a stimulus to get them started and this can be anything from a provocative 'starter' statement to a more structured and formal presentation. Throughout the ages, ability in public speaking has been considered a valuable skill, not least for its potential power to persuade large numbers of people to accept certain points of view. Despite this, or perhaps partly because of it, many of us are fearful of speaking in public. Have you ever felt apprehensive before having to talk to a group of people? How did you deal with this anxiety?

Many education systems have come to privilege the written word over the spoken one. (Would you say this is the case with the IB diploma?) Writing is durable, easily copied and thus can be examined at leisure. We have become accustomed to the relatively impersonal nature of writing, which allows us to concentrate on what has been written rather than who has written it. In the case of a presentation, given the much closer connection between message and speaker, a criticism of the message can be misinterpreted as a personal slur on the speaker. Alternatively, the speaker might be regarded as an impediment to understanding the message.

However, recent technological developments have set up new relationships between us and the spoken word. News bulletins slice up what people say into 'sound bites', easily taken out of the wider context of what was said as a whole. Perhaps we have become used to this phenomenon, so much so that our attention cannot span more than a few seconds of talk, beyond which we 'switch off'. (An interesting exercise is to measure the length of the 'sound bites' on different news channels.)

There is a worry that this 'laziness' is leaving us more vulnerable than ever to the sloppy acceptance of falsehoods and prejudices. While the rise of email over the past 10 to 15 years has been credited with a revival in writing as an everyday activity (albeit in a rather new form), electronic developments are making more audio and video communication available to the ordinary citizen – perhaps at the expense of text.

As a TOK student, you have the opportunity to explore the power of the spoken word in your TOK presentation. In addition to showing that you understand the nature of knowledge issues and can relate them to a situation in which knowledge is at work in the world, you will need to demonstrate your ability to communicate TOK ideas orally in the presence of your peers and teachers. This is your chance to be leader for the day.

The key dynamic of the TOK presentation

As you progress through your TOK course, you will acquire ever more practice in identifying and articulating knowledge issues. The key initial stage in planning your TOK presentation will be to build a bridge between a real-life situation and a knowledge issue.

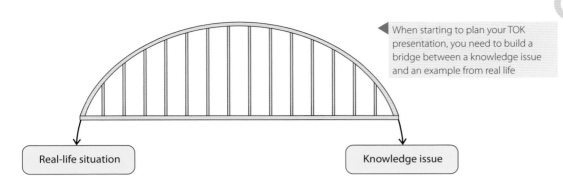

When starting to plan your TOK presentation, you need to build a bridge between a knowledge issue and an example from real life

Real-life situation

Knowledge issue

This bridge can be constructed from either end – you might start with the issue and search for the illustration, or begin with the concrete and strip it away to the underlying issue. It is possible that the two 'ends' will occur to you as a single act of recognition – you will 'see the TOK' in a situation as you come across it.

Although the real-life situation and knowledge issue are related, they must be clearly distinguished. If you can do this, then the following steps become achievable:

- State your knowledge issue clearly.
- Show how it arises from your selected real-life situation.
- Develop it.
- Demonstrate how it could be applied back to your real-life situation and others.

In this way, you can demonstrate why it is worthy of exploration. Without it, your treatment of the real-life situation will tend towards the descriptive, and this makes for poor TOK.

Exercise

Each case study below illustrates an attempt to identify a real-life situation and a knowledge issue, and to build a bridge between them. To what extent do you think each case is successful?

Case study A

Main focus: science

Scenario: starting from a clear knowledge issue; searching for a real-life situation

Stimulated by a general and spontaneous discussion that arises in their chemistry class, a group of three students chooses the following knowledge issue:

Given that the history of science is littered with theories that have been discarded, how can we have confidence in current scientific knowledge?

Encouraged by their teacher, who tells them that this is a promising knowledge issue, the group starts to search their collective knowledge for real-life situations to illustrate it. They succeed in identifying a number of examples of obsolete scientific theories but seem unsure that any particular one of them is strong and fertile enough to carry the weight of the whole presentation. Time is rather short and, in the midst of other academic obligations, they are unable to do much research. In their actual presentation, they flit from one example to another, just skimming the surface of each, hoping that this will suffice in convincing those present of the importance and relevance of the knowledge issue.

Case study B

Main focus: the arts

Scenario: a real-life situation from a personal hobby; deciding between clear knowledge issues

This student has decided to make her presentation on her own. This is largely because the real-life situation which she has identified has arisen out of her musical background which she pursues outside school; it is not something her class friends really share. While learning about the music of the Russian composer Dmitri Shostakovich, she comes across an article outlining his deeply problematic relationship with Stalin, who was the leader of the country at the time, and who judged the music in political terms (i.e. compatible or otherwise with communist ideology). This constitutes her real-life situation and a raft of knowledge issues quickly comes to her mind:

Does music convey knowledge? If so, what kind of knowledge? Is music different to the other arts in this respect? Should composers/artists be held responsible for the interpretations that others place on their work or the consequences that stem from these interpretations?

The student's teacher has strongly advised her to choose one issue as the central focus of her presentation while not abandoning the others. She has suggested that this can be achieved by selecting on the basis of how easily some of the others can be addressed as extensions of the chosen issue. Having read about the fates of some writers in the Soviet Union, she settles on:

What knowledge can music convey, as compared with other forms of art?

Case study C

Main focus: current affairs/history

Scenario: a real-life situation from a well-known 'historical' event; trying to crystallize a knowledge issue from it

This pair of students is interested in various explanations given by disparate sources for the destruction of the World Trade Center in New York on 11 September 2001. Having been encouraged to find something that interests them, they have become determined to use this situation at the heart of their presentation. This is mainly because they find conspiracy theories fascinating and their experiences with TOK have led them to the idea that outlandish suggestions are welcome! However, neither of them is finding it easy to articulate a knowledge issue that the situation exemplifies. Their teacher keeps prodding them about this, insisting that the real-life situation can be evaluated only in the light of a successfully identified knowledge issue. In the end, rather frustrated, they settle on:

To what extent can we trust an authority?

Unfortunately, this is a weakly-worded knowledge issue as it fails to guide discussion about what might constitute a reliable authority. It seems that the students are really more interested in the real-life situation itself (9/11) than any knowledge issues that might be extracted from it.

Case study D

Main focus: religion/science

Scenario: a real-life situation from a news article; many knowledge issues to choose from

A news article provides the focus for this group's presentation. This describes a decision by the broadcasting regulators of a country to prevent the transmission of TV programmes that purport to show miracles. Such programmes are to be banned unless the miracles they show are 'believable and provable'. This is the real-life situation. Crucially, the group realizes that the thrust of the presentation must be directed, not towards a discussion of whether miracles actually happen, but how one would go about trying to prove or disprove such occurrences. More broadly, what justification would be strong enough for us to believe that a miracle has taken place? The students characterize miracles as events in which scientific laws are suspended. This sets up a successful dynamic between the real-life situation and the central knowledge issue which they decide should be:

In what circumstances would we accept that known laws of physics have been breached?

There has been much debate within the group on the decision to choose this question, as it has been acknowledged that there are other possible knowledge issues that could support the presentation (for example, the obligations of broadcasters to the public). However, having read the assessment criteria carefully, the group has recognized the need to focus on one central issue and to assign the others more minor or supporting roles.

The knower's perspective

If you are clear about the nature of knowledge issues and real-life situations, there is a third concept that we need to examine before we move on.

The mission statement of the IB speaks about encouraging:

> *Students across the world to… understand that other people, with their differences, can also be right.*

One of the aims of the TOK course is to provide a setting for you to develop an awareness of different ways of approaching existing knowledge, and for constructing it yourself. You are encouraged to go further and try to identify what assumptions underlie these various perspectives on knowledge and what implications might arise from them. This process may make it easier for you to identify some of your own beliefs and assumptions about knowledge, and hence your own position amongst all of this diversity. The IB statement is not intended to mean that everyone, everywhere, is always necessarily 'right'; you can imagine some of the contradictions that would eventuate from this!

In the current assessment scheme for TOK, the 'knower's perspective' has been given a very high profile. This is not something to forget.

Appraisal of your work

It's crucial that you get the chance to discuss your forthcoming presentation with your teacher. This is an important opportunity to get some feedback on your intentions and it will help you to deliver a presentation that will not only earn a high score for you but also make a valuable contribution to the TOK course and thus help your fellow students.

The presentation assessment criteria and what they are measuring

As you plan your presentation, keep in mind the criteria by which your performance will be judged. To clarify the actual wording of the criteria here are a few notes for guidance.

Criterion A: Identification of knowledge issue (extraction)

In the case studies above, we have largely been dealing with how to address this first criterion as it is the key to the others. Briefly, you will score well if you formulate clearly and state your knowledge issue that you have extracted from your real-life situation. You must show how the issue and the situation are related and how the former arises out of the latter. Half the battle is getting this right. Notice how the title of this criterion refers to 'issue' in the singular – this is an important prompt.

Criterion B: Treatment of knowledge issues (understanding and development)

This criterion is intended to measure the degree to which your presentation shows that you understand your stated knowledge issue, and very likely other related knowledge issues as well that will arise as you explore and develop it – hence the plural 's' on the end of the title of this criterion. Successful development will provide evidence for a clear progression in your thinking, including logical argumentation.

Criterion C: Knower's perspective (your own engagement)

This criterion is concerned with your own direct involvement as a knower in your presentation. Throughout your preparation, you should aim for a mastery of the material you intend to present, such that you can think ahead and even anticipate what others might think of it. Then, in the actual performance, this 'ownership' of your work will be demonstrated through the arguments and examples that you deploy. Your manifest engagement with the topic will lead you naturally to show how it is significant to you as a knower.

Criterion D: Connections (alternative approaches)

Your own curiosity as a knower will have led you to the central knowledge issue of your presentation. Now Criterion D encourages you to take a step back from your own position and consider alternative approaches. These might rely on particular Ways of Knowing or Areas of Knowledge, or be based upon the assumptions that different individuals and groups adopt in their perspectives on knowledge. More often that not, each of these varying approaches will lead to wider implications for knowledge and give us insight into how we might approach other real-life situations beyond the one you chose for your presentation.

Exercise

Now return to the four case studies on pages 285–7. Evaluate the potential strengths and weaknesses in each case with reference to the four criteria. How would you develop each of the presentations in order to remedy any shortcomings?

Presenting skills

Let's return to the comparison of presentations and essays. Watching and listening are very different skills from reading (you could make a list of the differences). While the pace of progress is set by the reader in an essay (you can read slowly or quickly, stop for a cup of coffee, or 'cheat' and read the ending first, etc.), the pace is set by the presenter in a presentation, not the audience. In addition, there's no opportunity for your audience to go back and see something again, nor can anyone skip over a part to see the ending. This means that clear guidance will be needed from you as the presentation unfolds – guidance of a type that might not be needed in an essay. Listeners will need to be reminded of what has been said and perhaps forewarned of what is to come.

	Presentation	Essay
Pace	set by presenter	set by reader
Durability	ephemeral (gone when done)	indefinite (can be re-read)
Relevant audience skills	listening	reading

The table above shows why speech writers sometimes follow the maxim:

> *Tell them what you are going to say; then say it; then tell them what you have said.*

While your TOK presentation will ideally deepen your own understanding of TOK, and provide a stimulating intellectual experience for your audience, it is hoped that you will also develop skills in preparing and making it. After all, in your educational career you will be required to make other presentations of various kinds. So you might think of your work as having a wider usefulness in helping to develop your skills of public speaking, which will bolster your personal confidence.

Rhetoric: persuasion and exploration

Rhetoric was considered an important discipline in some curricula of the past but nowadays the word 'rhetoric' itself seems to have developed negative connotations. 'Well, that's just rhetoric,' some people say after having listened to someone speak – meaning that the speaker is more interested in persuasion than delivering information objectively. We speak of 'rhetorical questions' that are posed for effect (a literary device) rather than to solicit a diversity of answers. This emphasis on persuasion might be accepted in the context of a debate, where the object is to convince and win, but what about a TOK presentation? Isn't the idea here to explore rather than persuade? Don't we want dialogue and dialectic rather than debate?

It is clear that exploration and persuasion cannot be cleanly separated; what you say is intimately bound up with the way you say it so it is vital to think about these aspects of your presentation. If you are attempting to persuade your audience of the truth of a matter (rather than simply your convenient point of view), then persuasion quickly loses its negative connotation.

One thinker who has provided us with a helpful structure here is Aristotle who made distinctions between three aspects, or 'appeals' as he called them, of rhetoric:

- **ethos** – the credibility of the speaker as evaluated by the audience
- **pathos** – the emotional appeal made by the speaker to the audience
- **logos** – the logic of the speaker's arguments.

Aristotle believed that the most effective presentations contained a balance of these three attributes:

- credibility
- passion
- logic.

Try to keep this classification in mind as you read on.

The assessment criteria make specific reference to the use of arguments (C), demonstration of the topic's significance (C) and of implications in related areas (D). These attributes relate clearly to *logos*, and highlight the emphasis which the criteria have deliberately made towards giving credit for the content of the presentation. However, because *ethos* and *pathos* relate directly to your relationship with your audience, they play a crucial role in the success of your work, even though they do not appear to have direct counterparts in the formal assessment.

Passion and the audience

Pathos is often characterized as a way of altering and exploiting the emotional state of the audience, and this might be legitimate in many situations.

Once again, it could be argued that TOK, as a course that promotes reflection on knowledge issues, does not sit comfortably with brazen attempts to persuade people of particular points of view. On the other hand, in TOK we want you to deliver your (carefully considered) claims in a convincing fashion. So what exactly is the proper role of persuasion in a TOK presentation? As a rough checklist, you need to persuade your audience that:

- you are absorbed in your own work
- the topic is interesting and worth discussing
- there are different perspectives that exist on the topic
- you have made a personal intellectual journey during your preparation
- your conclusions, although perhaps contestable, are well-founded.

Credibility and the audience

Consider the questions below.

Who is going to be there?

Although there will be at least one TOK teacher present, your primary audience will be composed of other students. You may be able to take advantage of the fact that, unlike many other situations, you actually know all of your audience already! So take a few minutes to imagine them, sitting there, listening to you – put yourself in their shoes. What would make them interested in what you have to say? What will make them listen to you? They will have certain expectations about you and your presentation in advance, which you may wish to exploit.

Why do these students need your presentation?

Your answer to this question will guide you towards deciding which aspects of your presentation to emphasize. Ask yourself the question about your own presentation, 'So what?' What will your audience take from your work and find useful in the future? How will you show that the material in your presentation can be applied elsewhere? How will you be engaging and memorable?

What do the students in the audience already know?

You must pitch your presentation at the right level. Don't treat your audience as ignorant or you will waste time making unnecessary explanations and the listeners will quickly switch off. But it is more likely that you will credit your audience with too much advance knowledge about your topic! Once you have researched a topic, it is easy to underestimate the effort needed by others to comprehend it. Since your audience is made up of neither empty vessels nor expert authorities, where along this spectrum do they stand? You might consider trying to sound out a few people in advance.

It is important to think of your presentation as something that must be *interpreted* by your audience in the light of their existing knowledge, rather than as something that is *delivered* to them complete and self-contained. A presentation can only be judged as 'good' largely with respect to the ways in which it is tailored to its audience.

First impressions

Think about the numerous occasions when other people have presented material to you. How often have you made a snap judgement about whether or not you are going to give them all your attention and whether this effort is likely to be worthwhile? You will need to make an immediate impact – one that you can sustain. How can you win your audience's attention from the very start? We need to consider what you say and how you look.

Voice

Consider the following aspects of how you speak:

1 **Speed** – is your delivery slow enough? Try not to exceed 150 words per minute. Do you think everyone in the room can follow your line of thinking?

2 **Clarity** – are you enunciating every word clearly?

3 **Volume** – can you be heard by everyone in the room? The teachers may well be at the back and they can't give you credit for what they don't hear.

4 **Modulation** – are you speaking in a way that makes the material sound interesting? Does it sound as if you yourself are interested in what you are presenting?

With the help of some friends, practise addressing some of these aspects of your delivery.

Somewhere close to the beginning, you must relate the real-life situation and central knowledge issue of your presentation, although it need not be the very first thing you say. Remember once again that your familiarity with the real-life situation must not interfere with the communication of it to your audience.

Non-verbal communication

Also be aware of your non-verbal behaviour – what you do with your face and body while you are speaking. These are also forms of communication.

- Make your presentation standing up, unless there is some overriding reason why this is not appropriate or possible.
- Make sure that you have your audience's attention before you start – a pause beforehand can be effective.
- Make an effort to establish eye-contact with some members of the audience.
- Go closer to the audience to intensify your impact.
- Don't turn your back on the audience and don't talk to the wall.
- Don't read extensively from paper or spend time shuffling notes.
- If your group presentation calls for you to address another member of the group, think about how to do so while maintaining your relationship with the audience.
- Look and sound confident but never arrogant.

The organization of your presentation

One of the first decisions you have to make about your presentation is whether you want to do it on your own or with other students. What are the issues here? The expectation is that a presentation will last for 10 minutes, multiplied by the number of presenters (up to a maximum of about 30 minutes).

- **Working on your own:** this means that you have the advantage of total control over the presentation. It may be that this suits your general style. At the same time, consider the restriction of the 10-minute allocation – you have to be very organized in order to hit all the targets set by the assessment criteria in such a short period of time.
- **Working in a group:** this offers a number of contrasting advantages and concerns. The presentation can address the topic in more depth because the time available is longer. In addition, several heads can be better than one. Plus there is the advantage that different group members can be assigned different roles, although it's important that this doesn't detract from the overall coherence of the work.
- **Larger groups (four or five):** if you want to work as a group, what size would be best? The maximum permitted by the IBO is five (although your school may impose a lower limit). Although big groups may seem better ('many heads' again), you would need to keep in mind several aspects. Firstly, such a presentation will be expected to last for the full 30 minutes, so you need to ensure that your audience stays engaged for this time. Secondly, be careful when dividing up responsibilities between the group members – the presentation must remain an integrated whole and not fracture into a linear series of individual contributions. On the other hand, a large group will give you ample scope to explore your topic in depth.
- **Smaller groups (two or three):** pairs or trios constitute the middle option. Such smaller groups mean that different students can put forward alternative or opposing positions or perspectives – in a role play, for example. This dialectic can be a very powerful way of exploring knowledge issues. However, remember that it is important to draw together the fruits of this exploration – you could do this by commentating (reflecting) on the preceding dialogue (e.g. 'stepping out' of the role play). This is one way in which a group of three can divide up their roles in such a presentation.

Presentations	Advantages	Drawbacks
Individual	Total control of presentation	Exposition is short; hard to present divergent views
Smaller group	A natural 'dialectic' approach	A strong individual might dominate the direction of the presentation
Larger group	There are many contributors to bring ideas for the presentation	The presentation may fragment; audience fatigue

Presentation stages

However many presenters are involved, it's important to remember that your presentation will have different stages. One common structure that you might consider is:

introduction ⟶ development ⟶ conclusion

How might these stages be approached?

- **Introduction:** you might want to consider using one of your stronger speakers to introduce the presentation. Set out the 'landscape' of the presentation to come.
- **Development:** think about the various elements in the criteria. Do you need a branching argument that pursues counter claims and allows shifts in perspective? How do you intend to insert examples? If your presentation is lengthy, your audience's attention might flag; you may need to think about some interactive element, for example, to revitalize it.
- **Conclusion:** it might be worth returning to the strongest speaker to close the presentation, not least to give a sense of unity to the whole event (but remember that each member of the group must demonstrate their involvement).

Types of visual aid

It is easy to think of technology as something modern or new, and tempting to measure how 'advanced' a society might be in terms of the technology it uses (this could be an interesting assumption to examine in itself). But if we take a broad view, thinking of technology as a way of harnessing knowledge in order to master our environment, it is easy to see that even items such as basic clothing and the wheel are technological products. Our particular focus here is how technology can be employed in the service of storing and communicating knowledge.

You probably want to support what you say in your presentation with some kind of visual aid. Why might this be a good idea? What kind of aid might this be? Before you decide, remember the following: any technology you use must be *in the service* of the aims of the presentation, it must not become *the aim* of the presentation. Don't try to impress using technology unless the technology actually enhances the message. Here are some possibilities:

- transparent acetate sheets on an overhead projector
- a PowerPoint presentation on a data projector
- a photocopied handout
- a poster.

What factors govern the choice of what, if anything (or what combination), to use?

- **Overhead projector:** nowadays, this is considered a rather low-technology option. However, the advantages are that little can go wrong (except in places where electricity is unreliable); the drawbacks include lack of colour and various types of 'slide-building' that may be problematic.

- **PowerPoint presentation:** this is often regarded as the default visual-aid option. PowerPoint is an extremely powerful tool but it's important to be aware of its limitations and how to use it effectively. Slides need to be thought about from the perspective of the audience – with enough time given for reading and understanding each one (maybe a minimum of 30 seconds) and, for ease of reading individual slides, a word limit (possibly about 30 words).

- **Handout:** photocopied handouts perform a different role to the previous options – they can be read afterwards at leisure and, therefore, can be much more detailed than any kind of projection. Consider why a handout might be desirable or otherwise. To present additional material? To guide subsequent discussion?

- **Poster:** a poster is different to both projections (which are ephemeral) and handouts (that are distributed); it is an item that can endure and remain in place.

Other media can be included in your presentation – for example, video/DVD or audio – but it's vital to consider the role that these will play overall.

Plans, maps and rehearsals

Most people imagine plans to be restricted to the planning phase. But the structure of your presentation, and how its parts relate logically to each other, is something that needs to be shared with your audience during the actual delivery – listeners need a 'road map' that allows them to orient themselves with respect to what has been said and what is expected to come.

Don't make the mistake of assuming that 'it'll be alright on the night'. You need to rehearse your presentation and check the timing. With a group presentation, you need to practise how students will interact. You also need to get an idea of how much you will commit to memory – flashcards are an excellent idea but you must not read from a script.

Remember: reading aloud from a script is not allowed!

Summary of assessment and the presentation

Let's return to the diagram on page 278 and modify it for the presentation:

Assessment diagram for TOK presentation ▶

Key
A = discussion of initial ideas and presentation intentions between student and teacher (you should complete the planning form TK/PPD in advance)
B = formal assessment of presentation by teacher
C = self-evaluation by student on presentation marking form (you write this on form TK/PMF)

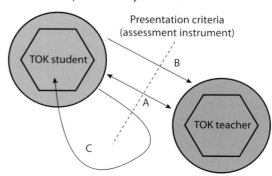

It is also worth mentioning that your school may be asked by the IB to record and send some presentations to be viewed by senior examiners. This is not common but it does happen in order to maintain the integrity of the scores awarded in different schools.

Essays: writing

We have examined and acknowledged the central role of speech and conversation in TOK and now we must turn to its written counterpart. Writing affords us some different tools for reflection and analysis and expands the range of possibilities for successful expression.

What is an essay? During your academic career to date, it is likely that you have written numerous items which were referred to as 'essays'. From time to time, teachers in various subjects have doubtless asked you to 'write an essay'; you might have been given some guidance in the form of oral instructions or perhaps a written scheme or framework. But have you ever stopped to consider what is meant more generally by an 'essay'? In the spirit of TOK, perhaps we should look more closely. Is it possible to describe the features of the essay and define it as a genre of writing (you may have attempted the task of genre definition in your literature course – with reference to poetry or drama, for example)?

When writing about the nature of essays, the British writer Aldous Huxley distinguished between three aspects, or 'poles':

1 The abstract, universal: general, perhaps derived from the factual (see next)
2 The factual, concrete: specific and verifiable
3 The personal, autobiographical: the writer giving something of him/herself

Huxley's idea can be represented like this

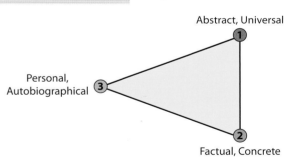

Although for Huxley an emphasis on all three 'poles' was not necessary in an essay, he considered a balance between them to be most desirable:

> *The most richly satisfying essays are those which make the best not of one, not of two, but of all the three worlds in which it is possible for the essay to exist.*

> From *Collected Essays* by Aldous Huxley

This model will prove helpful and we will return to examine it.

A short history of the essay

While there are pieces of writing from ancient times that we would recognize as essays, it is Michel de Montaigne (1533–92) of France whom we must credit with both the revival of the genre and the name by which it is known. Montaigne set out to document his ideas and opinions and subject them to critical analysis. He thought of each piece of his work as a means to attempt (*essayer* in French) to reach the truth about the matter in question, and thus it became known as an *essai*.

In his essays, Montaigne covers a multitude of topics – from friendship to cruelty, from education to lying, from smells to cannibals! Typically, he offers much of his own experiences and character in his writing and is thus sometimes considered to be the father of the informal essay. In contrast, the English philosopher and statesman Francis Bacon (1561–1626) was a famous early proponent of a more formal and impersonal style of essay writing. These versions of the essay can be thought of as alternative emphases within Huxley's scheme.

Informal essays have often dealt with literary topics but by the nineteenth century, essays had also become a common means of judging academic work, with a stress on formality. As such, they were suitable not only for assessing the understanding of ideas, but also of writing skills themselves. Content and form were thus closely tied together.

Exercise

At the time of writing, the Wikipedia entry on essays recognizes a number of different types including:
- the descriptive
- the narrative
- the 'compare and contrast'
- the persuasive
- the reflective
- the dialectic.

Can you find a location in the Huxley scheme for some of these?

The TOK essay

One reason for the popularity of the essay in academic assessment is the relative freedom that it affords in the presentation of ideas and argument. For a course such as TOK, which by its nature encourages different possibilities, this makes it a powerful and appropriate tool. In fact, Huxley's three 'poles' provide a very apt summary of many of the desired qualities in a TOK essay. The recognition of the importance of all three of them arguably serves to distinguish between essays in this course and in some others.

Choosing a Prescribed Title (PT)

Each year, the IB releases a set of ten prescribed titles for TOK (make sure that you have the correct list for your examination session). For your final IB assessment, you are required to respond to one of these, which will be assessed by an external TOK examiner. What is the best way of choosing the right PT for you?

First, examine the whole list. Think of it as a zoo – filled with individuals of different species, with varying characters, attractions and dangers. Firstly, you will notice that some of the titles are longer than others. Some titles make reference to particular course domains (Ways of Knowing, Areas of Knowledge) and some don't. It's important not to make any snap judgement about these differences, because your first impressions may turn out to be inaccurate and costly. Consider, for example, the following three titles:

1 'The arts deal in the particular, the individual and the personal while the sciences deal in the general, the universal and the collective.' To what extent does this statement obscure the nature of both Areas of Knowledge?

2 'Words are more treacherous and powerful than we think.' Evaluate the extent to which the characteristics Sartre claims for words affect – negatively or positively – different Areas of Knowledge.

3 Can we know something that has not yet been proven true?

© International Baccalaureate Organization 2003 and 2004

Let's look at each of the above in turn:

1 The first title is quite specific about course domains (two Areas of Knowledge) that must be addressed and names six attributes that they may or may not possess.

2 The second title requires a consideration of Areas of Knowledge (in relation to language as a Way of Knowing) but leaves the identity of them to the writer's discretion.

3 The third title is very short and includes a number of words which you are almost certain to have used frequently during the course (know, proven, true) but leaves the direction of treatment almost entirely open.

Whereas the second title offers a quotation attributed to a particular thinker, the first includes one that seems to be anonymous. The third offers none at all.

Limiting the discussion to just these three alternatives, which one is best for you?

1 The first title provides a clear framework for your essay – you could say that some of the work has been done for you. But of course this is only an advantage if you feel confident about tackling these particular Areas of Knowledge.

2 The second title gives you more choice but less structure – a half-way house.

3 The third allows a great deal of freedom but it's still expected that you will address course domains in some way, and you will have to create a framework that will allow you to do this successfully.

As for quotations, sometimes they are real, sometimes not, but it actually doesn't matter either way as the identity of any author should not be the focus of the treatment of the title (this is not necessarily the case with essay titles in other courses). Here, it is what *you* think about it that matters. So, often it is the case that longer titles provide more structure for you, whereas shorter ones possibly give you more scope for creativity but require that you lay the groundwork very carefully. The three examples discussed here could be thought of as representing three different categories of title.

Exercise

Try to place each of the following PTs in one of the suggested categories:

1 'All knowledge depends on the recognition of patterns or anomalies.' Discuss.

© International Baccalaureate Organization 1994

2 Compare and evaluate the ways in which literature on the one hand and the human sciences on the other may help us to know and understand human behaviour.

© International Baccalaureate Organization 2001

3 Is knowledge in mathematics and other Areas of Knowledge dependent on culture to the same degree and in the same ways?

© International Baccalaureate Organization 2004

4 Must all 'good explanations' allow for precise predictions?

© International Baccalaureate Organization 2001

Some titles encourage a treatment of how knowledge has developed over time:
- In what ways has technology expanded or limited the acquisition of knowledge?
  © International Baccalaureate Organization 2001

- 'Without a knowledge of the past, we would have no knowledge at all.' Evaluate this assertion with reference to any two of the following: (a) mathematics (b) natural sciences or human sciences (one choice) (c) history (d) the arts.
  © International Baccalaureate Organization 2000

Titles like this require either some existing knowledge about the history of certain disciplines or activities, or a willingness to research it.

There may also be a title that, at first glance, appears to be more about 'general studies' or 'current affairs':
- Which sources of knowledge – books, websites, the media, personal experience, authorities or some other – do you consider most trustworthy, and why?
  © International Baccalaureate Organization 2002

Be careful to consider how such a title can be firmly connected to core TOK concepts, such as knowledge, belief and truth, and to what constitutes a reliable authority through various Ways of Knowing, or in certain Areas of Knowledge. A major challenge in such a title is to keep the focus on TOK.

For all titles, it's vital that you identify the key terms that will need to play central roles in any response. Sometimes these are easy to find (they are identified below in italics):
- Do we have to learn to *think scientifically* in order to find the *truth*?
  © International Baccalaureate Organization 2001

- 'What distinguishes Areas of Knowledge from one another is not how *ideas* are *generated*, but how they are *evaluated*.' Do you agree?
  © International Baccalaureate Organization 2002

With other titles, the key terms tend to stretch into phrases:
- 'In science one tries to tell people, in such a way as to be understood by everyone, something that no one ever knew before. But in poetry, it's the exact opposite.' (P.A.M. Dirac) Do both the approaches suggested in the quotation enjoy equal success in expanding human knowledge?
  © International Baccalaureate Organization 2002

While such a title might seem rather complicated, the terms and phrases do provide quite a firm structure for your essay.

Exercise

What are the key terms in each of the following PTs?

1 One definition of knowledge is true belief based on strong evidence. What makes evidence 'strong' enough and how can this limit be established?
  © International Baccalaureate Organization 2004

2 'In order to find out how things really are, one must understand the filters through which one perceives the world.' Discuss and evaluate this claim.
  © International Baccalaureate Organization 2003

3 'For it is in the long run that, somehow, truth may survive – through the decay of untruth.' (John Lukacs) To what extent is this the case in different Areas of Knowledge and in your own experience?
  © International Baccalaureate Organization 2004

In all of these considerations, a close examination of the titles is likely to reveal advantages and drawbacks and you must try to align them with your own interests and aptitudes. What are your favourite exhibits in this zoo?

Having studied carefully the entire list of ten titles and identified their general features, you might narrow down your options to about three. Now take paper and pen and scribble down some rough ideas that come to mind for each of these provisionally chosen titles. Don't try to write in full sentences if they don't come easily; just record ideas and thoughts and connect them on the paper in any way that seems potentially helpful. What knowledge issues come to mind? Does your mind jump to situations from your own experience? Are there different ways to interpret the title and its key terms? Try to get a mix of general and specific points and let's try to relate these features to Huxley's model (look back to page 295).

The general (pole 1): knowledge issues

Whichever title you are looking at, you will need to find knowledge issues associated with it. For example:
- 'We are more likely to be mistaken in our generalizations than in our particular observations.' Do you agree?

One way to look at this is that generalizations are products of reasoning while observations are closely bound up with sense perceptions, so an underlying knowledge issue could be, Is reason or sense perception more reliable as a tool for constructing knowledge? A quick mental skim through your experiences in the TOK course might make you ponder whether the answer to the last question depends on the Area of Knowledge under consideration. Further thought might lead you to doubt that the two Ways of Knowing mentioned are completely independent, so you might ask, To what extent do conclusions reached in advance influence what we perceive? Or, is 'pure' perception ever possible? In this manner, knowledge questions can multiply and interlock.

The specific (pole 2): arguments and examples

Remember the rough rule from earlier on:
- Essays: more general (prescribed title) ⟶ more specific (arguments and examples)
- Presentations: more specific (real-life situation) ⟶ more general (knowledge issue)

In order to make your essay more concrete, you will need arguments and examples. These are ways to support the *knowledge claims* that you will inevitably make in your essay. For example, you may wish to *claim* that in science our conclusions are dependent on the scientific knowledge we already possess. You might support this by *arguing* that the power of science lies in its ability to generalize and, since we cannot observe everything, our prior knowledge determines what we end up observing and concluding from it. Or you might support your claim by referring to the *example* of a practical investigation you have carried out in which you chose to ignore certain outlying data that didn't fit the general pattern. You might address the question of why it is usually less unpalatable to ignore some of the experimental data than to modify what has been learned beforehand. It's possible you might decide to include both the above argument and the example.

Arguments and examples can be presented as stepping stones to a knowledge claim or as subsequent support for it. In an intellectually honest piece of work (rather than an attempt to impose a point of view on others), these will amount to the same thing, with the order in which they are presented being essentially a matter of style.

The author (pole 3): knower's perspective and 'ownership'

The third pole of Huxley's model concerns you as the author of your work. The examiner is looking for evidence that you not only understand what you are writing but appreciate it in the context of your own experiences and circumstances. The process of brainstorming ideas and actively connecting them is likely to lead ultimately to evidence of your 'ownership' of the material. This term does not mean that every thought you have is original to you; it simply refers to a mastery of your own material that becomes obvious in the way in which you wield it in your essay.

Appraisal of your work

You teacher will probably give you the opportunity to submit a draft of your work at some stage and will give you some feedback on it. This might be written or oral but, either way, make sure you understand what is being said and suggested. Such teacher input is very important but with some planning you can also employ yourself as a critic. One effective way of doing this is to put your draft away for a week or more and then revisit it. It is amazing how a little distance can reveal areas that need improvement.

Another way to create this critical distance is to conjure up three invisible readers. As you read through your own work, put yourself in the shoes of each of them in turn:
- A is quick-witted, critical but fair.
- B is slow and uncertain and gives up easily when the going gets tough.
- C is rather irreverent and has an eye for the comic, the incongruous, the unintended...

What does each of these imaginary readers have to say about your work? Are they appreciative or critical? Do they have positive or negative things to say to you? Listen to them in your head.

The essay assessment criteria and what they are measuring

As with your presentation, you will need to familiarize yourself with the criteria against which your essay performance will be judged. Here are a few notes for guidance, which should be read in conjunction with the actual descriptors:

- **Criterion A: Understanding knowledge issues (connections to the TOK course)**
  This criterion is concerned with the extent to which knowledge issues that are relevant to the title can be recognized and developed. These processes are expected to be set in the context of an appreciation of the TOK course and the domains that have been addressed during it – Ways of Knowing and Areas of Knowledge.

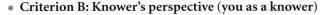

- **Criterion B: Knower's perspective (you as a knower)**
  The 'knower's perspective' has already been discussed on page 287. This criterion is there to reward the evidence that you can provide for an awareness of the perspectives of others and of your own. Try to do this by exploring the implications of these perspectives and by identifying some of the assumptions that underlie them. Examples are powerful tools in these processes.

- **Criterion C: Quality of analysis of knowledge issues (micro-level aspects)**
  It is fine to be able to recognize knowledge issues and the different perspectives that people have, including ourselves, but this will have limited value unless the specific related knowledge claims that you make are subjected to critical analysis. This is the broad purpose of the third criterion. Hence the reference in the descriptors to such aspects as detail, justification and coherence, and the treatment of counter-claims. The assessment of these items requires close scrutiny of what is written, so you can think of this as the 'micro-level' criterion.

- **Criterion D: Organization of ideas (macro-level aspects; facts/references)**
  In addition to this, essay writing also involves a different (or 'higher') level of organization – concerning the order in which ideas are presented, their clarity to the reader, paragraphing, etc. Performance of these aspects belongs in this criterion, along with the treatment of factual material – whether it is correct and, if it is not common knowledge, that the source is acknowledged. So there are two facets to this last area.

A note on examples

While the use of examples is explicitly mentioned in the descriptors for Criterion B, it should be noted that they can play a variety of roles in your essay. For example, a carefully selected example might act as a link between different domains of the course (A), or provide convincing justification for a claim made (C).

Exercise

Having inspected the assessment scheme in some detail, turn back to Huxley's model of essay structure on page 295. To what extent is it possible to locate each of the criteria within it? As with most ideas in life, you are unlikely to find an exact fit but even an approximation can be useful. Think about this: by paying insufficient attention to each of the three poles in turn, what effect might this have on the assessment of your essay?

Here is a suggested response to the previous activity. What do you think of it?

Huxley's model applied to TOK essay assessment

Abstract, Universal
Personal, Autobiographical
Factual, Concrete

Fine-tuning your essay

We have looked at:
- ways of getting started on the process of writing your essay
- what to do with your draft
- how to mould your draft for consistency with the assessment criteria.

There are some further points on the next page that may help you to reach the highest levels of achievement.

Exploration and argumentation: two approaches

A **thesis statement** is a frequent feature of more formal essays, although the popularity of this technique may vary between cultures and traditions. A thesis statement is a claim, made at an early stage in the essay, which is subsequently subjected to analysis. Essays that take this form are sometimes considered to be *argumentative* in the sense that the emphasis is on providing justification for the claim. Although counter-claims can be identified and examined, in this scheme they would probably be found less satisfactory than the original thesis and the essay's conclusion would mirror the original claim. By contrast, an *exploratory* essay might dispense with any thesis statement and proceed by examining a number of divergent possibilities. In the light of these investigations, a conclusion, possibly tentative, is finally drawn.

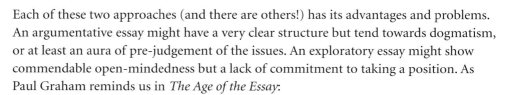

Thesis statement A claim made at an early stage in an essay which is then subjected to analysis.

Each of these two approaches (and there are others!) has its advantages and problems. An argumentative essay might have a very clear structure but tend towards dogmatism, or at least an aura of pre-judgement of the issues. An exploratory essay might show commendable open-mindedness but a lack of commitment to taking a position. As Paul Graham reminds us in *The Age of the Essay*:

> *The Meander (aka Menderes) is a river in Turkey. As you might expect, it winds all over the place. But it doesn't do this out of frivolity. The path it has discovered is the most economical route to the sea.*

> From *The Age of the Essay* by Paul Graham

Using this metaphor of the river, we can see that an essay might not have a linear structure but it still has a coherent logic to it. Clearly, there are attractive and essential aspects of both argumentation and exploration that you need to adopt. A thesis statement can be a very effective device but your essay can also work extremely well without one; both approaches are acceptable, although either way you need to provide a sense of purpose. Consider which works best for you.

Switching metaphors, we could say that the TOK essay invites a branching, rather than linear, argument. Arguments, sub-arguments and counter-arguments branch from the main trunk of the title and implications bud from these branches. This tree is constructed through argumentation and exploration.

Communication and style

Many IB students have a language other than English as their mother-tongue. If you are one of them, you may be reassured to know that the TOK examiners are looking for success in the communication of your ideas and not for a sophisticated literary style. However, it's clear that these two aspects of writing are not entirely separable, so in this situation you might benefit from asking another, carefully chosen, student to read your work and comment on whether anything in the wording could be improved.

In some parts of the world, students are taught to write essays in a particularly formal manner, avoiding the use of 'I' as a personal pronoun and even encouraging the use of the passive voice. Examiners are not looking for this and, indeed, are often encouraged to see the use of the first-person form as a part of the effort to address the 'knower's perspective'. Witness how Huxley's model makes room for this. At the same time, remember the need for balance. An essay that is liberally peppered with 'I' – the author as the knower – can appear self-obsessed. Whereas our Ways of Knowing may sometimes encourage us to think at a somewhat personal level, this should not blind us to our status as individual members of various communities which reach beyond us in important ways.

Academic honesty

Although your TOK essay is not strictly speaking a piece of research (in the sense that your Extended Essay is), it is essential to conform to the accepted standards of acknowledging other people's work. When you submit your final essay, you will be asked to sign a declaration relating to this. Your school may stipulate certain conventions about how to do this but, in any case, you must reference any facts or ideas that are not considered common knowledge. This is, of course, a judgement that you will have to make in each case but your teacher may be able to advise you. If in doubt, acknowledge!

Formatting

Your school might give you specific instructions about this but the general expectation is that you should follow these recommendations:
- Use a scholarly font, such as Times New Roman or Arial.
- Set the type size to 12-point.
- Set your paragraphing to 1.5 line spacing.
- Make sure that your chosen title and title number are at the top of the essay.
- Make sure your name is at the top and your candidate session number is on each page.
- Give an accurate word-count at the end of the essay.
- Don't use a page border (examiners need to make comments there).
- Set reasonable margins (for the same reason).
- Staple your essay together with the official cover sheet (TK/CS) on top.
- Read, complete and sign the relevant portions of the cover sheet.
- Don't use any bindings of any kind other than the staple.

Summary of assessment and the essay

Once again, let's return to the diagram on page 278 and this time modify it for the essay task:

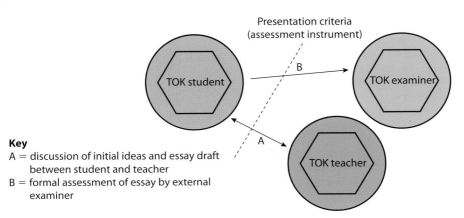

Presentation criteria
(assessment instrument)

TOK student

B

TOK examiner

A

TOK teacher

Key
A = discussion of initial ideas and essay draft between student and teacher
B = formal assessment of essay by external examiner

Assessment diagram for TOK essay

Today's world: *The Concord Review*

In this chapter, we have looked not only at the specific assessment requirements of the TOK course, but at the essay and presentation forms more generally. As you know, even within the IB diploma they are not confined to TOK alone. Just how valuable your skills in these areas might turn out to be is illustrated by the existence of *The Concord Review* – a journal that publishes outstanding work written by school students, many of whom are in the IB programme. The words of Will Fitzhugh, its founder and president, concerning the achievements of IB students, may prove instructive and inspirational.

Most of the writing students will be asked to do in college and at work is not creative writing, but non-fiction academic expository writing. Because writing in our high schools is so often in the hands of the English department, many high-school students only do writing that is personal, creative, or the five-paragraph essay these days. Even the AP courses do not require serious term papers.

International Baccalaureate students are very fortunate in the requirement that they write an Extended Essay for the Diploma. I have published history research papers by high school students from 35 countries since 1987 in *The Concord Review*, and many if not most of the ones from other countries have been IB Extended Essays.

In addition to being good preparation for the non-fiction expository writing tasks in their future, IB students benefit from studying something besides their own lives when they prepare for their Extended Essay.

Too many educators, but not in the IB Programs, often direct students' attention back onto themselves these days, and in the process block them from learning more about history and about the world they live in. This fosters ignorance and the various follies of solipsism. All too soon students will be caught up in the details of their daily work lives, and only a broad educational foundation can keep them aware of the wider concerns of their day. Reading for and preparing a good serious IB Extended Essay is a very helpful antidote to the risks of a too-narrow vision of what is important in life.

I am grateful for the many fine Extended Essays I have received in the last 20 years, and for the opportunity this task has offered to IB students to read more non-fiction and to think and write seriously about at least one important subject before they leave secondary school.

From *The Importance of Non-fiction Writing by School Students* by Will Fitzhugh

Ideal knower

Wole Soyinka (1934–)

Much of Wole Soyinka's work as a playwright, poet, writer, lecturer and activist has served to highlight various forms of injustice in the world, with consequences that have included imprisonment, periods of exile from his native Nigeria and the Nobel Prize in Literature. Sensitized from an early age to political issues, his work has suffered censorship by a number of government administrations – particularly those of the tumultuous 1960s before and during the failed attempt to establish an independent state of Biafra in the east of the country. In addition to Nigeria, he has lived for periods in the UK, Ghana and the US, and his forthright views on abuses of political office and individual human rights continue unabated. His consummate skills as a wordsmith render him a

Wole Soyinka

spokesman of immense stature in the world today; they provide a striking example of the power of the spoken and written word, not only to stimulate reflection and thought, but to bring about action. The success of knowledge at work in the world depends heavily on those who express it best.

The following extract is taken from the BBC Reith Lecture series which Soyinka was invited to deliver in 2004 (a lecture is an interesting cross-breed between an essay and a presentation!). As you read it, consider how he draws on his own knower's perspective as a Nigerian, writer and activist. Observe how he develops the key concepts of democracy and human dignity through example and argument by analogy. Note the clarity of the exposition; there is much worthy of emulation here.

We are trying get to grips with the concept 'dignity', and why it appears to mean so much to the sentient human, almost right from childhood. Why has it been entrenched in so many social documents across cultures, civilizations and political upheavals? Why was it given such prominence in the Charter that resulted from one of the bloodiest revolutions in human history – the French – was further enshrined in the document for the enthronement of peace after World War II, the Declaration of Universal Human Rights? In one form or the other, the quest for human dignity has proved to be one of the most propulsive elements for wars, civil strife and willing sacrifice. Yet the entitlement to dignity, enshrined among these 'human rights', does not appear to aspire to being the most self-evident, essential needs for human survival, such as food, or physical health. Compared to that other candidate for the basic impulse of human existence – self-preservation, it may even be deemed self-indulgent.

Considerations of this intangible bequest, human dignity, often reminds me of a rhetorical outburst in the United Nations by a Nigerian representative [who] challenged his listeners to combat in more or less the following words:

'What exactly is this Democracy that we're talking about? Can we eat Democracy? The government is trying to combat hunger, put food into people's stomachs and all we hear is Democracy, Democracy! What exactly is this democracy? Does it prevent hunger? Is it something we can put in the mouth and eat like food?'

I felt bound [to write] an article in response. I remarked I had dined in the cafeterias and restaurants of the United Nations on a number of occasions, and had never seen Democracy on the menu, or indeed on any menu in restaurants all over the world. So what, I demanded, was the point of that statement?

Well, Democracy as such may not be on the UN restaurant menu, it is nonetheless on its catering agenda. So is Human Dignity. Needless to say, both are inextricably linked. Indeed, Human Dignity appears to have been on everyone's menu from the most rudimentary society, recognized as such by philosophers who have occupied their minds with the evolution of the social order… What is worth noting for us today is simply the prodigious output of numerous minds on this theme, nearly all of which emphasize that the pursuit of dignity is one of the most fundamental defining aspects of human existence.

The Yoruba have a common saying: Iku ya j'esin lo. This translates literally as 'Sooner Death, than Indignity'. It is an expression that easily finds equivalents in numerous cultures, and captures the essence of self-worth, the sheer integrity of being that animates the human spirit, and the ascription of equal membership of the human community.

Over the course of history, the concept of human dignity has been variously characterized as arising out of our relationship with nature or various gods, our faculty of reason, or as an essential pre-condition for functioning society. Whichever view we adopt, reflecting on it enriches our understanding of what it means to be human, and empowers us to confer respect on each person and recognize their intrinsic worth. Perhaps we can regard it as the axiomatic basis for the adherence to acceptable standards of behaviour and the concept of human rights; maybe even our individual identities. It could be argued that, without a respect for human dignity, human knowledge loses its value. It could be for this reason that the IB Learner Profile speaks clearly of empathy and compassion towards others and the making of reasoned ethical decisions in the same breath as a respect for the dignity of individuals and communities.

Appendix

Solutions for Chapter 1: An introduction to Theory of Knowledge

Exercise, page 4

Logic (c)   Maths (a)
Economics (j)   Science (e)
History (d)   Psychology (f)
Ethics (b)   Politics (h)
Aesthetics (i)   Human sciences (g)

Solutions for Chapter 2: What is knowledge?

Exercise, page 19

Please note that 'D' indicates 'debatable'.

1 T	**10** T	**19** D
2 T	**11** T	**20** D
3 T	**12** F	**21** D
4 T	**13** F	**22** T
5 T	**14** F	**23** F
6 F	**15** T	**24** F
7 T	**16** T	**25** F
8 F	**17** T	
9 F	**18** F	

Exercise, page 28

a 2	**g** 2	**m** 1
b 2	**h** 1	**n** 2
c 1	**i** 2	**o** 1
d 1	**j** 2	**p** 2
e 1	**k** 1	**q** debatable
f 2	**l** 1	

Solutions for Chapter 7: Reason

First exercise, page 100

1 Consider:

p: he likes me q: he sends me roses

Hence the argument becomes: major premise: $p \Rightarrow q$

minor premise: q

conclusion: $\therefore p$

Below is the truth table representing the argument:

p	q	$p \Rightarrow q$	$(p \Rightarrow q) \wedge q$	$[(p \Rightarrow q) \wedge q] \Rightarrow p$
T	T	T	T	T
T	F	F	F	T
F	T	T	T	F
F	F	T	F	T

Notice that the last column of truth values are not all true.

The argument is invalid. Note that this argument is known as *the fallacy of the converse*.

It can be further noted that the converse of a statement does not necessarily follow from an original conditional. Consider the following:

Conditional: If $x = 2$, then $x^2 = 4$. (This statement is true)

Converse: If $x^2 = 4$, then $x = 2$. (This statement is not true as x could be -2)

2 Consider:

p: it rains q: she will wear her hat

Hence the argument becomes: major premise: $p \Rightarrow q$

minor premise: $\neg q$

conclusion: $\therefore \neg p$

The truth table representing the argument follows:

p	q	$\neg p$	$\neg q$	$p \Rightarrow q$	$(p \Rightarrow q) \wedge \neg q$	$[(p \Rightarrow q) \wedge \neg q] \Rightarrow \neg p$
T	T	F	F	T	F	T
T	F	F	T	F	F	T
F	T	T	F	T	F	T
F	F	T	T	T	T	T

The argument is valid and hence $(p \Rightarrow q) \equiv (\neg q \Rightarrow \neg p)$. This argument is known as *Modus tollens*.

Exercise, page 101

The original set of premises is given as:
1 All TOK teachers are promise breakers.
2 Promise breakers are untrustworthy.
3 One can always trust a person who wears clean socks.
4 Anyone who is not a sceptic wears clean socks.

These statements can be translated into the 'if … then …' form as follows:
1 If you are a TOK teacher, then you are a promise breaker.
2 If you are a promise breaker, then you are not trustworthy.
3 If you wear clean socks, then you are trustworthy.
4 If you are not a sceptic, then you wear clean socks.

These statements can be translated by using the contrapositive relationship:

$$(p \Rightarrow q) \equiv (\neg q \Rightarrow \neg p)$$

The results now become:
1 If you are a TOK teacher, then you are a promise breaker.
2 If you are a promise breaker, then you are not trustworthy.
3 If you are not trustworthy, then you do not wear clean socks.
4 If you do not wear clean socks, then you are a sceptic.

The transitivity property allows the reasoning to combine as:

TOK teacher $\Rightarrow$

      promise breaker $\Rightarrow$

            not trustworthy $\Rightarrow$

                  do not wear clean socks $\Rightarrow$

                       sceptic

Hence the conclusion is: *If you are a TOK teacher, then you are a sceptic.*

Solutions for Chapter 9: Mathematical knowledge

Bees and hives, Page 146

Some possible solutions to Howard Eve's axiomatics exercise are given below.

a Interpret the bees as six letters – A, B, C, D, E, F

Then identify the four hives as follows:

H1 (A, B, C)   H2 (A, D, E)   H3 (B, F, E)   H4 (C, F, D)

Each of the four postulates will satisfy the collection as shown above.

b To show independence of **P2** interpret four bees positioned at the vertex of a square. Hives are then formed by the side of each square.

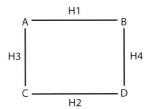

If each side of this square represents a hive then we have the following collection:

H1 (A, B)   H2 (C, D)   H3 (A, C)   H4 (B, D)

Note that **P1**, **P3** and **P4** are satisfied but **P2** is not. Also note that other variations of this solution are possible with multiples of four bees.

To show the independence of **P3**, interpret four bees positioned at the vertex and at the foot of an altitude of an equilateral triangle. The hives can be considered as the four rows along the sides and on the altitude of the triangle.

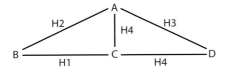

The sides and altitude of the triangle now form the following collection:

H1 (A, C)   H2 (A, B)   H3 (A, D)   H4 (B, C, D)

Postulates **P1**, **P2** and **P4** are satisfied with this collection but **P3** is not.

Note that we could also show that **P4** is independent. (Hint: place three bees in a triangle formation)

c A few theorems that could be deduced would include:
- There are exactly six bees.
- There are exactly three bees in each hive.
- For each bee, there is exactly one other bee not in the same hive with it.

BIBLIOGRAPHY

Abel, R. (1976). *Man is the Measure – A Cordial Invitation to the Central Problems of Philosophy.* London: The Free Press.

Anjelou, M. (1985). *Journey to Heartland.* Address delivered at the National Assembly of Local Arts, Cedar Rapids, Iowa, Jun 12.

Archer, M. (2002). *Art Since 1960.* London: Thames & Hudson.

Armstrong, K. (2006). *The Great Transformation.* London: Atlantic Books.

Ashe, G. (1979). *The Art of Writing Made Simple.* London: W. H. Allen.

Backhouse, R.E. (2002). *The Penguin History of Economics.* London: Penguin.

Bell, C. (1913). *Art.* London: Chatto and Windus.

Benckler, Y. (2007). *The Wealth of Networks.* Connecticut: Yale University Press.

Black, R. (2007). *Climate science: Sceptical About Bias.* BBC News, Nov 14.

Blackburn, S. (1999). *Think.* Oxford: Oxford University Press.

Blackburn, S. (2002). *Being Good.* Oxford: Oxford University Press.

Blackburn, S. (2004). *Lust.* Oxford/New York: The New York Public Library/Oxford University Press.

Blackburn, S. (2005). *Truth.* Oxford: Oxford University Press.

Bloomer, C.M. (1976). *The Principles of Visual Perception.* New York: Van Nostrand Reinhold Company.

Blurton, T.R. (1997). *The Enduring Image: Treasures from the British Museum.* London: The British Council.

Bok, S. (1997). *Lying: Moral Choice in Public and Private Life.* New York: Pantheon.

Booker, C. (2004). *The Seven Basic Plots: why we tell stories.* London: Continuum.

Boorstein, D.J. (1995). *Cleopatra's Nose.* New York: Vintage Press.

Brians, P., Gallway, M., Hughes, D., Hussein, A. and Low, R. (eds.) (1999). *Reading about the World,* Vol. 1. New York: Harcourt Brace Custom Publishing.

Bronowski, J. (1973). *The Ascent of Man: A Personal View.* London: BBC Publications.

Bruner, J. (1986). *Actual Minds, Possible Worlds.* Cambridge: Harvard University Press.

Carroll, L. (1998). *Alice's Adventures in Wonderland.* London: Penguin Classics.

Castells, M. (2002). *The Internet Galaxy.* Oxford: Oxford University Press.

Chalmers, A.F. (1982). *What is this thing called Science?* Milton Keynes: Open University Press.

Coate, L. (1995). *Ypres 1914–1918: A Study in History Around Us.* Horsham: D & L Educational Supplies.

Cole, K.C. (1985). Is there such a thing as scientific objectivity? *Discover Magazine,* April Edition.

Collingwood, R.G. (1946). *The Idea of History.* Oxford: Oxford University Press.

Cowley, G. (1996). The Biology of Beauty. *Newsweek,* Jun 3.

Damasio, A.R. (1994). *Descartes' Error: Emotion, Reason, and the Human Brain.* New York: Avon Books (Bard).

Damasio, A.R. (1999). *The Feeling of What Happens: Body, and Emotion In the Making of Consciousness.* New York: Harcourt, Inc.

Damasio, A.R. (2003). *Looking for Spinoza: Joy, Sorrow and the Feeling Brain.* New York: Harcourt, Inc.

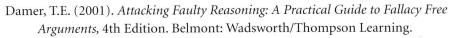

Damer, T.E. (2001). *Attacking Faulty Reasoning: A Practical Guide to Fallacy Free Arguments,* 4th Edition. Belmont: Wadsworth/Thompson Learning.

Darwin, C. (1859). *On the Origin of Species by Means of Natural Selection.* London: J. Murray.

Davis, P.J. and Hersh, R. (1981). *The Mathematical Experience,* 3rd Edition. Boston: Houghton Mifflin Company.

de Waal, F.B.M. (2007/8). Do Animals Feel Empathy? *Scientific American Mind,* December 2007/2008.

Dennett, D. (1991). *Consciousness Explained.* New York: Little, Brown & Co.

Di Stefano, B., Fukś, H. and Lawniczak, A. (2000). *Application of Fuzzy Logic in CA/LGCA Models as a Way of Dealing with Imprecise and Vague Data.* Conference proceedings of the Canadian Conference on Electrical and Computer Engineering, Halifax, Nova Scotia, Canada, May 7–10.

Durkheim, E. (1970). *Suicide: a study in sociology.* London: Routledge and Kegan Paul.

Economist, The (1994). Language Barriers. *The Economist,* Aug 19.

Economist, The (2002). Never the twain shall meet. *The Economist,* Jan 31.

Eiseman, F.B. Jr. (1990). *Bali Sekala and Niskala,* Vol. II. Singapore: Periplus.

Eves, H. (1990). *An Introduction to the History of Mathematics,* 6th Edition. Philadelphia: Saunders College Publishing.

Ferguson, M., Salter, M.J. and Stallworthy, J. (1996). *The Norton Anthology of Poetry,* 4th Edition. New York: W.W. Norton & Co.

Fernadez-Armesto, F. (2002). *Civilizations: Culture, Ambition and the Transformation of Nature.* New York: The Free Press.

Feyerabend, P. (1975). *Against Method.* London: Verso.

Feynman, R. (1981). *The Pleasure of Finding Things Out.* Interview with BBC Horizon.

Fischer, A. (2004). *The Logic of Real Arguments,* 2nd Edition. Cambridge: Cambridge University Press.

Fitzhugh, W. (2008). *The Importance of Non-fiction Writing by School Students,* Feb 9. Written by request.

Foer, J. (2007). Remember This. *National Geographic,* November 2007.

Garber, M. (2003). *Academic Instincts.* Princeton: Princeton University Press.

Gardner, H. (2000). *The Disciplined Mind.* New York: Penguin Books.

Gasset, J.O. (1962). *History as a System.* New York: W.W. Norton & Company.

Gay, K. (1989). *Bigotry.* New Jersey: Enslow Publishers.

Gerth, H.H. and Mills, C.W. (eds.) (1991). *Max Weber: Essays in Sociology.* New York: Routledge.

Giddens, A. (1972). *Politics and Sociology in the Thought of Max Weber.* Basingstoke: Palgrave Macmillan.

Giddens, A. (1999). *Runaway World.* New York: Routledge.

Gilligan, C. (1979). Woman's Place in Man's Life Cycle. *Harvard Education Review,* Vol. 49, No. 4, November 1979.

Gilligan, C. (1993). *In a Different Voice: Psychological Theory and Women's Development.* Cambridge: Harvard University Press.

Gladwell, M. (2005). *Blink: The Power of Thinking Without Thinking.* New York: Little, Brown.

Gleick, J. (1992). *Genius: The Life and Science of Richard Feynman.* New York: Pantheon.

Goleman, D. (2006). *Emotional Intelligence.* New York: Bantam.

Gombrich, E.H. (1969). *Art and Illusion: A Study in the Psychology of Pictorial Representation.* Princeton: Princeton University Press.

Gordon, R.G. Jr. (ed.) (2005). *Ethnologue: Languages of the World,* 15th Edition. Dallas: SIL International.

Gould, S.J. (1981). *The Mismeasure of Man.* New York: W.W. Norton & Company.

Gould, S.J. (2007). *The Richness of Life: the essential Stephen Jay Gould.* London: Vintage.

Gratzer, W. (2000). *The Undergrowth of Science: delusion, self-deception and human frailty.* Oxford: Oxford University Press.

Groopman, J. (2007). *How Doctors Think.* New York: Houghton Mifflin.

Hauser, M.D. (2006). *Moral Minds: How Nature Designed Our Universal Sense of Right and Wrong.* New York: Harper Perennial.

Hawking, S. (1988). *A Brief History of Time.* New York: Bantam Books.

Hayakawa, S.I. (1991). *Language in Thought and Action,* 5th Edition. New York: Harcourt Brace International.

Heaney, S. (2000). *Translation of Beowulf.* New York: Farrow, Strauss & Giroux.

Hersh, R. (2005). *18 Unconventional Essays on the Nature of Mathematics.* New York: Springer.

Hospers, J. (1956). *An Introduction to Philosophical Analysis.* London: Routledge and Kegan Paul.

Huxley, A. (1959). *Collected Essays.* London: Harper.

Keller, H. (1905). *The Story of My Life.* New York: Houghton Mifflin.

Kuhn, T.S. (1962). *The Structure of Scientific Revolutions.* Chicago: University of Chicago Press.

Kuhn, T.S. (1970). *The Structure of Scientific Revolutions.* Chicago: University of Chicago Press.

Kuper, J. and Kuper, A. (1985). *The Social Science Encyclopedia.* London: Routledge and Kegan Paul.

Lakoff, G. and Johnson, M. (1980). *Metaphors We Live By.* Chicago: The University of Chicago Press.

Lakoff, G. and Johnson, M. (1999). *Philosophy In the Flesh: The Embodied Mind and Its Challenge to Western Thought.* New York: Basic Books.

Lal, P. (2005). *The Mahabharata of Vyasa.* Calcutta: Writer's Workshop Press.

Lama, D. (2001). *Ethics for the New Millennium.* New York: Penguin Group USA.

Lamb, C. (1996). What the Whole World Likes Best. *The Sunday Times,* Dec 29.

Langer, S.K. (1942). *Philosophy in a New Key.* Cambridge: Harvard University Press.

Langer, S.K. (1958). The Cultural Importance of the Arts. In Andrews, M. F. (1958). *Aesthetic Form and Education.* Syracuse: Syracuse University Press, pp. 1–8.

Leighton, D. (2002). Searching for politics in an uncertain world. *Renewal,* Vol. 10, No.1, Winter.

Levin, P. and Topping, G. (2006). *Perfect Presentations!* Maidenhead: Open University Press.

Lewin, R. (1988). The Roots of Language and Consciousness. In Lewin, R. (ed.) *In The Age of Mankind.* Washington D.C.: Smithsonian Institution Press, pp. 170–86.

Lingstromberg, S. (1997). *The Standby Book.* Cambridge: Cambridge University Press.

Maira, S. (2002). Art: The Ultimate Luxury. *Design Today*, Dec 2002–Jan 2003.

Maley, A. and Duff, A. (1989). *The Inward Ear: poetry and language in the classroom.* Cambridge: Cambridge University Press.

McCarthy, P. and Hatcher, C. (2002). *Presentation Skills: the essential guide for students.* London: Sage.

Miller, C.D., Heeren V.E. and Hornsby, E.J. Jr. (1990). *Mathematical Ideas,* 6th Edition. Glenview: Scott Foresman.

Mithen, S. (1998). *The Prehistory of the Mind – a search for the origins of Art, Religion and Science.* London: Phoenix.

Montaigne, M. de. (1958). *Essays.* London: Penguin.

Moyne, J. and Coleman B. (trans.) (2001). *Unseen Rain, Quatrains of Rumi.* Boston/ London: Shambhala.

Mueller, S. (2007/8). Amputee Envy. *Scientific American Mind*, December 2007/January 2008.

Mukherjee, R. (1948). *The Social Function of Art.* Bombay: Hind Kitabs Ltd.

Nash C. et al. (1994). *Narrative in Culture – the Uses of Storytelling in the Sciences, and Literature.* London: Routledge.

National Academy of Engineering, Institute of Medicine, National Research Council and National Academy of Sciences. (1995). *On Being a Scientist: Responsible Conduct in Research,* 2nd Edition. Washington: National Academy Press.

Nicolelis, M. (2007/8). Living With Ghostly Limbs. *Scientific American Mind*, December 2007/January 2008.

Noë, A. (2004). *Action in Perception.* Cambridge: The MIT Press.

Noë, A. and Thompson, E. (eds.) (2002). *Vision and Mind.* Cambridge: Massachusetts Institute of Technology.

O'Brien, T. (1998). How to tell a True War Story. In Geyh, P. et al. (eds.) *Postmodern American Fiction: A Norton Anthology.* New York: W.W. Norton, pp. 174–183.

O'Hear, A. (1989). *An Introduction to the Philosophy of Science.* Oxford: Oxford University Press.

Oates, S.B. (1982). *Let the trumpet call.* New York: HarperCollins Publishers.

Peterson, A.D.C. and Prince of Wales, C.W. (1987). *Schools Across Frontiers: The Story of the International Baccalaureate and the United World Colleges.* Chicago and LaSalle: Open Court Publishing.

Phenix, P.H. (1966). *Realms of Meaning.* New York: McGraw-Hill.

Pinker, S. (1994). *The Language Instinct.* London, Penguin.

Pinker, S. (1997). *How the Mind Works.* New York: W.W. Norton & Co.

Pinker, S. (2002). *The Blank Slate: The Modern Denial of Human Nature.* New York: Viking.

Pinter, H. (1994). *The Birthday Party.* In Pinter, H. (1994). *Complete Works.* New York: Grove Press.

Polanyi, M. (1964). *Personal Knowledge: Towards a Post-Critical Philosophy.* Chicago: University of Chicago Press.

Popper, K. (1965). *Conjectures and Refutations: The Growth of Scientific Knowledge.* New York: Basic Books.

Popper, K. (2002). *Conjectures and Refutations.* New York: Routledge.

Postman, N. (1996). *The End of Education – Redefining the Value of School.* New York: Random House.

Pring, R. (1978). *Knowledge and Schooling.* Somerset, England: Open Books Publishing Ltd.

Quine, W.V. and Ullian, J. S. (1978). *The Web of Belief.* New York: Random House.

Rawls, J. (2003). *Justice as Fairness: A Restatement.* Cambridge: Harvard University Press.

Reid, L.A. (1926). Intellectual Analysis and Aesthetic Appreciation. *Journal of Philosophical Studies,* Vol. 1, No. 2, pp. 199–210.

Reid, L.A. (1952). Education and the Map of Knowledge. *British Journal of Educational Studies,* Vol. 1, No. 1, pp. 3–16.

Reid, L.A. (1964). Art, Truth and Reality. *The British Journal of Aesthetics,* Vol. 4, No. 4, pp. 321–331.

Reid, L.A. (1967). The Arts, Knowledge and Education. *British Journal of Educational Studies,* Vol. 15, No. 2, pp. 119–132.

Reid, L.A. (1981). Intuition and Art. *Journal of Aesthetic Education,* Vol. 15, No. 3, Special Issue: Aesthetic Education Conference 1980, pp. 27–28.

Roberts, D. (1996). *Minds at War: The poetry and experience of the First World War.* Guildford: Saxon Books.

Ross, R. (1957). *Symbols and Civilization: Science, Morals, Religion, Art.* New York: Harcourt, Brace & World, Inc.

Rumsfeld, D. (2002). *Department of Defense News Briefing,* Feb 12.

Russell, B. (1959). *The Problems of Philosophy.* New York: Oxford University Press.

Russell, B. (1999). *The Problems of Philosophy.* New York: Courier Dover Publications.

Ryan, A. (1970). *The Philosophy of the Social Sciences.* Basingstoke: Palgrave Macmillan.

Sagan, C. (1995). *The Demon Haunted World: Science as a Candle in the Dark.* New York: Random House.

Schick, T. (1997). The End of Science. *The Skeptical Inquirer,* March/April.

Schneider, S.H. (1996). *Laboratory Earth: the planetary gamble we can't afford to lose.* London: Phoenix.

Sims, R. (2001). How poksy are the arts? *Forum,* No. 45 (Nov).

Singapore Museum Trust (2008). *The Road to Nalanda.* Singapore: Exhibition Booklet.

Skinner, B.F. (1980). Science and Human Behaviour. In Block, N. (ed.) *Readings in the Philosophy of Psychology,* Vol. 1. Cambridge: Harvard University Press, pp. 40–41.

Smolin, L. (1997). *The Life of the Cosmos.* London: Wiedenfield & Nicholson.

Snow, C.P. (1993). *The Two Cultures.* Cambridge: Cambridge University Press.

Solomon, R.C. (2002). *The Big Questions: A Short Introduction to Philosophy.* Belmont, CA: Wadsworth Group/Thomson Learning.

Solzhenitsyn, A. (1970). *One Word of Truth.* Nobel Lecture 1970, translated by F.D. Reeve.

Staniszewski, M.A. (1995). *Believing Is Seeing: Creating the Culture of Art.* New York: Penguin Books.

Sterelny, K. (2001). *Dawkins versus Gould: Survival of the Fittest.* Cambridge: Icon.

Stoessinger, J.G. (1990). *Why Nations Go To War.* New York: St. Martin's Press.

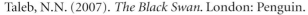

Taleb, N.N. (2007). *The Black Swan*. London: Penguin.

Tennant, R. (2006). The 5th Wave Cartoon. In Zegarelli, M. *Logic for Dummies*. Indianapolis: Wiley Publishing.

Thomas, L. (1980). On Science and Uncertainty. *Discover Magazine*, October.

Thurston, J.B. and Carraher, R.G. (1966). *Optical Illusions and the Visual Arts*. New York: Van Nostrand Reinhold Co.

Van Doren, C. (1991). *A History of Knowledge*. New York: Ballantine Books.

Van Emden, J. and Becker, L. (2004). *Presentation Skills for Students*. New York: Palgrave.

Weber, M. (1947). *The Theory of Social and Economic Organization*. London: William Hodge and Company.

Weber, M. (2001). *The Protestant Ethic and the Spirit of Capitalism*. London: Routledge.

Wharburton, N. (2000). *Thinking from A to Z,* 2nd Edition. New York: Routledge.

Wilson, E.O. (1998). *Conscilience: The Unity of Knowledge*. New York: Knopf.

Wilson, J. (1970). *Moral Thinking – A Guide for Students*. London: Heinemann Educational Books.

Witoelar, W. (2002). *No Regrets*. Melbourne: Equinox Press.

Wolpert, L. (1992). *The Unnatural Nature of Science*. Cambridge: Harvard University Press.

Worsley, P. (1997). *Knowledges: How different cultures view the world*. London: Profile Books.

Wriggens, S. and Hovey, X. (1996). *A Buddhist Pilgrim on the Silk Road*. Boulder: Westview Press.

Yoshiko, N. Yang, J. and Beal, T. (2001). Ghosts of the past: the Japanese history textbook controversy. *New Zealand Journal of Asian studies, 4 (2001), pp. 177–188.*

Zegarelli, M. (2006). *Logic for Dummies*. Indianapolis: Wiley Publishing.

Ziman, J. (2002). *Real Science – what it is and what it means*. Cambridge: Cambridge University Press.

Zinn, H. (2005). *A People's History of the United States: 1492–Present*. London: Harper Perennial.

Websites

To visit the following websites, visit www.heinemann.co.uk/hotlinks, enter the express code 4327P and click on the relevant weblink under Bibliography.

Ethnologue, Languages of the World. *Languages of Asia, Africa, and the Americas.* Please visit Hotlink 1.

Paulson, S. (2007). *Proud Atheists*. Please visit Hotlink 2.

Wynne, C. (2007). *Aping Language: a skeptical analysis of the evidence for nonhuman primate language*. Please visit Hotlink 3.

Briggs, H. (2007). *Chimps beat humans in memory test*. Please visit Hotlink 4.

Tong, J. (2004). *Shhhh, China's secret female language*. Please visit Hotlink 5.

Cody, E. (2004). *A language by women, for women*. Please visit Hotlink 6.

Emick, J. (2007). *Symbols of Taoism, Shinto, and Buddhism*. Please visit Hotlink 7.

Symbols.com. *Explore a World of Symbols*. Please visit Hotlink 8.

Netlingo.com. *The Internet Dictionary*. Please visit Hotlink 9.

Barnette, R. *(2008). Zeno's Coffeehouse*. Please visit Hotlink 10.

Brown, R.M. (2008). *Brainy Quote*. Please visit Hotlink 11.

Curtis, A. (2007). *The Power of Nightmares – The Rise of the Politics of Fear* (BBC Series film). Please visit Hotlink 12.

Holt, T. (2006). *Logical Fallacies*. Please visit Hotlink 13.

Janz, B. (2007). *The Reasoning Page*. Please visit Hotlink 14.

Shing, L.K. (2008). *Brainy Quote*. Please visit Hotlink 15.

Keystone Press Agency (2006). *English philosopher Bertrand Russell*. Please visit Hotlink 16.

LaBossiere, M. (2004). *Fallacies: Introduction*. Please visit Hotlink 17.

Le Bon, G. (1896). *A Crowd – A Study of the Popular Mind*. Please visit Hotlink 18.

Mesher, D. (1996). *Mission: Critical*. Please visit Hotlink 19.

Owen, W. (1917). *Dulce et Decorum Est*. Please visit Hotlink 20.

Poincre, H. (2007). *The Quotations Page*. Please visit Hotlink 21.

Wheeler, L.K. (2007). *Logical Fallacies Handlist*. Please visit Hotlink 22.

Whitehead, A.N. (2008). *Brainy Quote*. Please visit Hotlink 23.

Bauer, H.H. (1995). *Two Kinds of Knowledge: Maps and Stories*. Please visit Hotlink 24.

Bauer, H.H. (1990). *The antithesis*. Please visit Hotlink 25.

Brown, L.R. (2001). *Eco-Economy: Building an Economy for the Earth*. Please visit Hotlink 26.

Doxiadis, A. (2006). *Storytellers at the Crossroads: the challenge of narrative intelligence to identity, community and education*. Please visit Hotlink 27.

Harris, S. (2007). *Science Cartoons Plus – The Cartoons of S. Harris*. Please visit Hotlink 28.

Zalaya, R. and Barrallo, J. (2004). *Classification of Mathematical Sculpture*. Please visit Hotlink 29.

Dangerfield, R. (2004). *Proof Quotes and Quotations*. Please visit Hotlink 30.

Descartes, R. (2006). *Quotations about Mathematics and Education*. Please visit Hotlink 31.

O'Connor, J.J. and Robertson, E.F. (2006). Quotations by Albert Einstein. Please visit Hotlink 32.

Blondlot R.P. (2007). *Blondlot and N-rays*. Please visit Hotlink 33.

Brundtland, G.H. (2002). *Eastern Europe told to shackle tobacco*. Please visit Hotlink 34.

Lysenko, T. (2007). *Scientist: Trofim Denisovich Lysenko*. Please visit Hotlink 35.

United Nations Environment Programme. Please visit Hotlink 36.

Institute of International Studies: University of California, Berkeley (2008). *Conversations with History*. Please visit Hotlink 37.

Judith P. Zinnser's website. Please visit Hotlink 38.

Constable, C. (2000) *Truth in Painting*. Please visit Hotlink 39.

Garner, P. (2000). *The impact of photography on painting*. Please visit Hotlink 40.

O'Connor, J.J. and Robertson, E.F. (2003). *Mathematics and Art – Perspective*. Please visit Hotlink 41.

Wikipedia (2008). *Essay*. Please visit Hotlink 42.

Graham, P. (2004). *The Age of the Essay*. Please visit Hotlink 43.

International Baccalaureate (2008). *Mission and Strategy.* Please visit Hotlink 44.

International Baccalaureate (2008). *IB learner profile booklet.* Please visit Hotlink 45.

Lebech, M. (2008). *What is Human Dignity?* Please visit Hotlink 46.

Soyinka, W. (2004). *Reith Lectures 2004.* Please visit Hotlink 47.

The Concord Review (2007). Please visit Hotlink 48.

Gladwell, M. (2008). Gladwell.com. Please visit Hotlink 49.

Sullivan, A. (2007). *The Daily Dish: 'To see what is in front of one's nose needs a constant struggle'.* Please visit Hotlink 50.

Noë, A. (2008). *Psyche: an interdisciplinary journal of research on consciousness.* Please visit Hotlink 51.

Wikipedia (2008). *Wikipedia online encyclopedia.* Please visit Hotlink 52.

INDEX